Mometrix
TEST PREPARATION

Social Work ASWB Masters 2022-2023

450 Practice Questions

Exam Study Guide & LMSW Test Prep Secrets

4th Edition

Written and edited by the Mometrix Social Worker Certification Test Team

Printed in the United States of America

This paper meets the requirements of ANSI/NISO Z39.48-1992 (Permanence of Paper).

Paperback
ISBN 13: 978-1-5167-2072-9
ISBN 10: 1-5167-2072-5

FREE Study Skills Videos/DVD Offer

Dear Customer,

Thank you for your purchase from Mometrix! We consider it an honor and a privilege that you have purchased our product and we want to ensure your satisfaction.

As a way of showing our appreciation and to help us better serve you, we have developed Study Skills Videos that we would like to give you for FREE. These videos cover our *best practices* for getting ready for your exam, from how to use our study materials to how to best prepare for the day of the test.

All that we ask is that you email us with feedback that would describe your experience so far with our product. Good, bad, or indifferent, we want to know what you think!

To get your FREE Study Skills Videos, you can use the **QR code** below, or send us an **email** at studyvideos@mometrix.com with *FREE VIDEOS* in the subject line and the following information in the body of the email:

- The name of the product you purchased.
- Your product rating on a scale of 1-5, with 5 being the highest rating.
- Your feedback. It can be long, short, or anything in between. We just want to know your impressions and experience so far with our product. (Good feedback might include how our study material met your needs and ways we might be able to make it even better. You could highlight features that you found helpful or features that you think we should add.)

If you have any questions or concerns, please don't hesitate to contact me directly.

Thanks again!

Sincerely,

Jay Willis
Vice President
jay.willis@mometrix.com
1-800-673-8175

SCAN HERE

Mometrix
TEST PREPARATION
The World's #1 Test Preparation Company

Dear Future Exam Success Story

First of all, **THANK YOU** for purchasing Mometrix study materials!

Second, congratulations! You are one of the few determined test-takers who are committed to doing whatever it takes to excel on your exam. **You have come to the right place.** We developed these study materials with one goal in mind: to deliver you the information you need in a format that's concise and easy to use.

In addition to optimizing your guide for the content of the test, we've outlined our recommended steps for breaking down the preparation process into small, attainable goals so you can make sure you stay on track.

We've also analyzed the entire test-taking process, identifying the most common pitfalls and showing how you can overcome them and be ready for any curveball the test throws you.

Standardized testing is one of the biggest obstacles on your road to success, which only increases the importance of doing well in the high-pressure, high-stakes environment of test day. Your results on this test could have a significant impact on your future, and this guide provides the information and practical advice to help you achieve your full potential on test day.

Your success is our success

We would love to hear from you! If you would like to share the story of your exam success or if you have any questions or comments in regard to our products, please contact us at **800-673-8175** or **support@mometrix.com**.

Thanks again for your business and we wish you continued success!

Sincerely,
The Mometrix Test Preparation Team

TABLE OF CONTENTS

Introduction

Thank you for purchasing this resource! You have made the choice to prepare yourself for a test that could have a huge impact on your future, and this guide is designed to help you be fully ready for test day. Obviously, it's important to have a solid understanding of the test material, but you also need to be prepared for the unique environment and stressors of the test, so that you can perform to the best of your abilities.

For this purpose, the first section that appears in this guide is the **Secret Keys**. We've devoted countless hours to meticulously researching what works and what doesn't, and we've boiled down our findings to the five most impactful steps you can take to improve your performance on the test. We start at the beginning with study planning and move through the preparation process, all the way to the testing strategies that will help you get the most out of what you know when you're finally sitting in front of the test.

We recommend that you start preparing for your test as far in advance as possible. However, if you've bought this guide as a last-minute study resource and only have a few days before your test, we recommend that you skip over the first two Secret Keys since they address a long-term study plan.

If you struggle with **test anxiety**, we strongly encourage you to check out our recommendations for how you can overcome it. Test anxiety is a formidable foe, but it can be beaten, and we want to make sure you have the tools you need to defeat it.

Secret Key #1 – Plan Big, Study Small

There's a lot riding on your performance. If you want to ace this test, you're going to need to keep your skills sharp and the material fresh in your mind. You need a plan that lets you review everything you need to know while still fitting in your schedule. We'll break this strategy down into three categories.

Information Organization

Start with the information you already have: the official test outline. From this, you can make a complete list of all the concepts you need to cover before the test. Organize these concepts into groups that can be studied together, and create a list of any related vocabulary you need to learn so you can brush up on any difficult terms. You'll want to keep this vocabulary list handy once you actually start studying since you may need to add to it along the way.

Time Management

Once you have your set of study concepts, decide how to spread them out over the time you have left before the test. Break your study plan into small, clear goals so you have a manageable task for each day and know exactly what you're doing. Then just focus on one small step at a time. When you manage your time this way, you don't need to spend hours at a time studying. Studying a small block of content for a short period each day helps you retain information better and avoid stressing over how much you have left to do. You can relax knowing that you have a plan to cover everything in time. In order for this strategy to be effective though, you have to start studying early and stick to your schedule. Avoid the exhaustion and futility that comes from last-minute cramming!

Study Environment

The environment you study in has a big impact on your learning. Studying in a coffee shop, while probably more enjoyable, is not likely to be as fruitful as studying in a quiet room. It's important to keep distractions to a minimum. You're only planning to study for a short block of time, so make the most of it. Don't pause to check your phone or get up to find a snack. It's also important to **avoid multitasking**. Research has consistently shown that multitasking will make your studying dramatically less effective. Your study area should also be comfortable and well-lit so you don't have the distraction of straining your eyes or sitting on an uncomfortable chair.

The time of day you study is also important. You want to be rested and alert. Don't wait until just before bedtime. Study when you'll be most likely to comprehend and remember. Even better, if you know what time of day your test will be, set that time aside for study. That way your brain will be used to working on that subject at that specific time and you'll have a better chance of recalling information.

Finally, it can be helpful to team up with others who are studying for the same test. Your actual studying should be done in as isolated an environment as possible, but the work of organizing the information and setting up the study plan can be divided up. In between study sessions, you can discuss with your teammates the concepts that you're all studying and quiz each other on the details. Just be sure that your teammates are as serious about the test as you are. If you find that your study time is being replaced with social time, you might need to find a new team.

Secret Key #2 – Make Your Studying Count

You're devoting a lot of time and effort to preparing for this test, so you want to be absolutely certain it will pay off. This means doing more than just reading the content and hoping you can remember it on test day. It's important to make every minute of study count. There are two main areas you can focus on to make your studying count.

Retention

It doesn't matter how much time you study if you can't remember the material. You need to make sure you are retaining the concepts. To check your retention of the information you're learning, try recalling it at later times with minimal prompting. Try carrying around flashcards and glance at one or two from time to time or ask a friend who's also studying for the test to quiz you.

To enhance your retention, look for ways to put the information into practice so that you can apply it rather than simply recalling it. If you're using the information in practical ways, it will be much easier to remember. Similarly, it helps to solidify a concept in your mind if you're not only reading it to yourself but also explaining it to someone else. Ask a friend to let you teach them about a concept you're a little shaky on (or speak aloud to an imaginary audience if necessary). As you try to summarize, define, give examples, and answer your friend's questions, you'll understand the concepts better and they will stay with you longer. Finally, step back for a big picture view and ask yourself how each piece of information fits with the whole subject. When you link the different concepts together and see them working together as a whole, it's easier to remember the individual components.

Finally, practice showing your work on any multi-step problems, even if you're just studying. Writing out each step you take to solve a problem will help solidify the process in your mind, and you'll be more likely to remember it during the test.

Modality

Modality simply refers to the means or method by which you study. Choosing a study modality that fits your own individual learning style is crucial. No two people learn best in exactly the same way, so it's important to know your strengths and use them to your advantage.

For example, if you learn best by visualization, focus on visualizing a concept in your mind and draw an image or a diagram. Try color-coding your notes, illustrating them, or creating symbols that will trigger your mind to recall a learned concept. If you learn best by hearing or discussing information, find a study partner who learns the same way or read aloud to yourself. Think about how to put the information in your own words. Imagine that you are giving a lecture on the topic and record yourself so you can listen to it later.

For any learning style, flashcards can be helpful. Organize the information so you can take advantage of spare moments to review. Underline key words or phrases. Use different colors for different categories. Mnemonic devices (such as creating a short list in which every item starts with the same letter) can also help with retention. Find what works best for you and use it to store the information in your mind most effectively and easily.

Secret Key #3 – Practice the Right Way

Your success on test day depends not only on how many hours you put into preparing, but also on whether you prepared the right way. It's good to check along the way to see if your studying is paying off. One of the most effective ways to do this is by taking practice tests to evaluate your progress. Practice tests are useful because they show exactly where you need to improve. Every time you take a practice test, pay special attention to these three groups of questions:

- The questions you got wrong
- The questions you had to guess on, even if you guessed right
- The questions you found difficult or slow to work through

This will show you exactly what your weak areas are, and where you need to devote more study time. Ask yourself why each of these questions gave you trouble. Was it because you didn't understand the material? Was it because you didn't remember the vocabulary? Do you need more repetitions on this type of question to build speed and confidence? Dig into those questions and figure out how you can strengthen your weak areas as you go back to review the material.

Additionally, many practice tests have a section explaining the answer choices. It can be tempting to read the explanation and think that you now have a good understanding of the concept. However, an explanation likely only covers part of the question's broader context. Even if the explanation makes perfect sense, **go back and investigate** every concept related to the question until you're positive you have a thorough understanding.

As you go along, keep in mind that the practice test is just that: practice. Memorizing these questions and answers will not be very helpful on the actual test because it is unlikely to have any of the same exact questions. If you only know the right answers to the sample questions, you won't be prepared for the real thing. **Study the concepts** until you understand them fully, and then you'll be able to answer any question that shows up on the test.

It's important to wait on the practice tests until you're ready. If you take a test on your first day of study, you may be overwhelmed by the amount of material covered and how much you need to learn. Work up to it gradually.

On test day, you'll need to be prepared for answering questions, managing your time, and using the test-taking strategies you've learned. It's a lot to balance, like a mental marathon that will have a big impact on your future. Like training for a marathon, you'll need to start slowly and work your way up. When test day arrives, you'll be ready.

Start with the strategies you've read in the first two Secret Keys—plan your course and study in the way that works best for you. If you have time, consider using multiple study resources to get different approaches to the same concepts. It can be helpful to see difficult concepts from more than one angle. Then find a good source for practice tests. Many times, the test website will suggest potential study resources or provide sample tests.

Practice Test Strategy

If you're able to find at least three practice tests, we recommend this strategy:

Untimed and Open-Book Practice

Take the first test with no time constraints and with your notes and study guide handy. Take your time and focus on applying the strategies you've learned.

Timed and Open-Book Practice

Take the second practice test open-book as well, but set a timer and practice pacing yourself to finish in time.

Timed and Closed-Book Practice

Take any other practice tests as if it were test day. Set a timer and put away your study materials. Sit at a table or desk in a quiet room, imagine yourself at the testing center, and answer questions as quickly and accurately as possible.

Keep repeating timed and closed-book tests on a regular basis until you run out of practice tests or it's time for the actual test. Your mind will be ready for the schedule and stress of test day, and you'll be able to focus on recalling the material you've learned.

Secret Key #4 – Pace Yourself

Once you're fully prepared for the material on the test, your biggest challenge on test day will be managing your time. Just knowing that the clock is ticking can make you panic even if you have plenty of time left. Work on pacing yourself so you can build confidence against the time constraints of the exam. Pacing is a difficult skill to master, especially in a high-pressure environment, so **practice is vital**.

Set time expectations for your pace based on how much time is available. For example, if a section has 60 questions and the time limit is 30 minutes, you know you have to average 30 seconds or less per question in order to answer them all. Although 30 seconds is the hard limit, set 25 seconds per question as your goal, so you reserve extra time to spend on harder questions. When you budget extra time for the harder questions, you no longer have any reason to stress when those questions take longer to answer.

Don't let this time expectation distract you from working through the test at a calm, steady pace, but keep it in mind so you don't spend too much time on any one question. Recognize that taking extra time on one question you don't understand may keep you from answering two that you do understand later in the test. If your time limit for a question is up and you're still not sure of the answer, mark it and move on, and come back to it later if the time and the test format allow. If the testing format doesn't allow you to return to earlier questions, just make an educated guess; then put it out of your mind and move on.

On the easier questions, be careful not to rush. It may seem wise to hurry through them so you have more time for the challenging ones, but it's not worth missing one if you know the concept and just didn't take the time to read the question fully. Work efficiently but make sure you understand the question and have looked at all of the answer choices, since more than one may seem right at first.

Even if you're paying attention to the time, you may find yourself a little behind at some point. You should speed up to get back on track, but do so wisely. Don't panic; just take a few seconds less on each question until you're caught up. Don't guess without thinking, but do look through the answer choices and eliminate any you know are wrong. If you can get down to two choices, it is often worthwhile to guess from those. Once you've chosen an answer, move on and don't dwell on any that you skipped or had to hurry through. If a question was taking too long, chances are it was one of the harder ones, so you weren't as likely to get it right anyway.

On the other hand, if you find yourself getting ahead of schedule, it may be beneficial to slow down a little. The more quickly you work, the more likely you are to make a careless mistake that will affect your score. You've budgeted time for each question, so don't be afraid to spend that time. Practice an efficient but careful pace to get the most out of the time you have.

Secret Key #5 – Have a Plan for Guessing

When you're taking the test, you may find yourself stuck on a question. Some of the answer choices seem better than others, but you don't see the one answer choice that is obviously correct. What do you do?

The scenario described above is very common, yet most test takers have not effectively prepared for it. Developing and practicing a plan for guessing may be one of the single most effective uses of your time as you get ready for the exam.

In developing your plan for guessing, there are three questions to address:

- When should you start the guessing process?
- How should you narrow down the choices?
- Which answer should you choose?

When to Start the Guessing Process

Unless your plan for guessing is to select C every time (which, despite its merits, is not what we recommend), you need to leave yourself enough time to apply your answer elimination strategies. Since you have a limited amount of time for each question, that means that if you're going to give yourself the best shot at guessing correctly, you have to decide quickly whether or not you will guess.

Of course, the best-case scenario is that you don't have to guess at all, so first, see if you can answer the question based on your knowledge of the subject and basic reasoning skills. Focus on the key words in the question and try to jog your memory of related topics. Give yourself a chance to bring the knowledge to mind, but once you realize that you don't have (or you can't access) the knowledge you need to answer the question, it's time to start the guessing process.

It's almost always better to start the guessing process too early than too late. It only takes a few seconds to remember something and answer the question from knowledge. Carefully eliminating wrong answer choices takes longer. Plus, going through the process of eliminating answer choices can actually help jog your memory.

Summary: Start the guessing process as soon as you decide that you can't answer the question based on your knowledge.

How to Narrow Down the Choices

The next chapter in this book (**Test-Taking Strategies**) includes a wide range of strategies for how to approach questions and how to look for answer choices to eliminate. You will definitely want to read those carefully, practice them, and figure out which ones work best for you. Here though, we're going to address a mindset rather than a particular strategy.

Your odds of guessing an answer correctly depend on how many options you are choosing from.

Number of options left	5	4	3	2	1
Odds of guessing correctly	20%	25%	33%	50%	100%

You can see from this chart just how valuable it is to be able to eliminate incorrect answers and make an educated guess, but there are two things that many test takers do that cause them to miss out on the benefits of guessing:

- Accidentally eliminating the correct answer
- Selecting an answer based on an impression

We'll look at the first one here, and the second one in the next section.

To avoid accidentally eliminating the correct answer, we recommend a thought exercise called **the $5 challenge**. In this challenge, you only eliminate an answer choice from contention if you are willing to bet $5 on it being wrong. Why $5? Five dollars is a small but not insignificant amount of money. It's an amount you could afford to lose but wouldn't want to throw away. And while losing $5 once might not hurt too much, doing it twenty times will set you back $100. In the same way, each small decision you make—eliminating a choice here, guessing on a question there—won't by itself impact your score very much, but when you put them all together, they can make a big difference. By holding each answer choice elimination decision to a higher standard, you can reduce the risk of accidentally eliminating the correct answer.

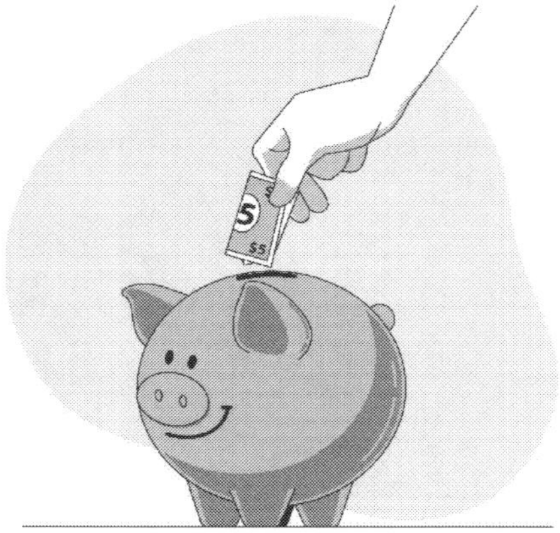

The $5 challenge can also be applied in a positive sense: If you are willing to bet $5 that an answer choice *is* correct, go ahead and mark it as correct.

Summary: Only eliminate an answer choice if you are willing to bet $5 that it is wrong.

Which Answer to Choose

You're taking the test. You've run into a hard question and decided you'll have to guess. You've eliminated all the answer choices you're willing to bet $5 on. Now you have to pick an answer. Why do we even need to talk about this? Why can't you just pick whichever one you feel like when the time comes?

The answer to these questions is that if you don't come into the test with a plan, you'll rely on your impression to select an answer choice, and if you do that, you risk falling into a trap. The test writers know that everyone who takes their test will be guessing on some of the questions, so they intentionally write wrong answer choices to seem plausible. You still have to pick an answer though, and if the wrong answer choices are designed to look right, how can you ever be sure that you're not falling for their trap? The best solution we've found to this dilemma is to take the decision out of your hands entirely. Here is the process we recommend:

Once you've eliminated any choices that you are confident (willing to bet $5) are wrong, select the first remaining choice as your answer.

Whether you choose to select the first remaining choice, the second, or the last, the important thing is that you use some preselected standard. Using this approach guarantees that you will not be enticed into selecting an answer choice that looks right, because you are not basing your decision on how the answer choices look.

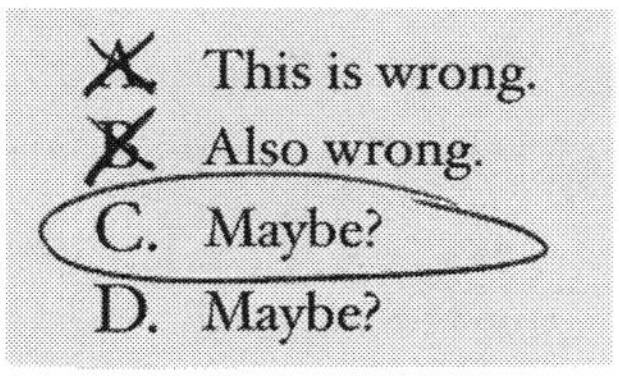

This is not meant to make you question your knowledge. Instead, it is to help you recognize the difference between your knowledge and your impressions. There's a huge difference between thinking an answer is right because of what you know, and thinking an answer is right because it looks or sounds like it should be right.

Summary: To ensure that your selection is appropriately random, make a predetermined selection from among all answer choices you have not eliminated.

Test-Taking Strategies

This section contains a list of test-taking strategies that you may find helpful as you work through the test. By taking what you know and applying logical thought, you can maximize your chances of answering any question correctly!

It is very important to realize that every question is different and every person is different: no single strategy will work on every question, and no single strategy will work for every person. That's why we've included all of them here, so you can try them out and determine which ones work best for different types of questions and which ones work best for you.

Question Strategies

✓ Read Carefully

Read the question and the answer choices carefully. Don't miss the question because you misread the terms. You have plenty of time to read each question thoroughly and make sure you understand what is being asked. Yet a happy medium must be attained, so don't waste too much time. You must read carefully and efficiently.

✓ Contextual Clues

Look for contextual clues. If the question includes a word you are not familiar with, look at the immediate context for some indication of what the word might mean. Contextual clues can often give you all the information you need to decipher the meaning of an unfamiliar word. Even if you can't determine the meaning, you may be able to narrow down the possibilities enough to make a solid guess at the answer to the question.

✓ Prefixes

If you're having trouble with a word in the question or answer choices, try dissecting it. Take advantage of every clue that the word might include. Prefixes and suffixes can be a huge help. Usually, they allow you to determine a basic meaning. *Pre-* means before, *post-* means after, *pro-* is positive, *de-* is negative. From prefixes and suffixes, you can get an idea of the general meaning of the word and try to put it into context.

✓ Hedge Words

Watch out for critical hedge words, such as *likely, may, can, sometimes, often, almost, mostly, usually, generally, rarely,* and *sometimes.* Question writers insert these hedge phrases to cover every possibility. Often an answer choice will be wrong simply because it leaves no room for exception. Be on guard for answer choices that have definitive words such as *exactly* and *always.*

✓ Switchback Words

Stay alert for *switchbacks.* These are the words and phrases frequently used to alert you to shifts in thought. The most common switchback words are *but, although,* and *however.* Others include *nevertheless, on the other hand, even though, while, in spite of, despite,* and *regardless of.* Switchback words are important to catch because they can change the direction of the question or an answer choice.

✓ FACE VALUE

When in doubt, use common sense. Accept the situation in the problem at face value. Don't read too much into it. These problems will not require you to make wild assumptions. If you have to go beyond creativity and warp time or space in order to have an answer choice fit the question, then you should move on and consider the other answer choices. These are normal problems rooted in reality. The applicable relationship or explanation may not be readily apparent, but it is there for you to figure out. Use your common sense to interpret anything that isn't clear.

Answer Choice Strategies

✓ ANSWER SELECTION

The most thorough way to pick an answer choice is to identify and eliminate wrong answers until only one is left, then confirm it is the correct answer. Sometimes an answer choice may immediately seem right, but be careful. The test writers will usually put more than one reasonable answer choice on each question, so take a second to read all of them and make sure that the other choices are not equally obvious. As long as you have time left, it is better to read every answer choice than to pick the first one that looks right without checking the others.

✓ ANSWER CHOICE FAMILIES

An answer choice family consists of two (in rare cases, three) answer choices that are very similar in construction and cannot all be true at the same time. If you see two answer choices that are direct opposites or parallels, one of them is usually the correct answer. For instance, if one answer choice says that quantity x increases and another either says that quantity x decreases (opposite) or says that quantity y increases (parallel), then those answer choices would fall into the same family. An answer choice that doesn't match the construction of the answer choice family is more likely to be incorrect. Most questions will not have answer choice families, but when they do appear, you should be prepared to recognize them.

✓ ELIMINATE ANSWERS

Eliminate answer choices as soon as you realize they are wrong, but make sure you consider all possibilities. If you are eliminating answer choices and realize that the last one you are left with is also wrong, don't panic. Start over and consider each choice again. There may be something you missed the first time that you will realize on the second pass.

✓ AVOID FACT TRAPS

Don't be distracted by an answer choice that is factually true but doesn't answer the question. You are looking for the choice that answers the question. Stay focused on what the question is asking for so you don't accidentally pick an answer that is true but incorrect. Always go back to the question and make sure the answer choice you've selected actually answers the question and is not merely a true statement.

✓ EXTREME STATEMENTS

In general, you should avoid answers that put forth extreme actions as standard practice or proclaim controversial ideas as established fact. An answer choice that states the "process should be used in certain situations, if..." is much more likely to be correct than one that states the "process should be discontinued completely." The first is a calm rational statement and doesn't even make a definitive, uncompromising stance, using a hedge word *if* to provide wiggle room, whereas the second choice is far more extreme.

✓ Benchmark

As you read through the answer choices and you come across one that seems to answer the question well, mentally select that answer choice. This is not your final answer, but it's the one that will help you evaluate the other answer choices. The one that you selected is your benchmark or standard for judging each of the other answer choices. Every other answer choice must be compared to your benchmark. That choice is correct until proven otherwise by another answer choice beating it. If you find a better answer, then that one becomes your new benchmark. Once you've decided that no other choice answers the question as well as your benchmark, you have your final answer.

✓ Predict the Answer

Before you even start looking at the answer choices, it is often best to try to predict the answer. When you come up with the answer on your own, it is easier to avoid distractions and traps because you will know exactly what to look for. The right answer choice is unlikely to be word-for-word what you came up with, but it should be a close match. Even if you are confident that you have the right answer, you should still take the time to read each option before moving on.

General Strategies

✓ Tough Questions

If you are stumped on a problem or it appears too hard or too difficult, don't waste time. Move on! Remember though, if you can quickly check for obviously incorrect answer choices, your chances of guessing correctly are greatly improved. Before you completely give up, at least try to knock out a couple of possible answers. Eliminate what you can and then guess at the remaining answer choices before moving on.

✓ Check Your Work

Since you will probably not know every term listed and the answer to every question, it is important that you get credit for the ones that you do know. Don't miss any questions through careless mistakes. If at all possible, try to take a second to look back over your answer selection and make sure you've selected the correct answer choice and haven't made a costly careless mistake (such as marking an answer choice that you didn't mean to mark). This quick double check should more than pay for itself in caught mistakes for the time it costs.

✓ Pace Yourself

It's easy to be overwhelmed when you're looking at a page full of questions; your mind is confused and full of random thoughts, and the clock is ticking down faster than you would like. Calm down and maintain the pace that you have set for yourself. Especially as you get down to the last few minutes of the test, don't let the small numbers on the clock make you panic. As long as you are on track by monitoring your pace, you are guaranteed to have time for each question.

✓ Don't Rush

It is very easy to make errors when you are in a hurry. Maintaining a fast pace in answering questions is pointless if it makes you miss questions that you would have gotten right otherwise. Test writers like to include distracting information and wrong answers that seem right. Taking a little extra time to avoid careless mistakes can make all the difference in your test score. Find a pace that allows you to be confident in the answers that you select.

✓ Keep Moving

Panicking will not help you pass the test, so do your best to stay calm and keep moving. Taking deep breaths and going through the answer elimination steps you practiced can help to break through a stress barrier and keep your pace.

Final Notes

The combination of a solid foundation of content knowledge and the confidence that comes from practicing your plan for applying that knowledge is the key to maximizing your performance on test day. As your foundation of content knowledge is built up and strengthened, you'll find that the strategies included in this chapter become more and more effective in helping you quickly sift through the distractions and traps of the test to isolate the correct answer.

Now that you're preparing to move forward into the test content chapters of this book, be sure to keep your goal in mind. As you read, think about how you will be able to apply this information on the test. If you've already seen sample questions for the test and you have an idea of the question format and style, try to come up with questions of your own that you can answer based on what you're reading. This will give you valuable practice applying your knowledge in the same ways you can expect to on test day.

Good luck and good studying!

Five-Week Study Plan

On the next few pages, we've provided an optional study plan to help you use this study guide to its fullest potential over the course of five weeks. If you have ten weeks available and want to spread it out more, spend two weeks on each section of the plan.

Below is a quick summary of the subjects covered in each week of the plan.

- Week 1: Human Development, Diversity, and Behavior in the Environment
- Week 2: Assessment and Intervention Planning
- Week 3: Interventions with Clients/Client Systems
- Week 4: Professional Relationships, Values, and Ethics
- Week 5: Practice Tests

Please note that not all subjects will take the same amount of time to work through.

Three full-length practice tests are included in this study guide. We recommend saving the third practice test and any additional tests for after you've completed the study plan. Take these practice tests without any reference materials a day or two before the real thing as practice runs to get you in the mode of answering questions at a good pace.

Week 1: Human Development, Diversity, and Behavior in the Environment

Instructional Content

First, read carefully through the Human Development, Diversity, and Behavior in the Environment chapter in this book, checking off your progress as you go:

- ❑ Human Growth and Development
- ❑ Human Behavior in the Social Environment
- ❑ Sexual Orientation
- ❑ Self-Image
- ❑ Discrimination
- ❑ Exploitation
- ❑ Culturally Competent Care
- ❑ Indicators of Substance Abuse
- ❑ Substance Use and Abuse
- ❑ Stress, Crisis, and Trauma
- ❑ Grief
- ❑ Concepts of Abuse
- ❑ Social and Economic Justice
- ❑ Globalization and Institutionalism

As you read, do the following:

- Highlight any sections, terms, or concepts you think are important
- Draw an asterisk (*) next to any areas you are struggling with
- Watch the review videos to gain more understanding of a particular topic
- Take notes in your notebook or in the margins of this book

After you've read through everything, go back and review any sections that you highlighted or that you drew an asterisk next to, referencing your notes along the way.

Week 2: Assessment and Intervention Planning

Instructional Content

First, read carefully through the Assessment and Intervention Planning chapter in this book, checking off your progress as you go:

- ❑ Biopsychosocial History and Collateral Data
- ❑ Pharmacologic Interventions
- ❑ Assessment Methods and Techniques
- ❑ Indicators for Risk to Self or Others
- ❑ Risk Management
- ❑ Psychiatric Disorders and Diagnosis
- ❑ Research

As you read, do the following:

- Highlight any sections, terms, or concepts you think are important
- Draw an asterisk (*) next to any areas you are struggling with
- Watch the review videos to gain more understanding of a particular topic
- Take notes in your notebook or in the margins of this book

After you've read through everything, go back and review any sections that you highlighted or that you drew an asterisk next to, referencing your notes along the way.

Week 3: Interventions with Clients/Client Systems

Instructional Content

First, read carefully through the Interventions with Clients/Client Systems chapter in this book, checking off your progress as you go:

- ❑ Therapeutic Relationships and Communication
- ❑ Interventions
- ❑ Family Therapy
- ❑ Group Work
- ❑ Case Management
- ❑ Out-of-Home Placement and Displacement
- ❑ Consultation and Collaboration
- ❑ Community Organization and Social Planning
- ❑ Program Development and Service Delivery
- ❑ Social Policy and Social Change
- ❑ Support Programs
- ❑ Leadership
- ❑ Supervision and Administration

As you read, do the following:

- Highlight any sections, terms, or concepts you think are important
- Draw an asterisk (*) next to any areas you are struggling with
- Watch the review videos to gain more understanding of a particular topic
- Take notes in your notebook or in the margins of this book

After you've read through everything, go back and review any sections that you highlighted or that you drew an asterisk next to, referencing your notes along the way.

Week 4: Professional Relationships, Values, and Ethics

Instructional Content

First, read carefully through the Professional Relationships, Values, and Ethics chapter in this book, checking off your progress as you go:

- ❑ Legal Issues and Client Rights
- ❑ Ethics
- ❑ NASW Code of Ethics: Ethical Responsibilities in Practice Settings
- ❑ Record-Keeping and Documentation
- ❑ Professional Development and the Use of Self

As you read, do the following:

- Highlight any sections, terms, or concepts you think are important
- Draw an asterisk (*) next to any areas you are struggling with
- Watch the review videos to gain more understanding of a particular topic
- Take notes in your notebook or in the margins of this book

After you've read through everything, go back and review any sections that you highlighted or that you drew an asterisk next to, referencing your notes along the way.

Week 5: Practice Tests

Your success on test day depends not only on how many hours you put into preparing, but also on whether you prepared the right way. It's good to check along the way to see if your studying is paying off. One of the most effective ways to do this is by taking practice tests to evaluate your progress. Practice tests are useful because they show exactly where you need to improve. Every time you take a practice test, pay special attention to these three groups of questions:

- The questions you got wrong
- The questions you had to guess on, even if you guessed right
- The questions you found difficult or slow to work through

This will show you exactly what your weak areas are, and where you need to devote more study time. Ask yourself why each of these questions gave you trouble. Was it because you didn't understand the material? Was it because you didn't remember the vocabulary? Do you need more repetitions on this type of question to build speed and confidence? Dig into those questions and figure out how you can strengthen your weak areas as you go back to review the material.

Practice Test #1

Now that you've read over the instructional content, it's time to take a practice test. Complete Practice Test #1. Take this test with **no time constraints**, and feel free to reference the applicable sections of this guide as you go. Once you've finished, check your answers against the provided answer key. For any questions you answered incorrectly, review the answer rationale, and then **go back and review** the applicable sections of the book. The goal in this stage is to understand why you answered the question incorrectly, and make sure that the next time you see a similar question, you will get it right.

Practice Test #2

Next, complete Practice Test #2. This time, give yourself **4 hours** to complete all of the questions. You should again feel free to reference the guide and your notes, but be mindful of the clock. If you run out of time before you finish all of the questions, mark where you were when time expired, but go ahead and finish taking the practice test. Once you've finished, check your answers against the provided answer key, and as before, review the answer rationale for any that you answered incorrectly and then go back and review the associated instructional content. Your goal is still to increase understanding of the content but also to get used to the time constraints you will face on the test.

As you go along, keep in mind that the practice test is just that: practice. Memorizing these questions and answers will not be very helpful on the actual test because it is unlikely to have any of the same exact questions. If you only know the right answers to the sample questions, you won't be prepared for the real thing. **Study the concepts** until you understand them fully, and then you'll be able to answer any question that shows up on the test.

Human Development, Diversity, and Behavior in the Environment

Human Growth and Development

Maslow's Hierarchy of Needs

American psychologist Abraham Maslow defined human motivation in terms of needs and wants. His hierarchy of needs is classically portrayed as a pyramid sitting on its base divided into horizontal layers. He theorized that, as humans fulfill the needs of one layer, their motivation turns to the layer above.

Level	Need	Description
Physiological	Basic needs to sustain life—oxygen, food, fluids, sleep	These basic needs take precedence over all other needs and must be dealt with first before the individuals can focus on other needs.
Safety and security	Freedom from physiological and psychological threats	Once basic needs are met, individuals become concerned about safety, including freedom from fear, unemployment, war, and disasters. Children respond more intensely to threats than adults.
Love/Belonging	Support, caring, intimacy	Individuals tend to avoid isolation and loneliness and have a need for family, intimacy, or membership in a group where they feel they belong.
Self-esteem	Sense of worth, respect, independence	To have confidence, individuals need to develop self-esteem and receive the respect of others.
Self-actualization	Meeting one's own sense of potential and finding fulfillment	Individuals choose a path in life that leads to fulfillment and contentment.

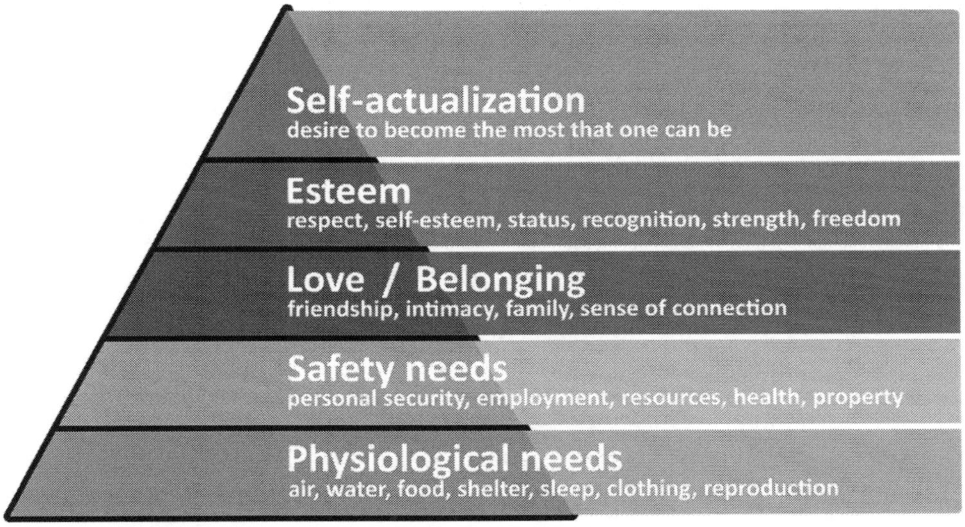

Review Video: Maslow's Hierarchy of Needs
Visit mometrix.com/academy and enter code: 461825

Freud's Psychoanalytic Theory

Motivational Forces of the Unconscious Mind That Shape Behavior

Freud's psychoanalytic theory postulates that behavior is influenced not only by environmental stimuli (i.e., physical influences) and external social constrains and constructs (i.e., taboos, rules, social expectations), but also by four specific unconscious elements as well. These elements exist only in the unconscious mind, and individuals remain substantively unaware of all the forces, motivations, and drives that shape their thoughts and behavioral decisions. The **four elements** are:

- Covert desires
- Defenses needed to protect, facilitate, and moderate behaviors
- Dreams
- Unconscious wishes

Review Video: Who was Sigmund Freud?
Visit mometrix.com/academy and enter code: 473747

Levels of the Mind

The three levels of the mind that Freud proposed include the following:

- The **conscious mind** is comprised of various ideas and thoughts of which we are fully aware.
- The **preconscious mind** is comprised of ideas and thoughts that are outside of immediate awareness, but can be readily accessed and brought into awareness.
- The **unconscious mind** is comprised of thoughts and ideas that are outside of our awareness and that cannot be accessed or brought into full awareness by personal effort alone.

Primary Focus of Psychoanalysis

The primary focus of psychoanalysis is on the unconscious mind and the desires, defenses, dreams and wishes contained within it. Freud proposed that the key features of the unconscious mind arise from experiences in the past and from problems in the development of the personality. Consequently, a focus on the unconscious mind requires the psychoanalytic process to also focus on the **past**—specifically on those repressed infant and childhood memories and experiences that served to create the desires, defenses, dreams, and wishes that invariably manifest through the thoughts and behaviors of every individual.

Freud's Structural Theory of Personality Development

Freud proposed a three-level structure of personality, composed of the id, the ego, and the super-ego:

Id	The level of personality that comprises basic instinctual drives and is the only part of personality present at birth. The id seeks immediate gratification of primitive needs (hunger, thirst, libido) and adheres to the "pleasure principle" (i.e., seek pleasure, avoid pain).
Ego	Develops secondarily and allows for rational thought, executive functions, and the ability to delay gratification. The ego is governed by the "reality principle" and mediates the desires of the id with the requirements of the external world.
Super-ego	Develops last and incorporates the higher concepts of morality, ethics, and justice into the personality, allowing concepts of right, wrong, and greater good to override base instincts and purely rational goals.

Review Video: How do the Id, Ego, and Superego Interact?
Visit mometrix.com/academy and enter code: 690435

Super-Ego, Conscience, and Ego Ideal

The **super-ego** is comprised of the conscience and the ego ideal, which are constructed from the restraints and encouragements provided by caregivers (parents, teachers, other role models). The **conscience** focuses on cognitive and behavioral restrictions (i.e., the "should nots") while the **ego ideal** focuses on perfection, including spiritual attainment and higher-order goals (the "shoulds" of thought and behavior).

The super-ego works in opposition to the id, produces feelings of guilt for inappropriate drives, fantasies, and actions, and encourages refinement, aspirations, and higher-order goals. Freud theorized that the super-ego emerges around age five, and is not the dominant feature of the personality in a healthy person (which would result in overly-rigid, rule-bound behavior).

The strongest part of the personality is the ego, which seeks to satisfy the needs of the id without disrupting the super-ego.

Psychosexual Stages of Development

Freud proposed that children develop through five stages that he referred to as the psychosexual stages of development. They are as follows:

Stage	Description
Oral (Birth to 1.5 years)	Gratification through mouth/upper digestive tract.
Anal (1.5 to 3 years)	The child gains control over anal sphincter and bowel movements.
Phallic (3 to 6 years)	Gratification through genitalia. Major task is resolution of Oedipal complex and leads to development of superego, which begins about age 4. During this time child's phallic striving is directed toward the opposite-sex parent and in competition with same-sex parent. Out of fear and love, child renounces desire for the opposite sex parent and represses sexual desires. Child then identifies with same-sex parent and internalizes their values, etc. This leads to development of superego and ability to experience guilt.
Latency (6 to 10 years)	Sublimation of the oedipal stage, expression of sexual-aggressive drives in socially acceptable forms
Genital (10 years to adulthood)	Acceptance of one's genitalia and concern for others' wellbeing.

Adult Personality Types

Freud's adult personality types are based on his psychosexual stages and include the following:

Personality Type	Characteristics
Oral	Infantile, demanding, dependent behavior; preoccupation with oral gratification.
Anal	Stinginess, excessive focus on accumulating and collecting. Rigidity in routines and forms, suspiciousness, legalistic thinking.
Phallic	Selfish sexual exploitation of others, without regard to their needs or concerns.

Processes and Stages Relevant to Development of the Personality

Freud identified two primary elements that contribute to the development of the personality:

1. Natural growth and maturational processes (biological, hormonal, and time-dependent processes)
2. Learning and experiential processes (coping with and avoiding pain, managing frustration, reducing anxiety, and resolving conflicts).

According to Freud, psychopathology will result if all 5 stages of psychosexual development are not fully mastered, or if fixation at a particular stage develops (resulting if needs at a particular stage are either over- or under-gratified). If significant developmental frustration is experienced in a later stage, the developmental process may fall back to an earlier stage by means of the defense mechanism known as regression.

Cathexis and Anti-Cathexis

According to Freud's theory, the individual's mental state emerges from the process of reciprocal exchange between two forces: cathexis and anti-cathexis:

- Freud used the term **cathexis** to refer to the psychic energy attached to an object of importance (i.e., person, body part, psychic element). He also used this term to refer to what he called urges, or psychic impulses (e.g., desires, wishes, pain), that drive human behavior.
- In contrast to the driving urges of cathexis, there is a checking force he referred to as **anti-cathexis**. It serves to restrict the urges of the id and also to keep repressed information in the unconscious mind.

ERIK ERIKSON'S PSYCHOSOCIAL STAGES OF DEVELOPMENT

Erik Erikson was one of the first theorists to address human development over the entire life span. The eight developmental stages in his theory of psychosocial development are:

Stage	Description
Trust vs. Mistrust (Birth to 1.5 years)	• Same ages as Freud's oral stage. • Infants develop a sense of trust in self and in others. • Psychological dangers include a strong sense of mistrust that later develops and is revealed as withdrawal when the individual is at odds with self and others.
Autonomy vs. Shame (1.5 to 3 years)	• Same ages as Freud's anal stage. • In this phase, rapid growth in muscular maturation, verbalization, and the ability to coordinate highly conflicting action patterns is characterized by tendencies of holding on and letting go. • The child begins experiencing an autonomous will, which contributes to the process of identity building and development of the courage to be an independent individual. • Psychological dangers include immature obsessiveness and procrastination, ritualistic repetitions to gain power, self-insistent stubbornness, compulsive meek compliance or self-restraint, and the fear of a loss of self-control.
Initiative vs. Guilt (3 to 6 years)	• Same ages as Freud's phallic stage. • Incursion into space by mobility, into the unknown by curiosity, and into others by physical attack and aggressive voice. • This stage frees the child's initiative and sense of purpose for adult tasks. • Psychological dangers include hysterical denial or self-restriction, which impede an individual from actualizing inner capacities.
Industry vs. Inferiority (6 to 11 years)	• Same as Freud's latency stage. • The need of the child is to make things well, to be a worker, and a potential provider. • Developmental task is mastery over physical objects, self, social transaction, ideas, and concepts. • School and peer groups are necessary for gaining and testing mastery. • Psychological dangers include a sense of inferiority, incompetence, self-restraint, and conformity.
Identity vs. Role Confusion (Adolescence)	• Same age range as Freud's genital stage. • Crucial task is to create an identity, reintegration of various components of self into a whole person—a process of ego synthesis. • Peer group is greatly important in providing support, values, a primary reference group, and an arena in which to experiment with various roles. • Psychological dangers include extreme identity confusion, feelings of estrangement, excessive conformity or rebelliousness, and idealism (a denial of reality, neurotic conflict, or delinquency).

Stage	Description
Intimacy vs. Isolation (Early adulthood)	• Task is to enter relationships with others in an involved, reciprocal manner. • Failure to achieve intimacy can lead to highly stereotyped interpersonal relationships and distancing. Can also lead to a willingness to renounce, isolate, and destroy others whose presence seems dangerous.
Generativity vs. Stagnation (Adulthood)	• Key task is to develop concern for establishing and guiding the next generation, and the capacity for caring, nurturing, and concern for others. • Psychological danger is stagnation. Stagnation includes caring primarily for oneself, an artificial intimacy with others, and self-indulgence.
Ego integrity vs. Despair (Late adulthood)	• Task is the acceptance of one's life, achievements, and significant relationships as satisfactory and acceptable. • Psychological danger is despair. Despair is expressed in having the sense that time is too short to start another life or to test alternative roads to integrity. • Despair is accompanied by self-criticism, regret, and fear of impending death.

The stages are hierarchical and build upon each other. The resolution of the fundamental "crisis" of each prior stage must occur before one can move on to the next stage of growth. Although individual attributes are primary in resolving the crisis associated with each stage, the social environment can play an important role as well.

Erikson's Ego Strength

The ego essentially mediates irrational impulses related to the id (drives, instincts, needs). The concept of ego strengths derives from Erikson's (1964, 1985) 8 psychosocial stages and includes hope, will, purpose, competence, fidelity, love, care, and wisdom. Ego strength results from the overcoming of crises in each stage of development and allows the individual to maintain good mental health despite challenges and cope with conflict. Ego strength is assessed through questioning and observation. Characteristics of **ego strength** include the ability to:

- Express a range of feelings and emotions without being overwhelmed by them
- Deal effectively with loss
- Gain strength from loss
- Continue to engage in positive and life-affirming activities
- Exhibit empathy and consideration of others
- Resist temptation and exercise self-control
- Admit responsibility for own actions and avoid blaming others
- Show acceptance of the self
- Set limits in order to avoid negative influences and outcomes

Jean Piaget's Theory of Cognitive and Moral Development

Key Concepts

Jean Piaget believed that development was progressive and followed a set pattern. He believed the child's environment, their interactions with others in that environment, and how the environment responds help to shape the child's cognitive development. **Key concepts of Piaget's theory of cognitive and moral development** are defined below:

- **Action** is overt behavior.
- **Operation** is a particular type of action that may be internalized thought.
- **Activity in Development** refers to the fact that the child is not a passive subject, but an active contributor to the construction of her or his personality and universe. The child acts on her or his environment, modifies it, and is an active participant in the construction of reality.
- **Adaptation** includes accommodation and assimilation. Accommodation entails adapting to the characteristics of the object. Assimilation is the incorporation of external reality into the existing mental organization.

Stages of Cognitive and Moral Development

The stages of Piaget's theory of cognitive and moral development are as follows:

Stage	Description
Sensorimotor (Birth to 2 years)	• Infant cannot evoke representations of persons or objects when they are absent—symbolic function. • Infant interacts with her or his surroundings and can focus on objects other than self. Infant learns to predict events (door opening signals that someone will appear). Infants also learn that objects continue to exist when out of sight and learn a beginning sense of causality.
Pre-operational (2 to 7 years)	• Developing of symbolic thought draws from sensory-motor thinking. • Conceptual ability not yet developed.
Concrete operational (7 to 11 years)	• Child gains capacity to order and relate experience to an organized whole. • Children can now explore several possible solutions to a problem without adopting one, as they are able to return to their original outlook.
Formal operational (11 years to adolescence)	• Child/youth can visualize events and concepts beyond the present and is able to form theories.

Lawrence Kohlberg's Theory of Moral Development

Lawrence Kohlberg's theory of moral development is characterized as the following:

- Kohlberg formulated his theory to extend and modify the work of Piaget, as he believed that moral development was a longer and more complex process. He postulated that infants possess no morals or ethics at birth and that moral development occurs largely independently of age. Kohlberg asserted that children's experiences shape their understanding of moral concepts (i.e., justice, rights, equality, human welfare).
- Kohlberg suggested a process involving three levels, each with two stages. Each stage reveals a dramatic change in the moral perspective of the individual.

- In this theory, moral development is linear, no stage can be skipped, and development takes place throughout the life span.
- Progress between stages is contingent upon the availability of a role model who offers a model of the principles of the next higher level.

Levels and Stages of Moral Development

The levels and stages of Kohlberg's theory of moral development are as follows:

Stage	Level	Description
1	Pre-conventional	The individual perspective frames moral judgments, which are concrete. The framework of Stage 1 stresses rule following, because breaking rules may lead to punishment. Reasoning in this stage is egocentric and not concerned with others.
2	Pre-conventional	Emphasizes moral reciprocity and has its focus on the pragmatic, instrumental value of an action. Individuals at this stage observe moral standards because it is in their interest, but they are able to justify retaliation as a form of justice. Behavior in this stage is focused on following rules only when it is in the person's immediate interest. Stage 2 has a mutual contractual nature, which makes rule-following instrumental and based on externalities. There is, however, an understanding of conventional morality.
3	Conventional	Individuals define morality in reference to what is expected by those with whom they have close relationships. Emphasis of this stage is on stereotypic roles (good mother, father, sister). Virtue is achieved through maintaining trusting and loyal relationships.
4	Conventional	In this stage, the individual shifts from basically narrow local norms and role expectations to a larger social system perspective. Social responsibilities and observance of laws are key aspects of social responsibility. Individuals in this stage reflect higher levels of abstraction in understanding laws' significance. Individuals at Stage 4 have a sophisticated understanding of the law and only violate laws when they conflict with social duties. Observance of the law is seen as necessary to maintain the protections that the legal system provides to all.
5	Post-conventional	The individual becomes aware that while rules and laws exist for the good of the greatest number, there are times when they will work against the interest of particular individuals. Issues may not always be clear-cut and the individual may have to decide to disregard some rules or laws in order to uphold a higher good (such as the protection of life).
6	Post-conventional	Individuals have developed their own set of moral guidelines, which may or may not fit with the law. Principles such as human rights, justice, and equality apply to everyone and the individual must be prepared to act to defend these principles, even if it means going against the rest of society and paying the consequences (i.e., disapproval or imprisonment). Kohlberg believed very few, if any, people reached this stage.

Parenting Styles

Although children are born with their own temperament, the parenting style they grow up with can influence how this temperament manifests over time.

Authoritarian (autocratic) parents desire obedience without question. They tend toward harsh punishments, using their power to make their children obey. They are emotionally withdrawn from their children and enforce strict rules without discussing why the rules exist. These children tend to have low self-esteem, be more dependent, and are introverted with poor social skills.

Authoritative (democratic) parents provide boundaries and expect obedience, but use love when they discipline. They involve their children in deciding rules and consequences, discussing reasons for their decisions, but they will still enforce the rules consistently. They encourage independence and take each child's unique position seriously. These children tend to have higher self-esteem, good social skills, and confidence in themselves.

Indulgent (permissive) parents stay involved with their children, but have few rules in place to give the children boundaries. These children have a difficult time setting their own limits and are not responsible. They disrespect others and have trouble with authority figures.

Indifferent (uninvolved) parents spend as little time as possible with their children. They are self-involved, with no time or patience for taking care of their children's needs. Guidance and discipline are lacking and inconsistent. These children tend toward delinquency, with a lack of respect for others.

Attachment and Bonding

Attachment is the emotional bond that develops between an infant and parent/caregiver when the infant responds to the nonverbal communication of the parent/caregiver and develops a sense of trust and security as the infant's needs are met. Nonverbal communication includes eye contact, calm and attentive facial expressions, tender tone of voice, touch, and body language.

Bonding is especially important during the child's first 3 years, and the failure to develop an attachment bond may impact the child's development and the family dynamics. Infants that have bonded generally exhibit stranger anxiety at about 6 months and separation anxiety by one year. While the parent/caregiver can nurture the emotional connection with the child at later ages, those infants who failed to attach in the first year may have increased difficulty doing so later. Children who have bonded with parents/caregivers tend to develop according to expectations, meeting expected milestones, while those who are deprived may exhibit growth and development delays and well as poor feeding.

Review Video: Factors in Development
Visit mometrix.com/academy and enter code: 112169

Learning Theory and Behavior Modification

Pavlov's Work

Pavlov learned to link experimentally manipulated stimuli (or conditioned stimuli) to existing natural, unconditioned stimuli that elicited a fixed, **unconditioned response**. Pavlov accomplished this by introducing the **conditioned response** just prior to the natural, unconditioned stimulus. Just before giving a dog food (an autonomic stimulus for salivation), Pavlov sounded a bell. The bell then became the stimulus for salivation, even in the absence of food being given. Many conditioned responses can be created through continuing reinforcement.

Skinner's Work

B. F. Skinner developed the **empty organism concept**, which proposes that an infant has the capacity for action built into his or her physical makeup. The infant also has reflexes and motivations that will set this capacity in random motion. Skinner asserted that the **law of effect** governs development. Behavior of children is shaped largely by adults. Behaviors that result in satisfying consequences are likely to be repeated under similar circumstances. Halting or discontinuing behavior is accomplished by denying satisfying rewards or through punishment. Skinner also theorized about **schedules of reinforcement**. He posited that rather than reinforcing every instance of a correct response, one can reinforce a fixed percentage of correct responses, or space reinforcements according to some interval of time. Intermittent reinforcement will reinforce the desired behavior.

Feminist Theory

Feminist theory views inequity in terms of gender with females as victims of an almost universal patriarchal model in which the sociopolitical, family, and religious institutions are dominated by males. Proponents of feminist theory focus on areas of interest to females, including social and economic inequality, power structures, gender discrimination, racial discrimination, and gender oppression. Feminists often point to the exclusion of women in the development of theories about human behavior, research, and other academic matters. Some feminists believe that oppression of women is inherent to capitalism, where females are often paid less than males, but others believe that it is inherent in all forms of government because they are all based on patriarchal models. Feminists recognize that gender, social class, and race are all sources of oppression with ethnic minorities and those in the lower social classes often suffering the most oppression. Feminists note that the idea that families headed by women are dysfunctional is based on patriarchal ideals.

Carol Gilligan's Morality of Care

Carol Gilligan's morality of care is the feminist response to Kohlberg's moral development theory. Kohlberg's theory was based on research only on men. Gilligan purports that a morality of care reflects women's experience more accurately than one emphasizing justice and rights. Key concepts include the following:

- **Morality of care** reflects caring, responsibility, and non-violence, while **morality of justice and rights** emphasizes equality.
- The two types of moralities give two distinct charges, to not treat others unfairly (justice/rights) and to not turn away from someone in need (care). Care stresses interconnectedness and nurturing. Emphasizing justice stems from a focus on individualism.
- **Aspects of attachment**: Justice/rights requires individuation and separation from the parent, which leads to awareness of power differences. Care emphasizes a continuing attachment to parent and less awareness of inequalities, not a primary focus on fairness.

Older Adulthood

How the Elderly Deal with Life Transitions

Typically, the elderly population seeks to cope with whatever problem comes their way without the benefit of mental health care. In 1991, Butler and Lewis developed a definition for **loss** in relation to the elderly. Elderly can experience a range of emotions whenever loss or death occurs. Examples of loss could be loss of friends, loss of significant others or spouse, a loss of social roles within the community, a loss of work or career, a loss of a prestigious role, a loss of income, a loss of physical vigor, or a loss of health. Some may experience personality changes or changes in sexual appetites.

Elderly people may have a situational crisis that puts a strain on their resources. The resiliency of this population is evident by the large number of seniors who live independently with only a little support. Only 4-6% live in nursing homes or assisted living facilities, and 10-15% receive homecare.

Factors Preventing the Elderly from Receiving Mental Health Services

While mental illness is often overestimated in the elderly population, it is still prevalent, with one in five elderly individuals experiencing some sort of mental illness. The most significant **mental illnesses** experienced by the elderly are anxiety, severe cognitive impairment, and mood disorders. Anxiety is the most prevalent of these problems. These numbers may be skewed by the fact that the elderly may not be seeking help when needed. Sadly, suicide rates are higher in this population than in any other population. The older a person gets, the higher the rate of suicide. Anxiety and depression cause much suffering in the elderly.

There are a number of factors that **prevent the elderly from receiving mental health services**. Part of the problem lies in the strong values which guide the elderly to solve their own problems. Other seniors feel they should keep quiet about private issues. Still others feel a negative connotation from past stigmas attached to those who needed mental health care. Baby boomers approaching old age have been bombarded with literature on psychology and healthy lifestyles. Therefore, the baby boomer generation may take on a healthier attitude about receiving the appropriate mental health care for their needs. A limited number of counselors, social workers and therapists are trained in geriatric care. Providers for the elderly have difficulties working with payment policies and insurance companies. In addition, seeing the client's aging problems may cause unpleasant personal issues about aging to surface for the provider.

Human Behavior in the Social Environment

Person-in-Environment Theory

The **person-in-environment** theory considers the influence the individual has on their environment and the influence that multiple environments (social, economic, family, political, cultural, religious, work, ethnic, life events) have on the individual. This is an interactive model that is central to social work and recognizes the impact of oppression and discrimination on the individual. The person-in-environment theory supports the goals of social work in providing personal care for the individual and furthering the cause of social justice. The person-in-environment theory is the basis for the strength-based perspective of social work in which the social worker focuses first on the personal strengths of the individual and the strengths within the person's environment. The social worker utilizes psychosocial interventions and assesses behavior on the basis of interactions between the individual and the environment because the person's life situation results from the relationship between the individual and the individual's environment.

Hildegard Peplau's Theory of Interpersonal Relations

Hildegard Peplau developed the theory of interpersonal relations in 1952, applying Sullivan's theory of anxiety to nursing practice, developing a framework for psychiatric nursing. The model, however, can be applied to other helping disciplines. The relationship comprises the helping professional (nurse or social worker), who has expertise, and the individual (client or patient), who wants relief from suffering/problems.

According to Peplau, the professional-individual relationship evolves through 4 phases:

Phase	Details
Preorientation	The helping professional prepares, anticipating possible reactions and interventions.
Orientation	Roles and responsibilities are clarified in the initial interview.
Working	The professional and individual explore together and promote the individual's problem-solving skills.
Termination	The final phase consists of summarizing and reviewing.

The helping professional uses process recording, which includes observing, interpreting, and intervening to help the individual, but also self-observation to increase self-awareness. Peplau believed that individuals deserved human care by educated helpers and should be treated with dignity and respect. She also believed that the environment (social, psychosocial, and physical) could affect the individual in a positive or negative manner. The helping professional can focus on the way in which individuals react to their problems and can help them to use those problems as an opportunity for learning and maturing.

Systems Theory

Systems theory derives its theoretical orientation from general systems theory and includes elements of organizational theory, family theory, group behavior theory, and a variety of sociological constructs. Key **principles** include the following:

- Systems theory endeavors to provide a methodological view of the world by synthesizing key principles from its theoretical roots.
- A fundamental premise is that key sociological aspects of individuals, families, and groups cannot be separated from the whole (i.e., aspects that are systemic in nature).
- All systems are interrelated, and change in one will produce change in the others.

- Systems are either open or closed: Open systems accept outside input and accommodate, while closed systems resist outside input due to rigid and impenetrable barriers and boundaries.
- Boundaries are lines of demarcation identifying the outer margins of the system being examined.
- Entropy refers to the process of system dissolution or disorganization.
- Homeostatic balance refers to the propensity of systems to reestablish and maintain stability.

Ecosystems Theory

Ecosystems (or life model) theory derives its theoretical orientation from ecology, systems theory, psychodynamic theory, behavioral theory, and cognitive theory. Key principles include the following:

- There is an interactive relationship between all living organisms and their environment (both social and physical).
- The process of adaptation is universal and is a reciprocal process by individuals and environments mutually accommodating each other to obtain a "goodness of fit."
- Changes in individuals, their environments, or both can be disruptive and produce dysfunction.
- This theory works to optimize goodness of fit by modifying perceptions, thoughts, responsiveness, and exchanges between clients and their environments.
- On a larger (community) level, treatment interventions by the ecosystems approach are drawn from direct practice and include educating, identifying and expanding resources, developing needed policies and programs, and engaging governmental systems to support requisite change.

Impact of Family on Human Behavior

Family Types

A **family** consists of a group of people that are connected by marriage, blood relationship, or emotions. There are many different variations when referring to the concept of family.

- The **nuclear family** is one in which two or more people are related by blood, marriage, or adoption. This type of family is typically parents and their children.
- The **extended family** is one in which several nuclear families related by blood or marriage function as one group.

A **household** consists of an individual or group of people residing together under one roof. The social worker will often interact with families on many different levels. This may involve meeting the family once during the client's session or establishing a long-term relationship with the family over the course of supporting a chronically ill client.

Functional Family

A functional family will be able to change roles, responsibilities, and interactions during a stressful event. This type of family can experience **nonfunctional behaviors** if placed in an acute stressful event; however, they should be able to reestablish their family balance over a period of time. The functional family will have the ability to deal with **conflict and change** in order to deal with negative situations without causing long-term dysfunction or dissolution of the family. They will have completed vital life cycle tasks, keep emotional contact between family members and across generations, over-closeness is avoided, and distance is used to resolve issues. When two members of the family have a conflict, they are expected to **resolve** this conflict between themselves and there is **open communication** between all family members. Children of a functional family are expected to achieve age-appropriate functioning and are given age-appropriate privileges.

FAMILY LIFE CYCLE

The family life cycle comprises the states typical individuals go through from childhood to old age. Stages include:

Stage	Details
Independence	Individuals begin to separate from the family unit and develop a sense of their place in the world. Individuals may begin to explore careers and become increasingly independent in providing for self needs. Individuals often develop close peer relationships outside of the family.
Coupling	Individuals develop intimate relationships with others and may live together or marry, moving toward interdependence, joint goal setting and problem-solving. Individuals learn new communication skills and may have to adjust expectations.
Parenting	Individuals make the decision to have or adopt children and adjust their lives and roles accordingly. Relationships may change and be tested, and parents may shift focus from themselves to their children.
Empty nest	Individuals may feel profound loss and stress at this change, especially since this is also the time when health problems of age and the need to care for parents arise. Relationships with children evolve.
Retirement	Individuals may undergo many changes and challenges and must deal with deaths of family and friends and their own mortality.

FAMILY LIFE EDUCATION

Family life education, which can include parenting and financial management classes, aims to give people the information and tools they need in order to strengthen family life. Approaches to family life education include:

- **Strength-based**: Assisting individuals to identify their strengths and those of their environment in order to increase their sense of personal power and engagement.
- **Cultural**: Focusing on cultural norms and the diverse needs of different populations as well as utilizing communication and activities that correspond to different cultures.
- **Selective**: Aiming at specific groups, such as LGBTQ parents or grandparents, in order to ascertain their unique needs and to provide appropriate education. Some programs may be designed for at-risk groups, such as those in court-ordered education programs because of abuse or neglect.
- **Universal**: Universal education focuses on all members of a particular population, such as all parents, despite differences among the parents. These programs often focus on general information, such as growth and development, and cover a range of topics.

EFFECTS OF MENTAL ILLNESS ON FAMILY

Families with a member that has a **chronic mental illness** will provide several functions that those without mentally ill members may not need. These functions can include providing support and information for care and treatment options. They will also monitor the services provided the family member and address concerns with these services. Many times, the family is the biggest **advocate** for additional availability of services for mental health clients. There can often be disagreements between the care providers and the family members concerning the dependence of the client within the family. Parents can often be viewed as overprotective when attempting to encourage a client's independence and self-reliant functioning. They will need support and reassurance if the individual leaves home. On the other hand, many parents will provide for their child for as long as they live. Once the primary care provider dies, the client may be left with no one to care for them and they may experience traumatic disruptions.

Developmental Model of Couples Therapy

The developmental model of couples therapy (Bader & Pearson) accepts the inevitable change in relationships and focuses on both individual and couple growth and development. The goal is to assist the couple to recognize their stage of development and to gain the skills and insight needed to progress to the next stage. Problems may especially arise if members of the couple are at different stages. Stages include:

Stage	Details
Bonding	Couples meet, develop a romantic relationship, and fall in love, focusing on similarities rather than differences. Sexual intimacy is an important component.
Differentiating	Conflicts and differences begin to arise, and couples must learn to work together to resolve their problems.
Practicing	Couples become more independent from each other, establish outside friendships, and develop outside interests.
Rapprochement	Couples move apart and then together again, often increasing intimacy and feeling more satisfied with the relationship.
Synergy	Couples become more intimate and recognize the strength of their union.

Anna Freud's Defense Mechanisms

According to Anna Freud, defense mechanisms are an unconscious process in which the ego attempts to expel anxiety-provoking sexual and aggressive impulses from consciousness. Defense mechanisms are attempts to protect the self from painful anxiety and are used universally. In themselves they are not an indication of pathology, but rather an indication of disturbance when their cost outweighs their protective value. Anna Freud proposed that defense mechanisms serve to protect the ego and to reduce angst, fear, and distress through irrational distortion, denial, and/or obscuring reality. Defense mechanisms are deployed when the ego senses the threat of harm from thoughts or acts incongruent with rational behavior or conduct demanded by the super-ego.

The following are terms that pertain to **Anna Freud's defense mechanisms**:

Compensation	Protection against feelings of inferiority and inadequacy stemming from real or imagined personal defects or weaknesses.
Conversion	Somatic changes conveyed in symbolic body language; psychic pain is felt in a part of the body.
Denial	Avoidance of awareness of some painful aspect of reality.
Displacement	Investing repressed feelings in a substitute object.
Association	Altruism; acquiring gratification through connection with and helping another person who is satisfying the same instincts.
Identification	Manner by which one becomes like another person in one or more respects; a more elaborate process than introjection.
Identification with the Aggressor	A child's introjection of some characteristic of an anxiety evoking object and assimilation of an anxiety experience just lived through. In this, the child can transform from the threatened person into the one making the threat.
Introjection	Absorbing an idea or image so that it becomes part of oneself.
Inversion	Turning against the self; object of aggressive drive is changed from another to the self, especially in depression and masochism.
Isolation of Affect	Separation of ideas from the feelings originally associated with them. Remaining idea is deprived of motivational force; action is impeded and guilt avoided.
Intellectualization	Psychological binding of instinctual drives in intellectual activities, for example the adolescent's preoccupation with philosophy and religion.
Projection	Ascribing a painful idea or impulse to the external world.
Rationalization	Effort to give a logical explanation for painful unconscious material to avoid guilt and shame.
Reaction Formation	Replacing in conscious awareness a painful idea or feeling with its opposite.
Regression	Withdrawal to an earlier phase of psychosexual development.
Repression	The act of obliterating material from conscious awareness. This is capable of mastering powerful impulses.
Reversal	Type of reaction formation aimed at protection from painful thoughts/feelings.
Splitting	Seeing external objects as either all good or all bad. Feelings may rapidly shift from one category to the other.
Sublimation	Redirecting energies of instinctual drives to generally positive goals that are more acceptable to the ego and superego.
Substitution	Trading of one affect for another (e.g., rage that masks fear)
Undoing	Ritualistically performing the opposite of an act one has recently carried out in order to cancel out or balance the evil that may have been present in the act.

Sexual Orientation

Sexuality

Sexuality is an integral part of each individual's personality and refers to all aspects of being a sexual human. It is more than just the act of physical intercourse. A person's sexuality is often apparent in what they do, in their appearance, and in how they interact with others. There are four main aspects of sexuality:

- **Genetic identity** or chromosomal gender
- **Gender identification** or how they perceive themselves with regard to male or female
- **Gender role** or the attributes of their cultural role
- **Sexual orientation** or the gender to which one is attracted

By assessing and attempting to conceptualize a person's sexuality, the social worker can gain a broader understanding of the client's beliefs and will be able to provide a more holistic approach to providing care.

Gender Identity

Gender identity is the gender to which the individual identifies, which may or may not be the gender of birth (natal gender). Most children begin to express identification and behaviors associated with gender between ages 2 and 4. The degree to which this identification is influenced by genetics and environment is an ongoing debate because, for example, female children are often socialized toward female roles (dresses, dolls, pink items). Societal pressure to conform to gender stereotypes is strong, so gender dysphoria, which is less common in early childhood than later, may be suppressed. At the onset of puberty, sexual attraction may further complicate gender identity although those with gender dysphoria most often have sexual attraction to those of the same natal gender, so a natal boy who identifies as a girl is more likely to be sexually attracted to boys than to girls. Later in adolescence, individuals generally experiment with sexual behavior and solidify their gender identity.

Influence of Sexual Orientation on Behaviors

The degree to which sexual orientation influences behavior may vary widely depending on the individual. For example, some gay males may be indistinguishable in appearance and general behavior from heterosexual males while others may behave in a stereotypically flamboyant manner. The same holds true for lesbians, with some typically feminine in appearance and behavior and others preferring a more masculine appearance. The typical heterosexual model (two people in a stable relationship) is increasingly practiced by homosexual couples while others prefer less traditional practices. Depending on the degree of acceptance that LGBTQ individuals encounter, they may hide their sexual orientation or maintain a heterosexual relationship in order to appear straight. LGBTQ individuals are at higher risk of depression and suicide, especially if they experience rejection because of their sexual orientation or have been taught that it is sinful. LGBTQ individuals with multiple sexual partners (especially males) are at increased risk for STDs, including HIV/AIDS.

Coming Out Process

The coming out process is the act of revealing LGBTQ sexual orientation to family and friends. This generally occurs during adolescence or early adulthood although some may delay coming out for decades or never do so. Individuals may come out to select groups of people. For example, friends may be aware of an individual's orientation but not family or co-workers. Coming out can be frightening for many people, especially if they have reason to fear rejection or fear for their safety. Stages in coming out typically progress in the following order:

Stage	Actions and feelings involved
Confusion	The individual may be unsure of feelings or be in denial.
Exploration	The individual begins to question orientation and wonder about LGBTQ people.
Breakthrough	The individual accepts the likelihood of being LGBTQ and seeks others of the same orientation.
Acceptance	The individual accepts orientation and begins to explore and read about the LGBTQ culture.
Pride	The individual begins to exhibit pride in orientation and may reject straight culture or exhibit stereotypically LGBTQ behaviors.
Synthesis	The individual comes to terms with the reality of the LGBTQ orientation, is at peace with their identity, and is generally out to family, friends, and co-workers.

Practice Issues When Working with LGBTQ Clients

Possible practice issues with LGBTQ clients include, but are not limited to, the following:

- Stigmatization and violence
- Internalized homophobia
- Coming out
- AIDS
- Limited civil rights
- Orientation vs. preference (biology vs. choice)

Problematic treatment models for treating gays and lesbians include the following:

- The moral model for treatment is religiously oriented and views homosexuality as sinful.
- Reparative or conversion psychotherapy focuses on changing a person's sexual orientation to heterosexual. Traditional mental health disciplines view this type of treatment as unethical and as having no empirical base.

Self-Image

Factors Influencing Self-Image

Factors influencing self-image include the following:

- **Spirituality**: Religious or spiritual beliefs may affect how individuals see their place in the world and their self-confidence. Individuals may gain self-esteem through secure beliefs and membership in a like group, but belief systems with a strong emphasis on sin may impair self-image.
- **Culture**: Individuals are affected (negatively and positively) by cultural expectations, especially if they feel outside of the norm.
- **Ethnicity**: Whether or not the individual is part of the dominant ethnic group may have a profound effect on self-image. Minority groups often suffer discrimination that reinforces the idea that they are less valuable than others.
- **Education**: Those with higher levels of education tend to have a better self-image than those without, sometimes because of greater unemployment and fewer opportunities associated with low education.
- **Gender**: Society often reinforces the value of males (straight) over females and LGBTQ individuals.
- **Abuse**: Those who are abused may often develop a poor self-image, believing they are deserving of abuse.
- **Media**: The media reinforces stereotypes and presents unrealistic (and unattainable) images, affecting self-image.

Body Image

Body image is the perception individuals have of their own bodies, positive or negative. An altered body image may result in a number of responses, most often beginning during adolescence but sometimes during childhood:

- **Obesity**: Some may be unhappy with their body image and overeat as a response, often increasing their discontent.
- **Eating disorders**: Some may react to being overweight or to the cultural ideal by developing anorexia or bulimia in an attempt to achieve the idealized body image they seek. They may persist even though they put their lives at risk. Their body image may be so distorted that they believe they are fat even when emaciated.
- **Body dysmorphic disorder**: Some may develop a preoccupation with perceived defects in their body image, such as a nose that is too big or breasts or penis that is too small. Individuals may become obsessed to the point that they avoid social contact with others, stop participating in sports, get poor grades, stop working, or seek repeated plastic surgery.

Discrimination

SYSTEMIC/INSTITUTIONALIZED DISCRIMINATION

Systemic or institutionalized discrimination is the unfair and unjust treatment of populations because of race, gender, sexual orientation, religion, disability, or any other perceived difference by society in general and by the institutions of society.

Institution	Evidence of racism, sexism, or ageism
Healthcare	Provision and access to care may be unequal. People often lack insurance or depend on Medicaid, which limits access. Lack of prenatal care results in higher rates of infant morbidity/mortality. People often develop chronic illnesses because of poor preventive care.
Employment	Discriminatory hiring practices limit employment and advancement opportunities, resulting in unemployment or low income, which can result in homelessness, substance abuse, or criminal activity.
Finances/Housing	People may be denied loans or face high interest rates, limiting their ability to buy homes, pay for education, and start businesses or resulting in high rates of debt. Low-cost housing is often in areas of high crime and gang activity, which is especially a risk for adolescents and the elderly.
Education	Children may attend substandard schools with few enrichment programs, putting them at a disadvantage as they progress through school and into job market or advanced education programs. Many students graduate without adequate skills or drop out.
Criminal justice	People of color are more likely to be arrested and to receive longer sentences for crimes.

EFFECTS OF DISCRIMINATION ON BEHAVIOR

Discrimination can result in significant effects, primarily negative, on its subjects:

- **Health problems**: Individuals may suffer from increased stress, anxiety, sadness, and depression. Individuals may develop stress-related disorders, such as hypertension or eating disorders. Individuals may not have access to adequate healthcare or insurance and often delay seeking medical help.
- **Substance abuse**: Individuals may seek relief from the stress of discriminatory actions by resorting to the use of alcohol or drugs in order to dull their feelings.
- **Violence/Conflict/Antisocial behavior**: Individuals may respond with anger and seek vengeance against perpetrators of discrimination (or entire groups representing these perpetrators). Adolescents, for example, may join gangs so that they feel accepted. Some individuals may resort to criminal activity, such as robbery.
- **Withdrawal**: Some individuals begin to pull inward and withdraw from social activities or engagement in work or school, leading to increasing failure and even further discrimination. Discrimination in employment and housing may lead to high rates of unemployment and homelessness.
- **Disenfranchisement**: Individuals may feel that they have no voice and may avoid voting or face obstacles to voting, such as lack of proper identification or transportation.

Ageism and Stereotypes of the Elderly

Ageism is an attitude toward the capabilities and experiences of old age which leads to devaluation and disenfranchisement. Some **stereotypes of the elderly** include the assumptions that all elderly individuals are:

- Asexual
- Rigid
- Impaired (psychologically)
- Incapable of change

Implications of Bias in Human Service Clinical Work

Health and mental health services express the ideology of the culture at large (dominant culture). This may cause harm to clients or reinforce **cultural stereotypes**. Examples of this include:

- **Minorities and women** often receive more severe diagnoses and some diagnoses are associated with gender.
- **African-Americans** are at greater risk for involuntary commitment.
- **Gays and lesbians** are sometimes treated with ethically questionable techniques in attempts to reorient their sexuality.

Immigrant Clients

Stresses Associated with Immigration

The process of **immigration introduces many stresses** that must be managed. They include the following:

- Gaining entry into and understanding a foreign culture
- Difficulties with language acquisition
- Immigrants who are educated often cannot find equivalent employment
- Distance from family, friends, and familiar surroundings

Consideration When Assessing Immigrant Clients' Needs

The following are considerations when assessing an immigrant's needs:

- Why and how did the client immigrate?
- Social supports the client has or lacks (community/relatives)
- The client's education/literacy in language of origin and in English
- Economic and housing resources (including number of people in home, availability of utilities)
- Employment history and the ability to find/obtain work
- The client's ability to find and use institutional/governmental supports
- Health status/resources (pre- and post-immigration)
- Social networks (pre- and post-immigration)
- Life control: Degree to which the individual experiences personal power and the ability to make choices

Key Concepts of Diversity and Discrimination

Key concepts of diversity and discrimination include the following:

Race	The concept of race first appeared in the English language just 300 years ago. Race has great social and political significance. It can be defined as a subgroup that possesses a definite combination of characteristics of a genetic origin.
Ethnicity	Ethnicity is a group classification in which members share a unique social and cultural heritage that is passed on from one generation to the next. It is not the same as race, though the two terms are used interchangeably at times.
Worldview	Worldview is an integral concept in the assessment of the client's experience. This can be defined as a way that individuals perceive their relationship to nature, institutions, and other people and objects. This comprises a psychological orientation to life as seen in how individuals think, behave, make decisions, and understand phenomena. It provides crucial information in the assessment of mental health status, assisting in assessment and diagnosis, and in designing treatment programs.
Acculturation	Acculturation is the process of learning and adopting the dominant culture through adaptation and assimilation.
Ethnic identity	Ethnic identity is a sense of belonging to an identifiable group and having historical continuity, in addition to a sense of common customs and mores transmitted over generations.
Social identity	Social identity describes how the dominant culture establishes criteria for categorizing individuals and the normal and ordinary characteristics believed to be natural and usual for members of the society.
Virtual/actual social identity	Virtual social identity is the set of attributes ascribed to persons based on appearances, dialect, social setting, and material features. Actual social identity is the set of characteristics a person actually demonstrates.
Stigma	Stigma is a characteristic that makes an individual different from the group, and is perceived to be an intensely discreditable trait.
Normalization	Normalization describes treating the stigmatized person as if he or she does not have a stigma.
Socioeconomic status	Socioeconomic status is determined by occupation, education, and income of the head of a household.
Prejudice	Prejudice is bias or judgment based on value judgment, personal history, inferences about others, and application of normative judgments.
Discrimination	Discrimination is the act of expressing prejudice with immediate and serious social and economic consequences.
Stereotypes	Stereotypes are amplified distorted beliefs about an ethnicity, gender, or other group, often employed to justify discriminatory conduct.
Oppressed minority	A group differentiated from others in society because of physical or cultural characteristics. The group receives unequal treatment and views itself as an object of collective discrimination.
Privilege	Advantages or benefits that the dominant group has. These have been given unintentionally, unconsciously, and automatically.
Racism	Generalizations, institutionalization, and assignment of values to real or imaginary differences between individuals to justify privilege, aggression, or violence. These societal patterns have the cumulative effect of inflicting oppressive or other negative conditions against identifiable groups based on race or ethnicity. Racism is pervasive, ubiquitous, and institutionalized.

Exploitation

Characteristics of Perpetrators of Exploitation

Characteristics of perpetrators of exploitation may vary widely, depending on the type of exploitation, making them difficult to identify.

- Many of those that are involved in **sex trafficking** are part of large criminal enterprises or have a history of criminal acts and antisocial behavior. The perpetrator may exhibit a domineering attitude, speaking for the victims and never leaving the victim unattended.
- Perpetrators of **elder exploitation** are usually family members or caregivers who take advantage of the victims financially. These perpetrators may appear as loving and caring or sometimes abusive. Business people may take advantage of the elderly by overcharging for goods and services, and some people use scams to get victims to pay or invest money.
- Those involved in **exploitation of child labor** are often in agriculture, working children (most often immigrants) for long hours in the fields at low wages.
- Perpetrators of **slavery/involuntary servitude** may come from cultures with different values, or may be individuals with personal values that allow them to take advantage of others.

Sexual Trafficking

Risk factors for sexual trafficking include being homeless or a runaway, being part of the LGBTQ community, being African American or Latino, having involvement in the child welfare system, having a substance use disorder, and being an illegal immigrant. **Sexual trafficking** may include the following:

- **Children**: Children may be bought or sold for sexual use or forced by family members, even parents, into sex trafficking. Runaways are often picked up on the street and offered shelter, and some children are lured through internet postings. Children who resist may be beaten or even killed. Young girls especially may serve in prostitution rings or be forced to participate in pornography. Many turn to substance abuse.
- **Adults**: Many adult victims begin as victims of sexual trafficking during childhood and continue into adulthood as part of prostitution rings or the pornography industry which they are afraid of or too dependent on to try to escape. Substance abuse is common, often used to self-treat depression or other mental health conditions. Physical abuse is common, as are high rates of STDs and HIV. Forced abortions are also common.

Financial Exploitation

Individuals (especially the elderly and disabled) who become unable to manage their own financial affairs become increasingly vulnerable to **financial exploitation**, especially if they have cognitive impairment or physical impairments that impair their mobility. Financial exploitation includes any of the following:

- Outright stealing of property or persuading individuals to give away possessions
- Forcing individuals to sign away property
- Emptying bank and savings accounts
- Using stolen credit cards
- Convincing the individual to invest money in fraudulent schemes
- Taking money for home renovations that are not done

Indications of financial abuse may be unpaid bills, unusual activity at ATMs or with credit cards, inadequate funds to meet needs, disappearance of items in the home, change in the provision of a will, and deferring to caregivers regarding financial affairs. Family or caregivers may move permanently into the client's home and take over without sharing costs. Clients may be unable to recoup losses and forced to live with reduced means and may exhibit shame or confusion about loss.

Exploitation of Immigration Status

People whose immigration status is illegal are especially at risk of exploitation because they have little recourse to legal assistance that doesn't increase the risk of deportation. Many have paid a high price to "coyotes" to smuggle them into the country and may have been robbed or sexually abused with impunity. Once in the United States, they are often hired at substandard wages and without benefits, including insurance. Many have little access to health care and may suffer from dental and health problems. Housing is often inadequate, and children may drop out of school or have poor attendance because parents move from place to place. Immigrants are often fearful of authorities. Mental health problems, such as depression and substance abuse, are common, but little treatment is available, and many immigrants come from cultures that consider mental illness a cause for shame. Legal immigrants who qualify for assistance may face similar problems, especially related to employment and housing, because of poor language skills and societal discrimination.

Culturally Competent Care

Theory of Cultural Relativism

Key concepts within the theory of cultural relativism include the following:

- Values, beliefs, models of behavior, and understandings of the nature of the universe must be understood within the cultural framework in which they appear.
- The outlines and limitations of normality and deviance are determined by the dominant culture.
- The behavioral norms and expressions of emotional needs of cultural minorities may be defined as abnormal in that they differ from those of the larger, dominant culture.

Behaviors and attitudes may be perceived differently if understood through a unique cultural context. It is important for a social worker to determine whether a client's abnormal or deviant behavior would be considered abnormal or deviant within the client's own culture, as well as in the client's self-assessment.

Cultural Competence

Development of Cultural Competence at the Organizational Level

The stages of development of cultural competency at the organization level are as follows:

1. **Cultural destructiveness**: This stage devalues different cultures and views them as inferior.
2. **Cultural incapacity**: The organization becomes aware of a need, but feels incapable of providing the required services, resulting in immobility.
3. **Cultural blindness**: Cultural blindness, or "colorblindness," lacks recognition of differences between cultural groups and denies the existence of oppression and institutional racism.
4. **Cultural pre-competency**: The organization starts to recognize the needs of different groups, seeking to recruit diverse staff and include appropriate training.
5. **Cultural competency**: Diversity issues are addressed with staff and clients. Staff is trained and confident with a range of differences.
6. **Cultural proficiency**: This is the ideal level of cultural competency and is represented by the ability to incorporate and respond to new cultural groups.

Measures of Cultural Competence

Measures of cultural competence include the following abilities:

- Ability to recognize the effects of cultural differences on the helping process
- Ability to fully acknowledge one's own culture and its impact on one's thoughts and actions
- Ability to comprehend the dynamics of power differences in social work practice
- Ability to comprehend the meaning of a client's behavior in its cultural context
- Ability to know when, where, and how to obtain necessary cultural information

Enhancing Cultural Competence

A social worker can enhance their cultural competence by doing the following:

- Reading applicable practice or scientific professional literature
- Becoming familiar with the literature of the relevant group(s)
- Identifying and consulting with cultural brokers
- Seeking out experiences to interact with diverse groups

Social workers must reflect on themselves, their own cultures, and how their cultures affect their way of thinking and moving in the world. Becoming aware of one's own biases and seeking to be open to differences in other cultures is a critical key in providing culturally competent care.

Cultural Sensitivity

Culturally Sensitive Practice for the Institution

Culturally sensitive practice for the institution includes practice skills, attitudes, policies, and structures that are united in a system, in an agency, or among professionals and allow that entity to work with cultural differences. It both values diversity (i.e., diverse staff, policies that acknowledge and respect differences, and regular initiation of cultural self-assessment) and institutionalizes diversity (i.e., the organization has integrated diversity into its structure, policies, and operations).

Culturally Sensitive Practice for Individual Social Workers

Culturally sensitive practice for the individual social worker describes an ability to work skillfully with cultural differences. It includes the following:

- Awareness and acceptance of differences
- Awareness of one's own cultural values
- Understanding the dynamics of difference
- Development of cultural competence
- An ability to adapt practice skills to fit the cultural context of the client's structure, values, and service

Cultural sensitivity is an ongoing process that requires continuing education, awareness, management of transference and counter-transference, and continuous skill development.

Characteristics of Culturally Sensitive Social Workers

Characteristics of the culturally sensitive social worker include the following:

- With regard for individuality and confidentiality, the social worker approaches clients in a respectful, warm, accepting, and interested manner.
- The social worker understands that opinions and experiences of both worker and client are affected by stereotypes and previous experience.
- The social worker is able to acknowledge their own socialization to beliefs, attitudes, biases, and prejudices that may affect the working relationship.
- The social worker displays awareness of cross-cultural factors that may affect the relationship.
- The social worker is able to communicate that cultural differences and their expressions are legitimate.
- The social worker is open to help from the client in learning about the client's background.

- The social worker is informed about life conditions fostered by poverty, racism, and disenfranchisement.
- The social worker is aware that a client's cultural background may be peripheral to the client's situation and not central to it.

Theories of Culturally Influenced Communication

Interpersonal communication is shaped by both culture and context. According to Hall's theory of communication, **high context communication styles** are used in Asian, Latino, African American, and Native American cultures in the US. In this style, there is a strong reliance on contextual cues and a flexible sense of time. This style is intuitive, and within it, social roles shape interactions, communication is more personal and affective, and oral agreements are binding.

According to Hall's theory, **low context communication styles** are used more in Northern European, white groups in the US. These styles tend to be formal and have complex codes. They tend to show a disregard for contextual codes and a reliance on verbal communication. In these styles, there is an inflexible sense of time, linear logic is used, and relationships are functionally based and highly procedural.

The worker should be aware of the potential for cross-cultural misunderstanding and that all cultures exhibit great diversity within themselves.

Use of Language and Communication to Become More Culturally Sensitive

Methods of communication for the social worker to become more culturally sensitive include the following:

- Learn to speak the target language
- Use interpreters appropriately
- Participate in cultural events of the group(s)
- Form friendships with members of different cultural groups than one's own
- Acquire cultural and historical information about cultural groups
- Learn about the institutional barriers that limit access to cultural and economic resources for vulnerable groups
- Gain an understanding of the socio-political system in the U.S. and the implications for majority and minority groups

Limitations in Cultural Sensitivity

Some cultural differences may be damaging or unacceptable. In these cases, there is a limit to which cultural sensitivity is applied. The worker needs to have a balanced approach to assess cultural norms within the context of American practices, norms, and laws. There are **illegal and unacceptable cultural practices** outside the limits of cultural sensitivity. These may include the following:

- Child labor
- Honor killings
- Private/family vengeance
- Slavery
- Infanticide
- Female genital mutilation
- Wife or servant beating
- Polygamy
- Child marriage
- Denial of medical care
- Abandonment of disabled children
- Extreme discipline of children

Barriers to Cross-Cultural Practice

Barriers to cross-cultural practice include the following:

- **Cultural encapsulation**: Ethnocentrism, color-blindness, false universals
- **Language barriers**: Verbal, nonverbal, body language, dialect
- **Class-bound values**: Treatment, service delivery, power dynamics
- **Culture-bound values**: Religious beliefs/practices, dietary preferences, choice of attire

Indicators of Substance Abuse

General Indicators of Substance Abuse

Many people with substance abuse (alcohol or drugs) are reluctant to disclose this information, but there are a number of indicators that are suggestive of substance abuse**:**

Physical signs include:

- Burns on fingers or lips
- Pupils abnormally dilated or constricted; eyes watery
- Slurring of speech or slow speech
- Lack of coordination, instability of gait, or tremors
- Sniffing repeatedly, nasal irritation, persistent cough
- Weight loss
- Dysrhythmias
- Pallor, puffiness of face
- Needle tracks on arms or legs

Behavioral signs include:

- Odor of alcohol or marijuana on clothing or breath
- Labile emotions, including mood swings, agitation, and anger
- Inappropriate, impulsive, or risky behavior
- Missing appointments
- Difficulty concentrating, short term memory loss, blackouts
- Insomnia or excessive sleeping
- Disorientation or confusion
- Lack of personal hygiene

Alcohol

Alcohol is described as follows:

- A liquid distilled product of fermented fruits, grains, and vegetables
- Can be used as a solvent, an antiseptic, and a sedative
- Has a high potential for abuse
- Small-to-moderate amounts taken over extended periods of time may have positive effects on health

Possible Effects of Alcohol

The following are **possible effects of alcohol use**:

- Intoxication
- Sensory alteration
- Reduction in anxiety

Particular Challenges of Diagnosis and Treatment of Alcohol Abuse

Challenges in **diagnostics and treatment of alcohol abuse** include the following:

- Alcohol is the most available and widely used substance.
- Progression of alcohol dependence often occurs over an extended period of time, unlike some other substances whose progression can be quite rapid. Because of this slow progression, individuals can deny their dependence and hide it from employers for long periods.
- Most alcohol-dependent individuals have gainful employment, live with families, and are given little attention until their dependence crosses a threshold, at which time the individual fails in their familial, social, or employment roles.
- Misuse of alcohol represents a difficult diagnostic problem as it is a legal substance. Clients, their families, and even clinicians can claim that the client's alcohol use is normative.
- After friends, family members, or employers tire of maintaining the fiction that the individual's alcohol use is normative, the individual will be more motivated to begin the process of accepting treatment.

Alcohol Use Assessment Tools

The **CAGE tool** is used as a quick assessment to identify problem drinkers. Moderate drinking, (1-2 drinks daily or one drink a day for older adults) is usually not harmful to people in the absence of other medical conditions. However, drinking more can lead to serious psychosocial and physical problems. One drink is defined as 12 ounces of beer/wine cooler, 5 ounces of wine, or 1.5 ounces of liquor.

- **C** – *Cutting down*: "Do you think about trying to cut down on drinking?"
- **A** – *Annoyed at criticism*: Are people starting to criticize your drinking?
- **G** – *Guilty feeling*: "Do you feel guilty or try to hide your drinking?"
- **E** – *Eye opener*: "Do you increasingly need a drink earlier in the day?

"Yes" on one question suggests the possibility of a drinking problem. "Yes" on ≥2 indicates a drinking problem.

The **Clinical Instrument for Withdrawal for Alcohol (CIWA)** is a tool used to assess the severity of alcohol withdrawal. Each category is scored 0-7 points based on the severity of symptoms, except #10, which is scored 0-4. A score <5 indicates mild withdrawal without need for medications; for scores ranging 5-15, benzodiazepines are indicated to manage symptoms. A score >15 indicates severe withdrawal and the need for admission to the unit.

1. Nausea/Vomiting
2. Tremor
3. Paroxysmal Sweats
4. Anxiety
5. Agitation
6. Tactile Disturbances
7. Auditory Disturbances
8. Visual Disturbances
9. Headache
10. Disorientation or Clouding of Sensorium

Alcohol Overdose

Symptoms of alcohol overdose include the following:

- Staggering
- Odor of alcohol on breath
- Loss of coordination
- Dilated pupils
- Slurred speech
- Coma
- Respiratory failure
- Nerve damage
- Liver damage
- Fetal alcohol syndrome (in babies born to alcohol abusers)

Alcohol Withdrawal and Treatment

Chronic abuse of ethanol (alcoholism) can lead to physical dependency. Sudden cessation of drinking, which often happens in the inpatient setting, is associated with **alcohol withdrawal syndrome**. It may be precipitated by trauma or infection and has a high mortality rate, 5-15% with treatment and 35% without treatment.

Signs and symptoms: Anxiety, tachycardia, headache, diaphoresis, progressing to severe agitation, hallucinations, auditory/tactile disturbances, and psychotic behavior (delirium tremens).

Diagnosis: Physical assessment, blood alcohol levels (on admission).

Treatment includes:

- **Medication**: IV benzodiazepines to manage symptoms; electrolyte and nutritional replacement, especially magnesium and thiamine.
- Use the **CIWA scale** to measure symptoms of withdrawal; treat as indicated.
- Provide an **environment** with minimal sensory stimulus (lower lights, close blinds) and implement fall and seizure precautions.
- **Prevention**: Screen all clients for alcohol/substance abuse, using CAGE or other assessment tool. Remember to express support and comfort to client; wait until withdrawal symptoms are subsiding to educate about alcohol use and moderation.

Psychosocial Treatments for Alcohol Abuse

The following are psychosocial treatments for alcohol abuse:

- Cognitive behavioral therapies
- Behavioral therapies
- Psychodynamic/interpersonal therapies
- Group and family therapies
- Participation in self-help groups

Cannabis

Cannabis is the hemp plant from which marijuana (a tobacco-like substance) and hashish (resinous secretions of the cannabis plant) are produced.

Possible Effects

Effects of cannabis include:

- Euphoria followed by relaxation
- Impaired memory, concentration, and knowledge retention
- Loss of coordination
- Increased sense of taste, sight, smell, hearing
- Irritation to lungs and respiratory system
- Cancer
- With stronger doses: Fluctuating emotions, fragmentary thoughts, disoriented behavior

Overdose and Misuse

Symptoms of cannabis **overdose** include:

- Fatigue
- Lack of coordination
- Paranoia

Cannabis **misuse** indications are as follows:

- Animated behavior and loud talking, followed by sleepiness
- Dilated pupils
- Bloodshot eyes
- Distortions in perception
- Hallucinations
- Distortions in depth and time perception
- Loss of coordination

Narcotics

Narcotics are drugs used medicinally to relieve pain. They have a high potential for abuse because they cause relaxation with an immediate rush. Possible effects include restlessness, nausea, euphoria, drowsiness, respiratory depression, and constricted pupils.

Misuse and Symptoms of Overdose

Indications of possible **misuse** are as follows:

- Scars (tracks) caused by injections
- Constricted pupils
- Loss of appetite
- Sniffles
- Watery eyes
- Cough
- Nausea
- Lethargy
- Drowsiness
- Nodding
- Syringes, bent spoons, needles, etc.
- Weight loss or anorexia

Symptoms of narcotic **overdose** include:

- Slow, shallow breathing
- Clammy skin
- Convulsions, coma, and possible death

Withdrawal Syndrome for Narcotics

The symptoms of narcotic **withdrawal** are as follows:

- Watery eyes
- Runny nose
- Yawning
- Cramps
- Loss of appetite
- Irritability
- Nausea
- Tremors
- Panic
- Chills
- Sweating

Depressants

Depressants are described below:

- Drugs used medicinally to relieve anxiety, irritability, or tension.
- They have a high potential for abuse and development of tolerance.
- They produce a state of intoxication similar to that of alcohol.
- When combined with alcohol, their effects increase and their risks are multiplied.

Possible Effects

Possible effects of depressant use are as follows:

- Sensory alteration, reduction in anxiety, intoxication
- In small amounts, relaxed muscles, and calmness
- In larger amounts, slurred speech, impaired judgment, loss of motor coordination
- In very large doses, respiratory depression, coma, death

Newborn babies of abusers may exhibit dependence, withdrawal symptoms, behavioral problems, and birth defects.

Misuse, Overdose, and Withdrawal

The following are indications of possible depressant **misuse**:

- Behavior similar to alcohol intoxication (without the odor of alcohol)
- Staggering, stumbling, lack of coordination
- Slurred speech
- Falling asleep while at work
- Difficulty concentrating
- Dilated pupils

Symptoms of an **overdose** of depressants include:

- Shallow respiration
- Clammy skin
- Dilated pupils
- Weak and rapid pulse
- Coma or death

Withdrawal syndrome may include the following:

- Anxiety
- Insomnia
- Muscle tremors
- Loss of appetite

Abrupt cessation or a greatly reduced dosage may cause convulsions, delirium, or death.

STIMULANTS

Stimulants are drugs used to increase alertness, relieve fatigue, feel stronger and more decisive, achieve feelings of euphoria, or counteract the down feeling of depressants or alcohol.

POSSIBLE EFFECTS

Possible effects include:

- Increased heart rate
- Increased respiratory rate
- Elevated blood pressure
- Dilated pupils
- Decreased appetite

Effects with high doses include:

- Rapid or irregular heartbeat
- Loss of coordination
- Collapse
- Perspiration
- Blurred vision
- Dizziness
- Feelings of restlessness, anxiety, delusions

MISUSE, OVERDOSE, AND WITHDRAWAL

Stimulant **misuse** is indicated by the following:

- Excessive activity, talkativeness, irritability, argumentativeness, nervousness
- Increased blood pressure or pulse rate, dilated pupils
- Long periods without sleeping or eating
- Euphoria

Symptoms of stimulant **overdose** include:

- Agitated behavior
- Increase in body temperature
- Hallucinations
- Convulsions
- Possible death

Withdrawal from stimulants may cause:

- Apathy
- Long periods of sleep
- Irritability
- Depression
- Disorientation

HALLUCINOGENS

Hallucinogens are described below:

- Drugs that cause behavioral changes that are often multiple and dramatic.
- No known medical use, but some block sensation to pain and their use may result in self-inflicted injuries.
- "Designer drugs," which are made to imitate certain illegal drugs, can be many times stronger than the drugs they imitate.

POSSIBLE EFFECTS

Possible effects of use:

- Rapidly changing mood or feelings, both immediately and long after use
- Hallucinations, illusions, dizziness, confusion, suspicion, anxiety, loss of control
- **Chronic use**: Depression, violent behavior, anxiety, distorted perception of time
- **Large doses**: convulsions, coma, heart/lung failure, ruptured blood vessels in the brain
- **Delayed effects**: flashbacks occurring long after use
- **Designer drugs**: possible irreversible brain damage

MISUSE AND OVERDOSE

The following are indications of hallucinogen **misuse**:

- Extreme changes in behavior and mood
- Sitting or reclining in a trance-like state
- Individual may appear fearful
- Chills, irregular breathing, sweating, trembling hands
- Changes in sensitivity to light, hearing, touch, smell, and time
- Increased blood pressure, heart rate, blood sugar

Symptoms of hallucinogen **overdose** include:

- Longer, more intense episodes
- Psychosis
- Coma
- Death

Steroids

Steroids are synthetic compounds closely related to the male sex hormone testosterone and are available both legally and illegally. They have a moderate potential for abuse, particularly among young males.

Possible Effects

Effects include:

- Increase in body weight
- Increase in muscle mass and strength
- Improved athletic performance
- Improved physical endurance

Misuse and Overdose

The following are indications of possible **misuse** of steroids:

- Rapid gains in weight and muscle
- Extremely aggressive behavior
- Severe skin rashes
- Impotence, reduced sexual drive
- In female users, development of irreversible masculine traits

Overdose of steroids includes the following:

- Increased aggressiveness
- Increased combativeness
- Jaundice
- Purple or red spots on the body
- Unexplained darkness of skin
- Unpleasant and persistent breath odor
- Swelling of feet, lower legs

Withdrawal Syndrome

Withdrawal syndrome may include the following:

- Considerable weight loss
- Depression
- Behavioral changes
- Trembling

Substance Use and Abuse

Pathophysiology of Addiction

Genetic, social, and personality factors may all play a role in the development of **addictive tendencies**. However, the main factor of the development of substance addiction is the pharmacological activation of the **reward system** located in the central nervous system (CNS). This reward systems pathway involves **dopaminergic neurons**. Dopamine is found in the CNS and is one of many neurotransmitters that play a role in an individual's mood. The mesolimbic pathway seems to play a primary role in the reward and motivational process involved with addiction. This pathway begins in the ventral tegmental area of the brain (VTA) and then moves forward into the nucleus accumbens located in the middle forebrain bundle (MFB). Some drugs enhance mesolimbic dopamine activity, therefore producing very potent effects on mood and behavior.

Theories of Substance Addiction

Theories of substance addiction include the following:

Theory of Addiction	Details
Exposure theory	According to this theory, once individuals begin to introduce a substance into their body, metabolic changes occur that result in increased dosages of the substance, leading to addiction. The exact mechanism as to how this occurs has not been identified.
Genetic theory	Children of individuals who misuse substances (alcohol or drugs) have a 3-4 times higher risk of becoming addicted, suggesting there is an inherited tendency toward addiction. However, the exact genes that may be implicated have not yet been identified and there is some controversy over this theory, which is based on family, sibling, and twin studies. This theory tends to apply to males more than females.
Adaptation theory	This theory postulates that social (peer pressure), environmental (availability, observation), and psychological factors (poor self-image, deficits) can lead individuals to addictions in accordance to their beliefs about the rewards the substances will provide.

Review Video: Addictions
Visit mometrix.com/academy and enter code: 460412

Etiologies of Substance Abuse

Substance abuse refers to the abuse of drugs, medicines, and/or alcohol that causes mental and physical problems for the abuser and family. Abusers use substances out of boredom, to hide negative self-esteem, to dampen emotional pain, and to cope with daily stress. As the abuse continues, abusers become unable to take care of their daily needs and duties. They lack effective coping mechanisms and the ability to make healthy choices. They struggle to identify and prioritize stress or choose positive behavior to resolve the stress in a healthy way. Some family members may act as codependents because of their desire to feel needed by the abuser, to control the person, and to stay with him or her. The social worker can help the family to confront an individual with their concerns about the person and their proposals for treatment. Family members can enforce consequences if treatment is not sought. Family members may also need counseling to learn new behaviors to stop enabling the abuser to continue substance abuse.

SUBSTANCE ABUSE AND SUBSTANCE DEPENDENCE

Substance abuse alone is considered a less severe condition than substance dependence. Substance abuse is **diagnosed** when:

- Major roles and obligations become impaired at home, school, or work.
- Legal problems ensue (e.g., arrests for driving while intoxicated or disorderly conduct).
- The abuse continues in spite of related interpersonal and social problems.

Substance dependence refers to the increased use of a substance in order to achieve intoxication, the presence of withdrawal symptoms when the substance is not used, and continued use in the face of efforts to stop. Medications that are sometimes prescribed to reduce substance use include disulfiram (Antabuse), which causes negative symptoms if alcohol is ingested and naltrexone (Trexan), a reward/receptor blocker for alcohol and opiates.

SUBSTANCE RELATED DISORDERS

Substance related disorders may be caused by abusing a drug, by medication side-effects, or by exposure to a toxin. These disorders involve substances including the following: caffeine, hallucinogens, alcohol, cannabis, stimulants, tobacco, inhalants, opioids, sedatives, hypnotics, and anxiolytics. Gambling is now also included in substance-related and addictive disorders, as evidence shows that the behaviors of gambling trigger similar reward systems as drugs. The severity of the particular substance use disorder can be determined by the presence of the number of symptoms, which may include substance/activity induced delirium, dementia, psychosis, mood disorders, anxiety disorder, sexual dysfunction, and sleep dysfunction. Substance intoxication or withdrawal includes behavioral, psychological, and physiological symptoms due to the effects of the substance. It will vary depending on type of substance.

FACTORS THAT CONTRIBUTE TO SUBSTANCE USE AND INFLUENCE THE DRUG OF CHOICE

Factors contributing to likelihood of substance abuse include the following:

- Early or regular use of "gateway" drugs (alcohol, marijuana, nicotine)
- Intra-familial disturbances
- Associating with substance-using peers

Factors influencing an individual's "**drug of choice**" include:

- Current fashion
- Availability
- Peer influences
- Individual biological and psychological factors
- Genetic factors (especially with alcoholism)

Clinical Disorders Commonly Found in Clients with Substance Use Disorders

The following are clinical disorders often found in those abusing substances:

- Conduct disorders, particularly the aggressive subtype
- Depression
- Bipolar disorder
- Schizophrenia
- Anxiety disorders
- Eating disorders
- Pathological gambling
- Antisocial personality disorder
- PTSD
- Other personality disorders

Harms Resulting from Substance Use/Abuse

The following are possible harms resulting from substance abuse:

- Substances that are illegally obtained are often associated with minor crimes, crimes against family members and the community, and prostitution.
- Alcohol is associated with domestic violence, child abuse, sexual misconduct, and serious auto accidents.
- All substances promote behavioral problems that may make it difficult for the individual to obtain/retain employment, or to sustain normal family relationships.

Injuries or illnesses that can result from substance use include:

- Physical damage
- Brain damage
- Organic failure
- Fetal damage when used by pregnant women
- Birth of drug exposed babies who require intensive therapy throughout childhood
- Altering of brain chemistry/permanent brain damage
- Effects on dopamine in brain, which directly effects mood

Harm Related to Method of Administration

Harm from illegal drug use related to their mode of administration includes:

- Unknown dosing, which can lead to drug overdose and death
- Using contaminated needles can cause staph infections, Hepatitis, or HIV/AIDS
- The use of inhalants, which are frequently toxic and can cause brain damage, heart disease, and kidney or liver failure

Substance Abuse Treatment

Substance use disorder treatment includes the following components:

- An assessment phase
- Treatment of intoxication and withdrawal when necessary
- Development of a treatment strategy

General treatment strategies include:

- Total abstinence (drug-free)
- Substitution, or the use of alternative medications that inhibit the use of illegal drugs
- Harm reduction

Goals of treatment are:

- Reducing use and effects of substances
- Abstinence
- Reducing the frequency and severity of relapse
- Improvement in psychological and social functioning

Stress, Crisis, and Trauma

STRESS

RELATIONSHIP BETWEEN STRESS AND DISEASE

Stress causes a number of physical and psychological changes within the body, including the following:

- Cortisol levels increase
- Digestion is hindered and the colon stimulated
- Heart rate increases
- Perspiration increases
- Anxiety and depression occur and can result in insomnia, anorexia or weight gain, and suicide
- Immune response decreases, making the person more vulnerable to infections
- Autoimmune reaction may increase, leading to autoimmune diseases

The body's **compensatory mechanisms** try to restore homeostasis. When these mechanisms are overwhelmed, pathophysiological injury to the cells of the body result. When this injury begins to interfere with the function of the organs or systems in the body, symptoms of dysfunction will occur. If the conditions are not corrected, the body changes the structure or function of the affected organs or systems.

PSYCHOLOGICAL RESPONSE TO STRESS

When stress is encountered, a person responds according to the threat perceived in order to compensate. The threat is evaluated as to the amount of harm or loss that has occurred or is possible. If the stress is benign (typical day-to-day burdens or life transitions) then a challenge is present that demands change. Once the threat or challenge is defined, the person can gather information, resources, and support to make the changes needed to resolve the stress to the greatest degree possible. Immediate psychological response to stress may include shock, anger, fear, or excitement. Over time, people may develop chronic anxiety, depression, flashbacks, thought disturbances, and sleep disturbances. Changes may occur in emotions and thinking, in behavior, or in the person's environment. People may be more able to adapt to stress if they have many varied experiences, good self-esteem, and a support network to help as needed. A healthy lifestyle and philosophical beliefs, including religion, may give a person more reserve to cope with stress.

IMPACT OF DIFFERENT KINDS OF STRESS

Everyone encounters stress in life and it impacts each person differently. There are the small daily "hassles," major traumatic events, and the periodic stressful events of marriage, birth, divorce, and death. Of these stressors, the daily stress that a person encounters is the one that changes the health status over time. Stressors that occur suddenly are the hardest to overcome and result in the greatest tension. The length of time that a stressor is present also affects its impact, with long-term, relentless stress, such as that generated by poverty or disability, resulting in disease more often. If there is **ineffective coping**, a person will suffer greater changes resulting in even more stress. The social worker can help clients to recognize those things that induce stress in their lives, find ways to reduce stress when possible, and teach effective coping skills and problem-management.

Crisis

Characteristics of a Crisis

A crisis occurs when a person is faced with a highly stressful event and their usual problem solving and coping skills fail to be effective in resolving the situation. This event usually leads to increased levels of anxiety and can bring about a physical and psychological response. The problem is usually an acute event that can be identified. It may have occurred a few weeks or even months before or immediately prior to the crisis and can be an actual event or a potential event. The crisis state usually lasts less than six weeks with the individual then becoming able to utilize problem solving skills to cope effectively. A person in crisis mode does not always have a mental disorder. However, during the acute crisis their social functioning and decision-making abilities may be impaired.

Types of Crises

Developmental

There are basically two different types of crises. These types include developmental or maturational crisis and situational crisis. A **developmental crisis** can occur during maturation when an individual must take on a new life role. This crisis can be a normal part of the developmental process. A youth may need to face and resolve crisis to be able to move on to the next developmental stage. This may occur during the process of moving from adolescence to adulthood. Examples of situations that could lead to this type of crisis include graduating from school, going away to college, or moving out on their own. These situations would cause the individual to face a maturing event that requires the development of new coping skills.

Situational

The second type of crisis is the **situational crisis**. This type of crisis can occur at any time in life. There is usually an event or problem that occurs, which leads to a disruption in normal psychological functioning. These types of events are often unplanned and can occur with or without warning. Some examples that may lead to a situational crisis include the death of a loved one, divorce, unplanned or unwanted pregnancy, onset or change in a physical disease process, job loss, or being the victim of a violent act. Events that affect an entire community can also cause an individual situational crisis. Terrorist attacks or weather-related disasters are examples of events that can affect an entire community.

Collecting a Trauma History

A trauma history should be collected from any client with a known history of physical/emotional abuse, accident involvement, or signs/symptoms of PTSD from known or unknown events. There are several methods of trauma history collection:

- **Trauma History Screen (THS)**: The client self-reports (via questionnaire) by responding with "Yes" or "No" to 14 event types and includes the number of times the event occurred. These events include abuse, accidents/natural disasters, military service, loss of loved ones, and life crises/transitions. Next, the client is prompted to respond to the question, "Did any of these things really bother you emotionally?" If the client responds with "Yes," they are then instructed to provide details about every event that bothered them.
- **Trauma History Questionnaire (THQ)**: Similar to the THS, this questionnaire requires the client to self-report experiences with 24 potentially traumatic events, and then to provide the frequency and details of each experience.

Grief

Impact of Grief on the Individual

Grief is an emotional response to loss that begins at the time a loss is anticipated and continues on an individual timetable. While there are identifiable stages of grief, it is not an orderly and predictable process. It involves overcoming anger, disbelief, guilt, and a myriad of related emotions. The grieving individual may move back and forth between stages or experience several emotions at any given time. Each person's grief response is unique to their own coping patterns, stress levels, age, gender, belief system, and previous experiences with loss.

Kubler-Ross's Five Stages of Grief

Kubler-Ross taught the medical community that the dying patient and family welcomes open, honest discussion of the dying process and felt that there were certain stages that patients and family go through while experiencing grief. The stages may not occur in order, but instead may vary, with stages sometimes being skipped. **Kubler Ross's stages of grief** include the following:

- **Denial**: The person denies the loss and tries to pretend it isn't true. During this time, the person may seek a second opinion or alternative therapies (in the case of a terminal diagnosis) or act as though the loss never occurred. They may use denial until they are better able to emotionally cope with the reality of the loss or changes that need to be made.
- **Anger**: The person is angry about the situation and may focus that rage on anyone or anything.
- **Bargaining**: The person attempts to make deals with a higher power to secure a better outcome to their situation.
- **Depression**: The person anticipates the loss and the changes it will bring with a sense of sadness and grief.
- **Acceptance**: The person accepts the loss and is ready to face it. The patient may begin to withdraw from interests and family.

Anticipatory Grief

Anticipatory grief is the mental, social, and somatic reactions of an individual as they prepare themselves for a perceived future loss. The individual experiences a process of intellectual, emotional, and behavioral responses in order to modify their self-concept, based on their perception of what the potential loss will mean in their life. This process often takes place ahead of the actual loss, from the time the loss is first perceived until it is resolved as a reality for the individual. This process can also blend with past loss experiences. It is associated with the individual's perception of how life will be affected by the particular diagnosis as well as the impending death. Acknowledging this anticipatory grief allows family members to begin looking toward a changed future. Suppressing this anticipatory process may inhibit relationships with the ill individual and contribute to a more difficult grieving process at a later time. However, appropriate anticipatory grieving does not take the place of grief during the actual time of death.

Disenfranchised Grief

Disenfranchised grief occurs when the loss being experienced cannot be openly acknowledged, publicly mourned, or socially supported. Society and culture are partly responsible for an individual's response to a loss. There is a social context to grief. If a person incurring the loss will be putting himself or herself at risk by expressing grief, disenfranchised grief occurs. The risk for disenfranchised grief is greatest among those whose relationship with the thing they lost was not known or regarded as significant. This is also the situation found among bereaved persons who are not recognized by society as capable of grief, such as young children, or needing to mourn, such as an ex-spouse or secret lover.

Grief vs. Depression

Normal grief is self-limiting to the loss itself. Emotional responses will vary and may include open expressions of anger. The individual may experience difficulty sleeping or vivid dreams, a lack of energy, and weight loss. Crying is evident and provides some relief of extreme emotions. The individual remains socially responsive and seeks reassurance from others.

By contrast, **depression** is marked by extensive periods of sadness and preoccupation often extending beyond two months. It is not limited to the single event. There is an absence of pleasure or anger and isolation from previous social support systems. The individual can experience extreme lethargy, weight loss, insomnia, or hypersomnia. Crying is absent or persistent and provides no relief of emotions. Professional intervention is often required to relieve depression.

Concepts of Abuse

Child Abuse

Physical Abuse of Children

Physical abuse of children is most often in the form of extreme physical discipline that exceeds normative community standards.

Physical indicators of physical abuse:

- Bruises or broken bones on an infant that lack an adequate explanation or that occur in unusual places
- Lacerations
- Fractures
- Burns in odd patterns
- Head injuries
- Internal injuries
- Open sores
- Untreated wounds or illnesses

Behavioral indicators of physical abuse:

- Child may be overly compliant, passive, or undemanding
- Child may be overly aggressive, demanding, or hostile
- Role reversal behavior
- Extremely dependent behavior (increased parental, emotional, and physical needs)
- Developmental delays

Sexual Abuse

Sexual abuse is defined as inappropriate and unsolicited sexual contact, molestation, or rape. Common **signs of sexual abuse** include:

- Genital injuries (abrasions, bruises, scars, tears, etc.)
- Blood in the underwear (from vaginal or rectal injuries)
- Complaints of genital discomfort or excessive grabbing of the genital area
- Any diagnosis of a sexually transmitted disease
- Frequent urinary tract and bladder infections
- Complaints of stomachache when coupled with other signs
- Abrasions or bruises to the thighs and legs
- Enuresis (bed-wetting) or encopresis (fecal soiling)
- Behavioral disturbances (acting out, self-destructive behavior, overly precocious or aggressive sexual behavior, promiscuity, etc.)
- Depression
- Eating disorders
- Fears and phobias
- Dissociation
- Any unexplained or sudden appearance of money, toys, or gifts

Child Neglect

Child neglect is the failure of a child's parent or caretaker (who has the resources) to provide minimally adequate health care, nutrition, shelter, education, supervision, affection, or attention. Also included in the definition of child neglect is the insufficient encouragement to attend school with consistency, exploitation by forcing to work too hard or long, or exposure to unwholesome or demoralizing circumstances.

Indicators of child neglect include the following:

- Abandonment
- Absence of sufficient adult supervision
- Inadequate clothing
- Poor hygiene
- Lack of sufficient medical/dental care
- Inadequate education
- Inadequate supervision
- Inadequate shelter
- Consistent failure, unwillingness, or inability to correct these indicators on the part of the caretaker

Elderly and Disabled Neglect and Abuse

The elderly and disabled are at risk for neglect and abuse when they have impaired mental processes or physical deficits that affect their ability to carry out activities of daily living. They are also at risk when there are caregiver problems such as:

- High amount of stress
- Substance abuse
- Physically abusive or violent
- Emotionally unstable or with mental illness
- Dependency on the elderly or disabled person for money, emotional support, or physical support

The social worker should act to help a caregiver cope more effectively to prevent abuse from occurring by providing an outlet for emotions and referring to resources. It's important to ask clients in private whether anyone prevents them from using medical assistive devices or refuses to help them with their daily activities. However, many will not admit to abuse. If there are risk factors present or signs of abuse, the social worker must act to preserve the safety of the individual. Most states require the reporting of elder abuse and neglect. The social worker should assist the person in accessing resources in the community to improve their living situation.

Identifying and Reporting Neglect of the Basic Needs of Adults

Neglect of the basic needs of adults is a common problem, especially among the elderly, adults with psychiatric or mental health problems, or those who live alone or with reluctant or incapable caregivers. In some cases, **passive neglect** may occur because an elderly or impaired spouse or partner is trying to take care of a client and is unable to provide the care needed, but in other cases, **active neglect** reflects a lack of caring which may be considered negligence or abuse. Cases of neglect should be reported to the appropriate governmental agency, such as adult protective services. Indications of neglect include the following:

- Lack of assistive devices, such as a cane or walker, needed for mobility
- Misplaced or missing glasses or hearing aids
- Poor dental hygiene and dental care or missing dentures
- Client left unattended for extended periods of time, sometimes confined to a bed or chair
- Client left in soiled or urine- and feces-stained clothing
- Inadequate food, fluid, or nutrition, resulting in weight loss

- Inappropriate and unkempt clothing, such as no sweater or coat during the winter and dirty or torn clothing
- A dirty, messy environment

Domestic Violence

Men, women, elderly, children, and the disabled may all be victims of **domestic violence**. The violent person harms physically or sexually and uses threats and fear to maintain control of the victim. The violence does not improve unless the abuser gets intensive counseling. The abuser may promise not to do it again, but the violence usually gets more frequent and worsens over time. The social worker should ask all clients in private about abuse, neglect, and fear of a caretaker. If abuse is suspected or there are signs present, the state may require reporting. The social worker should support the abused by doing the following:

- Give victims information about community hotlines, shelters, and resources
- Urge them to set up a plan for escape for themselves and any children, complete with supplies in a location away from the home
- Assure victims that they are not at fault and do not deserve the abuse
- Try to empower them by helping them to realize that they do not have to take abuse and can find support to change the situation

Assessment of Domestic Violence

According to the guidelines of the Family Violence Prevention Fund, assessment for domestic violence should be done for all adolescent and adult clients, regardless of background or signs of abuse. While females are the most common victims, there are increasing reports of male victims of domestic violence, both in heterosexual and homosexual relationships. The person doing the assessment should be informed about domestic violence and be aware of risk factors and danger signs. The interview should be conducted in private (special accommodations may need to be made for children <3 years old). The office, bathrooms, and examining rooms should have information about domestic violence posted prominently. Brochures and information should be available to give to clients. Clients may present with a variety of physical complaints, such as headache, pain, palpitations, numbness, or pelvic pain. They are often depressed, may appear suicidal, and may be isolated from friends and family. Victims of domestic violence often exhibit fear of spouse/partner, and may report injury inconsistent with symptoms.

Steps to Identifying Victims of Domestic Violence

The Family Violence Prevention Fund has issued guidelines for identifying and assisting victims of domestic violence. There are seven steps:

1. **Inquiry**: Non-judgmental questioning should begin with asking if the person has ever been abused—physically, sexually, or psychologically.
2. **Interview**: The person may exhibit signs of anxiety or fear and may blame oneself or report that others believe they are abused, but they disagree. The person should be questioned if they are afraid for their life or for their children.
3. **Question**: If the person reports abuse, it's critical to ask if the person is in immediate danger or if the abuser is on the premises. The interviewer should ask if the person has been threatened. The history and pattern of abuse should be questioned and if children are involved, whether the children are abused. Note: State laws vary, and in some states, it is mandatory to report if a child was present during an act of domestic violence as this is considered child abuse. The social worker must be aware of state laws regarding domestic and child abuse. All social workers are mandatory reporters.

4. **Validate**: The interviewer should offer support and reassurance in a non-judgmental manner, telling the client that the abuse is not their fault.
5. **Give information**: While discussing facts about domestic violence and the tendency to escalate, the interviewer should provide brochures and information about safety planning. If the client wants to file a complaint with the police, the interviewer should assist the person to place the call.
6. **Make referrals**: Information about state, local, and national organizations should be provided along with telephone numbers and contact numbers for domestic violence shelters.
7. **Document**: Record-keeping should be legal, legible, and lengthy with a complete report and description of any traumatic injuries resulting from domestic violence. A body map may be used to indicate sites of injury, especially if there are multiple bruises or injuries.

Injuries Consistent with Domestic Violence

There are a number of characteristic injuries that may indicate domestic violence, including the following:

- Ruptured eardrum
- Rectal/genital injury (burns, bites, or trauma)
- Scrapes and bruises about the neck, face, head, trunk, arms
- Cuts, bruises, and fractures of the face.

The pattern of injuries associated with domestic violence is also often distinctive. The bathing-suit pattern involves injuries on parts of body that are usually covered with clothing as the perpetrator inflicts damage but hides evidence of abuse. Head and neck injuries (50%) are also common. Abusive injuries (rarely attributable to accidents) are common and include bites, bruises, rope and cigarette burns, and welts in the outline of weapons (belt marks). Bilateral injuries of arms/legs are often seen with domestic abuse.

Defensive injuries are also indicative of abuse. Defensive injuries to the back of the body are often incurred as the victim crouches on the floor face down while being attacked. The soles of the feet may be injured from kicking at perpetrator. The ulnar aspect of hand or palm may be injured from blocking blows.

Mandatory Reporting

Mandated Reporting in Cases of Abuse

Social work is one of several professions that are under a **legal mandate to report cases of abuse**. It is not necessary to have witnessed the abuse, nor must one have incontrovertible evidence. Rather, there need only be sufficient cause to **suspect** in order for a report to be required. If the report is made in good faith, the reporting party is immune from liability—both from reporting (should the allegations prove unfounded) and from the liability that would otherwise accrue from any failure to report actual abuse. Abuse may be physical, emotional, sexual, or constitute neglect.

All states mandate the reporting of child abuse, and most mandate the reporting of dependent adult abuse (adults who are developmentally delayed and thus mentally infirm or elderly persons unable to protect themselves due to either physical or mental frailty). Where dependent abuse reporting is not mandated, complex situations may occur. Know state laws and seek advice when necessary.

Concerns When Reporting Incidents or Suspicions of Sexual Abuse

The following are concerns when reporting incidents or suspicions of sexual abuse:

- Perpetrators of these crimes can be highly motivated to obtain retractions and may threaten or use violence to do so.
- A major concern in developing immediate and long-term strategies for protection and treatment is the role of the non-abusing parent and his or her ability to protect the child.
- The victim may be safer if the worker does not notify the family when making the report.
- Great care must be taken by the worker with these cases.

Following up After Identifying Child, Dependent Adult, or Elder Adult Abuse

After abuse has been determined, a full report must be made to the appropriate agency, initially by telephone with a written report to follow. For social workers employed by such agencies, a follow-up plan of action must be determined. The level of risk must be evaluated, including the perpetrator's relationship to the victim, prior history of abusive behavior, and severity of harm inflicted, as well as the victim's age, health situation, cognitive capacity and psychological status, available support systems, and capacity for self-protection given that the abuse is now in the open.

Follow-up options include the following:

- Reports for criminal prosecution
- Home visits
- Removal from the home
- Alternative caregiver/guardian appointments through courts, etc.

Safety is the primary concern above all else.

Effects of Abuse on Individuals

The effects of abuse may vary widely depending on the type and extent of abuse and the resilience of the victim. Effects may include the following:

Physical	Victims may exhibit bruises, fractures, and pain. Long-term physical impairments from injuries may include disabilities from poorly healed fractures, hearing loss, other injuries, and traumatic brain injuries. Some clients may develop PTSD and remain hypervigilant and fearful.
Psychological	Victims may have little self-esteem and appear withdrawn and depressed or angry and aggressive. Over time, clients may become increasingly depressed and engage in self-destructive or antisocial behavior.
Sexual	Victims may try to hide or avoid sexuality or act overly sexualized. Many suffer from low self-esteem and fear, and some may develop PTSD.
Financial	Victims may feel shame for being taken advantage of or confused about what has happened, but if the financial abuse involves a great loss of savings, some victims may be forced to change their life situations, including housing.
Neglect	Victims may be unkempt, malnourished, unclean, and anxious. Victims may be depressed and fearful and may exhibit hoarding to compensate.

Social and Economic Justice

Children

Children in Poverty in the US

The following are basic facts/statistics relating to children in poverty in the US:

- Almost **one in six** children lives in poverty.
- **Minority** children under age six are much more likely than white children of the same age to live in poverty.
- Many of these children in poverty are **homeless** or are in the **child welfare system**.
- Fewer than one-third of all poor children below age six live solely on **welfare**.
- More than half of children in poverty have at least one **working parent**.
- Children of **single mothers** are more likely to live in poverty.
- Poor children have increased risk of **health impairment**.

Children in the Foster Care System

The following are some barriers that children in the foster care system face in this country:

- Children in foster care often go through frequent **relocations** due to rejection by foster families, changes in the family situation, returns to biological families and later returns to foster care, agency procedures, and decisions of the court. Additionally, many foster children experience **sexual and physical abuse** within the foster care system.
- Due to frequent changes in their situation, children in foster care may **change schools** multiple times, which can have an adverse impact on their academic achievement.
- Many youths age out of the foster care system at age 18; this can abruptly **end the relationships** with foster families and other supportive structures.
- Compared with children raised with their own families, children who have been through the foster care system have a higher incidence of **behavioral problems**, increased **substance abuse**, and greater probability of entering the **criminal justice system**.

Social Welfare Organizations

Approaches to Social Welfare Policy Making

The **rational approach to social welfare policy making** is an idealized and structured approach. It includes identifying and understanding a social problem, identifying alternative solutions and their consequences for consumers and society, and rationally choosing the best alternatives. The rational approach minimizes ideological issues.

The political approach recognizes the importance of compromise, power, competing interests, and partial solutions. Those who are most affected by social policies often have the least amount of political power to promote change. Those who have political power are often influenced by interests that are seeking to protect their own position. Policy makers are often concerned with retaining privilege and power. Without aggressive advocacy, the needs of the disadvantaged can become marginalized.

Administrative Challenges

Administrative challenges unique to social welfare organizations include the following:

- Clinical services can be difficult to assess objectively.
- It is difficult to evaluate prevention programs, as few techniques are able to measure events that have not occurred.
- Staff turnover is high due to low salary and burnout.
- Programs are often dependent on the political environment for funding.
- It can be difficult to implement systematization or routine work due to the flexibility often required when dealing with human problems.

Lesser Eligibility

This concept of lesser eligibility asserts that welfare payments should not be higher than the lowest paying job in society and derives from Elizabethan Poor Law. It suggests that economic and wage issues underlie the size of benefits and the availability of welfare. Some believe it is a way to control labor and maintain incentives for workers to accept low-paying or undesirable jobs that they might otherwise reject.

Challenges for Programs for Poor and Homeless People

One criticism of program development supposedly targeting homeless and poor people is that whereas programs affecting the middle class, such as Individual Development Accounts (IDAs), are put into operation upon conception, programs for poor people are first put through testing phases, with implementation taking years, if it happens at all. In program development for the poor, policies at the level of government may be at odds with actually implementing and carrying out a program.

Criminal Justice System

The criminal justice system includes agencies and processes involved in apprehending, prosecuting and defending, reaching a verdict, sentencing, and punishing offenders:

- **Law enforcement agencies**: These may include police, sheriffs, highway patrol, US Marshal service, FBI, DEA, ICE, and ATF. Law enforcement agencies may be local, state, or federal. Their purpose is to investigate and apprehend criminals.
- **Court system**: Prosecutors provide evidence against an individual, and defense attorneys attempt to discredit the evidence or otherwise provide a defense against the charges brought. Judges preside over court cases and may, in some cases, determine the verdict and sentence. In some states, judges determine if probable cause for arrest exists (preliminary hearing). A grand jury may meet in other state and federal cases to determine whether the evidence indicates probable cause.
- **Jail/prison systems**: Individuals may be incarcerated in local jails or state or federal prisons for varying duration of sentences.
- **Probation system**: Some individuals may receive probation instead of jail or prison time but must report regularly to probation officers and may have other requirements, such as attending rehab programs. Individuals released from jail or prison on parole may also enter the probation system for a specified period of time.

Criminal Justice Process

The criminal justice process includes the following:

- **Investigation** of a crime by law enforcement officers.
- **Probable cause** of a crime must be established in order to obtain a search warrant unless exigent circumstances exist.
- **Interrogation** may be carried out to obtain information on the suspect after the suspect receives the Miranda warning.
- An **arrest** may be made with or without a warrant in public places and with a warrant in private. After an arrest, the person must be charged or released within 24-48 hours (state laws vary).
- With federal cases and in some states, a grand jury decides whether **evidence supports probable cause**. In some states, this decision is made by a judge in a preliminary hearing.
- **Arraignment** involves presenting the charge in court and reading the charges to the individual.
- **Bail** may be set to allow the individual to remain out of jail.
- The case may be resolved by a **plea bargain or a trial** in which the evidence is presented, a **verdict** reached, and sentence determined.
- The individual may be eligible for **appeal** if found guilty.

Impact of Early Experience Within the Criminal Justice System

Early experience within the criminal justice system depends to some degree on the action taken. For example, an adolescent arrested for delinquent acts is more likely to reoffend if the sentence is punitive than if it is more lenient. Additionally, the child or adolescent may develop negative attitudes toward law enforcement and authority in general, and is more likely to commit crimes as an adult. Those who are incarcerated in juvenile facilities may suffer bullying and abuse from others, resulting in emotional and physical problems, and may receive inadequate education, limiting future educational and employment opportunities. Children in the juvenile justice system have high rates of depression, but mental health care and rehabilitation programs are often very limited. Children charged as adults may spend many years in juvenile facilities and then prison, and youth incarceration is one of the highest predictors of recidivism. Many youths are in juvenile detention because of non-violent offenses (such as drug use) but may be exposed to and influenced by more serious offenders.

Globalization and Institutionalism

Globalization

Globalization refers to the international integration and interaction of multiple systems, such as economics, communications, and trade. Considerations include the following:

- **International integration**: This term most often refers to financial and business affairs related to trade and investments. For example, one company may manufacture in the United States, Europe, and China and do business throughout the world. International integration is most successful when tariffs and quotas are eliminated or restricted in order to allow the free flow of goods. International integration may affect the cost of items to the client and may affect job opportunities.
- **Financial crisis**: Because of international integration, a financial crisis (devaluing currency, recession, inflation) in one country can have a profound effect on other countries. For example, the financial crisis that occurred in 2008-2009 resulted in high rates of unemployment and increased homelessness worldwide. The unemployed were unable to afford goods, causing businesses to fold or suffer losses, increasing unemployment, and increasing prices to the consumer.
- **Interrelatedness of systems**: Something that affects one system is likely to have an effect on other systems. For example, if a person works in a US factory that manufacturers equipment and a disaster occurs in the country from which the factory obtains materials, production may slow down and profits decrease, making it difficult for the company to obtain loans needed to finance operations, and the client may be laid off. Because the person has little or no income, they may be unable to make mortgage payments, resulting in the bank foreclosing, and the person becoming homeless.
- **Technology**: Knowledge flows with technology, and those countries with the most technological progress tend to have stronger economies and higher standards of living. Technology transfers have facilitated international integration and allowed instant sharing of information around the world, making inventory control, manufacturing, and delivery (shipping, ground, and air transport) more efficient.

Impact of Globalization on Environmental Crises and Epidemics

Globalization may have a profound effect on the following crises:

- **Environmental crises**: As industrialization moves into developing countries, pollution and stripping of natural resources follows. The increased worldwide demand for goods means that countries are motivated more by monetary gain than environmental concerns. Forests are decimated, water and air polluted, but the global community has been unable to reach a worldwide agreement on environmental planning, resulting in increasingly common environmental problems.
- **Pandemics**: Because of the rapid increase in international marketing and travel, it is now almost impossible to completely contain an outbreak that at one time may have been local, such as Ebola (which has killed over 11,000 people), HIV (which has killed over 35 million people), and most recently, the COVID-19 pandemic which is still active worldwide, killing half a million Americans in its first year. Additionally, health laws and practices vary widely, so not all populations have adequate preventive care or treatment. Thus, any outbreak can pose a worldwide threat. Viruses especially pose a grave threat because they readily mutate and treatment may be unavailable or inadequate.

Problems of Globalization Created by Modernization

Based on the idea that agrarian and impoverished countries would be improved by industrialization, **modernization** has been criticized for contributing to the problems of globalization. In globalization, multinational corporations have relocated their operations and jobs to less-developed regions where poverty remains the norm and average wages are extremely low. These corporations make higher profits, whereas workers in more-developed countries lose their jobs to workers in less-developed countries. Although the merits of this process in regard to workers in the less-developed countries can be debated, the effects on the previously employed workers in the more-developed countries are undeniably negative.

Institutionalism

Institutionalism is the idea that social interventions should be state run, and planning should be centralized in government. Reform is initiated through the electoral process, and a benevolent state would oversee reform efforts. Social services would be provided by the state as well. Critiques would include the assumption of a paternalistic and helpful state, run by individuals uninterested in personal power and gain at the expense of others. However, a counterargument may be the success of countries of northern Europe (e.g., Sweden, Denmark, and Norway) where institutionalism provides citizens with health care, free education, employment, childcare, and housing benefits.

Assessment and Intervention Planning

Biopsychosocial History and Collateral Data

Focuses of the Social Work Assessment

The social worker's assessment may focus on any or all of the following:

- **Intrapsychic** dynamics, strengths, and problems
- **Interpersonal** dynamics, strengths, and problems
- **Environmental** strengths and problems
- The **interaction and intersection** of intrapsychic, interpersonal, and environmental factors

The social worker's role in the assessment process is to ask questions, ask for elaboration and description in the client's response, observe client's behavior/affect, and organize data to create a meaningful psychosocial or diagnostic assessment.

Review Video: Life Stages in Client Assessment
Visit mometrix.com/academy and enter code: 535888

Steps of the Initial Social Work Assessment

The initial social work assessment is used to gain information about the client's needs (employment, rehabilitation, monetary support, housing, education, safety). It should include client goals and be the basis for intervention plans. Steps include the following:

1. Schedule an interview and review all pertinent documents (medical records, police reports, housing reports, previous social services records).
2. Utilize a theoretical framework as the basis for the assessment based on the needs of the client.
3. Utilize a standardized form if required by the agency.
4. Ask open-ended questions and avoid "why" questions, rapid questioning, or repeated questioning without pause for reflection. Utilize active listening.
5. Develop a problem list of things that may require intervention.
6. Outline interventions to assist with resolving the client's problems.
7. Assist the client to develop specific time-sensitive goals and outline the client's responsibilities.
8. Summarize the findings of the assessment and review the summary with the client.
9. Set up a follow-up interview.

Biopsychosocial History

The social work assessment must gather client information in a comprehensive, accurate, and systematic manner. A history is taken from clients and others (such as family members) to complete the assessment. Information relevant to the client's **biopsychosocial history** includes the following:

- **Appearance** of the client
- **Previous hospitalizations** and experience(s) with healthcare
- **Psychiatric history**: Suicidal ideation, psychiatric disorders, family psychiatric history, history of violence and/or self-mutilation

- **Chief complaint**: Client's perception of the problem
- **Use of complementary therapies**: Acupuncture, visualization, and meditation
- **Occupational and educational background**: Highest level of education, issues while in the school setting, employment record, retirement, and special skills
- **Social patterns**: Family and friends, living situation, typical activities, support system
- **Sexual patterns**: Orientation, practices, and problems
- **Interests and abilities**: Hobbies and sports
- **Current and past substance abuse**: Type, frequency, drinking pattern, use of recreational drugs, and overuse of prescription drugs
- **Ability to cope**: Stress reduction techniques
- **Physical, sexual, emotional, and financial abuse**: Older adults are especially vulnerable to abuse and may be reluctant to disclose out of shame or fear
- **Spiritual/cultural assessment**: Religious/Spiritual importance, practices, restrictions (such as blood products or foods), and impact on health and health decisions
- **Mental status**, gleaned from the following:
    - General attitude: Behavior and reaction to being interviewed
    - Mental activity: Logical or loosely associated
    - Speech profile: Normal, childlike, or pressured
    - Emotional state: Depressed, agitated, or calm
    - Level of consciousness: Alert or stuporous
    - Orientation: Normal or disoriented
    - Thought processes: Pressured thoughts (excessively rapid), flights of ideas, thought blocking, disconnected thoughts, tangentiality and circumstantiality, etc.
    - Judgment: Good, fair, poor, or none
    - Mood: Cooperative or agitated
    - Insight: Good, fair, poor, or none
    - Memory: Intact or presence of deficits

THE ROLE OF OBSERVATION IN ASSESSMENT

LEVELS OF OBSERVATION

One form of assessment involves nonstandard procedures that are used to provide individualized assessments. **Nonstandard procedures** include observations of client behaviors and performance. There are three **levels of observation** techniques that can be applied:

- The first level is **casual informational observation**, where the provider gleans information from watching the client during unstructured activities throughout the day.
- The second level is **guided observation**, an intentional style of direct observation accomplished with a checklist or rating scale to evaluate the performance or behavior seen.
- The third level is the **clinical level**, where observation is done in a controlled setting for a lengthy period of time. This is most often accomplished on the doctoral level with applied instrumentation.

Instruments Used During the Observation Process

The following instruments can be used in an observation:

- The **checklist** is used to check off behaviors or performance levels with a plus or minus sign to indicate that the behavior was observed or absent. The observer can converse with the client as they mark the checklist.
- The **rating scale** is a more complex checklist that notes the strength, frequency, or degree of an exhibited behavior. Likert scales are applied using the following ratings: 1. Never; 2. Rarely; 3. Sometimes; 4. Usually; and 5. Always. The evaluator of the behavior makes a judgment about whatever question has been asked on the rating scale.
- The **anecdotal report** is used to record subjective notes describing the client's behavior during a specified time or in a specified setting and is often applied to evaluate a suspected pattern.

Structured interviews, questionnaires, and personal essays or journals may also be useful in the observation process, depending on the client's ability to participate in these exercises.

Information Sources for Assessment

Information can also be collected from various external sources to contribute to the assessment of the client:

Source	Data Collected
Social services agency	Record of previous contact with the client and interventions made, as well as the reason for termination or continuation of the case.
Employer	History of employment, including the type of work, the duration, attendance record, skills needed for the jobs, problems encountered, and job-related injuries.
Medical records	Names of healthcare providers, diagnoses and treatments prescribed, medication list, history of chronic disorders and need for ongoing treatment and assessment.
Psychological records	Psychosocial assessment, diagnoses of mental health problems, types of therapies utilized, client goals, and recommendations for ongoing care.
Legal records	History of offenses and juvenile detention and adult incarceration/parole. Evidence of history of violence toward self or others.
School records	Attendance records indicate compliance with schooling, grades suggest cognitive ability, disciplinary actions may indicate behavioral problems. 504 plans and IEPs indicate students with disabilities and outline needs for special education and/or accommodations, auxiliary aids, and service.

Pharmacologic Interventions

Drugs for Schizophrenia and Psychotic Symptoms

Antipsychotic drugs are the drug of choice used to treat schizophrenia and psychotic symptoms. There are both older first-generation antipsychotic drugs and newer atypical/second generation antipsychotic drugs.

First-Gen Antipsychotics	Atypical/Second-Gen Antipsychotics
Haldol (haloperidol)	Clozaril (clozapine)
Thorazine (chlorpromazine)	Risperdal (risperidone)
Stelazine (trifluoperazine)	Seroquel (quetiapine)
Prolixin (fluphenazine)	Zyprexa (olanzapine)
Navane (thiothixene)	Abilify (aripiprazole)

Review Video: Anti-Psychotic Drugs: Clozapine, Haloperidol, Etc.
Visit mometrix.com/academy and enter code: 369601

Side Effects and Other Relevant Factors

A major drawback and potential side effect for the older antipsychotics (which are effective) is **tardive dyskinesia** (TD). TD is irreversible and causes involuntary movements of the face, tongue, mouth, or jaw. Other possible side effects for the older antipsychotics include **Parkinsonian syndrome** (tremor, shuffling gait, or bradykinesia) or **muscle rigidity**; these are reversible and can be counteracted with benztropine.

Among the newer antipsychotics, clozapine requires frequent blood testing due to the risk of **agranulocytosis**, a blood disorder that decreases white blood cells and increases the risk of infection. Though some atypical antipsychotics have much less risk of TD, they are very expensive and can cause weight gain, affect blood sugar, and affect the lipid profile.

Drugs for Bipolar Disorder

Bipolar disorder is treated with **mood stabilizers**:

- Lithium
- Tegretol (carbamazepine)
- Depakote (sodium valproate)
- Lamictal (lamotrigine)

Mood stabilizers can cause weight gain. Regular blood work is necessary to monitor for therapeutic drug levels and for potential side effects. Lithium can cause kidney or thyroid problems, and Tegretol and Depakote can cause problems with liver function.

Drugs for Unipolar Depression

Medications used for treating unipolar depression include the following:

Drug Classification	Brand Name (generic)
Selective serotonin reuptake inhibitors (SSRIs)	Prozac (fluoxetine) Zoloft (sertraline) Paxil (paroxetine) Luvox (fluvoxamine) Celexa (citalopram) Lexapro (escitalopram)
Atypical antidepressants	Effexor (venlafaxine) Wellbutrin (bupropion) Cymbalta (duloxetine)
Tricyclic antidepressants	Tofranil (imipramine) Elavil (amitriptyline)
MAO inhibitors (MAOIs)	Nardil (phenelzine) Parnate (tranylcypromine) Eldepryl (selegiline)

Side Effects and Other Relevant Factors

While antidepressants can be extremely effective in the treatment of unipolar depression, they also have many **side effects**, which both the social worker and client must be aware of:

- **SSRIs** have fewer side effects than other antidepressants, and one cannot overdose on SSRIs alone. SSRIs take several weeks to be effective, can cause a loss of libido, and can lose effectiveness after years of usage. In a few individuals, SSRIs can cause agitation, suicidal ideation, or manic symptoms (in which case, the prescriber should discontinue).
- Of the **atypical antidepressants**, Wellbutrin does not cause libido loss and is sometimes prescribed in combination with an SSRI to counter the sexual side effects or to increase the positive antidepressant effect of the SSRI. Cymbalta is recommended for depression linked with somatic complaints.
- **Tricyclic antidepressants** can cause side effects such as dry mouth, and an overdose can result in dangerous complications such as cardiac dysrhythmias. For this reason, tricyclic antidepressants are less commonly used today, but still have their place in treating depression in some clients.
- **MAO inhibitors** are also less commonly used to treat depression due to their required dietary limitations and possibly dangerous side effects (severe hypertension and serotonin syndrome). They are considered a third line treatment of depression for this reason.

Drugs for Anxiety

Drugs most often used for anxiety are **benzodiazepines**, including the following:

- Ativan (lorazepam)
- Xanax (alprazolam)
- Klonopin (clonazepam)
- Valium (diazepam)

Benzodiazepines are effective, short-acting, and quickly relieve anxiety. They should be used for as short a time as possible and in conjunction with appropriate therapeutic interventions because of their potential for abuse and addiction. In the elderly, long-term use of these drugs can cause psychotic symptoms that can be reversed by discontinuing their usage.

Drugs Used for Attention Disorders

Typical drugs used for attention disorders are either amphetamine-like or non-amphetamine like. The **amphetamine-like drugs** can be short- or long-acting and include the following:

- Ritalin (methylphenidate): Short-acting
- Ritalin LA: Long-acting
- Concerta (methylphenidate): Long-acting
- Adderall (dextroamphetamine-amphetamine): Short-acting
- Adderall XR: Long-acting

These medications relieve symptoms quickly and individuals can take them on selected days or partial days if desired. These have potential for abuse, can suppress appetite and cause weight loss, and can cause feelings of edginess similar to that resulting from excessive caffeine. Amphetamine-like drugs can also cause an increased heart rate.

The **non-amphetamine-like drug** most commonly used for attention disorders is Strattera (atomoxetine). Strattera is less appetite-suppressing; therefore, weight loss is less of a problem. This medication takes 2-4 weeks to be effective and must be taken every day. The client must be monitored for a rarely occurring liver problem. This drug has low risk for abuse.

Assessment Methods and Techniques

Methods of Psychological Testing

Various methods of psychological testing exist, which can be used in conjunction with one another, based on the client's needs:

- A **standardized test** is one in which the questions and potential responses from all tests can be compared with one another. Every aspect of the test must remain consistent.
- A **behavioral assessment** assumes that an individual can only be evaluated in relation to his or her environment. Behavioral assessments must include a stimulus, organism, response, and consequences (SORC).
- A **dynamic assessment** involves systematic deviation from the standardized test to determine whether the individual benefits from education. It is an interactive assessment that includes a process called "testing-teaching-retesting," in which an examinee is provided a problem to solve and their ability to solve it is assessed. They are then provided education to increase their sense of competence on the subject, and finally they are asked to solve the same problem again. In the retest, they are given sequence of stronger support (or "clues) to help solve the problem if needed, until it is solved. This reflects the client's ability to respond to education and apply it in problem solving; therefore, providing insight to the social worker on the client's need for intervention.
- **Domain-referenced testing** breaks evaluation into specific domains of ability—for instance, reading or math ability.

Assessment of Communication Skills

The social worker can assess communication skills through both interview and observation. Additionally, the social worker may provide the client with written information and ask the client to read and discuss the information to determine if the client has adequate ability to read and understand. The social worker should directly ask about which language the client communicates best with and whether there are problems, such as hearing deficit, that may impact communication so that accommodations can be provided. Techniques include the following:

- Ask questions to determine client's ability to understand and respond appropriately.
- Observe for signs of incongruence where words, body language, and tone of voice are inconsistent.
- Ask the client to summarize or restate information according to their understanding.
- Observe the client's ability to initiate and maintain conversation.
- Note the client's ability to understand and/or use metaphoric language.
- Observe the client's turn-taking and response to language cues.
- Note the client's use of appropriate nonverbal language, such as gestures and nodding head.

Assessment of Coping Abilities

Assessment of coping abilities is done through observation and interview and begins with determining if the client has developed effective coping strategies. The following should be considered as elements required for effective coping:

- **Habits that sustain good health**: Balanced diet, adequate exercise, adequate medical care, leisure activities, relaxation exercises
- **Satisfaction with life**: Work, family, activities, sense of humor, religious/spiritual belief, artistic endeavors
- **Support systems**: Family, friends, religious/spiritual affiliation, clubs, organizations, online supports
- **Healthy response to stressful circumstances**: Problem-solving as opposed to avoidance, utilizing support systems instead of blaming self and taking no positive action, reframing and realistically assessing positives and negatives rather than utilizing wishful thinking that everything will be alright

Mental Status Exam

Clients with evidence of dementia or short-term memory loss, often associated with Alzheimer's disease, should have cognition assessed. The **Mini-Mental State Exam (MMSE)** is commonly used. The MMSE requires the client to carry out specified tasks and scores on a scale of 0-9 based on their ability to do so:

Area Assessed	Tasks Performed
Memory	Remembering and later repeating the names of 3 common objects
Attention	Counting backward from 100 by increments of 7 or spelling "world" backward Following simple 3-part instructions, such as picking up a piece of paper, folding it in half, and placing it on the floor
Language	Naming items as the examiner points to them Repeating common phrases Reading a sentence and following directions Writing a sentence
Orientation	Providing the date and the location of the examiner's office, including city, state, and street address
Visual-Spatial Skills	Copying a picture of interlocking shapes

Scoring for the MMSE is as follows:

- 24-30: Normal cognition
- 18-23: Mild cognitive impairment
- 0-17: Severe cognitive impairment

INDICATORS OF SEXUAL DYSFUNCTION

Indicators of sexual dysfunction that may present upon assessment include the following:

- **History of promiscuity or prostitution**: Both may indicate that the client was sexually abused at one time or needed to resort to sex to gain income, acceptance, or to pay for drugs or alcohol.
- **Sexualized behavior**: In children and adolescents, this usually indicates sexual abuse. In adults, it often indicates that the individual uses the body as an expression of power.
- **Asexual behavior**: Client may dress or act in such a manner as to appear sexually unattractive as a means of self-protection.
- **Bragging**: Those who feel insecure about their sexuality may resort to bragging about sexual exploits.
- **Paraphilias**: Clients rarely admit to paraphilias (which usually have onset during adolescence), such as sadism, pedophilia, peeping, and exhibitionism, but may come in contact with social services as part of the criminal justice system.
- **Gender dysphoria**: Clients may bind breasts, tuck penis, or cross dress.

PSYCHIATRIC ILLNESS AND SEXUALITY

Many times, psychiatric illness can affect a person's sexuality. Mental illness, such as depression, can often decrease the client's sexual desire, while the manic client will often become hypersexual. Bipolar clients can experience a lack of sexual inhibition and may have many sexual affairs or act very seductively or overtly sexual. Psychotic clients may experience hallucinations or delusions of a sexual nature, and the schizophrenic client may exhibit inappropriate sexual behaviors such as masturbation in public. Clients residing in long-term care facilities must be kept safe from sexually transmitted diseases, unwanted pregnancies, and unwanted sexual advances or assaults from others. The social worker must be aware of these risks and provide support and advocacy accordingly.

INDICATORS OF BEHAVIORAL DYSFUNCTION

Indicators of behavioral dysfunction may be present upon assessment, including the following:

Indicator	Manifestations
Unkempt appearance	Sloppily dressed, dirty, smelly
Substance abuse	Burnt fingers, constricted pupils, needle tracks, runny nose, slurred speech, tremors, smell of alcohol
Labile emotions	May have sudden mood swings or outbursts of anger and may appear angry much of the time. May be wildly talkative or withdrawn and silent.
Self-injury	Signs of cutting, excessive piercings, picking at scabs, head banging
Counter-culture identification	May identify with extreme or marginal groups, or dress in the "uniform" of one of these groups.
Attitude	May be disrespectful, scatological, demanding, using expletives, and argumentative. May refuse to follow rules. May refuse to answer questions or respond to social worker.
Dishonesty	May lie and try to deceive. May have a history of stealing (shoplifting is common).
Truancy/Absence	May have a history of skipping classes or failing to attend school at all, running away, or staying out all night.

Indicators of Psychosocial Stress

Psychosocial stress (which occurs when one perceives a threat as part of social interaction with other individuals) causes a sympathetic nervous system response ("fight or flight") with the release of stress hormones (cortisol, adrenaline, dopamine), which can cause the heart rate and blood pressure to increase. Clients who are facing the need for resocialization (such as after incarceration), role change (after divorce, job loss), or situation change (foster care, rehab) are especially at risk for psychosocial stress. **Indicators** include the following:

Indicator	Manifestation
Self-injury	Signs of cutting, excessive piercings, picking at scabs
Speech alterations	Some may speak very quickly while others may say little or nothing
Demeanor	May be very withdrawn or nervous and agitated
Self-comforting measures	Licking lips, rubbing hands together, sitting with arms folded, taking deep breaths
Substance abuse	Use of alcohol or drugs to alleviate distress and provide an escape from problems
Stress-related ailments	Hypertension, headaches, GI upset
Sleep impairment	Insomnia or excessive drowsiness and sleep periods
Mental health issues	Depression is a common response to stress

Neuropsychological Assessments

The following tools are used to assess for psychological deficits caused by neurological disorders:

- The **Benton Visual Retention Test (BVRT)** assesses visual memory, spatial perception, and visual-motor skills in order to diagnose brain damage. The subject is asked to reproduce from memory the geometric patterns on a series of ten cards.
- The **Beery Developmental Test of Visual-Motor Integration (Beery-VMI-6)** assesses visual-motor skills in children; like the BRVT, it involves the reproduction of geometric shapes.
- The **Wisconsin Card Sorting Test (WCST)** is a screening test that assesses the ability to form abstract concepts and shift cognitive strategies; the subject is required to sort a group of cards in an order that is not disclosed to him or her.
- The **Stroop Color-Word Association Test (SCWT)** is a measure of cognitive flexibility; it tests an individual's ability to suppress a habitual reaction to stimulus.
- The **Halstead-Reitan Neuropsychological Battery (HRNB)** is a group of tests that are effective at differentiating between normal people and those with brain damage. The clinician has control over which exams to administer, though he or she is likely to assess sensorimotor, perceptual, and language functioning. A score higher than 0.60 indicates brain pathology.
- The **Luria-Nebraska Neuropsychological Battery (LNNB)** contains 11 subtests that assess areas like rhythm, visual function, and writing. The examinee is given a score between 0 and 2, with 0 indicating normal function and 2 indicating brain damage.
- The **Bender Visual-Motor Gestalt Test (Bender-Gestalt II)** is a brief examination that involves responding to 16 stimulus cards containing geometric figures, which the examinee must either copy or recall.

Assessment of Executive Function

Executive functions are cognitive features that control and regulate all other abilities and behaviors. These are higher-level abilities that influence attention, memory, and motor skills. They also monitor actions and provide the capacity to initiate, stop, or change behaviors, to set goals and plan future behavior, and to solve problems when faced with complex tasks and situations. Executive functions allow one to form concepts and think abstractly. Deficits in executive functioning are evident in the reduced ability to delay gratification, problems with understanding cause and effect (i.e., concrete thinking), poor organization and planning, difficulty following multi-step directions, perseveration with an idea in the face of superior information, and overall poor judgment. Various assessment tools exist to **evaluate executive functioning**, including the following:

- Trail making test
- WAIS-IV
- Clock drawing tests

When combined with observations and the social work assessment, these tests can expose deficiencies in executive function that may disrupt the client's ability to participate in daily activities. From this assessment, the social worker can identify needs and resources to better support the client.

Evaluation in the Assessment Process

Evaluation is the process of accumulating data in order to improve a person's ability to make a decision based on reliable standards. The accumulated data is given careful consideration and appraisal by the evaluator to ensure that it is complete and accurate. The evaluator must make some kind of interpretation or inference about the data that has been collected. This inference is known as a **value judgment** and is a common task for the social worker who uses a methodical and well-organized system to aid in their evaluation of the assessment process.

Indicators for Risk to Self or Others

Components of a Risk Assessment

A risk assessment evaluates the client's condition and their particular situation for the presence of certain risk factors. These risks can be influenced by age, ethnicity, spirituality, or social beliefs. They can include risk for suicide, harming others, exacerbation of symptoms, development of new mental health issues, falls, seizures, allergic reactions, or elopement. This assessment should occur within the first interview and then continue to be an ongoing process. The client's specific risks should be prioritized and documented, and then interventions should be put into place to protect this client from these risks.

Suicidal Ideation

Danger to the self or suicidal ideation occurs frequently in clients with mood disorders or depression. While females are more likely to attempt suicide, males actually successfully commit suicide 3 times more than females, primarily because females tend to take overdoses from which they can be revived, while males choose more violent means, such as jumping from a high place, shooting, or hanging. Risk factors include psychiatric disorders (schizophrenia, bipolar disorder, PTSD, substance abuse, and borderline personality disorder), physical disorders (HIV/AIDS, diabetes, stroke, traumatic brain injury, and spinal cord injury), and a previous violent suicide attempt. Passive suicidal ideation involves wishing to be dead or thinking about dying without making plans while active suicidal ideation involves making plans. Those with active suicidal ideation are most at risk. People with suicidal ideation often give signals, direct or indirect, to indicate they are considering suicide because many people have some ambivalence and want help. Others may act impulsively or effectively hide their distress.

Suicide Risk Assessment

A suicide risk assessment should be completed and documented upon initial interview, with each subsequent visit, and any time suicidal ideations are suggested by the client. This risk assessment should evaluate and score the following criteria:

- Would the client sign a contract for safety?
- Is there a suicide plan, and if so, how lethal is the plan?
- What is the elopement risk?
- How often are the suicidal thoughts?
- Have they attempted suicide before?

Any associated symptoms of hopelessness, guilt, anger, helplessness, impulsive behaviors, nightmares, obsessions with death, or altered judgment should also be assessed and documented. A higher score indicates a higher the risk for suicide.

Warning Signs of Suicide

The warning signs of suicide include the following:

- Depression
- Prior suicide attempts
- Family suicide history
- Abrupt increase in substance abuse
- Reckless and impulsive behavior
- Isolation
- Poor coping
- Support system loss
- Recent or anticipated loss of someone special
- Verbal expression of feeling out of control
- Preoccupation with death
- Behavioral changes not otherwise explained (a sudden changed mood from depressed to happy, the giving away of one's personal belongings, etc.)

Where **risk of suicide is suspected**, the client should be questioned directly about any thoughts of self-harm. This should be followed by a full assessment and history (particularly family history of suicide). Where the threat of suicide is not imminent and the client is amenable to intervention, a written "no-suicide contract" may be considered; the client will agree in the contract to contact the suicide hotline, the social worker, or some other specified professional. Where a client already has a plan, or has multiple risk factors, hospitalization must be arranged. If any immediate attempt has already been made, a medical evaluation must occur immediately.

Signs and Risk Factors of Client's Danger to Others

Violence and aggression are not uncommon among clients and pose a danger to others. Risk factors include mental health disorders, access to weapons, history of personal or family violence, abuse, animal cruelty, fire setting, and substance abuse. Violence and aggression should be handled as follows:

- **Violence** is a physical act perpetrated against an inanimate object, animal, or other person with the intent to cause harm. Violence often results from anger, frustration, or fear and occurs because the perpetrators believe that they are threatened or that their opinion is right and the victim is wrong. Violence may occur suddenly without warning or following aggressive behavior. Violence can result in death or severe injury if the individual attacks. The social worker must back away and seek safety.
- **Aggression** is the communication of a threat or intended act of violence and will often occur before an act of violence. This communication can occur verbally or nonverbally. Gestures, shouting, speaking increasingly loudly, invasion of personal space, or prolonged eye contact are examples of aggression requiring the client be redirected or removed from the situation.

Five-Phase Aggression Cycle

The five-phase aggression cycle is as follows:

Triggering	Client responds to a triggering event with anger or hostility. Client may exhibit anxiety, restlessness, and muscle tension. Other signs include rapid breathing, perspiration, loud angry voice, and pacing.
Escalation	Client's responses show movement toward lack of control. Client's face flushes and he or she becomes increasingly agitated, demanding, and threatening, often swearing, clenching fists, and making threatening gestures. Client is unable to think clearly or resolve problems.
Crisis	Client loses emotional and physical control. Client throws objects, hits, kicks, punches, spits, bites, scratches, screams, shrieks, and cannot communicate clearly.
Recovery	Client regains control. Client's voice lowers, muscle tension relaxes, and client is able to communicate more rationally.
Post-crisis	Client may attempt reconciliation. Client may feel remorse, apologize, cry, or become quiet or withdrawn. Client is now able to respond appropriately.

Managing Active Threats of Homicidality by Clients

A client may be deemed a threat to others if:

- Client makes a serious threat of physical violence.
- The threat is made against one or more specifically named individuals.

If the threat is made in the context of a social worker-client relationship, then a duty to protect is generated. In such a situation, a social worker is duty bound not only to notify appropriate authorities and agencies charged to protect the citizenry, but to also make a good-faith effort to warn the intended victim(s) or, failing that, someone who is reasonably believed to be able to warn the intended victim(s).

The duty to warn stems from the 1976 legal case *Tarasoff v. Regents of the University of California,* where a therapist heard a credible threat and called only law enforcement authorities, failing to notify the intended victim. The murder occurred, and the case was appealed to the California Supreme Court, from which the rubric of duty to protect an intended victim has been established.

Risk Management

Internal Controls That Minimize Risk

An agency minimizes risk internally through many different means, ranging from scheduling and infrastructure to excellence in supervision. Some examples of risk management include attending to the physical safety of workers and clients, ensuring that members of staff understand their ethical obligations, creating a work environment where cooperation and self-reflection are encouraged, and developing staff to the highest possible level of competence.

Policies and Procedures That Minimize Risk

Policies that help minimize risk may include rules about the number of staff present in the office or at particular interviews, when and how a worker should seek assistance from another staff member or from the police, and how the agency will respond to complaints or threats from clients or their acquaintances. When an issue of risk arises, agencies should have clearly defined ways of handling the problem. Training staff members in procedures concerning suicide prevention is one way to minimize risk; making sure they're current in their understanding of child protection laws is another. Documentation procedures can help an agency defend itself in cases of litigation.

Addressing Critical Incidents and Debriefing

Posttraumatic stress and vicarious posttraumatic stress can affect even the most balanced, educated worker, and many of the daily events of a social worker's life are difficult, unpleasant, and upsetting. Agencies have a duty to their employees to provide them with supervision, mental health care, and ways to process and work through **critical incidents**. Agencies should either have trained staff to manage debriefings after traumatic events or should contract with outside companies to provide those services. Employee assistance programs (EAPs), on-site supervision sessions targeted to the incident, and policies regarding time off for self-care after critical events are ways agencies can help employees regain and maintain their emotional stability.

Social Workers' Responsibilities to Clients and Community

Social workers have an **ethical obligation** to protect the identity of their clients and the duty to protect vulnerable members of the population. Confidentiality and informed consent documentation tell clients that if they intend to harm themselves or someone else, the social worker's ethical obligation is to get help, even at the expense of confidentiality. In ethical concerns, the word client could be expanded to mean every member of the population; protecting human rights and safety also includes the duty to warn, which extends to anyone the worker believes is in harm's way.

Quality Assurance

Quality assurance is an aspect of quality improvement and risk management and includes all processes involved in planning and operations to ensure that care provided is of high quality. **Quality assurance** (also referred to as quality control) includes those methods used to ensure compliance and a specific level of quality in providing services or products. Quality assurance includes devising standards as well as means of ensuring compliance through guidelines, protocols, and written specifications. One of the primary goals of quality assurance is to identify and correct errors that affect outcomes. Quality assurance reviews should be carried out on an ongoing basis, and reports should be issued so that staff members are aware of their progress in eliminating errors and working efficiently. Quality assurance units and personnel should be independent of the programs and processes they are reviewing in order to prevent bias and should use standardized and validated instruments for assessment purposes whenever possible.

Psychiatric Disorders and Diagnosis

DSM-5 Classifications

The major DSM-5 classifications are as follows:

- Neurodevelopmental disorders
- Schizophrenia spectrum and other psychotic disorders
- Bipolar and related disorders
- Depressive disorders
- Anxiety disorders
- Obsessive-compulsive and related disorders
- Trauma- and stressor-related disorders
- Dissociative disorders
- Somatic symptom and related disorders
- Feeding and eating disorders
- Elimination disorders
- Sleep-wake disorders
- Sexual dysfunctions
- Gender dysphoria
- Disruptive, impulse-control, and conduct disorders
- Substance-related and addictive disorders
- Neurocognitive disorders
- Personality disorders
- Paraphilic disorders
- Other mental disorders
- Medication-induced movement disorders
- Other conditions that may be a focus of clinical attention

Intellectual Disabilities

Very few (approximately 5%) cases of intellectual disability are **hereditary**. Hereditary forms of intellectual disability include Tay-Sachs, fragile X syndrome, and phenylketonuria. Most cases of intellectual disability (about 30%) are due to **mutations in the embryo** during the first trimester of pregnancy. Babies born with Down syndrome or those exposed to environmental toxins while in the uterus fall into this category. About 10% of cases of intellectual disability are due to **pregnancy or perinatal problems**, like fetal malnutrition, anoxia, and HIV. About 5% of those with intellectual disability have **general medical conditions** (like lead poisoning, encephalitis, or malnutrition) suffered during infancy or childhood. Approximately 20% are intellectually disabled because of either **environmental factors** or **other mental disorders** (e.g., sensory deprivation or autism). In the remaining 30%, etiology is **unknown**.

PKU

Phenylketonuria (PKU) is one cause of intellectual disability. It occurs when an infant lacks the enzyme to metabolize the amino acid phenylalanine, found in high-protein foods and aspartame sweetener. PKU is a rare recessive genetic disorder diagnosed at birth by a simple blood test. It affects mostly blue-eyed, fair babies. Expectant mothers can reduce the hazard of PKU by maintaining a diet low in phenylalanine. Untreated PKU typically leads to some form of intellectual disability. Some of the symptoms common to individuals with PKU are impaired motor and language development and volatile, erratic behavior. PKU can be treated if it is diagnosed in a timely fashion. Individuals must monitor their diet to keep phenylalanine blood levels at 2-10 mg/dL. Some phenylalanine is required for growth.

Down Syndrome

Down syndrome (Trisomy 21) occurs when a person has three #21 chromosomes instead of two. **Down syndrome** causes 20-30% of all cases of moderate and severe intellectual disability (1:800 births). Around 80% of Trisomy 21 pregnancies end in miscarriage. Classic physical characteristics associated with Down syndrome are slanted, almond-shaped eyes with epicanthic folds; a large, protruding tongue; a short, bent fifth finger; and a simian fold across the palm. Individuals with Down syndrome age rapidly. Medical conditions that often accompany Down syndrome and cause individuals to have a shorter life expectancy than normal, or poor quality of life, include heart lesions, leukemia, respiratory and digestive problems, cataracts, and Alzheimer's disease.

Communication Disorders

A number of disorders are lumped together under the heading of **communication disorders**:

- Language disorders
- Speech sound disorders
- Childhood-onset fluency disorders (stuttering)
- Social communications disorders

Childhood-onset fluency disorder (stuttering) typically begins between the ages of 2 and 7, and is more common in males than females. Research shows stuttering can be controlled through the removal of psychological stress in the home. Children who are constantly told not to stutter tend to stutter all the more. Many children find success through controlled and regular breathing exercises, accompanied by positive encouragement. In most cases, though, the child will spontaneously stop stuttering before the age of 16.

Many conditions that previously fell under the DSM-IV category of **pervasive developmental disorders** meet the criteria for **communication disorders** in DSM-5. Because autism spectrum disorder has social and communication deficits as part of its defining characteristics, it is important to note that communication disorders should not be diagnosed when there are repetitive behaviors or narrowed interests or activities.

Learning Disorders and Associated Conditions

A specific learning disorder is diagnosed as learning and academic difficulty, as evidenced by at least one of the following for at least six months (after interventions have been tried):

- Incorrect spelling
- Problems with math reasoning
- Problems with math calculation and number sense
- Difficulty reading
- Problems understanding what is read
- Difficulty using grammar and syntax

A child will be diagnosed with a learning disorder when he or she scores substantially lower than expected on a standardized achievement test and confirmed by a clinical assessment. The expectation for the child's score should be based on age, schooling, and intelligence, and the definition of "substantially lower" is a difference of two or more standard deviations. Learning disorders are frequently attended by delays in language development or motor coordination, attention and memory deficits, and low self-esteem. Learning disorders can be graded by severity as mild, moderate, or severe.

Prognosis and Etiology of Learning Disorders

Specific learning disorders include specific learning disorder with **impairment in reading**, specific learning disorder with **impairment in mathematics**, and specific learning disorder with **impairment in written expression**. Research has shown that boys are more likely to develop specific learning disorders with impairment in reading than girls. Although learning disorders are typically diagnosed during childhood or adolescence, they do not go away without treatment, and indeed may become more severe with time. Children who have a learning disorder with impairment in reading are far more likely than others to display antisocial behavior as an adult. At present, many researchers believe that reading disorders derive from problems with **phonological processing**.

Proposed **causes of learning disorders** include:

- Incomplete dominance and other hemispheric abnormalities
- Cerebellar-vestibular dysfunction
- Exposure to toxins, like lead

Autism Spectrum Disorder

Symptoms

There are two categories of symptoms necessary for a diagnosis of autism spectrum disorder. The first category is **deficits in social interaction and social communication**, which includes:

- Absence of developmentally appropriate peer relationships
- Lack of social or emotional reciprocity
- Marked impairment in nonverbal behavior
- Delay or lack of development in spoken language
- Marked impairment in the ability to initiate or sustain conversation
- Stereotyped or repetitive use of language or idiosyncratic language
- Lack of developmentally appropriate play

The other category of symptoms necessary for diagnosis of autism spectrum disorder is **restricted, repetitive patterns of behavior (RRBs), interests, and activities**. These include:

- Preoccupation with one or more stereotyped and restricted patterns of interest
- Inflexible adherence to nonfunctional routines or rituals
- Stereotyped and repetitive motor mannerisms
- Persistent preoccupation with the parts of objects

Diagnosis

Both categories of symptoms will be present in the ASD diagnosis. **Severity levels** are: **Level 1** (requiring support), **Level 2** (requiring substantial support), and **Level 3** (requiring very substantial support). Of note, ASD encompasses four disorders that were previously separate under DSM-IV: autistic disorder, Asperger's disorder, childhood integrative disorder, and pervasive developmental disorder. Individuals with ASD associated with other known conditions or environmental factors should have the diagnosis written: autism spectrum disorder associated with (name of condition).

Prognosis

Autism spectrum disorder (ASD) is frequently first suspected when an infant does not respond to his or her caregiver in an age-appropriate manner. Babies with ASD are not interested in cuddling, do not smile, and do not respond to a familiar voice. They are often misdiagnosed as profoundly deaf. The current scientific consensus is that four different disorders previously believed to be separate are actually just different **degrees** on the autism spectrum. Many children with ASD severity level 1 may escape diagnosis until a much later age. At the higher end of the spectrum (which was once referred to as Asperger's syndrome), individuals have impairment in social interactions and a limited repertoire of behaviors, interests, and activities, but they do not display other significant delays in language, self-help skills, cognitive development, or curiosity about the environment. They are extremely sensitive to touch, sounds, sights, and tastes, and have strong clothing preferences. The prognosis of the individual with ASD will largely depend on where they are on the spectrum. Unfortunately, even a small degree of improvement in ASD takes a great deal of work. Only one-third of children with autism will achieve some **independence** as adults. Those with ASD who have developed the ability to communicate verbally by age 5-6 and have an IQ over 70 have the best chance for future independence.

Characteristic Behavior Patterns

Some very noticeable, specific behavior patterns characteristic of autism spectrum disorder include:

- Lack of eye contact and disinterest in the presence of others
- Infants who rarely reach out to a caregiver
- Hand-flapping
- Rocking
- Spinning
- Echolalia (the imitating and repeating the words of others)
- Obsessive interest in a very narrow subject, like astronomy or basketball scores
- Heavy emphasis on routine and consistency, and violent reactions to changes in their normal environment

One half of people with autism remain mute for their entire lives. The speech that does develop may be abnormal. The majority of people with autism have an IQ in the intellectual disability range.

Etiology and Treatment

There are a few structural abnormalities in the brain that have been linked to autism spectrum disorders. These include a **reduced cerebellum** and **enlarged ventricles**. Research has also suggested that there is a link between autism and abnormal levels of **norepinephrine**, **serotonin**, and **dopamine**. The support for a genetic etiology of ASD has been increased by studies indicating that siblings of children with autism are much more likely have autism themselves. As for treatment, the most successful interventions focus on teaching individuals with autism the practical skills they will need to survive independently. Therapy should also include development of social skills and the reduction of undesirable behavior. Individuals with autism who reach a moderate level of functioning can be given direct vocational training.

Review Video: Autism
Visit mometrix.com/academy and enter code: 395410

ADHD

Diagnosis

Attention-deficit/hyperactivity disorder, commonly known as ADHD, can be diagnosed only if a child displays at least six symptoms of inattention or hyperactivity-impulsivity. Their onset must be before the age of 12, and they must have persisted for at least 6 months. The symptoms must not be motivated by anger or the wish to displease or spite others.

Inattentiveness Symptoms (must have 6 for diagnosis for children)	Impulsivity/Hyperactivity Symptoms (must have 6 for diagnosis for children)
• Forgetful in everyday activity • Easily distracted (often) • Makes careless mistakes and doesn't give attention to detail • Difficulty focusing attention • Does not appear to listen, even when directly spoken to • Starts tasks but does not follow through • Frequently loses essential items • Finds organizing difficult • Avoids activities that require prolonged mental exertion	• Frequently gets out of chair • Runs or climbs at inappropriate times • Frequently talks more than peer • Often moves hands and feet, or shifts position in seat • Frequently interrupts others • Frequently has difficulty waiting on turn • Frequently unable to enjoy leisure activities silently • Frequently "on the go" and seen by others as restless • Often finishes other's sentences before they can

Associated Features

Even though they are found to have **average or above-average intelligence**, children with ADHD typically score lower than average on **IQ tests**. Almost every child with ADHD will have some trouble in school, with about a quarter having major problems in **reading**. Also, **social adjustment** can be difficult for children with ADHD. Various reports give the co-diagnosis of Conduct Disorder with ADHD occurring 30-90% of the time. Other common co-diagnoses include **Oppositional Defiant Disorder**, **Anxiety Disorder**, and **Major Depression**. About half of all children who are diagnosed with ADHD are also suffering from a learning disorder.

Subtypes

There are three subtypes of ADHD:

- **Predominantly Inattentive Type** is diagnosed when a child has six or more symptoms of inattention and fewer than six symptoms of hyperactivity-impulsivity.
- **Predominantly Hyperactive-Impulsive Type** is diagnosed when there are six or more symptoms of hyperactivity-impulsivity and fewer than six of inattention.
- **Combined Type** is diagnosed when there are six or more symptoms of both hyperactivity-impulsivity and inattention.

ADHD is 4-9 times more likely to occur in boys than in girls, although the gender split is about half and half for Predominantly Inattentive Type. The rates of ADHD among adults appear to be about equal for both males and females.

Etiology

The theory that ADHD is a **genetic disorder** is supported by data that shows slightly higher rates of the disorder occur among biological relatives than among the general population, and there are higher rates among identical twins, rather than fraternal twins. ADHD is associated with structural abnormalities in the brain, like subnormal activity in the frontal cortex and basal ganglia, and a relatively small caudate nucleus, globus pallidus, and prefrontal cortex. Symptoms of ADHD vary widely, depending on the child's environment. Repetitive or boring environments encourage symptoms, as do those in which the child is given no chance to interact. One theory of ADHD asserts that it is the result of an inability to distinguish between important and unimportant **stimuli** in the environment.

Prognosis

The behavior of children with ADHD is likely to remain consistent until **early adolescence**, when they may experience diminished overactivity, but continue to suffer from attention and concentration problems. ADHD adolescents are much more likely to participate in antisocial behaviors and to abuse drugs. More than half of all children who are diagnosed with ADHD will continue to suffer from it as **adults**. These adults are more susceptible to divorce, work-related trouble, accidents, depression, substance abuse, and antisocial behavior. Children with ADHD who are co-diagnosed with Conduct Disorder are especially likely to have these problems later in life.

Treatment

Somewhat counterintuitively, central nervous system stimulants like **methylphenidate (Ritalin)** and **amphetamine (Dexedrine)** control the symptoms of ADHD. Side effects include headaches, gastrointestinal upset, anorexia, sleep difficulty, anxiety, depression, blood sugar and blood pressure increase, tics, and seizures. Research has consistently shown that **pharmacotherapy** works best when it is combined with **psychosocial intervention**. Many teachers have used the basic elements of **classroom management** to control the symptoms of ADHD. This involves laying out clear guidelines and contingencies for behavior, so that students do not have to speculate on what will happen in class or what they should be doing. Therapy that tries to increase the child's ability to **self-regulate behavior** has been shown to be less successful. It is always helpful when **parents** are involved in the treatment program.

Conduct Disorder

Diagnosis

Conduct disorder criteria are as follows:

Criteria A	Persistent pattern of behavior in which significant age-appropriate rules or societal norms are ignored, and others' rights and property are violated (theft, deceitfulness); aggression to people and animals and destruction of property are common. To meet diagnosis criteria individuals will display three of the fifteen possible symptoms over the course of a year. All the symptoms can be categorized as belonging to one of the four categories below: • Aggression to people or animals • Destruction of property • Deceitfulness or theft • Serious violations of rules
Criteria B	The patterns of behavior cause academic, social, or other impairments.
Criteria C	The behaviors couldn't better be classified as antisocial personality disorder.

Individuals with conduct disorder persistently violate either the rights of others or age-appropriate rules. They have little remorse about their behavior, and in ambiguous situations, they are likely to interpret the behavior of other people as hostile or threatening.

Etiology

According to Moffitt, there are two basic **types** of conduct disorder:

- **Life-course-persistent type** begins early in life and gets progressively worse over time. This kind of conduct disorder may be a result of neurological impairments, a difficult temperament, or adverse circumstances.
- **Adolescence-limited type** is usually the result of a temporary disparity between the adolescent's biological maturity and freedom. Adolescents with this form of conduct disorder may commit antisocial acts with friends. It is quite common for children with adolescence-limited conduct disorder to display antisocial behavior persistently in one area of life and not at all in others.

Treatment for Conduct Disorder and Oppositional Defiant Disorder

Research suggests that conduct disorder **interventions** are most successful when they are administered to preadolescents and include the immediate family members. Some therapists have developed programs of **parent therapy** to help adults manage the antisocial behavior of their children, as this has been demonstrated to have good success. Most programs advise rewarding good behavior and consistently punishing bad behavior.

Oppositional Defiant Disorder is similar to conduct disorder and is characterized by:

- Patterns of negative or hostile behavior towards authority figures
- Frequent outbreaks of temper and rages
- Deliberately annoying people
- Blaming others
- Spite and vindictiveness

This pattern of negative, hostile, defiant behavior, and vindictiveness however, is less serious violations of the basic rights of others that characterize conduct disorders. Behavior is motivated by interpersonal reactivity or resentful power struggle with adults.

Motor Disorders

Motor disorders are a type of neurodevelopmental disorder. **Motor disorders** can be classified as developmental coordination disorders, stereotypic movement disorders, and tic disorders. **Tic disorders** are further classified as Tourette's disorder, persistent motor or vocal tic disorder, and provisional tic disorder. **Tics** are defined in the DSM as "sudden, rapid, recurrent, nonrhythmic, stereotyped motor movements or vocalizations that feel irresistible yet can be suppressed for varying lengths of time."

Tourette's Syndrome

Tourette's syndrome is a neurological disorder characterized by at least one vocal tic and multiple motor tics that appear simultaneously or at different times, and appears before the age of 18. Those with **Tourette's syndrome** typically have multiple motor tics and one or more vocal tics. Those with chronic motor or vocal tic disorder have either motor or vocal tics. Individuals with Tourette's syndrome are likely to have obsessions and compulsions, high levels of hyperactivity, impulsivity, and distractibility.

Treatment

Most successful treatments for Tourette's syndrome include **pharmacotherapy**. The antipsychotics **haloperidol (Haldol)** and **pimozide (Orap)** are successful in relieving the symptoms of Tourette's syndrome because they inhibit the flow of dopamine in the brain; their success has led many scientists to speculate that Tourette's Disorder is caused by an excess of dopamine. In some cases, psychostimulant drugs amplify the tics displayed by the individual. In these cases, a doctor may treat the hyperactivity and inattention of Tourette's with **clonidine** or **desipramine**. The former of these is a drug usually used to treat hypertension, while the latter is typically used as an antidepressant.

ENURESIS AND ENCOPRESIS

Encopresis and enuresis make up the two major categories of elimination disorders. **Enuresis** is repeated urinating during the day or night into the bed or clothes at least twice a week for three or more months. Most of the time this urination is involuntary. Enuresis is diagnosed only when the child has reached an age at which continence can be reasonably expected (at least age five for DSM-5 criteria), and he or she does not have some other medical condition that could be to blame, like a urinary tract infection. Enuresis is treated with a night alarm, which makes a loud noise when the child urinates while sleeping. This is effective about 80% of the time, especially when it is combined with techniques like behavioral reversal and overcorrection. Desmopressin acetate (DDAVP) nasal spray, imipramine, and oxybutynin chloride (Ditropan) may help control symptoms. **Encopresis** is the involuntary fecal soiling in children who have already been toilet trained. Encopresis diagnosis cannot be made until the child is at least 4 years of age per DSM-5 criteria.

PICA AND RUMINATION DISORDER

Pica is the persistent eating of non-food substances such as paint, hair, sand, cloth, pebbles, etc. Those with **pica** do not show an aversion to food. In order to be diagnosed, the symptoms must persist for at least a month without the child losing an interest in regular food. Also, the behavior must be independent and not a part of any culturally acceptable process. Pica is most often manifested between the ages of 12 and 24 months. Pica has been observed in developmentally disabled children, pregnant women, and people with anemia.

Rumination disorder is the regurgitation and re-chewing of food.

AVOIDANT/RESTRICTIVE FOOD INTAKE DISORDER

DIAGNOSIS

The **criteria for avoidant/restrictive food intake disorder** are as follows:

Criteria A	A disruption in eating evidenced by not meeting nutritional needs and failure to gain expected weight or weight loss, nutritional deficiency requiring nutritional supplementation, or interpersonal interference.
Criteria B	This disruption is not due to lack of food or culture.
Criteria C	There does not appear to be a problem with the individual's body perception.
Criteria D	The disturbance can't be explained by another medical condition.

Anorexia Nervosa

Diagnosis

The characteristics of **anorexia nervosa** are:

Criteria A	Extreme restriction of food, lower than requirements, leading to low body weight
Criteria B	An irrational fear of gaining weight or behaviors that prevent weight gain, despite being at low weight
Criteria C	Distorted body image or a lack of acknowledgement of severity of current weight

A general standard used to determine the minimum healthy body weight is that it should be at least 85% of the norm for the individual's height and weight. People with restricting type anorexia lose weight through fasting, dieting, and excessive exercise. People with binging/purging type anorexia lose weight by eating a great deal and then either vomiting it or inducing immediate defecation with laxatives. People with anorexia are preoccupied with food. The physical symptoms of **starvation** are constipation, cold intolerance, lethargy, and bradycardia. The physical problems associated with **purging** are anemia, impaired renal function, cardiac abnormalities, dental problems, and osteoporosis.

Gender, Age, Etiology, and Treatment

The vast majority of people with anorexia are **female**, and the onset of anorexia is usually in **mid-to-late adolescence**. Onset may be associated with a stressful life event. Some studies associated anorexia with middle- and upper-class families that have a tendency towards competition and success. Girls with anorexia are likely to be introverted, nonassertive, and conscientious. Their mothers are likely to also be very concerned about food intake and weight. The immediate goal of any treatment program is to help the individual gain weight. Sometimes this requires hospitalization. **Cognitive therapy** is also often employed to correct the individual's misconceptions about healthy weight and nutrition.

Bulimia Nervosa

Diagnosis

The characteristics of **bulimia nervosa** are:

Criteria A	Cyclical periods of binge eating characterized by discretely consuming an amount of food that is larger than most individuals would eat in the same time period and situation. The individual feels a lack of control over the eating.
Criteria B	Characterized by binge eating followed by purging via self-induced vomiting/laxatives/fasting/vigorous exercise in order to prevent weight gain
Criteria C	At least one binge eating episode per week for three months
Criteria D	It is marked by a persistent over-concern with body shape and weight.
Criteria E	The eating and compensatory behaviors do not only occur during periods of anorexia nervosa.

Binges are often caused by interpersonal stress and may entail a staggering caloric intake. The **medical complications** associated with bulimia are fluid and electrolyte disturbances, metabolic alkalosis, metabolic acidosis, dental problems, and menstrual abnormalities.

GENDER, AGE, ETIOLOGY, AND TREATMENT

As with anorexia, the vast majority of people with bulimia are **female**. The onset is typically in **late adolescence** or **early adulthood**, and may follow a period of dieting. There are indications of a **genetic etiology** for bulimia. Also, there are links between bulimia and low levels of the endogenous opioid beta-endorphin, as well as low levels of serotonin and norepinephrine. The main point of any treatment for bulimia is encouraging the individual to get control of eating, and modifying unhealthy beliefs about body shape and nutrition. Treatment often involves **cognitive-behavioral techniques** like self-monitoring, stimulus control, cognitive restructuring, problem-solving, and self-distraction. Some antidepressants, like imipramine, have been effective at reducing instances of binging and purging.

ANXIETY DISORDERS

Types of anxiety disorders include the following:

Panic disorder	Recurrent brief but intense fear in the form of panic attacks with physiological or psychological symptoms
Specific phobia	Fear of specific situations or objects
Generalized anxiety disorder	Chronic psychological and cognitive symptoms of distress and excessive worry lasting at least 6 months
Separation anxiety disorder	Excessive anxiety related to being separated from someone the individual is attached to
Selective mutism	Inability to speak in social settings (when it would seem appropriate) though normally able to speak
Social anxiety disorder	Anxiety about social situations
Agoraphobia	Anxiety about being outside of the home or in open places

Review Video: Anxiety Disorders
Visit mometrix.com/academy and enter code: 366760

PANIC DISORDER

DIAGNOSIS

An individual may be diagnosed with **panic disorder** if he or she suffers recurrent unexpected panic attacks, and one of the attacks is followed by one month of either persistent concern regarding the possibility of another attack or a significant change in behavior related to the attack. **Panic attacks** are brief, defined periods of intense apprehension, fear, or terror. They develop quickly, and usually reach their greatest intensity after about ten minutes. Attacks must include at least 4 characteristic **symptoms**, which include:

- Palpitations or accelerated heart rate (tachycardia)
- Sweating
- Chest pain
- Nausea
- Dizziness
- Derealization
- Paresthesia (pins and needles or numbness)
- Shaking
- Shortness of breath
- Fear of losing control
- Fear of dying
- Chills or heat sensation
- Feeling of choking

Prevalence and Gender Issues

The consensus of research is that 1-2% of the population will suffer panic disorder at some point during their lives, and 30-50% of these individuals will also suffer **agoraphobia**. Panic disorder has a higher rate of diagnostic comorbidity when it is accompanied by agoraphobia. Panic disorder is far more likely to occur in **females** than males, and females with a panic disorder have a 75% chance of also having agoraphobia. There is a great deal of variation in the age of onset, but the most frequent ages of occurrence are in adolescence and the mid-30s. Children can experience the physical symptoms of a panic attack, but are unlikely to be diagnosed with panic disorder because they do not have the wherewithal to associate their symptoms with catastrophic feelings. The individual can be diagnosed with agoraphobia even if they are not diagnosed with panic disorder, but the two are commonly diagnosed together.

Treatment and Differential Diagnosis

The most effective treatment for panic attacks appears to be controlled in vivo exposure with response prevention, known as **flooding**. Flooding is typically accompanied by cognitive therapy, relaxation, breathing training, or pharmacotherapy. **Antidepressant medications** are often prescribed to relieve the symptoms of panic disorder. If stand-alone drug treatment is used, the risk of relapse is very high. Differential diagnoses for panic disorder include social phobia, and medical conditions like hyperthyroidism, hypoglycemia, cardiac arrhythmia, and mitral valve prolapse. Panic disorder can be distinguished from social phobia by the fact that attacks will sometimes occur while the individual is alone or sleeping.

Phobias

Diagnosis

A specific phobia is a marked and persistent fear of a particular object or situation, other than those associated with social phobia or agoraphobia. When an individual with a phobia is exposed to the feared object or event, he or she will have a panic attack or some other anxiety response. Adults with a specific phobia should be able to recognize that their fear is irrational and excessive. The onset of a specific phobia is typically in childhood or in the mid-20s. According to the DSM-5, there are five **subtypes** of specific phobia:

- Animal
- Natural environment
- Situational
- Blood-injection-injury
- Other

The blood-injection-injury subtype has different physical symptoms than the others. Individuals with blood-injection-injury phobia have a brief increase in heart rate and blood pressure, followed by a drop in both, often ending in a brief loss of consciousness (fainting). Other phobic reactions just entail the increase in heart rate and blood pressure, without loss of consciousness.

Distinguishing Symptoms of Agoraphobia

Symptoms that distinguish panic disorder from **agoraphobia** include the fear of being in a situation or place from which it could be difficult or embarrassing to escape, or of being in a place where help might not be available in the event of a panic attack. Agoraphobia usually manifests when the individual is alone outside of the home, is in a crowd, or is traveling in a train or automobile. Those who suffer from agoraphobia will typically go to great lengths to avoid problematic situations, or they will only be able to enter certain situations with a companion and under heavy distress. One of the main problems with agoraphobia is that it causes the individual to severely limit the places they are willing to go. These individuals often become reclusive.

Etiology and Treatment

The **two-factor theory** proposed by Mower asserts that phobias are the result of avoidance conditioning, when an individual associates a neutral or controlled stimulus with an anxiety-causing, unconditioned stimulus. The phobia reinforces a strategy of avoidance because it prevents anxiety (even though the neutral stimulus was not to blame for the anxiety in the first place). Another theory for the etiology of phobias is offered by **social learning theorists**, who state that phobic behaviors are learned by watching avoidance strategies used by one's parents. As with panic disorder, **in vivo exposure** is considered the best treatment for a specific phobia. **Relaxation and breathing techniques** are also helpful in dispelling fear and controlling physical response.

Generalized Anxiety Disorder

Individuals may be diagnosed with generalized anxiety disorder (GAD) if they have excessive anxiety about multiple events or activities. This anxiety must have existed for at least six months and must be difficult for the individual to control. The anxiety must be disproportionate to the feared event. Anxiety must include at least three of the following:

- Restlessness
- Fatigue on exertion
- Difficulty concentrating
- Irritability
- Muscle tension
- Sleep disturbance

The treatment for GAD usually entails a **multicomponent cognitive-behavioral therapy**, occasionally accompanied by pharmacotherapy. **SSRI** antidepressants and the anxiolytic buspirone have both demonstrated success in diminishing the symptoms of GAD.

Separation Anxiety Disorder

Onset

Many children who suffer from separation anxiety disorder will refuse to go to school, and may claim physical ailments to avoid having to leave the home. In some cases, the child will actually develop a headache or stomachache as a result of anxiety about separation from the home or from an individual to whom they are attached. The refusal to go to school may begin as early as 5 or as late as 12. If the separation anxiety occurs after the age of 10, however, it is quite possibly the result of depression or some more severe disorder. There are various treatment plans for separation anxiety disorder, all of which recommend that the child immediately resume going to school on a normal schedule.

Symptoms

Separation anxiety disorder is characterized by age-inappropriate and excessive anxiety that occurs when an individual is separated or threatened with separation from his or her home or family unit. In order to be diagnosed with separation anxiety disorder, the child must exhibit **symptoms** for at least four weeks and onset must be before the age of 18. Individuals with separation anxiety disorder will manifest some of the following symptoms:

- Excessive distress when separated from home or attachment figures
- Persistent fear of being alone
- Frequent physical complaints during separation

Children with separation anxiety tend to be from loving, stable homes. For many, the disorder begins to manifest after the child has suffered some personal loss.

Social Anxiety Disorder

The characteristics of social anxiety disorder or **social phobia** are a marked and persistent fear of social situations or situations in which the individual may be called upon to perform. Typically, the individual fears criticism and evaluation by others. The response to the feared situation is an immediate panic attack. Those with social phobia either avoid the feared situation or endure it with much distress. The fear and anxiety regarding these social situations have a negative impact on the individual's life, and is present for at least six months. Adults should be able to recognize that their fear is excessive and irrational. As with other phobias, social phobia is best treated with **exposure** in combination with **social skills and cognitive therapy**. Antidepressants and the beta-blocker propranolol are helpful for treating social phobia.

Obsessive-Compulsive Disorder

The following are the **criteria for obsessive-compulsive disorders:**

Criteria A	The individual exhibits obsessions, compulsions, or both. **Obsession**: continuous, repetitive thoughts, compulsions, or things imagined that are unwanted and cause distress. The individual will try to suppress thoughts, ignore them, or do a compulsive behavior. **Compulsion**: recurrent behavior or thought the individual feels obliged to perform after an obsession to decrease anxiety; however, the compulsion is usually not connected in an understandable way to an observer.
Criteria B	The obsessions and compulsions take at least one hour per day and cause distress.
Criteria C	The behavior is not caused by a substance.
Criteria D	The behavior could not better be explained by a different mental disorder.

Note if the criteria are met with good insight (individual realizes OCD beliefs are not true), poor insight (individual thinks the OCD beliefs are true), or absent insight (individual is delusional, truly believing OCD beliefs are true). Note if the individual has ever had tic disorder.

Other obsessive-compulsive and related disorders include:

- Body dysmorphic disorder
- Hoarding disorder
- Trichotillomania (hair-pulling disorder)
- Excoriation (skin-picking disorder)

Gender Issues, Etiology, and Treatment

OCD is equally likely to occur in adult males and adult females. The average age of onset is lower for males, so the rates of OCD among male children and adolescents are slightly higher than among females. Evidence suggests that OCD is caused by low levels of **serotonin**. Structurally, OCD seems to be linked to overactivity in the **right caudate nucleus**. The most effective treatment for OCD is exposure with response prevention in tandem with medication, usually either the tricyclic clomipramine or an SSRI. Therapies that provide help with stopping thought patterns seem to be especially successful in battling OCD. When drugs are used alone, there remains a high risk of relapse.

Review Video: Obsessive-Compulsive Disorder (OCD)
Visit mometrix.com/academy and enter code: 499790

PTSD

Diagnosis

An individual may be diagnosed with post-traumatic stress disorder (PTSD) if he or she develops symptoms after exposure to an extreme trauma. Examples of extreme trauma include: witnessing the death or injury of another person, experiencing injury to self, learning about the unexpected or violent death or injury of a family member or friend, or repeatedly being exposed to trauma (such as first responders or military soldiers). The traumatic event must elicit a reaction of intense fear, helplessness, or horror. The **characteristic symptoms** of PTSD are:

- Persistent re-experiencing of the event
- Persistent avoidance of stimuli associated with the trauma
- Persistent symptoms of increased arousal (difficulty concentrating, staying awake, or falling asleep)

These symptoms must have been present for at least a month; symptoms may not begin until three or more months after the event.

Treatment

The preferred treatment for PTSD is a **comprehensive cognitive-behavioral approach** that includes:

- Exposure
- Cognitive restructuring
- Anxiety management
- SSRIs to relieve symptoms of PTSD and comorbid conditions

Some psychologists criticize single-session psychological debriefings, because they believe one session amplifies the effects of a traumatic event. Another controversial therapy used to treat PTSD is eye movement desensitization and reprocessing; the positive benefits of this therapy may be more to do with the exposure that goes along with it than with the eye movements themselves.

Acute Stress Disorder

Acute stress disorder has symptoms similar to those of post-traumatic stress disorder. Acute stress disorder is distinguished by symptoms that occur for more than 3 days and but less than one month. An individual is diagnosed with acute stress disorder when he or she has 9 or more **symptoms** from any of the following 5 categories, which begin after the trauma:

- Intrusion
- Negative mood
- Avoidance symptoms
- Dissociative symptoms
- Arousal symptoms

An individual with acute stress disorder persistently relives the traumatic event, to the point where he or she takes steps to avoid contact with stimuli that bring the event to mind, and experiences severe anxiety when reminiscing about the event.

Review Video: What is Acute Stress Disorder?
Visit mometrix.com/academy and enter code: 538946

Additional Trauma- and Stressor-Related Disorders

Additional trauma- and stress-related disorders include:

Reactive attachment disorder	Child rarely seeks or responds to comfort when upset, usually due to neglect of emotional needs by caregiver (e.g., children who are institutionalized or in foster care). Reactive attachment disorder is characterized by a markedly disturbed or developmentally-inappropriate social relatedness in most settings. This condition typically begins before the age of five. In order to definitively diagnose this disorder, there must be evidence of pathogenic care, which may include neglect or a constant change of caregivers that made it difficult for the child to form normal attachments.
Disinhibited social engagement disorder	Child has decreased hesitations regarding interacting with unfamiliar adults. Does not question leaving normal caregiver to go off with a stranger.
Adjustment disorder	The individual has behavioral or emotional changes occurring within 3 months of a stressor. These changes cause distress for the individual and are disproportional to the actual stressor.

Somatoform Disorders

Conversion Disorder

Conversion disorder is a somatoform disorder characterized by either loss of bodily functions or symptoms of a serious physical disease. The individual becomes blind, mute, or paralyzed in response to an acute stressor. Occasionally, individuals develop hyperesthesia, analgesia, tics, belching, vomiting, or coughing spells. These symptoms do not conform to physiological mechanisms, and testing reveals no underlying physical disease. The sensory loss, movement loss, or repetitive physical symptoms are not intentional. The individual is not malingering to avoid work, or factitiously trying for financial gain. The symptoms of a conversion disorder can often be removed with **hypnosis** or **Amytal interview**. Some researchers believe that simply suggesting that these symptoms will go away is the best way to relieve them. The individual can develop complications, like seizures, from disuse of body parts.

Primary Gain, Secondary Gain, and Differential Diagnoses

The **etiology of conversion disorder** is explained in terms of two psychological mechanisms:

- A conversion disorder may be used for **primary gain** when the symptoms keep an internal conflict or need out of the consciousness.
- A conversion disorder is used for **secondary gain** when the symptoms help the individual avoid an unpleasant activity or obtain support from the environment.

In order to diagnose a conversion disorder, there must be evidence of *involuntary* psychological factors. Conversion disorder is occasionally confused with factitious disorder and malingering, both of which are voluntary.

Somatic Symptom Disorder

Somatic symptom disorder is a somatoform disorder, meaning that it suggests a medical condition but is not fully explainable by the medical condition, substance abuse, or other medical disorder. Individuals with somatic symptom disorder often describe their problems in dramatic, overstated, and ambiguous terms. They excessively worry or think about the symptoms and spend much time and energy worrying about health issues. Somatic symptom disorders cause clinically significant distress or impairment, and are not produced intentionally. A somatic symptom disorder involves recurrent multiple somatic complaints and though no one symptom has to be continuous, some symptoms are present for at least six months. Medical attention has been sought, but no physical explanation has been found.

Illness Anxiety Disorder

Individuals with illness anxiety disorder (formerly hypochondriasis) have an unrealistic preoccupation with having or getting a serious illness that is based on a misappraisal of bodily symptoms. This preoccupation is disproportional to symptoms or medical evidence. Individuals with illness anxiety disorder likely know a great deal about their condition, and frequently go to a number of different doctors searching for a professional opinion that confirms their own. They likely either experience frequent health related checks (either by doctors or by self-checks) or avoidance of doctors and healthcare facilities. The symptoms of this disorder have been present for at least six months, however the specific illness that the individual fears may change.

Delirium

Delirium is characterized by a clinically significant deficit in cognition or memory as compared to previous functioning. In order for delirium to be diagnosed, the individual must have disturbances in consciousness and either a change in personality or the development of perceptual abnormalities. These changes in cognition may appear as losses of memory, disorientation in space and time, and impaired language. The perceptual abnormalities associated with delirium include hallucinations and illusions. Delirium usually develops over a few hours or days, and may vary in intensity over the course of the days and weeks. If the cause of the delirium is alleviated, it may disappear for an extended period of time.

The **criteria** for delirium are as follows:

Criteria A	A disturbance in consciousness or attention
Criteria B	Develops over a short period of time, and fluctuates throughout the day
Criteria C	Accompanied by changes in cognition
Criteria D	Not better explained by another condition
Criteria E	Caused by a medical condition or is substance related

Five groups of people at **high risk** for delirium:

- Elderly people
- Those who have a diminished cerebral reserve due to major neurocognitive disorder (formerly dementia), stroke, or some other medical condition
- Post cardiotomy patients
- Burn patients
- Drug-dependent people who are in withdrawal

Delirium can also be **caused** by:

- Systemic infections
- Metabolic disorders
- Fluid and electrolyte imbalances
- Postoperative states
- Head trauma
- Long hospital stays, such as those in the intensive care unit

The **treatment** for delirium usually aims at curing the underlying cause of the disorder and reducing the agitated behavior. Antipsychotic drugs can be good for reducing agitation, delusions, and hallucinations, while providing a calm environment can decrease the appearance of agitation.

Neurocognitive Disorders

Major and minor neurocognitive disorders (NCD) may be due to any of the following: Alzheimer's disease, Frontotemporal lobar degeneration, Lewy body disease, vascular disease, traumatic brain injury, substance or medication use, HIV Infection, prion disease, Parkinson's disease, Huntington's disease, another medical condition, and multiple etiologies. **Criteria** are as follows:

Criteria A	A change in cognitive ability from baseline. This information can be determined by the individual, a well-informed significant other, family member, or caretaker, or it can be determined by neuropsychology testing.
Criteria B	For a major neurocognitive disorder, the cognitive change interferes with ADLs and independence. For a minor neurocognitive disorder, the cognitive change doesn't interfere with normal ADLS and independence, if accommodations are used.
Criteria C	The cognitive change cannot be defined as delirium only.
Criteria D	The cognitive change is not better described as another mental disorder.

Differential Diagnosis

Some of the cognitive symptoms of major depressive disorder are very similar to those of **neurocognitive disorders**. Indeed, this kind of depression is frequently referred to as pseudodementia. One difference is that the **cognitive deficits** typical of neurocognitive disorders will get progressively worse, and the individual is unlikely to admit that he or she has impaired cognition.

Pseudodementia, on the other hand, typically has a very rapid onset and usually causes the individual to become concerned about his or her own health. There are also differences in the quality of memory impairment in these two conditions: Individuals with **neurocognitive disorders** have deficits in both recall and recognition memory, while individuals who are **depressed** only have deficits in recall memory.

Diagnosis

Individuals who suffer from neurocognitive disorders are likely to manifest a few **cognitive deficits**, most notably memory impairment, aphasia, apraxia, agnosia, or impaired executive functioning. Depending on the etiology of the neurocognitive disorders, these deficits may get progressively worse or may be stable.

These individuals could have both **anterograde** and **retrograde amnesia**, meaning that they find it difficult both to learn new information and to recall previously learned information. There may be a decrease in language skill, specifically manifested in an inability to recall the names of people or things. Individuals may also have a hard time performing routine motor programs, and may be unable to recognize familiar people and places. Abstract thinking, planning, and initiating complex behaviors are difficult.

Neurocognitive Disorder Due to Alzheimer's Disease

Particular kinds of **Alzheimer's disease** have been linked with specific genetic abnormalities. For instance, those with early-onset familial Alzheimer's often have abnormalities on **chromosome 21**, while individuals whose onset is later are likely to have irregularities on **chromosome 19**. Those with Alzheimer's disease have also been shown to have significant **aluminum deposits** in brain tissues, a malfunctioning **immune system**, and a low level of **acetylcholine**. Some of the drugs used to treat Alzheimer's increase the cholinergic activity in the brain. These drugs, which include the trade names **Cognex** and **Aricept**, can temporarily reverse cognitive impairment, though these improvements are not sustained when the drugs are removed.

Stages of Alzheimer's Disease

Over half of all cases of neurocognitive disorder are caused by Alzheimer's disease. Alzheimer's begins slowly and may take a long time to become noticeable. Researchers have outlined **three stages** of Alzheimer's disease:

- **Stage 1** usually comprises the first 1-3 years of the condition. The individual suffers from **mild anterograde amnesia**, especially for declarative memories. He or she is likely to have **diminished visuospatial skill**, which often manifests itself in wandering aimlessly. Also common to this stage are indifference, irritability, sadness, and anomia.
- **Stage 2** can stretch between the second and tenth years of the illness. The individual suffers increasing **retrograde amnesia**, restlessness, delusions, aphasia, acalculia, ideomotor apraxia (the inability to translate an idea into movement), and a generally flat mood.
- In **Stage 3** of Alzheimer's disease, the individual suffers **severely impaired intellectual functioning**, apathy, limb rigidity, and urinary and fecal incontinence. This last stage usually occurs between the eighth and twelfth years of the condition.

Alzheimer's disease is quite difficult to diagnose directly, so it is usually only diagnosed once all the other possible causes of major neurocognitive disorder (formerly dementia) have been eliminated. A brain biopsy that indicates extensive neuron loss, amyloid plaques, and neurofibrillary tangles can give solid evidence of Alzheimer's disease. Individuals who develop Alzheimer's disease usually only live about ten years after onset. The disease is more common in females than males, and is more likely to occur after the age of 65.

Treatment

Though Alzheimer's disease is a degenerative condition with no known cure, there are a number of different **treatments** that can provide help to those who suffer from the disease:

- Group therapy that focuses on orienting the individual in reality and encourages him or her to reminisce about past experiences
- Antidepressants, antipsychotics, and other pharmacotherapy
- Behavioral techniques to fight the agitation associated with Alzheimer's
- Environmental manipulation to improve memory and cognitive function
- Involving the individual's family in interventions

Neurocognitive Disorder Due to HIV Infection

Individuals with AIDS develop a particular form of neurocognitive disorder. In its early stages, the **Human Immunodeficiency Virus** causes major neurocognitive disorder (formerly dementia), which appears as forgetfulness, impaired attention, and generally decelerated mental processes. **Neurocognitive disorders** due to HIV progresses include poor concentration, apathy, social withdrawal, loss of initiative, tremor, clumsiness, trouble with problem-solving, and saccadic eye movements. One of the ways that neurocognitive disorders due to HIV is distinguished is by motor slowness, the lack of aphasia, and more severe forms of depression and anxiety. It shares these features with neurocognitive disorders due to Parkinson's and Huntington's diseases.

Neurocognitive Disorder Due to Vascular Disease

In order to be diagnosed with neurocognitive disorder due to **vascular disease**, the individual must have **cognitive impairment** and either **focal neurological signs** or **laboratory evidence of cerebrovascular disease**. Neurocognitive disorder has varying symptoms, depending on where the brain damage lies. Focal neurological signs may include exaggerated reflexes, weaknesses in the extremities, and abnormalities in gait. Symptoms gradually increase in severity. Risk factors for vascular neurocognitive disorder are hypertension, diabetes, tobacco smoking, and atrial fibrillation. In some cases, an individual may be able to recover from neurocognitive disorder due to vascular disease. Stroke victims, for instance, will notice a great deal of improvement in the first six months after the cerebrovascular accident. Most of this improvement will be in their physical, rather than cognitive, symptoms.

Neurocognitive Disorder Due to Huntington's disease

Individuals with **Huntington's disease** suffer degeneration of the GABA-producing cells in their substantia nigra, basal ganglia, and cortex. This inherited disease typically appears between the ages of 30 and 40. The **affective symptoms** of Huntington's disease include irritability, depression, and apathy. After a while, these individuals display **cognitive symptoms** as well, including forgetfulness and dementia. Later, **motor symptoms** emerge, including fidgeting, clumsiness, athetosis (slow, writhing movements), and chorea (involuntary quick jerks). Because the affective symptoms appear in advance of the cognitive and motor symptoms, many people with Huntington's are misdiagnosed with depression. Individuals in the early stages of Huntington's are at risk for suicide, as they are aware of their impending deterioration, and will have the loss of impulse control associated with the disease.

Neurocognitive Disorder Due to Parkinson's Disease

The following symptoms are commonly associated with neurocognitive disorder due to **Parkinson's disease**:

- Bradykinesia (general slowness of movement)
- Resting tremor
- Stoic and unmoving facial expression
- Loss of coordination or balance
- Involuntary pill-rolling movement of the thumb and forefinger
- Akathisia (violent restlessness)

Most people with Parkinson's will suffer from **depression** at some point during their illness, and 20-60% will develop major neurocognitive disorder (formerly dementia). Research indicates that those with Parkinson's have a deficiency of **dopamine-producing cells** and the presence of **Lewy bodies** in their substantia nigra. Many doctors now believe that there is some **environmental cause** for Parkinson's, though the etiology is not yet clear. The medication L-dopa (Dopar, Larodopa) alleviates the symptoms of Parkinson's by increasing the amount of dopamine in the brain.

Schizophrenia

Diagnosis

Schizophrenia is a psychotic disorder. Psychotic disorders are those that feature one or more of the following: delusions, hallucinations, disorganized speech or thought, or disorganized or catatonic behavior. Schizophrenia **diagnostic criteria** are as follows:

Criteria A	Diagnosis requires at least two of the following symptoms, one being a core positive symptom: • Hallucinations (core positive symptom) • Delusions (core positive symptom) • Disorganized speech (core positive symptom) • Severely disorganized or catatonic behavior • Negative symptoms (i.e., avolition, diminished expression)
Criteria B	Individual's level of functioning is significantly below level prior to onset.
Criteria C	If the individual has not had successful treatment there are continual signs of schizophrenia for more than six months.
Criteria D	Depressive disorder, bipolar disorder, and schizoaffective disorder have been ruled out.
Criteria E	The symptoms cannot be attributed to another medical condition or a substance.
Criteria F	If the individual has had a communication disorder or Autism since childhood, a diagnosis of schizophrenia is only made if the individual has hallucinations or delusions.

Etiology

Both twin and adoption studies have suggested that there is a **genetic component** to the etiology of schizophrenia. The rates of instance (concordance) among first-degree biological relatives of people with schizophrenia are greater than among the general population. **Structural abnormalities** in the brain linked to schizophrenia are enlarged ventricles and diminished hippocampus, amygdala, and globus pallidus. **Functional abnormalities** in the brain linked to schizophrenia are hypofrontality and diminished activity in the prefrontal cortex. An abnormally large number of the people with schizophrenia in the Northern Hemisphere were born in the late winter or early spring. There is speculation that this may be because of a link between prenatal exposure to influenza and schizophrenia.

Schizophrenia and Dopamine

For many years, the professional consensus was that schizophrenia was caused by either an excess of the neurotransmitter **dopamine** or oversensitive **dopamine receptors**. The **dopamine hypothesis** was supported by the fact that antipsychotic medications that block dopamine receptors had some success in treating schizophrenia, and by the fact that dopamine-elevating amphetamines amplified the frequency of delusions. The dopamine hypothesis has been somewhat undermined, however, by research that found elevated levels of norepinephrine and serotonin, as well as low levels of GABA and glutamate in schizophrenics. Some studies have shown that clozapine and other atypical antipsychotics are effective in treating schizophrenia, even though they block serotonin rather than dopamine receptors.

Positive Symptoms

The symptoms of schizophrenia may be **positive, negative,** or **disorganized**. Positive symptoms are **delusions** and **hallucinations**. Delusions are false beliefs that are held despite clear evidence to the contrary. The delusions suffered by a schizophrenic usually fall into one of three categories:

- **Persecutory**, in which the person believes that someone or something is out to get him or her.
- **Referential**, in which the person believes that messages in the public domain (like song lyrics or newspaper articles) are specifically directed at him or her.
- **Bizarre**, in which the person imagines that something impossible has happened.

The most common sensory mode for hallucinations is sound, specifically the audition of voices.

Disorganized and Negative Symptoms

For many psychologists, the classic characteristic of schizophrenia is **disorganized speech**. Disorganized speech manifests as:

- Incoherence
- Free associations that make little sense
- Random responses to direct questions

Disorganized behavior manifests as:

- Shabby or unkempt appearance
- Inappropriate sexual behavior
- Unpredictable agitation
- Catatonia and decreased motor activity

Negative symptoms of schizophrenia include:

- Restricted range of emotions
- Reduced body language
- Lack of facial expression
- Lack of coherent thoughts
- Inability to make conversation
- Avolition (the inability to set goals or to work in a rational, programmatic manner)

Catatonia

Criteria for catatonia includes at least three of the following:

- Catalepsy
- Defying or refusing to acknowledge instruction
- Echolalia
- Echopraxia
- Little to no verbal response
- Grimacing
- Agitation
- Semi-consciousness
- Waxy flexibility
- Posturing
- Mannerism
- Stereotypy

Associated Features

Features commonly associated with schizophrenia are:

- Inappropriate affect
- Anhedonia (loss of pleasure)
- Dysphoric mood
- Abnormalities in motor behavior
- Somatic complaints

One of the more troublesome aspects of schizophrenia is that the afflicted individual rarely has any insight into his or her own condition and so is unlikely to **comply** with treatment. People with schizophrenia often develop substance dependencies, especially to nicotine. Though many people believe that those with schizophrenia are more likely to be violent or aggressive than individuals in the general population, there is no statistical information to support this assertion. The onset of schizophrenia is typically during the ages of 18-25 for males and 25-35 for females. Males are slightly more likely to develop the disorder.

Prognosis and Differential Diagnosis

Individuals typically develop schizophrenia as a **chronic condition**, with very little chance of full remission. Positive symptoms of schizophrenia tend to decrease in later life, though the negative symptoms may remain. The following factors tend to **improve prognosis**:

- Good premorbid adjustment
- Acute and late onset
- Female gender
- Presence of a precipitating event
- Brief duration of active-phase symptoms
- Insight into the illness
- Family history of mood disorder
- No family history of schizophrenia

Differential diagnoses for schizophrenia include bipolar and depressive disorders with psychotic features, schizoaffective disorder, and the effects of prolonged and large-scale use of amphetamines or cocaine.

Treatment

Treatment for schizophrenia begins with the administration of **antipsychotic medication**. Antipsychotics are very effective at diminishing the positive symptoms of schizophrenia, though their results vary from person to person. Antipsychotics have strong side effects, however, including tardive dyskinesia. Medication is more effective when it is taken in combination with psychosocial intervention. Many people with schizophrenia are prone to relapse if they receive a great deal of criticism from family members, so it may be a good idea to initiate **family therapy** in which the level of expressed emotion in the family is discussed. Those who are recovering from schizophrenia also benefit from **social skills training** and **help with employment**.

Schizoaffective Disorder

The **criteria** for schizoaffective disorder are as follows:

Criteria A	For diagnosis the individual must have at least two of the following symptoms, one being a core positive symptom. The individual will experience the symptoms during a continuous period of illness during which there will also be a significant manic or depressive mood episode. • Hallucinations (known as a core positive symptom) • Delusions (known as a core positive symptom) • Disorganized speech (known as a core positive symptom) • Severely disorganized or catatonic behavior • Negative Symptoms (such as avolition or diminished expression)
Criteria B	Individual experiences hallucinations or delusions for at least two weeks during illness that do not occur during a significant depressive or manic mood episode.
Criteria C	The individual experiences significant depressive or manic mood symptoms for most of the time of the illness.
Criteria D	The symptoms cannot be attributed to another medical condition or a substance.

Schizophreniform Disorder

The **criteria** for schizophreniform disorder are as follows:

Criteria A	Diagnosis requires at least two of the following symptoms, one being a core positive symptom: • Hallucinations (known as a core positive symptom) • Delusions (known as a core positive symptom) • Disorganized speech (known as a core positive symptom) • Severely disorganized or catatonic behavior • Negative Symptoms (such as avolition or diminished expression)
Criteria B	An illness of at least one month but less than six months duration.
Criteria C	Depressive disorder, bipolar disorder, and schizoaffective disorder have been ruled out.
Criteria D	The symptoms cannot be attributed to another medical condition or a substance.

Brief Psychotic Disorder

Brief psychotic disorder is characterized as a delusion that has sudden onset and lasts less than one month. Brief psychotic disorder is a classification of the schizophrenia spectrum and other psychotic disorders.

Criteria A	At least one of the following symptoms: delusions, hallucinations, disorganized speech, or catatonic behavior.
Criteria B	The symptoms last more than one day but less than one month. The individual does eventually return to baseline functioning.
Criteria C	The disorder cannot be attributed to another psychotic or depressive disorder.

Delusional Disorder

Delusional disorder is typified by the presence of a persistent delusion. Delusion may be persecutory type, jealous type, erotomanic type (that someone is in love with delusional person), somatic type (that one has physical defect or disease), grandiose type, or mixed.

The following are the **criteria** for delusional disorder:

Criteria A	The individual experiences at least one delusion for at least one month or longer.
Criteria B	The individual does not meet criteria for schizophrenia.
Criteria C	Functioning is not significantly impaired, and behavior except dealing specifically with delusion is not bizarre.
Criteria D	Any manic or depressive episodes are brief.
Criteria E	The symptoms cannot be attributed to another medical condition or a substance.

It should be specified if the delusions are bizarre. Severity is rated by the quantitative assessment measure "Clinician-Rated Dimensions of Psychosis Symptom Severity."

Bipolar Disorders

Documentation and Gender Influences

Bipolar disorders should be documented with current (or most recent) features, whether manic, hypomanic, or major depressive episode noted. The current severity of mild, moderate, or severe should also be noted as well as any applicable specifiers. Partial or full remission should be noted when applicable. Example: bipolar I disorder, current episode manic, moderate severity, with anxious distress. Bipolar **specifiers** include:

- With anxious distress
- With melancholic features
- With peripartum onset
- With seasonal pattern
- With psychotic features
- With catatonia
- With atypical features
- With mixed features
- With rapid cycling

Bipolar II is distinguished from Bipolar I by the fact that the individual has never had either a manic or a mixed episode. Males and females develop Bipolar I disorder equally, but Bipolar II is much more common for females. On average, the age of onset for the first manic episode is the early 20s.

Etiology and Treatment

Among all mental disorders, Bipolar I and II disorders are the most clearly linked to **genetic factors**. Identical twins are overwhelmingly more likely to develop the disease than are fraternal twins. Research suggests a traumatic event may precipitate the first manic episode, although later manic episodes do not need to be preceded by a stressful episode. The most effective treatment for Bipolar I and II is **lithium**. Lithium reduces manic symptoms and eliminates mood swings for more than 50% of individuals. One major problem with lithium is that it works so well, many individuals consider themselves cured and stop taking it, causing a relapse. Pharmacotherapy is most effective when combined with psychotherapy. Individuals who do not respond to lithium treatment are given **anticonvulsants** like carbamazepine or divalproex sodium. Anticonvulsants are also used in lieu of lithium for individuals who have rapid cycling or dysphoric mania.

Bipolar I Disorders

The **criteria** for bipolar I disorder are as follows:

Criteria A	The individual must meet the criteria (listed below) for at least one manic episode. The manic episode is usually either proceeded or followed by an episode of major depression or hypomania.
Criteria B	The episode cannot be explained by schizophrenia spectrum and other psychotic disorders criteria.

The manic episode **criteria** are as follows:

Criteria A	An episode of significantly elevated, demonstrative, or irritable mood. There is significant goal-directed behaviors, activities, and an increase in the amount of energy the individual normally has. These symptoms are present for most of the day and last at least one week.
Criteria B	During the period described in criteria A, the individual will experience 3 of the following symptoms (if the individual presents with only an irritable mood, 4 of the following symptoms need to be present for diagnosis): • Less need for sleep • Excessive talking • Inflated self-esteem • Easily distracted • Flight of ideas • Engages in activities that have negative consequences • Engages in either goal directed activity or purposeless activity
Criteria C	The episode causes significant impairment socially.
Criteria D	The symptoms cannot be attributed to a substance.

Bipolar II Disorders

The **criteria** for bipolar II disorder are as follows:

Criteria A	The individual has had one or more major depressive episodes and one or more hypomanic episodes.
Criteria B	The individual has never experienced a manic episode.
Criteria C	The episode doesn't meet criteria for schizophrenia spectrum or other psychotic disorder.
Criteria D	The depressive episodes or alterations between the two moods cause significant impairment socially or functionally.

A **hypomanic episode** is severe enough to be a clear departure from normal mood and functioning, but not severe enough to cause a marked impairment in functioning, or to require hospitalization. The **criteria** for hypomania are as follows:

Criteria A	An episode of significantly elevated, demonstrative, or irritable mood. There are significant goal-directed behaviors, activities, and an increase in the amount of energy the individual normally has. These symptoms are present for most of the day and last at least 4 days.
Criteria B	During the period described in criteria A, the individual experiences 3 of the following symptoms (if the individual presents with only an irritable mood, 4 of the following symptoms need to be present for diagnosis): • Less need for sleep • Excessive talking • Inflated self-esteem • Easily distracted • Flight of ideas • Engages in activities that have negative consequences • Engages in goal directed activity or purposeless activity
Criteria C	The episode causes a change in the functioning of the individual.
Criteria D	The episode causes changes noticeable by others.
Criteria E	The episode does not cause social impairments.
Criteria F	The symptoms cannot be attributed to a substance.

Cyclothymic Disorder

Cyclothymic disorder is characterized by chronic, fluctuating mood with many hypomanic and depressive symptoms, which are not as severe as either bipolar I or bipolar II. The **criteria** are as follows:

Criteria A	The individual experiences a considerable number of hypomania symptoms without meeting all the criteria for hypomanic episodes and experiences depressive symptoms that do not meet the criteria for major depressive episode for two years or more (can be for one year or more in <18 years of age).
Criteria B	During the above time period, the individual exhibits the symptoms more than half of the time and they are never symptom free for more than two months at a time.
Criteria C	The individual has not met the criteria for manic, hypomanic, or major depressive episodes.
Criteria D	The episode doesn't meet criteria for schizophrenia spectrum or other psychotic disorder.
Criteria E	The symptoms cannot be attributed to a substance.
Criteria F	The episodes cause significant impairment socially or functionally.

Major Depressive Disorder

Major Depressive Episode

The **criteria** for a major depressive episode are as follows:

Criteria A	The individual experiences 5 or more of the following symptoms during 2 consecutive weeks. These symptoms are associated with a change in their normal functioning. (Note: Of the presenting symptoms, either depressed mood or loss of ability to feel pleasure must be included to make this diagnosis.): • Depressed mood • Loss of ability to feel pleasure or have interest in normal activities • Decreased aptitude for thinking • Thoughts of death • Fatigue (daily) • Inappropriate guilt or feelings of worthlessness • Observable motor agitation or psychomotor retardation • Weight loss or gain of more than 5% in one month • Hypersomnia or Insomnia (almost daily)
Criteria B	The episode causes distress or social or functional impairment.
Criteria C	The symptoms cannot be attributed to a substance or another condition or disease.
Criteria D	The episode does not meet the criteria for schizophrenia spectrum or other psychotic disorder.
Criteria E	The individual does not meet criteria for manic episode or a hypomanic episode.

Diagnosis and Gender

Major depressive disorder is diagnosed when an individual has one or more major depressive episodes without having a history of manic, hypomanic, or mixed episodes. There are a few different **specifiers** (categories of associated features) for major depressive disorder issued by the DSM-5:

- With anxious distress
- With melancholic features
- With peripartum onset
- With seasonal pattern
- With psychotic features
- With catatonia
- With atypical features
- With mixed features

Some studies estimate that 20% of women will have symptoms worthy of a diagnosis of major depressive disorder after giving birth.

From the beginning of adolescence on, the rate of major depressive disorder is about twice as great for females as for males. Before adolescence, the rates are about the same. Most major depressive disorders occur in the mid-twenties.

Cognitive-Behavioral Etiologies

Three major cognitive-behavioral etiologies have been offered for major depressive disorder:

- The **learned helplessness model** proposed by Seligman suggests afflicted individuals have been exposed to uncontrollable negative events in the past and have a tendency to attribute negative events to internal, stable, and global factors.
- **Rehm's self-control model** suggests depression occurs in individuals who obsess over negative outcomes, set extremely high standards for themselves, blame all of their problems on internal failures, and have low rates of self-reinforcement coupled with high rates of self-punishment.
- **Beck's cognitive theory** suggests depression is the result of negative and irrational thought and beliefs about the depressive cognitive triad (the self, the world, and the future).

Prognosis and Catecholamine Hypothesis

The severity and duration of a major depressive episode varies from case to case, but symptoms usually last about six months before remission to full function. 20-30% of individuals have lingering symptoms for months or years. About 50% of individuals experience more than one episode of major depression. Oftentimes, multiple episodes are precipitated by some severe psychological trauma. The **catecholamine hypothesis** suggests major depressive episodes are due to a deficiency of the neurotransmitter norepinephrine. The **indolamine hypothesis** proposes that depression is caused by inferior levels of serotonin.

Etiology

Besides the catecholamine and indolamine hypotheses, there are a few other proposed ideas for the etiology of major depressive disorder. Some researchers speculate depression is caused by **hormonal disturbances**, like an increased level of cortisol. Cortisol is one of the stress hormones secreted by the adrenal cortex. Other researchers speculate there is a connection between depression and diminished new cell growth in certain regions of the brain, particularly the subgenual prefrontal cortex and hippocampus. The **subgenual prefrontal cortex** is the part of the brain associated with the formation of positive emotions. Many antidepressant drugs seem to stimulate new growth in the **hippocampus**.

Symptoms

Symptoms of major depressive disorder vary with age. For **children**, common symptoms are:

- Somatic complaints
- Irritability
- Social withdrawal

Male preadolescents often display aggressive and destructive behavior. When **elderly** individuals develop a major depressive disorder, it manifests as memory loss, distractibility, disorientation, and other cognitive problems. Many major depressive episodes are misdiagnosed as major neurocognitive disorder (formerly dementia). It is very common in non-Anglo cultures for the symptoms of depression to be described solely in terms of their somatic content. Latinos, for instance, frequently complain of jitteriness or headaches, while Asians commonly complain of tiredness or weakness.

Treatment

The typical treatment program for major depressive disorder combines antidepressant drugs and psychotherapy. Three classes of **antidepressant medication** are commonly prescribed:

- **Selective serotonin reuptake inhibitors (SSRIs)** are prescribed for melancholic depressives; they have a lower incidence of serious adverse side effects than do tricyclics.
- **Tricyclics (TCAs)**, are prescribed for classic depression, involving vegetative bodily symptoms, a worsening of symptoms in the morning, acute onset, and short duration of moderate symptoms.
- **Monoamine oxidase inhibitors** are prescribed as a last resort for individuals who have an unorthodox depression that includes phobias, panic attacks, increased appetite, hypersomnia, and a mood that worsens as the day goes on.

Depressive Disorder with Seasonal Pattern

Depressive disorder with seasonal pattern, formerly called seasonal affective disorder (SAD), is a depressive disorder that afflicts people in the Northern Hemisphere from October to April. Symptoms of this disorder are hypersomnia, increased appetite, weight gain, and an increased desire for carbohydrates. Research suggests this disorder is caused by circadian and seasonal increases in the level of melatonin production by the pineal gland from lack of sunlight. Affected individuals are treated with phototherapy (exposure to full-spectrum white light for several hours each day), aerobic exercise, and SSRIs.

Persistent Depressive Disorder

The **criteria** for persistent depressive disorder are the following:

Criteria A	For at least two years, the individual experiences for most of a day, more days than they don't experience it, a depressed mood.
Criteria B	The individual experiences 2 or more of the following when depressed: • Low self-esteem • Decreased appetite or overeating • A feeling of hopelessness • Fatigue • Difficulty concentrating • Insomnia or hypersomnia
Criteria C	During the episode the individual has not had relief from symptoms for longer than 2 months at once.
Criteria D	The individual may have met the criteria for a major depressive disorder.
Criteria E	The individual does not meet criteria for cyclothymic disorder, manic episode, or hypomanic episode.
Criteria F	The episode does not meet the criteria for schizophrenia spectrum or other psychotic disorder.
Criteria G	The symptoms cannot be attributed to a substance.
Criteria H	The symptoms cause distress or impairment socially or functionally.

Of those with persistent depressive disorder, 25-50% of individuals show sleep EEG abnormalities. Women are 2-3 times more likely to suffer from persistent depressive disorder than men. Around 75% of individuals with persistent depressive disorder develop major depressive disorder within 5 years. First degree relatives are likely to also suffer major depression or persistent depressive disorder. Treatment programs for persistent depressive disorder usually include a combination of **antidepressant drugs** (especially fluoxetine) and either **cognitive-behavioral therapy or interpersonal therapy**.

Suicide Statistics and Correlates

Gender, Race, and Marital Status

Statistics indicate that 4-5 times as many males as females successfully commit **suicide**. However, females attempt suicide about 3 times as often as males. The reason for this disparity is that men tend to employ more violent means of self-destruction, including guns, hanging, and carbon monoxide poisoning. Among racial and ethnic groups, the suicide rate is highest among whites. The exception is **American Indian** and **Alaskan Natives** aged 15-34, for whom suicide is the second leading cause of death. As for **marital status**, the highest rates of suicide are among divorced, separated, or widowed people. The suicide rate for single people trails that of those groups, but it remains higher than the suicide rate for married people.

History, Age, and Drugs of Choice

Suicide is the eighth leading cause of death for **males** in the United States, and sixteenth for **females**. Indicators that a person is at risk for a suicide attempt include:

- Previous suicide attempt in 60-80% of cases
- Warning issued by the prospective suicide in 80% of cases

Drug suicides are the most common (>70% annually). In order of preference, suicides use: Sedatives (especially benzodiazepines), antidepressants, opiates, prescription analgesics, and carbon monoxide from car exhaust. The most likely persona to commit a successful suicide is a male, Caucasian, 45-49 years of age. Women are more likely to be saved from an attempted suicide through treatment at an Emergency Department. The average age of those saved is 15-19. A sharp increase in suicides aged 10-19 may be due to the increased use of antidepressants, which now carry an FDA black box warning. Around 25% of suicide attempts by seniors over age 65 are successful.

Psychiatric Disorders and Biological Correlates

Most of those who commit suicide are suffering from some mental disorder, most commonly **major depressive disorder** or **bipolar disorder**. Suicide associated with depression is most likely to occur within three months after the symptoms of depression have begun to improve. The risk of suicide among adolescents with depression increases greatly if the adolescent also has conduct disorder, ADHD, or is a substance abuser, particularly of inhaled solvents. As for biological correlates, people who commit suicide have been found to have low levels of **serotonin** and **5HIAA** (a serotonin metabolite). Individuals at risk for suicide need immediate psychological intervention and a 24-hour suicide watch.

Cognitive Correlates and Life Stress

Research into suicide has indicated that **hopelessness** is the most common predictor of an inclination to self-destruction. It is a more accurate predictor even than the intensity of depressive symptoms. **Self-assigned or society-assigned perfectionism** has also been blamed for suicide. Many suicides are preceded by some **traumatic life event**, like the end of a romantic relationship or the death of a loved one. For adolescents, the most common precipitant of suicide is an **argument with a parent or rejection by a boyfriend or girlfriend**. Among adolescents, the common warning signs of suicide are talking about death, giving away possessions, and talking about a reunion with a deceased individual.

Factitious Disorder

An individual diagnosed with factitious disorder (FD) intentionally manifests physical or psychological symptoms to satisfy an intrapsychic need to fill the role of a sick person. The individual with FD presents the illness in an exaggerated manner and avoids interrogation that might expose the falsity. These individuals may undergo multiple surgeries and invasive medical procedures. They often hide insurance claims and hospital discharge forms. A disturbing variation of FD is **factitious disorder imposed on another** (sometimes referred to as Munchausen's syndrome by proxy), in which a caregiver intentionally produces symptoms in another individual. Usually, a mother makes her young child ill.

Malingering vs. Factitious Disorder

Malingering is feigning physical symptoms to avoid something specific, like going to work, or to gain a specific reward. Consider malingering as a possibility when:

- A person obtains a medical evaluation for legal reasons or to apply for insurance compensation.
- There is marked inconsistency between the individual's complaint and the objective findings, or if the individual does not cooperate with a diagnostic evaluation or prescribed treatment.
- The individual has an antisocial personality disorder.

Malingering contrasts with factitious disorder because in FD the individual does not feign physical symptoms for personal gain or to avoid an adverse event, but does it with no obvious external rewards.

Dissociative Disorders

Dissociative disorders are a disruption in consciousness, identity, memory, or perception of the environment that is not due to the effects of a substance or a general medical condition. These are all characterized by a disturbance in the normally integrative functions of identity, memory, consciousness, or environmental perception.

Dissociative identity disorder (previously multiple personality disorder)	Two or more personalities exist within one person, with each personality dominant at a particular time.
Dissociative amnesia	Inability to recall important personal data, more than forgetfulness. It is not due to organic causes and comes on suddenly.
Depersonalization/derealization disorder	Feeling detached from one's mental processes or body, as if one is an observer.

Cultural influences can cause or amplify some of the symptoms of dissociative disorders, so take these into account when making a diagnosis. For instance, many religious ceremonies try to foster a dissociative psychological experience; individuals participating in such a ceremony may display symptoms of dissociative disorder without requiring treatment.

Dissociative Amnesia

Individuals may be diagnosed with dissociative amnesia if they have more than one episode in which they are unable to remember important personal information, and this memory loss cannot be attributed to ordinary forgetfulness. The gaps in the individual's memory are likely to be related to a traumatic event. The three most common patterns of dissociative amnesia are:

- **Localized**, in which the individual is unable to remember all events around a defined period
- **Selective**, in which the individual cannot recall some events pertaining to a circumscribed period
- **Generalized**, in which memory loss spans the individual's entire life

It should be specified if this is with dissociative fugue, a subtype of dissociative amnesia, which is a purposeful travel that is associated with amnesia.

Dissociative Fugue and Depersonalization Disorder

A **dissociative fugue** is a subtype of dissociative amnesia and is an abrupt, unexpected, purposeful flight from home, or another stressful location, coupled with an inability to remember the past. The individual is unable to remember his or her identity and assumes a new identity. Fugues are psychological protection against extreme stressors like bankruptcy, divorce, separation, suicidal or homicidal ideation, and rejection. Fugues happen in wars, natural disasters, and severe accidents. Fugues affect 2 in every 1,000 Americans. There will be no recollection of events that occur during the fugue. Individuals in a fugue state may seem normal to strangers. Dissociative fugue is a specifier that can be used with dissociative amnesia.

Depersonalization/derealization disorder is diagnosed when an individual has recurrent episodes in which he or she feels detached from his or her own mental processes or body or to the surroundings. In order to be diagnosed, this condition must be intense enough to cause significant distress or functional impairment.

Sexual Dysfunctions

A sexual dysfunction is any condition in which the sexual response cycle is disturbed or there is pain during sexual intercourse, and this causes distress or interpersonal difficulty. **Types** of sexual dysfunctions:

- Delayed ejaculation
- Erectile disorder
- Female orgasmic disorder
- Female sexual interest/arousal disorder
- Genito-pelvic pain/penetration disorder
- Male hypoactive sexual desire disorder
- Premature ejaculation
- Substance-induced sexual dysfunction

Male erectile disorder is the inability to attain or maintain an erection. This condition is linked to diabetes, liver and kidney disease, multiple sclerosis, and the use of antipsychotic, antidepressant, and hypertensive drugs. **Orgasmic disorders** are any delay or absence of orgasm after the normal sexual excitement phase. Premature ejaculation is orgasm that occurs with a minimum of stimulation and before the person desires it. Premature ejaculation may be in part due to deficiencies in serotonin.

Physical and Psychological Components and Treatments

Any individual with sexual dysfunction should be given a medical evaluation for diabetes, pelvic scars, kidney disease, hypertension, and drug interactions. Use sleep studies to determine if an impotent male gets an erection at night, and determine whether the cause of impotence is physical or psychological. **Psychological impotence** can be treated with cognitive-behavioral therapy. Sex therapy is most helpful in treating premature ejaculation. Sensate focus is used to reduce performance anxiety and increase sexual excitement. Kegel exercises, which strengthen the pubococcygeus muscle, can improve sexual pleasure. As for pharmacotherapy, Viagra is helpful in attaining and maintaining erections.

Genito-Pelvic Pain/Penetration Disorder and Categories of Sexual Dysfunctions

Genito-pelvic pain/penetration disorder is persistent difficulty with genital pain associated with sexual intercourse or involuntary spasms in the pubococcygeus muscle in the vagina, which make it difficult to have sexual intercourse, or fear or anxiety related to anticipation of pain during intercourse. Sexual dysfunctions are categorized as lifelong or acquired, and generalized or situational, depending on their cause. **Generalized dysfunctions** occur with every sexual partner in all circumstances. **Situational dysfunctions** only occur under certain circumstances. The cause may be psychological, physical, or both.

Paraphilic Disorders

Paraphilic disorders are intense, recurrent sexual urges or behaviors involving either nonhuman objects, non-consenting partners (including children), or the suffering or humiliation of oneself or one's partner. **Common paraphilias** include:

- Fetishistic disorder
- Transvestic disorder
- Pedophilic disorder
- Exhibitionistic disorder
- Voyeuristic disorder
- Sexual masochism disorder
- Sexual sadism disorder
- Frotteuristic disorder (rubbing against a non-consenting person)

The most common **treatment** for paraphilia was previously in vivo aversion therapy, but now it is more common for treatment to include covert sensitization, in which the imagination is given aversion therapy. The medication Depo-Provera has been found to relieve paraphiliac symptoms for many men, although this relief ceases as soon as the man stops taking the drug.

Gender Dysphoria

DSM-5 defines gender dysphoria (formerly gender identity disorder) as a marked incongruence between one's expressed gender and assigned gender that causes significant distress or impairment over a period of at least 6 months. Informally, gender dysphoria is used to describe a person's persistent discomfort and disagreement with their assigned gender. DSM-5 criteria for diagnosis in **children** include:

- Strong desire to be of the other gender or insistence that one is the other gender
- Strong preference for clothing typically associated with the other gender
- Strong preference for playing cross-gender roles
- Strong preference for activities stereotypical of the other gender and rejection of those activities stereotypical of one's assigned gender
- Strong preference for playmates of the other gender
- Strong dislike of one's own sexual anatomy
- Strong desire for the sex characteristics that match one's expressed gender

DSM-5 criteria for diagnosis in **adolescents and adults** include:

- Marked incongruence between expressed gender and one's existing primary and secondary sex characteristics
- Strong desire to rid oneself of these sex characteristics for this reason
- Strong desire for the sex characteristics of the other gender
- Strong desire to be of the other gender and to be treated as such
- Strong conviction that one's feelings and reactions are typical of the other gender

Sleep-Wake Disorders

Sleep-wake disorders include the following:

Insomnia disorders	Difficulty falling asleep, staying asleep, or early rising without being able to go back to sleep.
Hypersomnolence disorder	Sleepiness despite getting at least 7 hours with difficulty feeling awake when suddenly awoke, lapses of sleep in the day, feeling unrested after long periods of sleep.
Narcolepsy	Uncontrollable lapses into sleep, occurring at least three times each week for at least 3 months.
Obstructive sleep apnea hypopnea	Breathing related sleep disorder with obstructive apneas or hypopneas.
Central sleep apnea	Breathing related sleep disorder with central apnea.
Sleep-related hypoventilation	Breathing related sleep disorder with evidence of decreased respiratory rate and increased CO_2 level.
Circadian rhythm sleep-wake disorder	Sleep wake disorder caused by a mismatch between the circadian rhythm and sleep required by person.
Non-rapid eye movement sleep arousal disorder	Awakening during the first third of the night associated with sleep walking or sleep terrors.
Nightmare disorder	Recurring distressing dreams that are well remembered and cause distress.
Rapid eye movement sleep behavior disorder	Arousal during REM sleep associated with motor movements and vocalizing.
Restless legs syndrome	The need to move legs due to uncomfortable sensations, usually relieved by activity.

Review Video: Chronic Insomnia
Visit mometrix.com/academy and enter code: 293232

Adjustment Disorders

Adjustment disorders appear as maladaptive reactions to one or more identifiable psychosocial stressors. In order to make the diagnosis, the onset of symptoms must be within three months of the stressor, and the condition must cause impairments in social, occupational, or academic performance. The symptoms do not align with normal grief or bereavement. Symptoms remit within six months after the termination of the stressor or its consequences. The adjustment disorder should be specified with at least one of the following:

- Depressed mood
- Anxiety
- Mixed anxiety and depressed mood
- Disturbance of conduct
- Mixed disturbance of emotions and conduct

Personality Disorders

Personality disorders occur when an individual has developed personality traits so maladaptive and entrenched that they cause personal distress or interfere significantly with functioning.

The DSM-5 lists five **traits** involved in personality disorders:

- Neuroticism
- Extraversion/introversion
- Openness to experience
- Agreeableness/antagonism
- Conscientiousness

The following are the **criteria** for personality disorders:

Criteria A	Long-term pattern of maladaptive personality traits and behaviors that do not align with the individual's culture. These traits and behaviors will be found in at least two areas: • Impulse control • Inappropriate emotional intensity or responses • Inappropriately interpreting people, events, and self • Inappropriate social functioning
Criteria B	The traits and behaviors are inflexible and exist despite changing social situations.
Criteria C	The traits and behaviors cause distress and impair functioning.
Criteria D	Onset was adolescence or early adulthood and has been enduring.
Criteria E	The behaviors and traits are not due to another mental disorder.
Criteria F	The behaviors and traits are not due to a substance.

Cluster A, B, and C Personality Disorders

Personality disorders are **clustered** into three groups:

Cluster A (eccentric or odd disorders)	**Cluster B** (dramatic or excessively emotional disorders)	**Cluster C** (fear- or anxiety-based disorders)
Paranoid	Antisocial	Avoidant
Schizoid	Borderline	Dependent
Schizotypal	Histrionic	Obsessive-Compulsive
	Narcissistic	

Paranoid Personality Disorder

Paranoid personality disorder is a pervasive pattern of distrust and suspiciousness that involves believing the actions and thoughts of other people to be directed antagonistically against oneself. In order to make the diagnosis, the individual must have at least four of the following **symptoms**:

- Suspects that others are somehow harming him or her
- Doubts the trustworthiness of others
- Reluctant to confide in others
- Suspicious without justification about fidelity of one's partner
- Reads hidden meaning into remarks or events
- Consistently has grudges
- Believes there are attacks on his or her character that others present do not perceive

Schizoid Personality Disorder

Schizoid personality disorder is characterized by a pervasive lack of interest in relationships with others and limited range of emotional expression in contacts with others. Four of these **symptoms** must be present:

- Avoidance of or displeasure in close relationships
- Always chooses solitude
- Little interest in sexual relationships
- Takes pleasure in few activities
- Indifference to praise or criticism
- Emotional coldness or detachment
- Lacks close friends except first-degree relatives

Schizotypal Personality Disorder

Schizotypal personality disorder is characterized by pervasive social deficits, oddities of cognition, perception, or behavior. Diagnosis requires five of the following:

- Ideas of reference
- Odd beliefs or magical thinking
- Lack of close friends except first-degree relatives
- Bodily illusions
- Suspiciousness
- Social anxiety (excessive)
- Inappropriate or constricted affect
- Peculiarities in behavior or appearance

ANTISOCIAL PERSONALITY DISORDER

Antisocial personality disorder is a general lack of concern for the rights and feelings of others. In order to receive a diagnosis of antisocial personality disorder, the individual must:

- Be at least 18
- Have had a history of conduct disorder before age 15
- Have shown *at least three* of the following symptoms before the age of 15:
    - Failure to conform to social laws and norms
    - Deceitfulness
    - Impulsivity
    - Reckless disregard for the safety of self and others
    - Consistent irresponsibility
    - Lack of remorse
    - Irritability or aggressiveness

Antisocial personality disorder may also include an inflated opinion of self, superficial charm, and a lack of empathy for others.

BORDERLINE PERSONALITY DISORDER

Borderline personality disorder is a pervasive pattern of instability in social relationships, self-image, and affect, coupled with marked impulsivity. A diagnosis of borderline personality disorder requires five of the following **symptoms**:

- Frantic efforts to avoid being abandoned
- A pattern of unstable and intense personal relationships, in which there is alternation between idealization and devaluation
- Instability of self-image
- Potentially self-destructive impulsivity in at least two areas
- Recurrent suicide threats or gestures
- Affective instability
- Chronic feelings of emptiness
- Inappropriate anger
- Paranoid ideation or dissociative symptoms

The changes in self-identity may manifest as shifts in career goals and sexual identity; impulsivity may manifest as unsafe sex, reckless driving practices, and substance abuse.

Borderline personality disorder is most common in people between the ages of 19 and 34. Most individuals see substantial improvement over a period of 15 years. Impulsive symptoms are the first to recede.

Review Video: Borderline Personality Disorder
Visit mometrix.com/academy and enter code: 550801

Dialectical behavior therapy (DBT) is often used to treat borderline personality disorder; it combines cognitive-behavioral therapy with the assumption of Rogers that the individual must accept his or her problem before any progress can be made. There are three basic strategies associated with dialectical behavior therapy:

- Group skills training
- Individual outpatient therapy
- Telephone consultations

Regular DBT has reduced the number of suicides and violent acts committed by individuals with borderline personality disorder.

Histrionic Personality Disorder

Histrionic personality disorder is excessive emotionality and attention-seeking behavior. Five **symptoms** from the following list must be present:

- Annoyance or discomfort when not receiving attention
- Inappropriate sexual provocation
- Rapidly shifting and shallow emotions
- Vague and impressionistic speech
- Exaggerated expression of emotion
- Easily influenced by others
- Believes relationships are more intimate than they actually are
- Uses physical appearance to draw attention to self

Narcissistic Personality Disorder

Narcissistic personality disorder is grandiose behavior along with a lack of empathy and a need for admiration. The individual must exhibit five of these **symptoms** for diagnosis:

- Grandiose sense of self-importance
- Fantasies of own power and beauty
- Belief in personal uniqueness
- Need for excessive admiration
- Sense of entitlement
- Exploitation of others
- Lack of empathy
- Envious of others or believes other envy him or her
- Arrogant behaviors

Avoidant Personality Disorder

Avoidant personality disorder is a pervasive pattern of social inhibition, feelings of inadequacy, and hypersensitivity to negative evaluation. A person with avoidant personality disorder exhibits at least four of these **symptoms**:

- Avoiding work or school activities that involve interpersonal contact
- Unwillingness to associate with any person who may withhold approval
- Preoccupation with concerns about being criticized or rejected
- Conception of self as socially inept, inferior, or unappealing to others
- General reluctance to take personal risks or engage in dangerous behavior
- Does not reveal self in intimate relationships, due to fear of shame
- Not able to excel in new situations due to fear of inadequacy

Dependent Personality Disorder

Dependent personality disorder is excessive reliance on others. A diagnosis of dependent personality disorder requires five of these **symptoms**:

- Difficulty making decisions without advice
- Need for others to assume responsibility for one's actions
- Fear of disagreeing with others
- Difficulty self-initiating projects
- Feelings of helplessness or discomfort when alone
- Goes to great lengths to get support from others
- Seeks new relationships when an old one ends
- Preoccupied with the thought of having to care for self

Obsessive-Compulsive Personality Disorder

Obsessive-compulsive personality disorder is a persistent preoccupation with organization and mental or interpersonal control. Four of these **symptoms** are required for the diagnosis of obsessive-compulsive personality disorder:

- Preoccupation with rules and details
- Perfectionism that interferes with progress
- Excessive devotion to work
- Counterproductive rigidity about beliefs and morality
- Inability to throw away old objects
- Reluctance to delegate authority to others
- Rigid or stubborn
- Hoards money without spending

Behavioral Pediatrics

Disclosure

Behavioral pediatrics, otherwise known as pediatric psychology, has become a more popular field because research revealed that many psychological disorders originate in childhood. For the most part, a pediatric mental health provider should be open with the child about his or her condition. Children may need some psychological help if they are to undergo any major medical procedures. Providers must relay any information related to the mental or medical condition in language the child can understand. **Multicomponent cognitive-behavioral interventions**, in which the child is given information about his or her condition and armed with some coping strategies, are especially helpful.

Hospitalization, Compliance, and School Adjustment

Children who need to be **hospitalized** for a significant period of time are especially at risk of developing psychological problems, in large part because they have been separated from their families. Children and adolescents are generally less **compliant** with medical regimens. This may be because of poor communication, parent-child problems, or a general lack of skill. For adolescents, peer pressure and the desire for social acceptance may motivate noncompliance with potentially embarrassing medical programs. Children with serious medical conditions are more likely to have trouble **adjusting to school**. Problems may be caused by the illness itself, by the frequent absences it necessitates, or by the social stigma of illness. Some treatments, like chemotherapy, are associated with deficits in neurocognitive functioning and greater risk of learning disabilities.

Research

Research Process

The key steps in the research process are as follows:

1. **Problem or issue identification**: Includes a literature review to further define the problem and to ensure that the problem has not already been studied
2. **Hypothesis formulation**: Creating a clear statement of the problem or concern, worded in a way that it can be operationalized and measured
3. **Operationalization**: Creating measurable variables that fully address the hypothesis
4. **Study design selection**: Choosing a study design that will allow for the proper analysis of the data to be collected

Data

Objective vs. Subjective Data

Both **subjective (qualitative)** and **objective (quantitative)** data are used for research and analysis, but the focus is quite different:

Subjective Data	Objective Data
Subjective data depend on the opinions of the observer or the subject. Data are described verbally or graphically, depending upon observers to provide information. Interviews may be used as a tool to gather information, and the researcher's interpretation of data is important. Gathering this type of data can be time-intensive, and it usually cannot be generalized to a larger population. This type of information gathering is often useful at the beginning of the design process for data collection.	Objective data are observable and can be tested and verified. Data are described in terms of numbers within a statistical format. This type of information gathering is done after the design of data collection is outlined, usually in later stages. Tools may include surveys, questionnaires, or other methods of obtaining numerical data.

Data Collection

Key points in data collection include the following:

- Data should ideally be collected close to the time of intervention (delays may result in variation from forgetfulness, rather than from the intervention process).
- Frequent data collection is ideal, but subject boredom or fatigue must be avoided as well. Thus, make the data collection process as easy as possible (electronic devices can sometimes help).
- Keep the data collection process short to increase subject responsiveness.
- Standardize recording procedures (collect data at the same time, place, and method to enhance ultimate data validity and reliability).
- Choose a collection method that fits the study well (observation, questionnaires, logs, diaries, surveys, rating scales, etc.) to optimize the data collection process and enhance the value of the data obtained.

Study Designs

Selecting a Study Design

Key considerations that guide the selection of a study design include the following:

- **Standardization**: Whether or not data can be collected in an identical way from each participant (eliminating collection variation)
- **Level of certainty**: The study size needed to achieve statistical significance (determined via power calculations)
- **Resources**: The availability of funding and other resources needed
- The **time frame** required
- The capacity of subjects to provide **informed consent** and receiving **ethics approval** via Human Subjects Review Committees and Institutional Review Boards

Common Study Designs

The three common study designs used in the research process include the following:

- An **exploratory research design** is common when little is known about a particular problem or issue. Its key feature is flexibility. The results comprise detailed descriptions of all observations made, arranged in some kind of order. Conclusions drawn include educated guesses or hypotheses.
- When the variables chosen have already been studied (e.g., in an exploratory study), further research requires a **descriptive survey design**. In this design, the variables are controlled partly by the situation and partly by the investigator, who chooses the sample. Proof of causality cannot be established, but the evidence may support causality.
- **Experimental studies** are highly controlled. Intervening and extraneous variables are eliminated, and independent variables are manipulated to measure effects in dependent variables (e.g., variables of interest)—either in the field or in a laboratory setting.

Ethical Concerns with Study Design Selection

Ethical concerns involved with selecting a study design include the following:

- Research must not lead to harming clients.
- Denying an intervention may amount to harm.
- Informed consent is essential.
- Confidentiality is required.

Single System Study Designs

Evaluation of the efficacy and functionality of a practice is an important aspect of quality control and practice improvement. The most common approach to such an evaluation is the **single system study approach**. Selecting one client per system ($n = 1$), observations are made prior to, during, and following an intervention.

The **research steps** are:

1. Selection of a problem for change (the target)
2. Operationalizing the target into measurable terms
3. Following the target during the baseline phase, prior to the application of any intervention
4. Observing the target and collecting data during the intervention phase, during which the intervention is carried out (There may be more than one phase of data collection.)

Data that are repeatedly collected constitute a single system study "time series design." Single system designs provide a flexible and efficient way to evaluate virtually any type of practice.

Basic Single System Design and Additional Types of Case Study or Predesigns

The most basic single system design is the **A-B design**. The baseline phase (A) has no intervention, followed by the intervention phase (B) with data collection. Typically, data are collected continuously through the intervention phase. Advantages of this design include the following:

- Versatility
- Adaptability to many settings, program styles, and problems
- Clear comparative information between phases

A significant limitation, however, is that causation cannot be demonstrated.

Three additional types of **case study or predesigns** are:

- **Design A**, an observational design with no intervention
- **Design B,** an intervention-only design without any baseline
- **Design B-C**, a "changes case study" design (where no baseline is recorded, a first intervention [B] is performed and then changed [C] and data are recorded)

Common Single System Experimental Designs

Common single system experimental designs are described below:

- The **A-B-A design** begins with data collection in the pre-intervention phase (A) and then continuously during the intervention phases (B). The intervention is then removed (returning to "A") and data are again collected. In this way an experimental process is produced (testing without, with, and then again without intervention). Inferences regarding causality can be made, and two points of comparison are achieved. However, the ethics of removing a successful intervention leaves this study poorly recommended.
- The **A-B-A-B study** overcomes this failure by reintroducing the intervention ("B") at the close of the study. Greater causality inferences are obtained. However, even temporary removal of a successful intervention is problematic (especially if the client drops out at that time), and this design is fairly time-consuming.
- The **B-A-B design** (the "intervention repeat design") drops the baseline phase and starts and ends with the intervention (important in crisis situations and where treatment delays are problematic), saving time and reducing ethical concerns.

Sampling

Terms Used in Sampling

In sampling, the following concepts are considered:

- A **population** is the total set of subjects sought for measurement by a researcher.
- A **sample** is a subset of subjects drawn from a population (as total population testing is usually not possible).
- A **subject** is a single unit of a population.
- **Generalizability** refers to the degree to which specific findings obtained can be applied to the total population.

Sampling Techniques

The following are types of sampling techniques:

Simple random sampling	Any method of sampling wherein each subject selected from a population has an equal chance of being selected (e.g., drawing names from a hat).
Stratified random sampling	Dividing a population into desired groups (age, income, etc.) and then using a simple random sample from each stratified group.
Cluster sampling	A technique used when natural groups are readily evident in a population (e.g., residents within each county in a state). The natural groups are then subjected to random sampling to obtain random members from each county. The best results occur when elements within clusters are internally heterogeneous and externally (between clusters) homogeneous, as the formation of natural clusters may introduce error and bias.
Systematic sampling	A systematic method of random sampling (e.g., randomly choosing a number *n* between 1 and 10—perhaps drawing the number from a hat) and then selecting every *n*th name of a randomly generated or already existing list (such as the phone book) to obtain a study sample.

Measurements

Categories of Measurement

The four different categories of measurement are as follows:

Nominal	Used when two or more named variables exist (male/female, pass/fail, etc.)
Ordinal	Used when a hierarchy is present but when the distance between each value is not necessarily equal (e.g., first, second, third place)
Interval	Hierarchal values that are at equal distance from each other
Ratio	One value divided by another, providing a relative association of one quantity in terms of the other (e.g., 50 is one half of 100)

Statistics and Measures of Central Tendency

A statistic is a numerical representation of an identified characteristic of a subject.

- **Descriptive statistics** are mathematically derived values that represent characteristics identified in a group or population.
- **Inferential statistics** are mathematical calculations that produce generalizations about a group or population from the numerical values of known characteristics.

Measures of central tendency identify the relative degree to which certain characteristics in a population are grouped together. Such measures include:

- The **mean**, or the arithmetic average
- The **median**, or the numerical value above which 50% of the population is found and below which the other 50% is located
- The **mode**, or the most frequently appearing value (score) in a series of numerical values

Review Video: Mean, Median, and Mode
Visit mometrix.com/academy and enter code: 286207

Measures of Variability and Correlation

Measures of variability (or variation) include the following:

- The **range**, or the arithmetic difference between the largest and the smallest value (idiosyncratic "outliers" often excluded)
- The **interquartile range**, or the difference between the upper and lower quartiles (e.g., between the 75th and 25th percentiles)
- The **standard deviation,** or the average distance that numerical values are dispersed around the arithmetic mean

Correlation refers to the strength of relatedness when a relationship exists between two or more numerical values, which, when assigned a numerical value, is the **correlation coefficient** (*r*). A perfect (1:1) correlation has an *r* value of 1.0, with decimal values indicating a lesser correlation as the correlation coefficient moves away from 1.0. The correlation may be either positive (with the values increasing or decreasing together) or negative (if the values are inverse and move opposite to each other).

Review Video: Standard Deviation
Visit mometrix.com/academy and enter code: 419469

Statistical Significance

Statistical tests presume the null hypothesis to be true and use the values derived from a test to calculate the likelihood of getting the same or better results under the conditions of the null hypothesis (referred to as the "observed probability" or "empirical probability," as opposed to the "theoretical probability"). This likelihood is referred to as **statistical significance**. Where this likelihood is very small, the null hypothesis is rejected. Traditionally, experimenters have defined a "small chance" at the 0.05 level (sometimes called the 5% level) or the 0.01 level (1% level). The Greek letter alpha (α) is used to indicate the significance level chosen. Where the observed or empirical probability is less than or equal to the selected alpha, the findings are said to be "statistically significant," and the research hypothesis would be accepted.

Tests

Three examples of tests of statistical significance are:

- The **chi square test** (a nonparametric test of significance), which assesses whether or not two samples are sufficiently different to conclude that the difference can be generalized to the larger population from which the samples were drawn. It provides the degree of confidence by which the research hypothesis can be accepted or rejected, measured on a scale from 0 (impossibility) to 1 (certainty).
- A ***t*-test** is used to compare the arithmetic means of a given characteristic in two samples and to determine whether they are sufficiently different from each other to be statistically significant.
- **Analysis of variance**, or **ANOVA** (also called the "***F* test**"), which is similar to the *t*-test. However, rather than simply comparing the means of two populations, it is used to determine whether or not statistically significant differences exist in multiple groups or samples.

Statistical Error

Types of statistical error include the following:

- **Type I error**: Rejecting the null hypothesis when it is true
- **Type II error**: Accepting the null hypothesis when it is false and the research hypothesis is true (concluding that a difference doesn't exist when it does)

Data Analysis

Data analysis involves the examination of testing results within their context, assessing for correlations, causality, reliability, and validity. In testing a hypothesis (the assertion that two variables are related), researchers look for correlations between variables (a change in one variable associated with a change in another, expressed in numerical values). The closer the correlation is to +1.0 or –1.0 (a perfect positive or negative correlation), the more meaningful the correlation. This, however, is not causality (change in one variable responsible for change in the other). Since all possible relationships between two variables cannot be tested (the variety approaches infinity), the "null hypothesis" is used (asserting that no relationship exists) with probability statistics that indicate the likelihood that the hypothesis is "null" (and must be rejected) or can be accepted. Indices of "reliability" and "validity" are also needed.

Reliability and Validity

Reliability refers to consistency of results. This is measured via test–retest evaluations, split-half testing (random assignment into two subgroups given the same intervention and then comparison of findings), or in interrater situations, where separate subjects' rating scores are compared to see if the correlations persist.

Validity indicates the degree to which a study's results capture the actual characteristics of the features being measured. Reliable results may be consistent but invalid. However, valid results will always be reliable. **Methods for testing validity** include the following:

Concurrent validity	Comparing the results of studies that used different measurement instruments but targeted the same features
Construct validity	The degree of agreement between a theoretical concept and the measurements obtained (as seen via the subcategories of (a) convergent validity, the degree of actual agreement on measures that should be theoretically related, and (b) discriminant validity, the lack of a relationship among measures which are theoretically not related)
Content validity	Comprising logical validity (i.e., whether reasoning indicates it is valid) and face validity (i.e., whether those involved concur that it appears valid)
Predictive validity	Concerning whether the measurement can be used to accurately extrapolate (predict) future outcomes

Review Video: Testing Validity
Visit mometrix.com/academy and enter code: 315457

Interventions with Clients/Client Systems

Therapeutic Relationships and Communication

Conditions Required for a Positive Therapeutic Relationship

In order for a social worker to establish a **positive therapeutic relationship**, he or she must express non-possessive warmth and concern, genuineness, appropriate empathy, nonjudgmental acceptance, optimism regarding prospects for change, objectivity, professional competence, ability to communicate with a client, and self-awareness. Self-disclosure should be used only purposefully and for the client's benefit.

For clients to contribute to a positive therapeutic environment, they must have hope and courage to undertake change processes, be motivated to change, and trust in the worker's interest and skill. They must also be dealt with as an individual and not a case, personality type, or category. Clients must be able to express themselves, to make their own choices, and to change at their own pace.

Professional Objectivity in Social Worker-Client Relationship

Objectivity requires remaining neutral when making judgements. Because of the nature of social work, a large part of evaluation tends to be subjective and not easily quantified, but these evaluations can then reflect the social worker and the social worker's biases. The goal should be to make objective observations as much as possible—reporting what is seen and heard rather than the subjective opinion about those things. In order to ensure that opinions are objective, specific parameters should be developed for decision making. For example, when evaluating a client's socioeconomic status, judging by language and appearance may produce one opinion while judging according to occupation and income may produce another (and probably more accurate) opinion. The way a social worker measures may also reflect biases. For example, measuring gender by male and female only suggests a subjective rejection of other choices, such as non-binary or transgender.

Principles of Communication

Communication involves the conveying of information, whether verbally or nonverbally, between individuals and has two key aspects: sending and receiving information. Each of these requires unique skills, and effective communication requires proficiency in both. **Essential principles of communication** include:

- All aspects of communication must be considered and interpreted in any exchange.
- Communication may be written, verbally spoken, or nonverbally delivered via body language, gestures, and expressions.
- Not all communication is intentional, as unintentional information may also be conveyed.
- All forms of communication have limits, further imposed by issues of perception, unique experiences, and interpretation.
- Quality communication accounts for issues of age, gender, ethnicity/culture, intellect, education, primary language, emotional state, and belief systems.
- Optimum communication is active (or reflective), using strategies such as furthering responses (nodding, etc.), paraphrasing, rephrasing, clarification, encouragement ("tell me more"), partialization (reducing long ideas into manageable parts), summarization, feelings reflection, exploring silence, and nonverbal support (eye contact, warm tone, neutral but warm expressions, etc.).

Quality Communication with Clients

The following are key rules for quality communication with clients:

- Don't speak for the client; instead allow the client to fully express him or herself.
- Listen carefully and try diligently to understand.
- Don't talk when the client is speaking.
- Don't embellish; digest what the client has actually said, not what was presumed to be said.
- Don't interrupt, even if the process is slow or interspersed with long pauses.
- Don't judge, criticize, or intimidate when communicating.
- Facilitate communication with open-ended questions and a responsive and receptive posture.
- Avoid asking "why" questions, which can be perceived as judgmental.
- Communicate using orderly, well-planned ideas, as opposed to rushed statements.
- Moderate the pace of speech and adjust expressions to fit the client's education, intellect, and other unique features.
- Ask clarifying questions to enhance understanding.
- Attend to nonverbal communication (expression, body language, gestures, etc.).
- Limit closed-ended and leading questions.
- Avoid "stacked" (multi-part) questions that can be confusing.

Congruence in Communication

Congruence in communication is consistently communicating the same message verbally and nonverbally. The individual's words, body language, and tone of voice should all convey the same message. If they do not, then the communication is incongruent, and the receiver cannot trust the communication. For example, if a person says, "I really want to help you," in a very harsh tone of voice and with an angry affect, the communication is incongruent, and the message may actually be perceived as the exact opposite of the words spoken. Communication is also incongruent if the individual gives a series of conflicting messages: "I'm going to get a job," "Why should I work?" "I know I need to work," "There's no point in taking a low-paying job." The social worker must be alert to the congruence of client communication in order to more accurately assess the client as well as be aware of personal congruence of communication when interacting with client. This helps to ensure that the social worker can cultivate a relationship built on trust.

Active Listening

Active listening techniques include the use of paraphrasing in response, clarification of what was said by the client, encouragement ("tell me more"), etc. Key **overarching guidelines** include the following:

- Don't become preoccupied with specific active listening strategies; rather, concentrate on reducing client resistance to sharing, building trust, aiding the client in expanding his or her thoughts, and ensuring mutual understanding.
- The greatest success occurs when a variety of active listening techniques are used during any given client meeting.
- Focus on listening and finding ways to help the client to keep talking. Active listening skills will aid the client in expanding and clarifying his or her thoughts.
- Remember that asking questions can often mean interrupting. Avoid questioning the client when he or she is midstream in thought and is sharing, unless the questions will further expand the sharing process.

Allowing Clients Uninterrupted Opportunities to Speak

There are many reasons to limit a client's opportunities to speak. Time may be inadequate, the workload may be impacted, the client may seem distracted or uninterested in sharing, etc. However, only by **allowing the client to divulge his or her true feelings** can the worker actually know and understand what the client believes, thinks, feels, and desires.

Barriers to client sharing include the following:

- **Frequent interruptions**: Instead, the social worker might jot a short note to prompt a question later.
- **Supplying client words**: A client may seem to have great difficulty finding words to express his or her feelings and the social worker may be tempted to assist. However, this may entirely circumvent true expression, as the client may simply say, "Yes, that's it," rather than working harder to find his or her true feelings.
- **Filling silence**: Long pauses can be awkward. The social worker may wish to fill the silence, but in so doing he or she may prevent the client from finding thoughts to share.

Utilizing Nonverbal Communication

To facilitate the sharing process it is important for a social worker to present as warm, receptive, caring, and accepting of the client. However, the social worker should also endeavor not to bias, lead, or repress client expressions by an inappropriate use of **nonverbal** cues. Frowning, smiling, vigorous nodding, etc., may all lead clients to respond to the social workers' reactions rather than to disclose their genuine feelings and thoughts. To this end, a social worker will endeavor to make good eye contact, use a soft tone of voice, present as interested and engaged, etc., but without marked expressions that can influence the dialogue process. Sitting and facing the client (ideally without a desk or other obstruction in between), being professionally dressed and groomed, sitting close enough to be engaging without invading the client's space, and using an open posture (arms comfortable in the lap or by the sides, rather than crossed over the chest) can all facilitate the communication process.

Leading Questions

Leading questions are those that predispose a particular response. For example, saying, "You know that it is okay to ask questions, don't you?" is a strongly leading question. While it may seem an innocuous way to ensure that someone feels free to ask questions, it may not succeed in actually eliciting questions. Instead, ask the client directly, "What questions do you have?" This way of asking not only reveals that questions are acceptable, but is much more likely to encourage the client to openly share any confusion he or she is having.

Even less forceful leading questions can induce a bias. For example, when a couple comes in for counseling, the social worker asking, "Would you like to sit over here?" could prevent the social worker from seeing how they elect to arrange themselves in relation to the social worker and each other (a very revealing element in the relationship). Instead, the worker might simply say, "Feel free to sit anywhere you'd like." Avoiding leading questions is an important skill in the communication process.

Obtaining Sensitive Information from Clients

Sensitive information includes that involving sexual activity, abuse, intimate partner violence, substance abuse, and mental health issues. Clients are more likely to answer questions truthfully if they have developed a relationship of trust with the questioner. **Methods of obtaining sensitive information** include the following:

- Embedding the questions in a series of questions in context: "Do you spend time with your friends?" "Are your friends sexually active?" "Do you think you are more or less sexually active than your friends?" "How many sexual partners have you had?"
- Asking for facts and not opinions
- Using familiar language and terminology
- Asking for permission to question, "Do you mind if I ask you about..." and explaining the reason for questioning, "In order to plan for your medical care, I need to ask you about..."
- Using a scale (1 to 10) rather than asking for detailed information
- Explaining what kinds of information can remain confidential and what kinds cannot (such as child abuse)

Interventions

Principles of Treatment Planning

Goals and Objectives

The treatment plan is used to set goals and objectives and to monitor progress. **Goals** are considered broad-based aims that are more general in nature (e.g., becoming less anxious, developing improved self-esteem), while **objectives** are the fundamental steps needed to accomplish the identified goals. Because objectives are used to operationalize goals, they must be written with considerable clarity and detail (questions of who, what, where, when, why, and how should be carefully answered). Properly constructed objectives must be based upon the client's perception of needs, as opposed to a clinician's bias, whenever possible. Finally, the treatment plan should be revised and updated as often as necessary to ensure that it remains an effective guiding and monitoring tool.

Length of Time Needed to Accomplish Goals

While the length of time required to accomplish certain goals is largely dependent on the individual client, there are general expectations to time requirements based on the goals desired to be met:

- **Extended periods of time for treatment** are needed for those approaches that focus on personality change.
- **Shorter-term treatment** is called for in those approaches that focus on behavioral change, cognitive change, or problem solving. Examples are crisis intervention, task-centered treatment, cognitive therapy, and behavioral treatment.

Clinical Practice in Social Work

Clinical practice in social work requires a master's degree to actively diagnose and treat clients, but must be understood at all levels of social work. Clinical practice has the following focuses:

- Seeks to **improve the internalized negative effects** of environmental factors including stress from health, vocation, family, and interpersonal problems.
- The worker assists individuals, couples, and families to **change** feelings, attitudes, and coping behaviors that hinder optimal social functioning.
- Practice is conducted in both **agencies and private practice**.
- Practice is differentiated from other practices by its **goal** of helping individuals change, facilitating personal adjustment, treating emotional disorders and mental illness, or enhancing intrapsychic or interpersonal functioning.
- Like all social work practice, **assessment** is psychosocial, focused on the person-in-environment, and has the goal of enhancing social functioning.

Theoretical Bases

The theoretical bases of clinical practice are as follows:

- The **psychosocial approach** focuses on intrapsychic and interpersonal change.
- The **problem-solving approach** seeks to solve distinct problems, based on psychosocial and functional approaches.
- The **behavior modification approach** seeks symptom reduction of problem behaviors, learning alternative positive behaviors.
- **Cognitive therapy** focuses on symptom reduction of negative thoughts, distorted thinking, and dysfunctional beliefs.

- The **crisis intervention approach** is the brief treatment of reactions to crisis in order to restore client's equilibrium.
- **Family therapy** treats an entire family system and sees the individual symptom bearer as indicative of a problem in the family as a whole.
- **Group therapy** is a model in which group members help and are helped by others with similar problems, receive validation for their own experiences, and test new social identities and roles.
- In the **narrative therapy** approach, the stories clients tell about their lives reveal how they construct perceptions of their experiences. The worker helps client construct alternative, more affirming stories.
- The **ecological or life model** focuses on life transitions, environmental pressures, and maladaptation between the individual and the family or environment. Focuses on interaction and interdependence of people and environments.
- The **task-centered approach** focuses on completing tasks to strengthen self-esteem and restore usual capacity for coping.

Assumptions and Knowledge Base

Clinical practice assumes that individual behavior, growth, and development are brought about by a complex interaction of psychological and environmental factors.

The **required knowledge base** for the implementation of clinical practice in social work is as follows:

- An understanding of the theories of personality development
- An understanding of systems theory
- Knowledge of clinical diagnoses (DSM-5)
- An understanding that significant influences on the individual are socio-cultural factors including ethnicity, immigration status, occupation, race, gender, sexual orientation, and socioeconomic class

Assessment Process

The assessment process in clinical practice is as follows:

- Determine the **presenting problem**.
- Determine if there is a **match** between the problem and available services.
- Ongoing **data collection and reassessment** to enhance understanding of client's problems.
- The worker's role is to ask **questions** and ask for elaboration and description, observe client's behavior and affect, and organize data to create a meaningful psychosocial or diagnostic assessment.
- Sources of data other than client include **interviews** with family members, home visits, and contacts with teachers, clergy, doctors, social agencies, and friends.
- **Clinical diagnosis**: A product of the clinical social worker's understanding of the client's problems based on the data collected. It categorizes the client's functioning. Also includes relevant medical illnesses or physical conditions and their influence on client's emotional life and functioning.

Key Concepts

Key concepts used in clinical practice include the following:

Direct influence	The worker continually seeks to understand the client's view of self and situation.
Exploration	The worker offers advice and suggestions in order to influence the client.
Confrontation	The worker challenges the client to deal with inconsistencies between her or his words and actions, maladaptive behaviors, or resistance to treatment or change.
Clarification	The worker questions, repeats, or rephrases material the client discusses. The worker must be sensitive to the client's defensiveness.
Universalization	The normalization of problems. Problems are presented as a part of the human condition in order to help the client see them as less pathological.
Ventilation	The client's airing of feelings associated with the information presented about self and the situation. May alleviate the intensity of the client's feelings or feeling that they are alone in those feelings. The worker may need to help the client distinguish times when ventilation is useful and when it may increase intensity of feelings.
Catharsis	The release of tension or anxiety through reliving and intentionally examining early life, repressed, or traumatic experiences.

Behavior Modification Approach

Theoretical Bases

The theoretical bases of the behavior modification approach to social work practice are as follows:

- **Early classical conditioning research** (Pavlov)
- **Behavior modification theory**: Operant conditioning (Skinner, Thorndike, Watson, Dollard & Miller, Thomas)
- **Social learning theory**: Observing, imitating, modeling (Bandura)

Assumptions About Human Behavior

The following are assumptions this approach makes about human behavior:

- One can know a person only through the observable. Behavior can be explained by learning theory. Theory of the unconscious is unnecessary.
- A person has learned, dysfunctional behaviors rather than emotional illness. No presumptions about psychiatric illness.
- One expresses dysfunctional behavior in symptoms. Symptoms are defined as the observed individual behaviors that are labeled as deviant or problematic. Once the symptoms are removed, there are no remaining underlying problems.
- High priority goes to research and empirically based knowledge.

Motivations for Change and the Means Through Which Change Occurs

The motivations for change in behavior modification include the following:

- Disequilibrium
- Anxiety
- Conscious desire to eliminate a symptom
- Agreement to follow a behavior modification program

The following are the means through which change occurs:

- **Operant or voluntary behavior** that is increased by positive or negative reinforcement and decreased by withholding reinforcement or punishing.
- **Involuntary behavior** that is increased or decreased by conditioning.
- Change depends upon environmental conditions or events that precede, are connected with, or follow the behavior.
- As a result of observing and imitating in a social context, modeling occurs; this is not learned by reward and punishment.

Operant Behavior and Respondent Behavior

Operant behavior is controlled by consequences of that behavior. Actions preceding or following the behavior need to be changed. **Respondent behavior** is behavior which is brought out by a specific stimulus. The individual must be desensitized to the stimuli, for example, in the case of phobias.

Treatment Planning

Treatment planning in the behavioral modification approach is as follows:

1. **Prioritize problems**. Identify maintaining conditions for selected problems.
2. Engage client in establishing goals for change.
3. **Establish baseline data** regarding the frequency of behavior.
4. Develop written or oral **contract**.

Cognitive Therapy Approach

Theoretical Base and Assumptions About Human Behavior

The theoretical bases of the cognitive therapy approach are as follows:

- Albert Ellis' rational-emotive behavior therapy
- Aaron Beck's cognitive theory

Assumptions made by the cognitive therapy approach include:

- Mental distress is caused by the maladaptive and rigid ways we construe events, not by the events themselves.
- Negative automatic thoughts are generated by dysfunctional beliefs. These beliefs are set in motion by activating events, and they trigger emotional consequences. Future events are interpreted through the filter of these belief systems.
- Negative affect and symptoms of psychological disorders follow negative automatic thoughts, biases, and distortions.
- Irrational thinking carries the form of systematic distortions.

Motivations for Change and Means Through Which Change Occurs

The motivations for change in the cognitive therapy approach include:

- Disequilibrium
- Anxiety
- Desire to live without a symptom
- Agreement to work toward changing thought patterns

The following are means through which change occurs:

- Structured sessions
- Exploring and testing cognitive distortions and basic beliefs
- Homework between sessions, which allows the client to practice changes in thinking in a natural environment
- Changes in feelings and behaviors in the future come about through changes in the way the client interprets events

Assessment Process and Role of Therapeutic Relationship

The following are conducted during the assessment in the cognitive therapy approach:

- List the client's cognitive distortions (e.g., catastrophizing, minimizing, negative predictions, mind-reading, overgeneralization, personalization)
- List the client's negative automatic thoughts and dysfunctional beliefs

The roles of the therapeutic relationship in cognitive therapy are as follows:

- The worker is a teacher, ally, and coach.
- The worker is active, directive, and didactic.

Treatment Planning Process and Treatment Skills and Techniques

The treatment planning process is described below:

- Establish baseline data measuring client's negative automatic thoughts, distortions, and dysfunctional beliefs. How often do these thoughts occur and under what circumstances?
- Create target goals for change and alternative ways of thinking.
- Agree to contract for goals, homework, and time frame of treatment.

Treatment skills and techniques are as follows:

- Short term treatment
- A focus on symptom reduction
- Using a rational approach, focused on concrete tasks in sessions and for homework
- Per **Albert Ellis**: Be forcefully confrontive in order to reveal the client's thought system, get the client to see how that system defeats them, and work to change the thoughts that make up that system.
- Per **Aaron Beck**: A gentler, more collaborative approach. Help the client restructure their interpretations of events. "What is the evidence for this idea?" or "Is there another way to look at this situation?" Social skill building, group therapy, and milieu treatment are utilized.

Task-Centered Approach

Theoretical Bases and Assumptions About Human Behavior

The theoretical bases for the task-centered approach are as follows:

- Learning theory
- Cognitive and behavioral theory
- High priority on research-based practice knowledge

Assumptions of the task-centered approach include:

- An individual is not influenced solely by internal or unconscious drives, nor controlled solely by environmental forces.
- The client usually is able to identify her or his own problems and goals.
- The client is the primary agent of change and is a consumer of services.
- The worker's role is to help the client achieve the changes that they decide upon and are willing to work on.

Motivations for Change and Means Through Which Change Occurs

The following are motivations for change in the task-centered approach:

- A temporary breakdown in coping influences the client to seek help
- A conscious wish for change
- Strengthening of self-esteem through task completion

The following are means through which change occurs:

- Clarification of the problem or problems
- Steps taken to resolve or alleviate problems
- Changes in environment

Process of Assessment and Role of Therapeutic Relationship

The assessment process in the task-centered approach is described below:

- Examination and clarification of problems are primary. The problem must be one that concerns the client and is amenable to treatment.
- The worker and client create a rationale for resolution of the problem and note potential treatment benefits.

The role of therapeutic relationship in the task-centered approach to practice is described below:

- The relationship is not an objective in itself, but is a means of augmenting and supporting problem solving. Transference and countertransference aspects are minimized.
- The social worker expects that the client will work on agreed upon tasks and activities to resolve problems and provides acceptance, respect, and understanding.
- The social worker and the client have a collaborative relationship. The social worker seeks the client's input at all stages. The client is the consumer and the social worker is the authority with expertise who works on the client's behalf.

Treatment Planning and Contraindications

Treatment planning in the task-centered approach is described below:

- A **contract** must state an agreement upon what will be worked on, the social worker's and the client's willingness to engage in the work, and the limits of the treatment (time, etc.). The contract can be formal, oral, or written; it is dynamic and can be renegotiated.
- Both the worker and client agree on a specific **definition** of the problem(s) to be worked on and the changes sought in the process. This is expressed in both behavioral and measurable terms.

The task-centered approach is **inappropriate** for the following clients:

- Clients who are interested in existential issues, life goals, or discussion of stressful events.
- Clients who are unwilling or unable to use the structured approach to tasks.
- Clients who have problems that are not subject to resolution or improvement by problem-solving.
- Clients who are involuntary; some clients' treatment is mandated.

Systems Theory Approach

Theoretical Bases

The theoretical bases to the systems theory approach are as follows:

- This approach is based on general system theory applied to social work treatment.
- Systems theory is a framework that a worker can use with any of the practice approaches in order to help the client establish and maintain a steady state.

Key Concepts in System Theory

Boundary	Organizational means by which the parts of a system can be differentiated from their environment and which differentiates subsystems
Open and closed systems	Indicates whether boundary between a system and its environment is open or closed
Subsystem	Subset of the entire system
Entropy	Randomness, chaos, disorder in a system that causes a system to lose energy faster than it creates or imports it
Homeostasis	Changes a system makes in order to maintain an accustomed balance

Assumptions About Human Behavior and Motivations for Change

Assumptions of the systems theory approach are as follows:

- Individuals have potential for **growth and adaptation** throughout life. They are active, problem solving and purposeful.
- Individuals can be understood as **open systems** which interact with other living systems and the nonliving environment.
- All systems are **interdependent**. Change in one system brings about changes in the others. Additionally, change in a subsystem brings about changes in other subsystems.
- Change occurs in the **individual**, in the **environment**, or in the **interaction** between the individual and the environment.

Assessment and Role of the Therapeutic Relationship

A key assumption in the assessment process of the systems theory approach is that problems do not belong to the individual, but instead belong to the interaction of the behaviors or social conditions that create disequilibrium.

The role of therapeutic relationship in the systems theory approach is as follows:

- Depending on the problem and target of change, the relationship may be supportive, facilitative, collaborative, or adversarial. The worker may intervene on behalf of the client with individuals, the social support network, or the larger system.
- The relationship offers feedback to the client and to other systems.

Treatment Planning

Treatment planning in the systems theory approach is as follows:

- Planning begins with establishing specific goals, their practicability, and their priority.
- Target systems for intervention are identified in collaboration with the client.
- A specific contract is developed with the client or other systems that may be involved in the change process.

Psychosocial Approach

Basic Tenets and Theoretical Bases

The basic tenets of the psychosocial approach include the following:

- Problem-solving
- Crisis intervention
- Task-centered casework
- Planned short-term treatment

The following are the theoretical bases of this approach:

- **Psychoanalytic theory** (Sigmund Freud)
- **Ego Psychology**: Psychoanalytic base, with focus on ego functions and adaptation; defense mechanisms (Anna Freud); adaptations to an average expected environment (Hartmann); ego mastery and development through the life cycle (Erikson); separation or individuation (Margaret Mahler)
- **Social Science Theories**: Role, family and small group, impact of culture, communication theory, systems theory
- **Biological theories**: Ecological, homeostasis, behavioral genetics, medical model

Review Video: Psychoanalytic Approach
Visit mometrix.com/academy and enter code: 162594

Assumptions About Human Behavior

The following are assumptions about human behavior that the psychosocial approach to practice makes:

- The individual is always seen in the context of the environment, interacting with social systems (such as family), and influenced by earlier personal experiences.
- Conscious vs. unconscious and rational vs. irrational motivations govern individual behavior.
- Individuals can change and grow under fitting conditions throughout the life cycle.

Motivations for Change and Means Through Which Change Occurs

The following are motivations for change according to the psychosocial approach to practice:

- Disequilibrium, which induces anxiety and releases energy to change
- Conscious and unconscious needs and wishes
- Relationship with the worker (or group in group treatment)

The means through which change occurs include the following:

- Development of insight and resolution of emotional conflicts
- Corrective emotional experience in relationship with the worker
- Changes in affective, cognitive, or behavioral patterns that induce changes in interpersonal relationships
- Changes in the environment

Assessment

Assessment in the psychosocial approach has the following characteristics:

- Outlines the client's presenting problem and resources for addressing it.
- Determines if there is an appropriate match between the presenting problem and available services
- Begins in first interview and continues throughout treatment
- **Dynamic components**: Determining how different characteristics of the client and important relationships interact to influence his or her total functioning
- **Etiological components**: Determining the causative factors that produced the presenting problem and that influence the client's previous attempts to deal with it
- **Clinical components**: Articulation of the client's functioning (i.e., mental status, coping strategies and styles, a clinical diagnosis if pertinent)

Role of Therapeutic Relationship

The role of the therapeutic relationship in the psychosocial approach is as follows:

- Mindful use of the relationship can **motivate** and create energy to change.
- Relationship should foster a **corrective** emotional experience.
- Client and **client's needs** are central. Self-disclosure by worker is used purposefully and only for client's benefit.
- Some **transference dynamics** may hamper treatment, but generally they should be seen and used as potential vehicles for promoting client self-understanding and changing problematic interpersonal patterns.
- To deal with possible **countertransference**, the worker should be self-aware, seek supervision and consultation to decrease countertransference reactions, and use her or his own therapy for dealing with countertransference.
- The worker should be aware that they may be perceived as more competent than the client and as the expert who is there to fix the client's problems. This can be **disempowering** to the client and works against a strengths perspective.

Components and Phases of Treatment Planning

The following are components of treatment planning:

- Development of a unique treatment plan based on the client's situation.
- Client goals and their practicality, given the client's abilities, strengths, and weaknesses, as well as availability of relevant services.
- Treatment plan is directed at changing the individual, the environment, or the interaction between the two.

The phases of treatment are as follows:

Phase	Focus
Engagement or assessment	Applicant becomes client; increasing motivation; initial resistance; establishing work relationship; assessment; informed consent re: confidentiality; roles, rights, and responsibilities of the client and worker
Contracting or goal setting	Mutual understanding between client and worker with regard to goals, treatment process, nature of roles and relationship, and intended time of treatment
Ongoing treatment and interventions	Working toward improving previously agreed upon problems; major focus is on current functioning and conscious experience; dealing with ongoing resistance, transference, and countertransference
Termination	Potential for growth, reiterate major themes of treatment, experience feelings about relationship ending

Narrative Therapy Approach

Theoretical Bases and Assumptions About Human Behavior

The theoretical bases of the narrative therapy approach are as follows:

- Narrative therapy draws on the work of Michael White of the Dulwich Centre in Australia.
- It utilizes a variety of individual and personality theories, as well as social psychological approaches.
- It focuses on the stories people tell about their lives. These stories are interpreted through their subjective personal filters.
- Interventions are designed to reveal and reframe the ways clients structure their perceptions of their experiences.

Assumptions made about human behavior in the narrative therapy approach are as follows:

- Individuals' behaviors come from their interpretations of experiences.
- Subjective meanings influence actions. Meanings derived from interpretations of experience determine specifics of action.
- Narrative therapy is concerned with the telling and re-telling of the preferred stories of people's lives, as well as the performance and re-performance of these stories.

Assessment and Role of Therapeutic Relationship

Assessment in narrative therapy is characterized as the following:

- **Mapping how the problem influences the client's life and relationships**: How does the problem affect the client(s)?
- **Mapping the influence of the person or family in the life of the problem**: Clients start to see themselves as authors or co-authors of their own stories.
- This therapy builds on **strengths and abilities** of families and individuals rather than seeking weaknesses and deficits.

The role of the therapeutic relationship in the narrative therapy approach is as follows:

- The worker is co-constructor of new narratives.
- The relationship is a partnership; the authority of the therapist is minimized. Partnership does not use techniques that result in clients feeling coerced or manipulated.
- Relationship seeks and is an agent of client empowerment. The worker offers an optimistic, future-oriented perspective that builds on the client's abilities and strengths in moving toward change. Emphasizes client's possibilities, strengths, and resources.
- Worker guides therapeutic conversations to create new possibilities, fresh options, and opportunities to reframe the client's realities.

Treatment Planning

Treatment planning in narrative therapy includes the following:

- Together, the worker and client establish clear goals for their work.
- The worker and client divide out and work on small, specific, limited goals.
- The approach avoids a medical (disease) model that seeks explanations for problems or ascribes pathology to the family system.

Problem-Solving Approach

Theoretical Bases

The theoretical bases for the problem-solving approach to social work practice are as follows:

- **Psychodynamic, with major influence from ego psychologists**: Erik Erikson (capacity for change throughout life), Robert White (coping, adaptation, mastery of environment), Heinz Hartmann (use of the conflict-free ego).
- **Social science theory**: Role theory, problem solving theory (John Dewey).

Assumptions About Human Behavior

Assumptions that the problem-solving approach to social work practice makes about human behavior include the following:

- Individuals are engaged in life-long problem-solving and adaptation to maintain, rebuild, or achieve stability, even as circumstances change.
- The individual is viewed as a whole person; the focus, however, is on the person in relation to a problem.
- Individuals have or can develop the motivation and ability to change.
- This perspective does not see the individual as sick or deficient, but instead as in need of help to resolve life problems.

- Each individual has a reachable moment at a time of disequilibrium, at which point they can most successfully mobilize motivation and capacity.
- An individual's cognitive processes can be engaged to solve problems, to achieve goals, and to grow emotionally.
- An individual has both rational/irrational and conscious/unconscious processes, but cognitive strengths can control irrationality.

Motivations for Change and Means Through Which Change Occurs

The following are motivations for change according to the problem-solving approach:

- Disequilibrium between reality and what the client wants
- Conscious desire to achieve change
- Positive expectations based on new life possibilities
- The strength of a supportive relationship and positive expectations of the worker

The means through which change occurs are as follows:

- Improved problem-solving skills. These may produce changes in personality or improved functioning, but these are secondary to problem resolution.
- Gratification, encouragement, and support that result from improvement in the problem situation. This and the worker's emotional support increase the possibility of change.
- Repetition and practice (drilling) of the problem-solving method increases possibility for replication of effective strategies in new situations.
- Insight, resolution of conflicts, and changes in feelings.
- Problem resolution concerning changes in the individual, the environment, and the interaction between the two.

Assessment

Assessment in the problem-solving approach is focused on the following:

- Focus first on **identifying the problem** and the aspects of the person or environment that can be involved in problem solving
- Assess **motivation, capacity, and opportunity (MCO)** of the client to resolve the problem
- Include a **statement of the problem** (objective facts and subjective responses to them), precipitating factors, and prior efforts to resolve it
- A **combined activity** of worker and client

Role of Therapeutic Relationship

The role of the therapeutic relationship in the problem-solving approach is as follows:

- Mindful and continual use of **the supportive social work relationship** to motivate clients to engage in problem resolution.
- The worker is an expert in **problem-solving methodology** and guides clients through steps of problem resolution. The relationship grows as worker and client work on problems jointly.
- Work is focused on **practical problem solving**; therefore, transference and countertransference are less likely. These are only addressed if they are interfering with the work.

Components and Elements of Treatment Planning

The following are components of treatment planning according to the problem-solving approach:

1. **Psychosocial**: Derived from an evaluation of the problem and the client's motivation, capacity, and opportunities (MCO).
2. **Functional**: The function of the agency serves as a boundary of service (i.e., adoption agency, mental health service)
3. **Interagency**: Using resources from other agencies in a network of services designed to help the client.

The **four P's** are the basic elements involved in treatment: A **person** has a **problem** and comes to a **place** for help given through a **process**:

1. Clearly identify the problem and the client's subjective response to it
2. Select a part of the problem that has possibility for resolution, identify possible solutions, and assess their achievability in light of MCO
3. Engage client's ego capacities
4. Determine steps or actions to be taken by the worker and client to resolve or alleviate the problem
5. Help the client carry out problem-solving activities and determine their effectiveness
6. Termination

Ecological or Life Model Approach

Theoretical Bases

The following are the theoretical bases of the ecological/life model approach:

- Ecology
- Systems theory
- Stress, coping, and adaptation theory
- Psychodynamic, behavioral, and cognitive theory

This approach follows a conceptual framework that has its focus on the **interaction and interdependence of people and environments**. It provides service to individuals, families, and groups within a community, organizational, and cultural environment.

Assumptions About Human Behavior and the Motivation for Change

Ecological/life model assumptions about human behavior are as follows:

- The individual is active, purposeful, and capable of problem solving. They have potential for growth and adaptation throughout life.
- There are three areas of life experience in which problems occur: life transitions, environmental pressures, and maladaptive lack of "fit" between the individual and a larger entity (the family, the community).
- Each individual client system depends upon or is interdependent with other systems.

The motivation for change in this approach stems from changes that the individual wants in relation to herself or himself, the environment, or the interplay between the two.

The worker's relationship with the client is based on mutuality, trust, and authenticity. Depending on the goal of the intervention, the worker and client relationship may be supportive, collaborative, or adversarial.

Crisis Intervention Approach

Theoretical Base

The theoretical bases for the crisis intervention approach are as follows:

- **Psychodynamic therapy**, particularly ego psychology (Freud, Erikson, Rapoport) and Lindemann's work on loss and grief
- **Intellectual development** (Piaget)
- **Social science**: stress theory, family structure, role theory

Sources of Trauma

Trauma can be introduced into an individual's life through various means:

- The trauma victim experiences a **threat** to her or his physical integrity or life. The trauma experience confronts a person with an extreme situation of fear and helplessness.
- Trauma may be **chronic** and repeated or may take the form of one event of short duration.
- Many of the symptoms related to PTSD and domestic violence are self-protective attempts at **coping** with **realistic threats**.

Motivations for Change and Means Through Which Change Occurs

The motivations for change in the crisis intervention approach are as follows:

- Disequilibrium caused by a stressful event or situation
- Energy, which is made available by anxiety about the situation
- A supportive relationship

The following are the means through which change occurs:

- Challenging old coping patterns and a reorganization of coping skills
- Growth, which occurs as the ego develops a larger repertoire of coping skills and organizes them into more complex patterns

Assessment and Motivations for Change

The general assessment process in the crisis intervention approach is as follows:

- **Exploring the stress producing event or situation**, the individual's response to it, and responses to past crises
- Characteristic signs, phases, and patterns of adaptation and maladaptation to **crisis** (e.g., PTSD)
- Because of the need for quick action, a highly focused assessment that emphasizes **current state** of functioning and internal and environmental supports and deficits

Assessment in the crisis intervention approach also must be specific to the crisis experienced:

- **Assessment for PTSD**: Evaluate the nature of the trauma; the strengths and limitations that pre-date the trauma; the impact of trauma on the client's emotional life, self-esteem, and functioning; and whether the client remains at risk and the possible need for self-protective measures.
- **Assessment for domestic violence**: Evaluate if the client is still at risk and if practical protective measures are required. Legal reporting is not required for adult-adult domestic violence, however, if children are at risk as witnesses or victims the worker must make a report to child protective services.

Motivations for change in the crisis intervention approach are as follows:

- Reality-based fear and the need for protection
- Symptoms including depression, anxiety, dissociation, and low self-esteem

Role of Therapeutic Relationship

The role of the therapeutic relationship in trauma-based social work is described below:

- For clients with PTSD, the worker is a protective presence. The worker guides the pace of treatment in order to avoid flooding the client with excessive traumatic memories that would promote regression. The worker creates an emotionally safe therapeutic space in which to remember and process the trauma.
- For clients who have experienced domestic violence, the worker may be a therapist, case manager, court-based victim's advocate, or broker to obtain services.

Phases of Treatment and Treatment Skills and Techniques

The phases of treatment in the crisis intervention approach are as follows:

1. Identify events that brought on the crisis.
2. Promote awareness of impact of crisis, both cognitive and emotional.
3. Manage affect leading to tension discharge and mastery.
4. Seek resources in networks (individual, family, social) and in community.
5. Identify specific tasks associated with healthy resolution of crisis.

The following are the treatment skills and techniques for this approach:

- **Brief treatment.** Like the crisis itself, treatment is time limited.
- **Present- and future-oriented.** Treatment can deal with the past, however, only to resolve old conflicts if they prevent work on the present crisis.
- Uses all **psychosocial and problem-solving techniques**, but reorders them; clinician is active, directive, and at times authoritative.

Coping Mechanisms When Experiencing Loss or Trauma

Coping mechanisms available to assist clients after their experiencing loss or trauma include:

- **Emotion-focused strategies**: Used to reduce anxiety and help the individual avoid obsessing over problems. Strategies include progressive relaxation exercises, guided imagery, controlled breathing, and distractions (such as listening to music, playing a musical instrument, reading, and playing video games). Clients may use mindfulness to try to recognize unhealthy emotional responses and modify them. Exercise may help to distract the client from problems and increase sense of wellbeing. Rational coping, in which the client faces the problem directly rather than avoiding it, can lessen the long-term emotional effects.
- **Problem-focused strategies**: Used to resolve or ameliorate problems. Strategies include learning and applying various problem-solving methods, engaging in role playing, and learning organizational skills, such as more effective time management and making and adhering to schedules. Clients may change environments to one that is less stressful or dangerous, and may seek social support of friends or professionals.

PTSD Treatment

PTSD treatment consists of the following:

- Psychodynamic therapy
- Dialectical behavioral therapy (DBT): teaches skills to cope with intense feelings, reduce symptoms of PTSD, and enhance respect for self and quality of life
- EMDR (Eye Movement Desensitization and Reprocessing)
- Group therapy (support or DBT)

Treating Victims of Domestic Violence

Domestic violence treatment is as follows:

- Develop a safety plan for safe shelter, etc. to protect victim from perpetrator.
- Do not assess or treat domestic violence in marital or family therapy sessions as this may increase risk to the victim, inhibit revealing the violence history, and enrage the perpetrator.

Review Video: Counseling: Domestic Abuse
Visit mometrix.com/academy and enter code: 530581

Clinical Work with Children

Children are typically referred to treatment for symptoms or behavioral problems. The child's underlying conflicts reveal themselves through play and verbally in free expression. Play is the child's form of symbolic communication, an emulation of the real world, and the child's psychological reality.

Theoretical Bases

The theoretical base for the treatment of children is found in:

- Normal child development theory
- Psychosocial development theory (Sigmund Freud, Anna Freud, Erikson)
- Attachment theory
- Object relations theory

Motivations for Change

Motivations for change when treating children are as follows:

- If child is in alternative placement (foster care, etc.), the child's behavior may be seen as problematic by the agency or worker and treatment interventions may be sought
- The child is unhappy with peer relations or may be socially immature
- Unsatisfactory school adjustment (grades, problems with authority)
- Conflict with parents (struggle to cope with dysfunctional family or problems in parents' marriage)
- Feelings of anger, unhappiness
- Self-destructive behaviors such as cutting or eating disorders

Role of Therapeutic Relationship

The role of the therapeutic relationship when treating children in social work practice is as follows:

- Worker as a therapist: provides a safe environment in which the worker can follow child's lead, show child acceptance, and create an environment for free expression
- Worker as advocate
- Worker as case manager and care coordinator
- Worker as protective service worker
- Worker as adoption and foster care specialist
- Worker as school guidance counselor

Assessment and Treatment Planning

Assessment seeks to understand the child's inner feelings and conflicts, the parent-child interaction, the family dynamics and interactions, and practical difficulties and any environmental problems. Assessment will be sensitive to multi-problem families and will be culturally competent.

Treatment planning for children is as follows:

- Build on strengths, focus on areas where functioning is problematic (individual difficulties, family dysfunction, environmentally generated crises)
- Support adaptive behavior
- Set realistic goals and emphasize the issues that directly affect the care of the child
- Clarify the projected length of time of treatment; ongoing reevaluation
- Build relationship through management of concrete problems

Maltreated or Traumatized Children

Treatment Planning

Treatment planning for social work practice with a maltreated or traumatized child is discussed below:

- The principal goal is **protecting the child** from further harm and **halting** any further abuse, neglect, or sexual exploitation immediately and conclusively. This may require temporary or permanent removal of an offending caretaker or household member, or removal of the child from the home to a safe place.
- The secondary goal is creating conditions that **ensure that abuse or neglect does not recur** after supervision and treatment are terminated. This may include prosecution or incarceration of the offending party and evaluation of the non-offending parent's long-term capacity and motivation to protect the child.
- The official agency can and will use **legal authority** to ensure compliance with agency directives when necessary. The worker should be aware that the possibility of the child's removal may be the primary concern of the parent and may lead to panic, dissembling, or flight.
- Treatment's goal is to help parents learn **parenting and relational skills** that can change parental behavior and the child's responses.

Role of Therapeutic Relationship

The role of the therapeutic relationship in social work practice with maltreated or traumatized children is discussed below:

- The worker is to establish trust and a working relationship with the family and build parental self-esteem.
- Treatment issues include the parents confusing the worker's clinical role with the role of child protective services and the parents viewing the clinician as a hostile part of the legal system, rather than as a trusted helper.
- Communication can be inhibited by the perception of coercion, which can also limit the treatment's effectiveness. Both parent and child may become unwilling to reveal potentially damaging facts.
- Worker should openly discuss mandated reporting obligations and responsibility to inform child protective services.

Geriatric Social Work

Theoretical Bases

The theoretical bases of geriatric social work include the following:

- Psychodynamic theory
- Ego psychology
- Family systems theory
- Life-span development theory (Wieck)
- Continuity theory
- Normal aging and demographics of the aging population
- Impact of chronic illness and physical or cognitive limitations

Assumptions About Human Behavior

The following are assumptions geriatric social work makes about human behavior:

- Growth occurs throughout the life span, including during old age.
- Individuals are inherently adaptive and are capable of managing the disruptions, discontinuities, and losses that are characteristic of old age.
- Our culture demands and values independence. This can present a conflict with accepting the increasing need for help in old age.
- The younger generation's caring for the older may be seen as role reversal and may be challenging to both generations. Dependency in the aged, however, has a different meaning than dependency in childhood.
- Supportive services are preferable to institutional care whenever possible.
- Ageist assumptions or an individual's living in an institutional setting are not reasons to compromise self-determination or confidentiality.
- Individuals age in different ways.

Motivations for Change and Means Through Which Change Occurs

Motivations for change in geriatric social work include:

- The need for individuals to adapt to longer periods of old age and retirement as life expectancy increases. With a longer period of old age comes increased risk for chronic illness and physical or cognitive limitations.
- There is a greater need for multiple types of social services, supported housing, and care options.
- Adult children are also affected by their parents' aging and may need help dealing with the emotional impact or with care planning.

Change occurs through:

- Individual, couples, or family treatment
- Support groups or group therapy
- Recreational programs
- Education

Assessment and Treatment Planning

Assessment in geriatric social work is concerned with:

- The presenting problem and the client's resources for resolving it
- When adult children are involved, the intergenerational dynamics and resources and the relevance and impact of family history on present functioning
- The presence and effect of chronic illness and physical or cognitive limitations
- Home safety
- Medications, their influence on functioning, and negative side effects
- The need for supportive services or institutional care
- ADLs (bathing, dressing, etc.) and IADLs (cooking, driving, etc.)

Treatment planning is concerned with:

- **Interventions**, solutions that offer choice and support the older adult's highest level of functioning.
- **Promoting independence** by planning home modifications through home-safety assessment and planning for assistive devices through assessing physical or cognitive limitations.

Role of Therapeutic Relationship

The role of the therapeutic relationship is as follows:

- Individual, couple, or multi-generational family therapist
- Case manager
- Advocate
- Care planner (working with older adults and their children to determine level of care needed and options)
- Guardian (for the older adult who the court has declared mentally incompetent)
- Conservator (for the older adult who the court has declared incompetent to handle his or her own financial affairs)
- Educator
- Group therapist or leader
- Program planner

Strategic Considerations

The following are strategic practice issues to be considered when working with older adults:

- Role reversal (worker often younger than client)
- Physiological changes
- Variation in physical and mental decline
- Clients often have experienced multiple losses
- Clients are often involuntary
- Respect and formality can be important to client
- Differences in generational perceptions: socialization around problems, values, and mores and attitudes toward receiving help, charity, and counseling
- Two categories of older adults: young-old (60-80) and old-old or frail-old (80+)

Clinical Considerations

The clinical considerations the worker should make in practice with older adults are as follows:

- Shorter interviews, possibly more frequent
- Varied questioning styles
- The worker is more active, directive, and demonstrative
- Home visits may be preferred to office visits
- Consider roles and attitudes of relatives and caretakers
- Awareness of possibility for abuse or exploitation
- Access to social services or other publicly funded programs
- Possible hearing impairment and need to make responses shorter, louder, and slower
- Reminiscence is an important style of communication

Additional Therapeutic Interventions and Considerations

Preventive Measures in Social Work

Gerald Caplan's (1964) **model for prevention** includes three types of preventive measures:

- **Primary**: The focus is on helping people to cope with stress and decreasing stressors in the environment, specifically targeting at-risk groups. Examples include teaching parenting skills to parents; providing support services to the unemployed; providing food, shelter, and other services to the homeless; and teaching about the harmful effects of drugs and alcohol to schoolchildren.
- **Secondary**: The focus is on identifying problems early and beginning treatment in order to shorten the duration of the disorder. Examples include follow-up for clients at risk for recurrence, staffing rape crisis centers, providing suicide hotlines, and referrals as needed.
- **Tertiary**: The focus is on preventing complications and promoting rehabilitation through teaching clients socially-appropriate behaviors. Examples include teaching the client to manage daily living skills, monitoring effectiveness of outpatient services, and referring clients to support services.

Systematic Desensitization and Flooding

Systematic desensitization is a therapy used to treat anxiety disorders, typically those caused by a specific stimulus. The client is progressively exposed to anxiety-inducing objects, images, or situations, or is asked to imagine them, and is then encouraged to practice relaxation or other coping techniques to manage or eliminate the anxiety. Once the client learns to cope with a given level of exposure, the intensity of the exposure is increased and the process is repeated. This continues until the client is successfully desensitized to the stimulus.

Flooding is an extreme form of desensitization by exposure. While typical systematic desensitization gradually increases the intensity of the stimulus, flooding jumps directly to the final stage. The client is subjected to the full intensity of the anxiety-inducing stimulus for a prolonged period of time, sometimes several hours. Part of the reasoning for this method is that all of the physiology-based fear responses can only affect the person for limited time, and once the client is no longer affected, they will be better able to train themselves not to fear the stimulus.

Contracting or Goal Setting

The **contract** is compatible with various models of social work practice and is not limited to an initial working agreement, but is part of the total treatment process. The contract is helpful in facilitating the client's action in problem solving, maintaining focus, and continuing in therapy. The contract is an explicit **agreement** between the client and the worker concerning target problems, goals, strategies of social work intervention, and distinguishing the roles and tasks of the client and the worker. The contract includes mutual agreement, differentiated participation, reciprocal accountability, explicitness, realistic agreement, and flexibility. It is difficult to contract with **involuntary clients** who do not acknowledge or recognize problems, who see the worker as unhelpful, or who are severely disturbed or intellectually disabled. The worker should openly acknowledge the difficulty for both the client and worker in mandated treatment and negotiate a contract within those realities.

SUPPORTING/SUSTAINING, PARTIALIZATION, AND RESISTANCE

Supporting/sustaining, partialization, and resistance as they relate to clinical practice are as follows:

- **Supporting/sustaining**: The worker conveys confidence in, interest in, and acceptance of the client in order to decrease the client's feelings of anxiety, poor self-esteem, and low self-confidence. The worker uses interest, sympathetic listening, acceptance of the client, reassurance, and encouragement.
- **Partialization**: Helping the client to break down problems or goals into smaller, more manageable elements in order to decrease the client's sense of overwhelm and increase the client's empowerment. Discrete elements of the problem or goal can then be prioritized as more manageable or more important.
- **Resistance**: An unconscious defense against painful or repressed material. Resistance can be conveyed through silence, evasiveness, balking at worker's suggestions, or by wanting to end treatment prematurely. The worker should recognize and understand resistance as a chance to learn more about the client and work more deeply with the client to help him or her face resistance and use it effectively.

INTERPRETATION

Through interpretation, the social worker offers the psychodynamic meaning of the client's thoughts, feelings, and fantasies, particularly about the origins of problem behaviors. **Interpretation** seeks to improve the client's insight and work through difficult material by deepening and expanding the client's awareness. Interpretation may entail the following:

- Exposing **repressed** (unconscious) or **suppressed** (conscious) information
- Making connections between the **present** and the **past** to help the client see present distortions more clearly
- Integrating information from **different sources**, so that the client can gain a more realistic perspective

Interpretation should not be used with clients who are **emotionally fragile**.

COMPLEMENTARY THERAPEUTIC APPROACHES

Complementary therapeutic approaches involve interventions that differ from traditional social work practice and are adjunctive to primary interventions. Complementary therapies should be utilized with informed consent on the client's part and in the client's best interest, ensuring that professional boundaries are not breached. **Complementary therapeutic approaches** in social work generally focus on mind-body interventions to reduce stress as they are non-invasive and easily mastered:

- **Relaxation exercises**: Progressive muscle relaxation (Jacobson), tensing and relaxing muscles to bring about full-body relaxation.
- **Mindfulness**: Focusing on moment-to-moment state of awareness of self and mental activity to increase awareness of thoughts and feelings and to learn to refocus them.
- **Meditation**: Practicing to calm and clear the mind in order to reduce anxiety.
- **Cognitive reframing**: Replacing irrational thoughts with more rational ones to increase self-esteem.
- **Guided imagery**: Envisioning calming and relaxing images to reduce anxiety and discomfort.
- **Journaling**: Keeping a daily journal to help identify and modify daily stressors.
- **Controlled breathing (diaphragmatic)**: Using breath control to focus the mind and reduce anxiety.

MINDFULNESS

Mindfulness is a form of meditation based on Buddhist beliefs that focus on a constant moment-to-moment state of awareness of the self and mental activity. **Mindfulness** has been adapted from the spiritual to secular practice in the West. The purpose of mindfulness is to accept thoughts nonjudgmentally and to examine them as they pass through the mind, recognizing that thoughts are just thoughts and that the individual has the power to take negative thoughts (e.g., "I'm worthless") and replace them with positive ones (e.g., "I'm a hard worker"). The individual focuses not only on thoughts but on feelings and sensations (sounds, smells, sights, touch) in order to increase client awareness and to balance physical, spiritual, and mental health. Mindfulness-based therapy (Kabat-Zinn) utilizes Hatha Yoga and controlled breathing to help individuals concentrate without distractions. Mindfulness is helpful to reduce anxiety and stress and prevent recurrence of depression. Over time, individuals often develop a less negative internal dialog and a more positive attitude.

SELF-MANAGEMENT TECHNIQUES

Self-management techniques that clients can utilize include:

- **Harm reduction**: This strategy is used to reduce harmful behaviors, especially related to drug abuse and sexual behavior. The strategies that reduce the negative impact of the behaviors include providing clean needles to addicts, providing free condoms and other birth control, and using medications (such as methadone) to reduce cravings.
- **Limit setting**: This strategy is used to reduce risky behavior and avoid crises with the intent to teach and guide rather than to discipline. Limits are agreed upon, and when behavior escalates or limits exceeded, a positive choice is offered and the individual is reminded of the consequences of choices.
- **Anger management**: These strategies are used to help individuals control their tempers. Strategies include thinking before responding, utilizing time outs, using "I" statements, expressing anger when calm, exercising, suggesting resolutions to problems, avoiding holding grudges, and seeking help when needed.
- **Stress management**: These strategies help the individual relieve stress and anxiety. Strategies include meditating, deep breathing, focusing on the here-and-now, exercising (yoga is especially relaxing), utilizing self-hypnosis and relaxation exercises (including progressive muscle relaxation), utilizing acupressure (tapping meridian points) or aromatherapy, and engaging in hobbies or enjoyable activities.

Self-Monitoring

Self-monitoring involves the awareness of emotions and actions in order to promote healthy behaviors. It is especially useful for clients who are disorganized, lack attention to details, exhibit repetitive behaviors, such as tapping of the foot or clearing the throat, or fail to carry out needed actions (such as class participation). Techniques include the following:

- Identifying those behaviors that the individual wants or needs to modify.
- Establishing an intervention system, such as responding to cues or indicators that require intervention.
- Helping the client to recognize triggers for behaviors and developing strategies to avoid them.
- Developing a method of keeping track of progress, such as a checklist or graph, to provide positive reinforcement.
- Assisting the client to plan ahead in order to avoid negative behaviors. For example, if a client needs to avoid drinking, the client may need to leave a party and arrange for transportation early to avoid temptation.

Transference and Countertransference

Transference is the client's unconscious redirection of feelings for another person toward the worker in an attempt to resolve conflicts attached with that relationship or relationships. The worker should help the client understand transference, how it relates to relationships in her or his past, and how it may be contributing to present difficulties in relationships.

Countertransference is the worker's unconscious redirection of feelings for another person or relationship toward the client. The worker should understand her or his own countertransference reactions, be aware of their presence and consequences, and use supervision or therapy to gain greater understanding of them and not impose them on the client.

Termination of Treatment

Termination offers an opportunity to rework previously unfinished issues. Frequently, earlier symptoms of the presenting problem resurface at this time. The worker should not necessarily use this reemergence as a reason to continue treatment, but the worker and client should work during the termination period to strengthen earlier gains. Termination offers an opportunity for growth in dealing with loss and endings. The worker should acknowledge, verbalize, and manage feelings about endings (such as anger, abandonment, sadness, etc.). Termination can be an opportunity to reassess the meaning of previous losses in the client's life. Termination provides a chance to evaluate the treatment and the treatment relationship. What goals were met or unmet? What was effective or ineffective? Which client resources outside of treatment may continue after termination?

Factors Affecting How Client Approaches Termination

Factors affecting how the client will approach termination include the following:

- The degree of the **client's participation** in the treatment process.
- The degree of the **client's success and satisfaction**.
- **Earlier losses** the client may have experienced.
- Mastery of the **separation-individuation stage** of development in early life.
- The **reason** treatment is ending: if the worker is leaving or if ending is seen as against client's wishes or as a rejection, termination may be more intense.
- The **timing** of termination—is it occurring at a difficult or favorable moment in the client's life?
- Is termination part of a plan to **transfer** client's work to a new worker? If so, worker and client should use this time to put together ideas about focus and goals for next treatment relationship.

Worker's Role in Termination Process

The social worker's role in the termination process is as follows:

- Plan sufficient **time** for termination. In long-term treatment this would be four to eight sessions.
- **Inform the client** if the work is ending prematurely.
- Be aware of worker's own **countertransference** attitudes and behaviors about termination.
- Continue to be **sensitive, observant, empathic, and responsive** to the client's response to termination.
- Encourage the client's **dealing** with the experience of termination. **Confront** client's inappropriate and dysfunctional coping with the experience.
- Promote the client's **belief** in their ability to care for themself and direct their own life.
- Present the possibility for **future contact** at times of difficulty.
- Go over the **client's resources** (internal and environmental) that the client can draw on before making the decision to reenter treatment.

Family Therapy

GOALS OF FAMILY THERAPY

Family therapy is a therapeutic modality theorizing that the patient's psychiatric symptoms are a result of **pathology within the patient's family unit**. This dysfunction is due to problems within the system, usually arising from conflict between marital partners. Psychiatric problems result from these behaviors. This conflict is expressed by:

- **Triangulation**, which manifests itself by the attempt of using another family member to stabilize the emotional process
- **Scapegoating**, which occurs when blaming is used to shift focus to another family member

The **goals** of family therapy are:

- To allow family members to recognize and **communicate their feelings**
- To determine the **reasons for problems** between marital partners and to **resolve** them
- To assist parents in **working together** and to strengthen their **parental authority**
- To help define and clarify **family expectations and roles**
- To learn more and different **positive techniques for interacting**
- To achieve **positive homeostasis** within the family
    - Homeostasis means remaining the same, or maintaining a functional balance. Homeostasis can occur to maintain a dysfunctional status as well.
- To enhance the family's **adaptability**
    - Adaptability is maintaining a balanced, positive stability in the family. A prerequisite for balanced stability, and a basic goal of family therapy, is to help the client family develop strategies for dealing with life's inevitable changes. Morphogenesis is the medical term often applied to a family's ability to react functionally and appropriately to changes.

THEORETICAL APPROACHES TO FAMILY THERAPY

Four theoretical approaches to family therapy are **strategic**, **behavioral**, **psychodynamic**, and **object relations** theories:

- A **strategic approach** to family therapy was proposed by Jay Haley. Haley tried to map out a different strategic plan for each type of psychological issue addressed. With this approach, there is a special treatment strategy for each malady.
- A **behavioral approach** uses traditional behavior-modification techniques to address issues. This approach relies heavily on reinforcement strategies. B.F. Skinner is perhaps the most famous behaviorist. This approach relies on conditioning and often desensitizing as well.
- The **psychodynamic approach** attempts to create understanding and insight on the part of the client. Strategies may be diverse, but in all of them the counselor-therapist acts as an emotional guide, leading the client to a better understanding of mental and emotional mechanisms. One common example is Gestalt therapy.
- **Object relations theory** asserts that the ego develops attachment relationships with external and internal objects. A person's early relationships to objects (which can include people) may result in frustration or rejection, which forms the basis of personality.

Strategic Family Therapy

Strategic family therapy (Haley, 1976) is based on the following concepts:

- This therapy seeks to learn what **function** the symptom serves in the family (i.e., what payoff is there for the system in allowing the symptom to continue?).
- **Focuses**: Problem-focused behavioral change, emphasis of parental power and hierarchical family relationships, and the role of symptoms as an attribute of the family's organization.
- Helplessness, incompetence, and illness all provide **power positions** within the family. The child uses symptoms to change the behavior of parents.

Jay Haley tried to develop a strategy for each issue faced by a client. Problems are isolated and treated in different ways. A family plagued by alcoholism might require a different treatment strategy than a family undermined by sexual infidelity. Haley was unusual in that he held degrees in the arts and communication rather than in psychology. Haley's strategies involved the use of directives (direct instructions). After outlining a problem, Haley would tell the family members exactly what to do. If John would bang his head against the wall when he was made to do his homework, Haley might tell a parent to work with him and to be there while he did his homework.

Virginia Satir and the Esalen Institute's Experiential Family Therapy

Virginia Satir and the Esalen Institute's experiential family therapy draws on sociology, ego concepts, and communication theory to form **role theory concepts**. Satir examined the roles of "rescuer" and "placatory" that constrain relationships and interactions in families. This perspective seeks to increase intimacy in the family and improve the self-esteem of family members by using awareness and the communication of feelings. Emphasis is on individual growth in order to change family members and deal with developmental delays. Particular importance is given to marital partners and on changing verbal and nonverbal communication patterns that lower self-esteem.

Satir's Communication Impediments

Satir described four issues that impede communication between family members under stress. Placating, blaming, being overly reasonable, and being irrelevant are the **four issues which blocked family communication**, according to Virginia Satir:

- **Placating** is the role played by some people in reaction to threat or stress in the family. The placating person reacts to internal stresses by trying to please others, often in irrational ways. A mother might try to placate her disobedient and rude child by offering food, candy, or other presents on the condition that he stop a certain behavior.
- **Blaming** is the act of pointing outwards when an issue creates stress. The blamer thinks, "I'm very angry, but it's your fault. If I've wrecked the car, it's because you made me upset when I left home this morning."
- **Irrelevance** is a behavior wherein a person displaces the potential problem and substitutes another unrelated activity. A mother who engages in too much social drinking frequently discusses her split ends whenever the topic of alcoholism is brought up by her spouse.
- Being overly reasonable, also known as being a **responsible analyzer** is when a person keeps his or her emotions in check and functions with the precision and monotony of a machine.

Murray Bowen's Family Systems Theory

Bowen's family systems theory focuses on the following concepts:

- The role of **thinking versus feeling/reactivity** in relationship/family systems.
- Role of **emotional triangles**: The three-person system or triangle is viewed as the smallest stable relationship system and forms when a two-person system experiences tension.
- **Generationally repeating family issues***:* Parents transmit emotional problems to a child. (Example: The parents fear something is wrong with a child and treat the child as if something is wrong, interpreting the child's behavior as confirmation.)
- **Undifferentiated family ego mass**: This refers to a family's lack of separateness. There is a fixed cluster of egos of individual family members as if all have a common ego boundary.
- **Emotional cutoff**: A way of managing emotional issues with family members (cutting off emotional contact).
- Consideration of thoughts and feelings of **each individual family member** as well as seeking to understand the family network.

Review Video: Bowen Family Systems
Visit mometrix.com/academy and enter code: 591496

Family System Theory Assumptions About Human Behavior

Family systems theory makes several basic assumptions:

- Change in one part of the family system brings about change in other parts of the system.
- The family provides the following to its members: unity, individuation, security, comfort, nurturance, warmth, affection, and reciprocal need satisfaction.
- Where family pathology is present, the individual is socially and individually disadvantaged.
- Behavioral problems are a reflection of communication problems in the family system.
- Treatment focuses on the family unity; changing family interactions is the key to behavioral change.

Motivations for Change and Means Through Which Change Occurs

The **motivations for change** according to Bowen's family systems theory are as follows:

- **Disequilibrium** of the normal family homeostasis is the primary motivation for change according to this perspective.
- The family system is made up of three subsystems: the marital relationship, the parent-child relationship, and the sibling relationship. **Dysfunction** that occurs in any of these subsystems will likely cause dysfunction in the others.

The **means for change** in the family systems theory approach is the family as an interactional system.

Contributions to Family Systems Theory

The **psychodynamic theory** emphasizes multi-generational family history. Earlier family relations and patterns determine current ones. Distorted relations in childhood lead to patterns of miscommunication and behavioral problems. Interpersonal and intrapersonal conflict beneath apparent family unity results in psychopathology. Social role functioning is influenced by heredity and environment.

Don Jackson, a major contributor to family therapy, focuses on **power relationships**. He developed a theory of double-bind communication in families. Double-bind communication occurs when two conflicting messages communicated simultaneously create or maintain a no-win pathological symptom.

Assessment and Treatment Planning in the Family Systems Theory

Assessment in family systems theory includes the following:

- Acknowledgement of **dysfunction** in the family system
- **Family hierarchy**: Who is in charge? Who has responsibility? Who has authority? Who has power?
- Evaluation of **boundaries** (around subsystems, between family and larger environment): Are they permeable or impermeable? Flexible or rigid?
- How does the **symptom** function in the family system?

Treatment planning is as follows:

- The therapist creates a mutually satisfactory contract with the family to establish service boundaries.
- Bowenian family therapy's goal is the differentiation of the individual from the strong influence of the family.

Sal Minuchin's Structural Family Therapy

Sal Minuchin's structural family therapy seeks to strengthen boundaries when family subsystems are enmeshed, or seeks to increase flexibility when these systems are overly rigid. Minuchin emphasizes that the family structure should be hierarchical and that the parents should be at the top of the hierarchy.

Joining, enactment, boundary making, and mimesis are four techniques used by Salvador Minuchin in structural family counseling:

- **Joining** is the worker's attempt at greeting and bonding with members of the family. Bonding is important when obtaining cooperation and input.
- Minuchin often had his clients enact the various scenarios which led to disagreements and conflicts within families. The **enactment** of an unhealthy family dynamic would allow the therapist to better understand the behavior and allow the family members to gain insight.
- **Boundary making** is important to structural family therapies administered by Salvador Minuchin, because many family conflicts arise from confusion about each person's role. Minuchin believed that family harmony was best achieved when people were free to be themselves yet knew that they must not invade the areas of other family members.
- **Mimesis** is a process in which the therapist mimics the positive and negative behavior patterns of different family members.

Therapeutic Methods Employed by Carl Whitaker

Carl Whitaker, known as the dean of family therapy, developed **experiential symbolic family therapy**. Whitaker would freely interact with other family members and often played the part of family members who were important to the dynamic. He felt that experience, not information and education, had the power to change family dynamics.

Whitaker believed that in family therapy, theory was also less important than experience and that co-therapists were a great aid to successful counseling. Co-therapists freed one of the counselors to participate more fully in the counseling sessions. One counselor might direct the flow of activity while the other participated in role playing. The "psychotherapy of the absurd" is a Whitaker innovation which was influenced by the "theatre of the absurd," a popular existential art form at the time. In this context, the absurd is the unreasonable exaggeration of an idea, to the point of underscoring the underlying meaninglessness of much of human interaction. A person who repeated a neurotic or destructive behavior, for example, was being absurd. The **psychotherapy of the absurd**, as Whitaker saw it, was a method for bringing out repeated and meaningless absurdities. A person pushing against an immovable brick wall, for example, might eventually understand the psychological analogy to some problem behavior.

Theories of Causality

Multiple theories of causality exist in the interpretation of family dynamics, which are then applied to the selection of therapeutic interventions. While linear causality (the concept that one cause equals one effect) uses a direct line of reasoning and is commonly used in individual counseling, **circular/reciprocal causality** is often used in family therapy and refers to the dynamic interactions between family members. Think of a situation in which one member of a family (a father, perhaps) has a severe emotional problem accompanied by violent and angry outbursts. The father periodically assaults his teenage son. Reciprocal or circular causality would apply in this family situation, since the father's angry behavior resonates throughout the family, causing different problems for each person. The spouse might feel inadequate to protect her son and sink into a depression. The other children would suffer, too, from anxiety and fear that the same treatment would befall them. Owing to circular causality, a single cause can have many effects.

Paradoxical Intervention Strategies

Paradoxical intervention strategies involve the use of the client's disruptive behavior as a treatment itself, requiring the client to put the behavior in the spotlight to then motivate change. This technique tries to accomplish the opposite of what it suggests on the surface. Interventions include the following:

- **Restraining** is advising that a negative behavior not be changed or be changed only slightly or slowly. This can be effectively used in the context of couples therapy when a couple is struggling with intimacy issues. The therapist may challenge the couple to refrain from sexual intimacy for a period of time, thus removing certain stressors from that dynamic, possibly resulting in a positive intimate experience that occurs naturally and spontaneously.
- **Positioning** is characterizing a negative behavior in an even more negative light through the use of exaggeration. "David, do you feel you are not terrifying your family enough with your reckless driving or that you ought to drive faster in order to make them worry more about your wellbeing? Perhaps that way you will know that they care about you," says the therapist using positioning as a technique. It is important that the social worker use this technique only with great care, as it can be harmful to clients with a negative self-image. It is generally used in situations where the client is behaving in a certain negative way in order to seek affirmation or attention.
- **Prescribing the symptom** is another paradoxical technique used by therapists to obtain an enlightened reaction from a client. A therapist using this technique directs the client to activate the negative behavior in terms that are absurd and clearly objectionable. 'John, I want you to go out to that sidewalk overpass above the freeway and yell as loud as you can at the cars passing below you. Do it for at least four hours." The therapist prescribes this activity to cure his client's dangerous tendency toward road rage.
- **Relabeling** is recasting a negative behavior in a positive light in order to get an emotional response from the client. "Perhaps your wife yells at you when you drink because she finds this behavior attractive and wants your attention," the therapist might say. The therapist might even support that obviously illogical and paradoxical argument by pointing out invented statistics, which support the ridiculous assertion.

Extinction, Time Out, and Thought Stopping

Behavior modification is a term used in facilities like schools and jails to bring behavior into line with societal or family rules:

- **Extinction** is the process of causing a behavior to disappear by providing little or no reinforcement. It is different from punishment, which is negative reinforcement rather than no reinforcement at all. Very often, a student will be removed from the general population and made to sit alone in a quiet room. In schools, this goes by various names, but is often called in-school suspension (ISS). It is hoped that, through lack of reinforcement and response from outside, the offensive behavior will become extinct.
- **Time out** is another extinction technique, generally applied to very young children. A disobedient child will be isolated for a specified, usually short time whenever he or she misbehaves. The method's operant mechanism assumes that we are all social animals and require the reinforcement of the outside world. Deprived of this, we adapt by altering our behavior.
- **Thought stopping** is a learned response which requires the participation and cooperation of the client to change a negative behavior. When it is successful, the client actively forbids negative thoughts from entering his or her mind.

Specific Family Therapy Interventions

Family Therapy Interventions Used with OCD

Family therapy interventions used with **obsessive-compulsive disorder (OCD) patients** include therapy oriented to develop expression of thoughts and impulses in a manner that is appropriate. This approach assumes that family members often:

- Attempt to avoid situations that trigger OCD responses
- Constantly reassure the patient (which often enables the obsession)

Family therapy to address these issues involves:

- Remaining neutral and not reinforcing through encouragement
- Avoiding attempts to reason logically with patient

Family Therapy Interventions for Panic Disorders

Family dynamics and therapy interventions for **panic disorders** include:

- Patients with agoraphobia may require the presence of family members to be constantly in close proximity, resulting in marital stress and over-reliance on the children.
- Altered role performance of the afflicted member results in family and social situations that increase the responsibility of other family members.
- The family must be educated about the source and treatment of the disorder.
- The goal of family therapy is to reorganize responsibilities to support family change.

Functional Family Therapy for Adolescents with Antisocial Behavior

Functional family therapy (FFT) is designed for adolescents (11–17 years of age) with **antisocial behavior**. FFT uses the principles of family systems theory and cognitive-behavioral therapy and provides intervention and prevention services. While the therapy has changed somewhat over the past 30 years, current FTT usually includes three phases:

1. **Engagement/motivation**: The therapist works with the family to identify maladaptive beliefs to increase expectations for change, reduce negativity and blaming, and increase respect for differences. Goals are to reduce dropout rates and establish alliances.
2. **Behavior change**: The therapist guides the parents in using behavioral interventions to improve family functioning, parenting, and conflict management. Goals are to prevent delinquent behavior and build better communication and interpersonal skills.
3. **Generalization**: The family learns to use new skills to influence the systems in which they are involved, such as school, church, or the juvenile justice system. Community resources are mobilized to prevent relapses.

Multisystemic Therapy for Adolescents with Antisocial Behavior

Multisystemic therapy (MST) is a **family-focused program** designed for adolescents (11–17 years of age) with antisocial and delinquent behaviors. The primary goal is **collaboration** with the family to develop strategies for dealing with the child's behavioral problems. Services are delivered in the family's natural environment rather than at a clinic or office with frequent home visits, usually totaling 40–60 hours over the course of treatment. Sessions are daily initially and then decrease in frequency. A variety of different therapies may be used, including family therapy, parent training, and individual therapy. Therapists use different approaches but adhere to basic principles, including focusing on the strength of the systems, delivering appropriate treatment for developmental level, and improving family functioning. The goals of therapy are to improve family relations and parenting skills, to engage the child in activities with nondelinquent peers, and to improve the child's grades and participation in activities, such as sports.

Therapeutic Methods for Counseling an Adolescent With Behavioral Problems

When an **adolescent's behavior** is a problem, some parents have him or her sign an agreement to perform in a specified manner. The agreement may state that a reward will be provided to the adolescent so long as the contract is upheld. The therapist can help parents and children write an effective contract. Another time-honored method of behavior conditioning is the withholding of leisure activity until chores are done. In a family therapy session, the therapist might advise stating the case like this: "Your television has a parental guide lock which will not be turned on unless you can demonstrate that all your homework is complete."

Role of Therapeutic Relationship in Family therapy

The **role of the therapeutic relationship** in family therapy is as follows:

- The social worker interacts in the here and now with the family in relation to current problems.
- The social worker is a consultant to the family.
- The social worker's role differs according to school of thought:
  - **Structural**: Dysfunctional interaction is actively challenged.
  - **Strategic and Systemic**: The worker is very active.
  - **Milan School**: Male/female clinicians are co-therapists; a team observes from behind a one-way mirror and consults and directs their co-therapists with the clients.
  - **Psychodynamic**: The worker facilitates self-reflection and understanding of multi-generational dynamics and conflicts.
  - **Satir**: The worker models caring, acceptance, love, compassion, nurturance in order to help clients face fears and increase openness.

Key Concepts of Family Therapy

Key **concepts of family therapy** include the following:

Behavior modeling	The manner in which a child bases his or her own behavior on the behavior of his or her parents and other people. In other words, a child will usually learn to identify acceptable behaviors by mimicking the behavior of others. Some children may have more difficulty with behavior modeling than others.
Boundaries	The means of organization through which system parts can be differentiated both from their environment and from each other. They protect and improve the differentiation and integrity of the family, subsystems, and individual family members.
Collaborative therapy	Therapy in which a different worker sees each spouse or member of the family.
Complementary family interaction	A type of family relationship in which members present opposite behaviors that supply needs or lacks in the other family member.
Complementarity of needs	Circular support system of a family, in which reciprocity is found in meeting needs; can be adaptive or maladaptive.
Double-bind communication	Communication in which two contradictory messages are conveyed concurrently, leading to a no-win situation.
Family of origin	The family into which one is born.
Family of procreation	The family which one forms with a mate and one's own children.
Enmeshment	Obscuring of boundaries in which differentiation of family subsystems and individual autonomy are lost. Similar to Bowen's "undifferentiated family ego mass." Characterized by "mind reading" (partners speak for each other, complete each other's sentences).
Heritage	The set of customs, traditions, physical characteristics, and other cultural artifacts that a person inherits from his or her ancestors.
Homeostasis	A state of systemic balance (of relationships, alliances, power, authority).
Identified patient	The "symptom bearer" in the family.
Multiple family therapy	Therapy in which three or more families form a group with one or more clinicians to discuss common problems. Group support is given and problems are universalized.
Scapegoating	Unconscious, irrational election of one family member for a negative, demeaned, or outsider role.

Group Work

Social Work Values in Group Practice

The underlying values of social work practice with groups include:

- Every individual has dignity and worth.
- All people have a right and a need to realize their full potential.
- Every individual has basic rights and responsibilities.
- The social work group acts out democratic values and promotes shared decision making.
- Every individual has the right of self-determination in both setting and achieving goals.
- Positive change is made possible by honest, open, and meaningful interaction.

Purposes and Goals of Group Practice

Group practice takes a multiple-goal perspective to solving individual and social problems and is based on the recognition that group experiences have many important functions and can be designed to achieve any or all of the following:

- Provide restorative, remedial, or rehabilitative experiences
- Help prevent personal and social distress or breakdown
- Facilitate normal growth and development, especially during stressful times in the life cycle
- Achieve a greater degree of self-fulfillment and personal enhancement
- Help individuals become active, responsible participants in society through group associations

Advantages of Group Work

Advantages of group work include the following:

- Members can help and identify with others dealing with similar issues and situations.
- Sometimes people can more easily accept help from peers than from professionals.
- Through consensual validation, members feel less violated and more reassured as they discover that their problems are similar to those of others.
- Groups give opportunities to members to experiment with and test new social identities and roles.
- Group practice is not a replacement for individual treatment. Group work is an essential tool for many workers and can be the method of choice for some problems.
- Group practice can complement other practice techniques.

Review Video: What are the Benefits of Group Work?
Visit mometrix.com/academy and enter code: 375134

Importance of Relationships in Group Work

Establishing meaningful, effective relationships in group work is essential, and its importance cannot be overemphasized. The worker will form multiple changing relationships with individual group members, with sub-groups, and with the group as a whole. There are multiple other parties who have a stake in members' experiences, such as colleagues of the worker, agency representatives, relatives, friends, and others. The worker will relate differentially to all of those individuals.

Types of Social Work Groups

The different types of social work groups are as follows:

- **Educational groups**, which focus on helping members learn new information and skills.
- **Growth groups**, which provide opportunities for members to develop a deeper awareness of their own thoughts, feelings, and behavior, as well as develop their individual potentialities (i.e., values clarification, consciousness-raising, etc.).
- **Therapy groups**, which are designed to help members change their behavior by learning to cope with and improve personal problems and to deal with physical, psychological, or social trauma.
- **Socialization groups**, which help members learn social skills and socially acceptable behaviors and help members function more effectively in the community.
- **Task groups**, which are formed to meet organizational, client, and community needs and functions.

Group Structure and Group Properties

Group structure refers to the patterned interactions, network of roles and statuses, communications, leadership, and power relationships that distinguish a group at any point in time.

Group properties are attributes that characterize a group at any point in time. They include:

- Formal vs. informal structure
- Primary group (tight-knit family, friends, neighbor)
- Secondary relationships (task centered)
- Open vs. closed
- Duration of membership
- Autonomy
- Acceptance-rejection ties
- Social differentiation and degrees of stratification
- Morale, conformity, cohesion, contagion, etc.

Closed Groups vs. Open Groups

Groups can be either closed or open, serving different functions and purposes:

Closed Groups	Open Groups
• Convened by social workers. • Members begin the experience together, navigate it together, and end it together at a predetermined time (set number of sessions). • Closed groups afford better opportunities than open groups for members to identify with each other. • Closed groups provide greater stability to the helping situation, and they allow the stages of group development progress more powerfully. • Closed groups provide a greater amount and intensity of commitment due to the same participants being counted on for their presence.	• Open groups allow participants to enter and leave according to their choice. • A continuous group can exist, depending on the frequency and rate of membership changes. • The focus shifts somewhat from the whole group process to individual members' processes. • With membership shifts, opportunities to use the group's social forces to help individuals may be reduced. The group will be less cohesive, and therefore less available as a therapeutic instrument. • The social worker is kept in a highly central position throughout the life of the group, as he or she provides continuity in an open structure.

Short-Term Groups and Formed Groups

Some circumstances call for the formation of short-term and/or formed groups:

Short-Term Groups	Formed Groups
• Short-term groups are formed around a particular theme or in order to deal with a crisis. • Limitations of time preclude working through complex needs or adapting to a variety of themes or issues. • The worker is in the central position in a short-term group.	• Deliberately developed to support mutually agreed-upon purposes. • Organization of the group begins with the realization of a need for group services. • The purpose is established by an identification of common needs among individuals in an agency or worker caseload. • The group is worker-guided in interventions and timing by an understanding of individual and interpersonal behavior related to the group's purpose. • It is advisable to have screening, assessment, and preparation of group members in formed groups. • Different practice requirements for voluntary and non-voluntary groups exist, as members will respond differently to each.

Small Group Theory

System Analysis and Interactional Theory of Small Groups

The system analysis and interactional theory of small groups is a broadly used framework for understanding small groups. In this framework, small groups are living systems that consist of interacting elements that function as a whole. In this framework, a social system is a structure of relationships or a set of patterned interactions. System concepts help maintain a focus on the whole group, and explain how a group and its sub-groups relate functionally to larger environments. This framework describes how interaction affects status, roles, group emotions, power, and values.

Social System Concepts and General Systems Concepts

The following are **social system concepts** used in the system analysis and interactional theory of small group work:

- **Boundary maintenance**: Maintaining group identities and separateness
- **System linkages**: Two or more elements combine to act as one
- **Equilibrium**: Maintaining a balance of forces within the group

General systems concepts used in the system analysis and interactional theory of small group work are as follows:

- **Steady state**: The tendency of an open system to remain constant but in continuous exchange
- **Equifinality**: The final state of a system that can be reached from different initial conditions
- **Entropy**: The tendency of a system to wear down and move toward disorder

Symbolic Interactionism

Symbolic interactionism is characterized by the following:

- Emphasizes the **symbolic nature** of people's relationships with others and the external world versus a social system analysis that emphasizes form, structures, and functions.
- Group members play a part in determining their own actions by recognizing symbols and **interpreting meaning**.
- Human action is accomplished mainly through the process of **defining and interpreting situations** in which people act. The worker uses such concepts to explain how individuals interact with others, and to understand the following:
    - The role of the individual as the primary resource in causing change
    - The significance of social relationships
    - The importance of self-concept, identification, and role identity in group behavior
    - The meanings and symbols attributed to group interactions

Gestalt Orientations and Field Theory

Gestalt psychology played a major part in the development of group dynamics. Contrasting with earlier psychologies that stressed elementary sensations and associations, Gestalt theorists viewed experiences not in isolation, but as perpetually organized and part of a **field** comprised of a system of co-existing, interdependent factors. Group dynamics produced a plethora of concepts and variables:

- Goal formation
- Cohesion
- Group identification and uniformity
- Mutual dependency
- Influences and power
- Cooperation and competition
- Productivity

Group dynamics (or group processes) provide a helpful framework of carefully defined and operationalized relevant group concepts.

Sociometry

Sociometry, inspired by the work of J. L. Moreno, is both a general theory of human relations and a specific set of practice techniques (psychodrama, sociodrama, role playing).

- Sociometric tests are devised to measure the affectivity factor in groups.
- Quality of interpersonal attraction in groups is a powerful force in rallying group members, creating feelings of belonging, and making groups sensitive to member needs.

Cognitive Consistency Theory and Balance Theory

The basic assumption of **cognitive consistency theory** is that individuals need to organize their perceptions in ways that are consistent and comfortable. Beliefs and attitudes are not randomly distributed but rather reflect an underlying coherent system within the individual that governs conscious processes and maintains internal and psychosocial consistency.

According to the balance theory, processes are balanced when they are consistent with the individual's beliefs and perceptions. Inconsistency causes imbalance, tension, and stress, and leads to changing perceptions and judgments which restore consistency and balance. The group worker incorporates varying ideas from these orientations. Some stress the need for the group to be self-conscious and to study its own processes, emphasizing that cognition is apparent in contracting, building group consciousness, pinpointing or eliminating obstacles, and sharing data.

Social Reinforcement and Exchange Theory

The **social reinforcement and exchange theory** in regard to group work is summarized as follows:

- Social exchange theorists propose that members of groups are motivated to seek **profit** in their interactions with others (i.e., to maximize rewards and minimize costs).
- Analysis of interactions within groups is done in terms of a series of **exchanges or tradeoffs** group members make with each other.
- The individual member is the **primary unit of analysis**. Many of the core concepts of this theory are merely transferred to the group situation and do not further the understanding of group processes.

Group Formation

Elements in the Group Formation Process

The key elements in the group formation process include the following:

- The worker makes a clear and uncomplicated statement of purpose that includes both the members' stakes in coming together and the agency's (and others') stakes in serving them.
- The worker's part should be described in as simple terms as possible.
- Identify the members' reactions to the worker's statement of purpose and how the worker's statement connects to the members' expectations.
- The worker helps members do the work necessary to develop a working consensus about the contract.
- Recognize goals and motivations, both manifested and latent, stated and unstated.
- Recontract as needed.

Worker's Role in Group Member Selection

The worker's process of selecting members for a group is as follows:

- The worker explains **reasons** for meeting with group applicants.
- The worker elicits applicants' **reactions** to group participation.
- The worker assesses applicants' **situations** by engaging them in expressing their views of the situation and goals in joining the group.
- The worker determines **appropriateness** of applicants for the group, accepts their rights to refuse membership, and provides orientation upon acceptance into the group.

Heterogeneity vs. Homogeneity in Group Formation

Issues of heterogeneous vs. homogenous group formation include the following:

- A group ought to have sufficient homogeneity to provide stability and generate vitality.
- Groups that focus on socialization and developmental issues or on learning new tasks are more likely to be homogeneous.
- Groups that focus on disciplinary issues or deviance are more likely to be heterogeneous.
- The composition and purposes of groups are ultimately influenced or determined by agency goals.

Beginning Phase of Group Process

Intervention Skills

Intervention skills of the social worker that are used in the **beginning phase** of group process include the following:

- The worker must tune into the needs and concerns of the members. Member cues may be subtle and difficult to detect.
- The worker must seek members' commitment to participate through engagement with members.
- The worker must continually assess the following:
  - Members' needs/concerns
  - Any ambivalence/resistance to work
  - Group processes
  - Emerging group structures
  - Individual patterns of interaction
- The worker must facilitate the group's work.

Facilitating the Group's Work

The social worker's role in facilitating group process is as follows:

- Promote **member participation and interaction**.
- Bring up **real concerns** in order to begin the work.
- Help the group keep its **focus**.
- Reinforce observance of **rules** of the group.
- Facilitate **cohesiveness** and focus the work by **identifying emerging themes**.
- Establish worker **identity** in relation to group's readiness.
- **Listen** empathically, **support** initial structure and rules of the group, and **evaluate** initial group achievements.
- Suggest **ongoing tasks or themes** for the subsequent meeting.

Stressors

The following are stressors that the worker might experience in the beginning phase of group process:

- Anxiety regarding gaining acceptance by the group
- Integrating group self-determination with an active leadership role
- Fear of creating dependency and self-consciousness in group members which would deter spontaneity
- Difficulty observing and relating to multiple interactions
- Uncertainty about the worker's own role

Middle Phase of Group Process

Intervention skills of the social worker used in the **middle phase** of group process include the following:

- Judge when work is being avoided
- Reach for opposites, ambiguities, and what is happening in the group when good and bad feelings are expressed
- Support different ways in which members help each other
- Partialize larger problems into more manageable parts
- Generalize and find connections between small pieces of group expression and experience
- Facilitate purposeful communication that is invested with feelings
- Identify and communicate the need to work and recognize when work is being accomplished by the group

Ongoing Group Development

Group development refers to the ongoing group processes that influence the progress of a group, or any of its sub-groups, over time. Group development typically involves changing structures and group properties that alter the quality of relationships as groups achieve their goals. Understanding group development gives social workers a blueprint for interventions that aid the group's progression toward attaining goals. A danger in using development models is in the worker forcing the group to fit the model, rather than adapting interventions for what is occurring in the group. A complex set of properties, structures, and ongoing processes influence group development. Through processes that are repeated, fused with others, modified, and reinforced, movement occurs.

MODELS OF GROUP PRACTICE

LINEAR STAGE MODELS OF GROUP DEVELOPMENT

There are many models of group development, often describing the group's process through a series of **linear stages** in which the group progresses predictably from one to another.

Tuckman's five stages of group development are as follows:

1. **Form**: Group comes together, rules are established and agreed upon, and members are relatively subdued and hesitant.
2. **Storm**: Expression of feelings begins by the members who still feel individual versus members of the group; there may be resistance to cues by the social worker or signs of cynicism.
3. **Norm**: A sense of unity and teamwork prevails; members begin to interact with and encourage one another.
4. **Perform**: A sense of hierarchy dissipates as the member take control of the group process and feel empowered in an open and trusting team environment.
5. **Adjourn**: The team recognizes time for closure, some members may mourn the loss of the group and need guidance and support for next steps, and reflection on progress and celebration of accomplishments occur.

The **Boston Model** (Garland, Jones, & Kolodny) of group development is as follows:

1. **Preaffiliation stage**: Consists of regulation by the worker, expressions of concern or anxiety, heavy dependence on the worker, hesitant disclosure of personal goals, clarification of purpose, timeline, and roles
2. **Power and control stage**: Consists of limit setting, clarification, and the use of the program
3. **Intimacy stage**: Consists of handling transference, rivalries, and a degree of uncovering
4. **Differentiation stages**: Consist of clarification of differential and cohesive processes, and group autonomy
5. **Separation**: Consists of a focus on evaluation, handling ambivalence, and incorporating new resources

The **Relational Model**, developed by Schiller, in regard to group development in groups of women, is as follows:

- Preaffiliation
- Establishing a relational base
- Mutuality and interpersonal empathy
- Challenge and change
- Separation and termination

SOCIAL GOALS MODEL

The social goals model of group practice is as follows:

- The primary focus is to influence a wide range of small group experiences, to facilitate members' identifying and achieving of their own goals, and to increase social consciousness and social responsibility.
- It assumes a rough unity between involvement in social action and the psychological health of the individual. Early group work was concerned with immigrant socialization and emphasized principles of democratic decision making, in addition to tolerance for difference.

- The methodology is focused on establishing positive relationships with groups and members, using group processes in doing with the group rather than for the group, identification of common needs and group goals, stimulation of democratic group participation, and providing authentic group programs stemming from natural types of group living.

Remedial/Rehabilitative Model

The remedial/rehabilitative model of group practice is as follows:

- It uses a medical model and the worker is focused primarily on **individual change**.
- This model includes **structured** program activities and exercises.
- It is more commonly found in organizations concerned with **socialization**, such as schools, and in those concerned with treatment and social control (inpatient mental health treatment, etc.).
- Practice techniques in this model focus on **stages** of treatment.
    - **Beginning**: Intake, group selection, diagnosis of each member, and setting specific goals.
    - **Middle**: Planned interventions. Worker is central figure and uses direct means to influence group and members. Worker is spokesperson for group values and emotions. Worker motivates and stimulates members to achieve goals.
    - **Ending**: Group members have achieved maximum gains. Worker helps clients deal with feelings about ending. Evaluation of work, possible renegotiation of contract.

Reciprocal Interactional or Mediating Model

The reciprocal interactional or mediating model of group practice can be summarized as follows:

- The social worker is referred to as a **mediator** and participates in a network of reciprocal relationships. Goals are developed mutually through contracting process. The interaction and insight of group members is the primary force for change in what is seen as a "mutual aid" society.
- **Worker's task**: Help search for common ground between group members and the social demands they experience, help clients in their relationships with their own social systems, detect and challenge obstacles to clients' work, and contribute data.
- **Phases** of intervention:
    - **Tuning in or preparation for entry**: The worker helps the group envision future work, but makes no diagnosis. The worker is also sensitive to members' feelings.
    - **Beginning**: The worker engages group in contracting process, and the group establishes clear expectations.
    - **Middle**: The middle phase consists of searching for common ground, discovering/challenging obstacles, data contribution, sharing work visions, and defining limits/requirements
    - **Ending**: Finally, the worker is sensitive to his or her own reactions and members' reactions and helps members evaluate the experience and consider new beginnings.

Freudian/Neo-Freudian Approach

The Freudian/Neo-Freudian approach to group practice is as follows:

- Groups consist of 8-10 members.
- Interaction is mainly through discussion.
- Group members explore feelings and behavior, and interpret unconscious processes.
- The worker uses interpretation, dream analysis, free association, transference relations, and working through.
- This approach aims to help group members re-experience early family relationships, uncover deep-rooted feelings, and gain insight into the origins of faulty psychological development.

Tavistick Group-Centered Models

The Tavistick "group as a whole" group-centered model for group practice is as follows:

- This approach derives from Wilfred Bion's work with leaderless groups. Bion developed analytic approaches that focused on the **group as a whole**.
- Latent group feelings are represented through the group's prevailing emotional states or **basic assumption cultures**.
- The therapist is referred to as a **consultant**. The consultant does not suggest an agenda, establishes no rules and procedures, but instead acts as an observer. A major role of the consultant is to alert members to ongoing group processes and to encourage study of these processes.
- The consultant encourages members to explore their experiences as group members through **interaction**.

Group Therapy Methods

Process Groups

Irvin Yalom's "here-and-now" or process groups are characterized by the following:

- Yalom stressed using clients' **immediate reactions** and discussing members' **affective experiences** in the group.
- Process groups have relatively unstructured and spontaneous sessions.
- Process groups emphasize **therapeutic activities**, like imparting information, or instilling hope, universality, and altruism.
- The group can provide a **rehabilitative narrative** of primary family group development, offer socializing techniques, provide behavior models to imitate, offer interpersonal learning, and offer an example of group cohesiveness and catharsis.

Moreno's Psychodrama Group Therapy

Moreno's psychodrama group therapy is summarized as follows:

- **Spontaneous drama techniques** contribute to powerful therapy to aid in the release of pent-up feelings and to provide insight and catharsis to help participants develop new and more effective behaviors.
- The five **primary instruments** used are the stage, the client or protagonist, the director or therapist, the staff of therapeutic aides or auxiliary egos, and the audience.
- Psychodrama group therapy can begin with a **warm-up**. The warm-up uses an assortment of techniques such as self-presentations, interviews, interaction in the role of the self and others, soliloquies, role reversals, doubling techniques, auxiliary egos, mirroring, multiple doubles, life rehearsals, and exercises.

Behavioral Group Therapies

Behavioral group therapies are characterized by the following:

- The **main goals** are to help group members eliminate maladaptive behaviors and learn new behaviors that are more effective. Behavioral groups are not focused on gaining insight into the past, but rather on current interactions with the environment.
- It is one of the few research-based approaches.
- The worker utilizes **directive techniques**, provides information, and teaches coping skills and methods of changing behavior.
- The worker arranges **structured activities**. The primary techniques used include restructuring, systematic desensitization, implosive therapies, assertion training, aversion techniques, operant-conditioning, self-help reinforcement and support, behavioral research, coaching, modeling, feedback, and procedures for challenging and changing conditions.

Influencing the Group Process

Influencing group process in group work methodology can be done through the following:

- The worker's ability to recognize, analyze, understand, and influence group process is necessary and vital. The group is a system of relationships rather than a collection of individuals. This system is formed through associations with a unique and changing quality and character (this is known as group structures and processes).
- Processes that the worker will be dealing with include understanding group structures, value systems, group emotions, decision-making, communication/interaction, and group development (formation, movement, termination).

Externalizing

The worker must be prepared to help individual members profit from their experiences in and through the group. Ultimately, what happens to group members and how they are influenced by the group's processes determines the success of any group experience, not how the group itself functions as an entity. The worker should give attention to helping members relate beyond the group (**externalizing**), to encouraging active participation and involvement with others in increasingly wider spheres of social living. This should occur even when the group is relatively autonomous.

Programming

The importance of programming in group work methodology is as follows:

- The worker uses activities, discussion topics, task-centered activities, exercises, and games as a part of a planned, conscious process to address individual and group needs while achieving group purposes and goals.
- Programming should build on the needs, interests, and abilities of group members and should not necessitate a search for the unusual, esoteric, or melodramatic.
- Social work skills used in implementing programs include the following: initiating and modifying program plans to respond to group interests, self-direction, responsibility, drawing creatively upon program resources in the agency and environment, and developing sequences of activities with specific long-range goals.
- Using program activities is an important feature of group practice.

Contracting Working Agreements in Group Work

Only if group members are involved in clarifying and setting their own personal and common group goals can they be expected to be active participants on their own behalf. **Working agreements** consider not only worker-member relationships, but also others with a direct or indirect stake in the group's process. Examples would be agency sponsorship, collaborating staff, referral and funding sources, families, caretakers, and other interested parties in the public at large.

The following are the **social worker's role in contracting**:

- Setting goals
- Determining membership
- Establishing initial group structures and formats

All three of these elements require skillful management by the worker.

Analyzing Group Processes

The following are categories for analyzing group work:

- Communication processes
- Power and influence
- Leadership
- Group norms and values
- Group emotion
- Group deliberation and problem solving

Group Practice with Special Populations

Groups for Serious Mental Illness

Group work with clients who have serious mental illness should include the following elements:

- **Clearly defined programs** that use psychosocial rehabilitation approaches (not psychotherapeutic).
- Focus on making each group session **productive and rewarding** for group members.
- **Themes** addressed include dealing with stigma, coping with symptoms, adjusting to medication side effects, dealing with problems (family, relationships, housing, employment, education, etc.), and real and imagined complaints about mental health treatment organizations.
- Many groups in community-based settings focus on helping members learn **social skills** for individuals with limited or ineffective coping strategies.
- Mandated groups in **forensic settings** are highly structured and focus on basic topics such as respect for others, responsibility for one's behavior, or staying focused.

Chemical Dependency Groups

Group work for chemical dependency focuses on the following:

- Group work is the treatment of choice for **substance use disorder**.
- Guidelines for these groups include maintaining confidentiality, using "I" statements, speaking directly to others, never speaking for others, awareness of one's own thoughts and feelings, honesty about thoughts and feelings, and taking responsibility for one's own behavior.
- Types of groups used include:
  - **Orientation groups** that give information regarding treatment philosophy/protocols.
  - **Spiritual groups** that incorporate spirituality into recovery.
  - **Relapse prevention groups** that focus on understanding and dealing with behaviors and situations that trigger relapse.
  - **AA and NA self-help groups** utilize the principles and philosophies of 12-step programs. For family and friends, **Nar-Anon** and **Al-Anon groups** provide support.

Parent Education Groups

Parent education groups are used in social agencies, hospitals, and clinics. They are often labeled as psycho-ed groups or parent training groups and use a cognitive-behavioral approach to improve the parent-child relationship. Parent education groups are often structured to follow manuals or curricula. Their main focus is helping parents improve parent-child interactions, parent attitudes, and child behaviors.

Abused Women's Groups

Abused women's groups can be described as follows:

- Provide a warm, accepting, and caring environment in which members can feel secure.
- Structured for consciousness raising, dispelling false perceptions, and resource information.
- Common themes these groups explore include the use of power which derives from the freedom to choose, the need for safety, the exploration of resources, the right to protection under the law, and the need for mutual aid.
- Basic principles of these groups include respect for women, active listening and validation of members' stories, ensuring self-determination and individualization, and promoting group programs that members can use to demonstrate their own strength and achieve empowerment.
- For post-group support, groups typically seek to utilize natural supports in the community.

Groups for Spouse Abusers

Groups for spouse abusers (perpetrators of domestic violence) are explained below:

- Work with this population is typified by resistance and denial.
- Clients have difficulty processing guilt, shame, or abandonment anxiety and tend to convert these feelings into anger.
- These clients have difficulties with intimacy, trust, mutuality, and struggle with fear of abandonment and diminished self-worth.
- Mandatory group treatment is structured. It is designed to challenge male bonding that often occurs in such groups.
- Including spouses/victims in these groups is quite controversial in clinical literature.

Groups for Sex Offenders

Groups for sex offenders are summarized below:

- Typically, membership in these groups is ordered by the court. There is no assurance of confidentiality, as workers may have to provide reports to the courts, parole officers, or other officials.
- Clients typically deny wrongdoing, test workers, and are often resistant.
- In groups with voluntary membership, confidentiality is extremely important, as group members often express extreme fear of exposure.
- Prominent themes include denial, victim-blaming, blaming behavior on substances, blaming behavior on uncontrollable sex drives/needs.
- Treatment emphasizes the importance of conscious control over drives/needs, regardless of their strength or if they are natural.
- A culture of victimization is strongly discouraged.

Groups for Children of Alcoholics

Groups for children of alcoholics are discussed below:

- Individuals who grow up with parents who abuse alcohol and/or drugs often learn to distrust others as a survival strategy. They become used to living with chaos and uncertainty and with shame and hopelessness.
- These individuals commonly experience denial, secrecy, and embarrassment.
- They may have a general sense of fearfulness, especially if they faced threats of violence, and tend to have rigid role attachment.
- Treatment in these groups requires careful planning, programming, and mutual aid in the form of alliances with parental figures and other related parties in order to create a healthy environment that increases the individual's safety and ability to rely on self and others.

Groups for Sexually Abused Children

Groups for sexually abused children are summarized below:

- The worker must pay particular attention to her or his own attitudes toward sexuality and the sexual abuse of children.
- Important in these groups are contracting, consistent attendance, and clearly defined rules and expectations.
- Clients may display control issues and may challenge the worker's authority.
- Confidentiality is not guaranteed.
- Termination can be a particularly difficult process.
- Common themes that come up include fear, anger, guilt, depression, anxiety, inability to trust, and delayed developmental/socialization skills.
- Programming can include ice breaking games, art, body drawings, letter writing, and role playing.

Termination of Group Process

Group members' experience of termination and the worker's role in helping group members to cope with the ending of the group are discussed below:

- Group members may have feelings of loss and may desire to minimize the painful feelings they are experiencing.
- Members may experience ambivalence about ending.
- The social worker will:
  - Examine her or his own feelings about termination
  - Focus the group on discussing ending
  - Help individuals express their feelings of loss, relief, ambivalence, etc.
  - Review achievements of the group and members
  - Help members prepare to cope with next steps
  - Assess members' and group's needs for continued services
  - Help members with transition to other services

METHODS OF FORESTALLING OR DEALING WITH TERMINATION

The following are group members' methods of forestalling or dealing with termination:

- **Simple denial**: A member may forget ending, act surprised, or feel "tricked" by termination.
- **Clustering**: Members may physically draw together, also called super-cohesion.
- **Regression**: Reaction can be simple-to-complex. Earlier responses reemerge, outbursts of anger, recurrence of previous conflicts, fantasies of wanting to begin again, attempts to coerce the leader to remain, etc.
- **Nihilistic flight**: Members may reject and perform rejection-provoking behavior.
- **Reenactment and review**: Members begin recounting or reviewing earlier experiences in detail or actually repeating those experiences.
- **Evaluation**: Members assess meaning and worth of former experiences.
- **Positive flight**: There is a constructive movement toward self-weaning. Members find new groups, etc.

Case Management

Linking and Monitoring in Case Management

At times, the social worker may take the role of case manager for certain clients or populations. Case managers must **link** clients with the service providers and resources needed, to the extent appropriate resources are available. Case managers are also responsible for helping clients overcome any obstacles in using the resources they are provided. When a client is unable to articulate his or her own needs, case managers must advocate and speak for them to get the assistance required. If necessary, help from an agency's administrative staff may be needed to fully address the services required.

High-quality continuous **monitoring** is a key case management function. Good working relationships between case managers, clients, and direct service providers are essential to ensure a successful monitoring and accommodation process. Changes in plans and linkages may at times become necessary, as the client and/or available services may change and evolve.

Balancing Cases Among Social Workers

Cases should be balanced in the equitable distribution of time requirements and the proportional distribution of the social workers' experience or expertise. Variables to take into consideration in assigning caseloads include the amount of risk to clients (and the self-care required by social workers in high-intensity cases), the complexity of cases, the nature of the problem being addressed, and factors such as paperwork and travel time of the social worker. Highly intense cases should be assigned to staff workers with the experience to handle them, but concentrating such emotionally-draining work on a few members of staff will also increase burnout and put these valuable team members at increased risk. Increasing training opportunities and providing consistent supervision for staff members can help create a stronger, more highly functioning team.

Connecting the Client to Direct Service Providers

The goal of case management is to ensure that clients with multiple issues receive the comprehensive services and aid they need in a timely and effective manner. In the role of case manager, the social worker does not provide direct services; instead, they connect the client to direct service providers. The social worker is responsible for all the services provided by the direct service agency engaged. Thus, the social worker and the agency staff need a close working relationship, to ensure that all client needs are being met. While all areas of health and human services use case managers, they are especially utilized for the mentally ill, the elderly, and the disabled, as well as in matters of child welfare. Having one case manager responsible for all the needs of a client provides clients with the one-on-one attention they need and prevents them from falling between the cracks because too many direct service people are involved.

CASE PRESENTATION

The case presentation is the primary way the social worker can communicate his or her knowledge of the client to others. The challenge is to create a comprehensive, factual document that's also manageably brief and to the point. The **elements of a case presentation** include the following:

- Identifying information such as age, gender, culture, and economic status
- Family history
- Personal and social history
- Medical and psychological diagnoses
- The presenting problem(s) in terms of assessments, diagnoses, and current mental status
- A summary of the social worker's impression of the client
- Theories about potential ways of helping the client, treatment plans, and goals

Out-of-Home Placement and Displacement

Out-of-Home Displacement

Out-of-home displacement may have varying effects on clients and client systems:

- **Natural disasters***:* Some clients may develop PTSD and have recurring nightmares or fears regarding the disaster, especially if it was particularly frightening or the individual or family members experienced injuries. Some may experience depression and withdrawal. Living situations may change if the home was damaged or destroyed, sometimes forcing clients into sharing homes with others, living in substandard housing, or being homeless. Some may have to move away from schools, neighborhoods, and friends.
- **Homelessness**: Many clients that are homeless develop depression and low self-esteem and may engage in substance abuse. Children may attend school irregularly, have difficulty studying, and lack adequate clothing and nutrition. They may be bullied by other children aware of their circumstances. Families may be separated and children placed in separate shelters or foster care. Risk of injuries and chronic disease increases.

Out-of-Home Placement

Out-of-home placements may have varying effects on clients and client systems, depending on the age, duration, and reason:

- **Hospitalization**: Both children and adults may feel fearful and anxious. Children, especially, may feel abandoned or rejected and may regress (bed wetting, thumb sucking). Children may be compliant out of fear when alone but cry and express feelings when parents or other caregivers are present. Adolescents may resent the lack of privacy, isolation, and loss of control. Adults may be concerned about the family unit and loss of income.
- **Foster care**: Children may have difficulty attaching and may become depressed or exhibit behavioral issues (anger or aggression). Developmental delays are common, and children often have poor educational backgrounds, resist studying, get low grades, or must repeat grades. Children may act out or become withdrawn after family visits.
- **Residential care**: Those in residential care may suffer from abuse or molestation because of inadequate supervision. Adults may have an increased risk of falls and injuries. Clients of all ages may become withdrawn and regress because of a lack of personal attention and caring. Small children, especially, may exhibit growth and developmental delays.

Follow-up After Placing Child in Out-of-Home Placement

Follow-up after placing a child in out-of-home placement may vary according to the state regulations, age of the child, type of placement, and the child's specific plan of care, but common **follow-up activities** include:

- Making regularly scheduled visits to observe the child and caregivers in the home environment
- Ensuring that the child's special needs, such as for medical care or counseling, are met
- Assessing the caregiver's communication with the child, disciplinary actions, and attention to special needs, such as giving medications and providing a special diet
- Recording compliance with court ordered actions required of the child (such as rehabilitation for an adolescent drug abuser) or the parents (such as attendance at child development or anger management classes or testing free of alcohol and drugs)
- Monitoring health and education, including school records of grades and attendance
- Ensuring that support services are provided to the caregivers as needed
- Sending periodic reports to the court

Permanency Planning

Permanency planning for permanent placement should begin when the child is admitted to the care of child protective services (CPS) and the initial plan of care is developed. Permanent placement may include reunification, foster care, kinship placement, adoption, residential care facility, group home, or transition to adult living. **Elements of permanency planning** include:

- Assessing the child and the child's needs as well as those of the potential caregivers
- Reviewing any previous CPS records
- Noting any previous history with the juvenile justice system and reviewing records
- Preparing the child by engaging them in the process as appropriate for their age through explaining options, showing photographs, and asking for the child's input
- Reviewing health and education records (including lists of schools attended and grades) to ascertain the child's needs and the need for interventions or support services
- Establishing permanency goals and target dates
- Attending permanency hearings and providing justification for termination of parental rights when appropriate

Consultation and Collaboration

Social Workers Role in the Healthcare Team

Components, Goals and Attributes

Social workers may be involved on hospital units and play a critical role in the healthcare team, working amongst other disciplines to care for a client. Key components, goals, and attributes of the **interdisciplinary treatment and healthcare team** include:

- **Components**: Interdisciplinary treatment employs the talents of multiple professionals to design a comprehensive treatment plan, with each team member having input based on his or her specialty. The client is included as a member of this team.
- **Goals**: The intention is to develop appropriate interventions for each client, which are to be consistently implemented and assessed on a regular basis by everyone involved in the client's care.
- **Attributes**: Dedication to the team, collective accountability, common goals and intervention viewpoints, egalitarian leadership, decision making by consensus, open communication, and open and free examination of roles and relationships.

Typical Members

Typical members of a healthcare team may include:

- **Dietitian**: Provides ethnically relevant dietary recommendations, is aware of the psychological importance of food, understands the psychology of eating disorders, and is aware of food-drug interactions (such as MAOI's and grapefruit juice, etc.).
- **Nurse**: Responsible for around-the-clock care, activities of daily living (ADLs), and security of client and staff. Clinical nurse specialists may perform individual, family, or group psychotherapy.
- **Ministry**: Aids and supports the spiritual beliefs of the client and family and may provide marital or personal counseling.
- **Psychiatry**: Diagnoses and treats mental health conditions using counseling and/or medication, responsible for admission and discharge, and may provide individual, group, or family therapy.
- **Psychology**: Performs diagnostic testing, provides treatment plans, and may provide individual, family, or group therapy.
- **Social Work**: Evaluates how family, social, and environmental factors contribute to the client's problems, and collaborates with internal and external agencies to set up a support system for the client's goals.
- **Volunteer Agencies**: Organizations that provide ancillary support to individuals with mental health problems.

Team Meetings

Interdisciplinary team meetings occur as a gathering of several disciplines to coordinate care and services for the client. During these meetings, the client's diagnosis, current issues, family support, medication, and progress are all discussed, as well as any other issues that may arise. Additionally, many team meetings collectively gather information that will be used in the future for when the client is eventually discharged to other services or home. The disciplines that may be present at meetings in addition to the social worker include the physician or psychiatrist, nurse, pharmacist, occupational or physical therapist, nutritionist, and case manager. Each team member presents on the topics of their expertise as they relate to the client in order to produce a full picture of the client, and therefore create a holistic approach to the client's care.

Promoting Collaboration

Promoting collaboration and assisting others to understand and use the resources and expertise of others requires a commitment both of time and effort. Examples of promoting collaboration include the following:

- Coaching others on methods of collaboration, which can include providing information in the form of **handouts** about effective communication strategies and **modeling** this type of communication with the staff being coached.
- **Team meetings** are commonly held on hospital units and provide an opportunity to model collaboration and suggest the need for outside expertise to help with planning client care plans.
- Selecting a **diverse group** for teams or inviting those with expertise in various areas to join the team when needed can help team members to appreciate and understand how to use the input of other resources.

Collaboration with External Agencies

The social worker must initiate and facilitate collaboration with external agencies because many have direct impacts on client care and needs:

- **Industry** can include other facilities sharing interests in the client's care or pharmaceutical companies. The social worker may have a dialog with drug companies about their products and how they are used in specific populations because many medications are prescribed to women, children, or the aged without validating studies for dose or efficacy.
- **Payors** have a vested interest in containing health care costs, so providing information and representing the interests of the client is important.
- **Community groups** may provide resources for clients and families, both in terms of information and financial or other assistance.
- **Political agencies** are increasingly important as new laws are considered about social work case load and infection control in many states.
- **Public health agencies** are partners in health care with other facilities and must be included, especially in issues related to communicable disease.

Conflict Resolution

Conflict is an almost inevitable product of collaboration with the client and other team members, and the social worker must assume responsibility for **conflict resolution**. While conflicts can be disruptive, they can produce positive outcomes by forcing people to listen to different perspectives and opening dialogue. The social worker should make a plan for dealing with conflict resolution. The best time for conflict resolution is when differences emerge but before open conflict and hardening of positions occur. The social worker must pay close attention to the people and problems involved, listen carefully, and reassure those involved that their points of view are understood.

Steps to conflict resolution are as follows:

1. Allow both sides to present their side of the conflict without bias, maintaining a focus on opinions rather than individuals
2. Encourage cooperation through negotiation and compromise
3. Maintain the focus, providing guidance to keep the discussions on track, and avoid arguments
4. Evaluate the need for renegotiation, formal resolution process, or a third party
5. Utilize humor and empathy to diffuse escalating tensions
6. Summarize the issues, outlining key arguments
7. Avoid forcing resolution if possible

Managing a Consultation

Consultation is a natural part of working in human services, as clients often present with multiple needs that call on different specialties. Managing a consultation prevents complications when the following steps are taken:

1. The **client's permission** should be obtained for the social worker to share relevant information with the consultant.
2. The consultation should have a **clearly defined purpose**: The nature of the problem should be identified as completely as possible.
3. The **role of the consultant** should also be defined and understood by all parties.
4. The **process should be outlined**, with understanding reached as to its time considerations and the limits of the consulting role.

Issues of Communication That Influence Case Consultation

Case consultation involves communication between a social worker and a direct service provider. The client could be an individual, family, or community. To be successful, consultation must have a purpose, a problem, and a process. The person requesting the consultation has the right to decline help, so the consultant must have high-value ideas to gain the trust of the consultee. An effective consultation process requires that the consultee determine the need for consultation and initiate the request for consultation, then the consultant and consultee must collaborate in assessing the problem, determine a plan for help, negotiate contracts, have a mutual list of objectives, determine the action to be taken, implement the plan, and measure and report the outcomes in a clear and concise manner. Communication is at the core of the process, so the consultant must have quality communication and problem-solving skills to be successful.

Networking and Consultation

Networking and consultation can help the social worker get the best help for the client while also reducing stress on the social worker. Building a network of professionals whose expertise overlaps and complements one's own will save time and effort when it becomes necessary to locate services and information outside one's own sphere of expertise. Establishing a personal-professional relationship allows one to partner with others, possibly sidestepping red tape and wait times, to get assistance for clients. Perhaps just as important is that the social worker has a group of outside experts whose advice they can trust, just as those experts can trust the social worker.

Community Organization and Social Planning

Social Planning and Program Development

Community Practice Model of Social Planning

The community practice model of social planning as discussed by Weil and Gamble states that social planning is for the purpose of coordinating, developing, and growing social services and policies. Often considered highly technical, the process has moved over time from being in the hands of experts to being community driven, with concomitant increases in community participation, cohesion, proactive activity, empowerment, and sustainability.

Social planning can be participatory and community led, or it may take place in fundraising organizations such as the United Way. It may involve making physical changes to the environment, such as the revitalization of buildings, and it may involve increasing quality of life for members of particular sectors, such as the aged or the mentally ill.

Community Resources, Outreach, and Advocacy

Social planning encompasses a range of activities that may serve to connect people with established **resources** or increase their access to those resources. Establishing or increasing accessibility may require social workers to first get community members to buy into the project, which may prove difficult when members have been let down by projects or agencies before.

When a would-be **advocate** finds their potential sector to be apathetic, angry, and mistrustful, the frustration the advocate experiences is rational but not helpful. Fostering participation first requires a connection that establishes enough hope, trust, and motivation to get community members in on the ground floor. Without this initial participation, it's highly unlikely that members will feel empowered by the process or willing to take part in it. Thus, **community outreach** becomes a vital, ongoing strategy for social planning agendas.

Importance of Networking in the Community

Creating a program usually requires coordination among various groups. Establishing and maintaining **networks** among agencies and community leaders is important in not only identifying community needs, but also eliciting ideas for solutions and motivating community members to participate. Community leaders are an important resource because they know the problems and potentials of their communities while maintaining their own connections to individuals in those communities. With a finger on the pulse of a neighborhood, they can advise social workers in program development and delivery, preventing problems that would be unanticipated by service providers from outside that community. Connecting active community leaders to external resources may create a situation in which the social worker's role is primarily that of supporter and liaison to other agencies, while the community does the work of the program.

Involvement of Community Members and Participants in Program Development

Community or sector members can be involved at the earliest stages of program development by being part of the needs assessments and by providing information about the environment in which the program is to take place, two important elements of program development. Participants can also be active in recruiting others to the program, monitoring and reporting obstacles and possible solutions, and providing regular feedback. Feeling an ownership in a program gives participants the chance to create real, positive changes. In this way, what may start as a small community program may evolve over time into more comprehensive community organization.

Involvement of Beneficiaries in Program Development

Modern social work practice includes the recruitment and involvement of potential **beneficiaries**, ideally as experts in regard to identifying problems, suggesting solutions, and being involved in the process not only as beneficiaries but as important sources of monitoring, feedback, and evaluation. In this process, social workers may act as advocates and solution-focused advisors, problem-solvers, and connectors, while participants share the challenges and excitement of full participation. The larger the project, the greater the need for social workers' expertise in mediation and negotiation as many groups with conflicting agendas, values, and needs come together in one program.

Steps of Promoting Community Change

Mark Homan's *Promoting Community Change: Making it Happen in the Real World, 6th Edition* (2016) examines community-based planning as a process with multiple levels of consideration. According to Homan, the social worker must consider the following when attempting to **promote community change**:

- **Know the community**: Understand perspectives about the community, assess the community's needs and currently available resources, and conduct community-based participatory research.
- **Utilize powerful planning**: Identify one's own discomforts and opportunities, identify one's vision and goals based on potentiality, identify current obstacles and resources, identify time frames and people who can handle specific tasks, create indicators to show task completion, and measure both effectiveness and indicators of trouble.
- **Raise other resources**: Create a budget and ask for what is needed, fundraise, gain contributions from others, utilize the internet in fundraising, receive funding from private and public organizations, and utilize grant writing.
- **Get the word out**: Identify the populations that need to be reached, send messages that are controlled (but be aware of messages that others can control), and utilize e-organizing.
- **Build an organized effort**: Understand that organizations are built around issues, develop the organization, understand structural limitations, utilize small group processes, understand the steps of incorporation, and sustain the organization.
- **Take action**: Utilize action strategies and tactics (confrontation, negotiation, collaboration, co-optation, and advocacy), know the strategies and tactics that an opponent may use, and understand the commandments of change.

Approaches for Working with Communities and Larger Systems

Social workers may be called upon to work for **change and progress in large systems**, such as in school districts, in multi-site agencies, and with governmental entities. In such situations, there are two key approaches:

- The **horizontal approach** is used in working with centralized agencies and in communities. It involves bringing key participants (stakeholders) into the process of problem identification, consensus building, goal setting, and implementation and monitoring of an improvement process.
- The **vertical approach** is used when there is a need to reach outside or beyond the community or centralized entity environment. This approach involves learning about hierarchical levels of leadership in government, charitable organizations, grant-funding institutions, etc., and then collaborating with key leaders in problem identification, consensus building, goal setting, and program implementation and monitoring to achieve the necessary goals. An understanding of systems theory and eco-systems (or life model) theory can aid in this process.

The Social-Psychological Area of Community

There are several interpretations of the social-psychological area of community.

- One is the belief that people of a community are bound together by an existing **area of interest**. They feel connected based on goals they share, needs, values, and activities that makeup the feeling of community.
- Another is the belief that there is a **personal-psychological community** within each individual. This is the view from one person that reflects what the community is like. Children and lower-class individuals tend to view community as having more narrow boundaries than middle- and upper-class adults do.
- Another view is the **cultural-anthropological view of community**, which looks at community as a form of social living that is defined by attitudes, norms, customs, and behaviors of those living in the community.

Community Organization Practice

Tasks/Goals

The following are **tasks and goals** of community organization practice:

- Change public or private **priorities** in order to give attention to problems of inequality and social injustice
- Promote **legislative change** or public funding allocation
- Influence **public opinions** of social issues and problems
- Improve **community agencies/institutions** in order to satisfy needs of the community better
- Develop **new ways** to address community problems
- Develop **new services** and coordinate existing ones
- Improve community **access** to services
- Set up new **programs** and services in response to new or changing needs
- Develop the capacity of **grassroots citizen groups** to solve community problems and make claims on public resources for under-served communities
- Seek justice for oppressed **minorities**

Values

The following are **values** of community organization practice:

- Working with, not for, clients to enhance their participatory skills
- Developing leadership, particularly the ability to foresee and act on problems
- Strengthening communities so that they are better able to deal with future problems
- Redistributing resources in order to enhance the resources of the disadvantaged
- Planning changes in systematic and scientific ways
- Rational problem-solving process: studying the problem, defining it, considering possible solutions, creating a plan, then implementing and evaluating the plan
- Advancing the interests of the disadvantaged in order for them to have a voice in the process of distribution of social resources

Differences from Other Forms of Social Work Practice

Differences between community organization practice (COP) and other forms of social work practice include the following:

- COP highlights knowledge about social power, social structure, social change, and social environments.
- COP acknowledges the reciprocal process between the individual and the social environment. It seeks to influence and change the social environment as it is seen as the source and likely solution for many problems.
- In the view of COP, social problems result from structural arrangements rather than from personal inadequacies. Consequently, the reallocation of resources and social power leads to changes in the community and eventually in individuals.

Underlying Assumptions

Assumptions that underlie community organization practice include the following:

- Members of the community want to improve their situation.
- Members of the community are able to develop the ability to resolve communal and social problems.
- Community members must participate in change efforts rather than have changes imposed on them.
- A systems approach which considers the total community is more effective than imposing programs on the community.
- One goal of participation in community organization initiatives involving social workers is education in democratic decision-making and promoting skills for democratic participation.
- The organizer enables members to address community problems independently, in part through their learning, analytic, strategic, and interpersonal skills.

Utilization of Tactics in Community Organization

Various tactics should be utilized when approaching community organization and community program development:

- **Collaborative tactics** include problem solving, joint action, education, and mild persuasion. They require a perceived consensus in goals, power equality, relatively close relationships, and cooperation/sharing.
- **Campaign tactics** include hard persuasion, political maneuvering, bargaining/negotiation, and mild coercion. They require perceived differences in goals, inequality in power, and intermediate relationships.
- **Contest tactics** include public conflict and pressure. They require public conflict, disagreement concerning goals, uncertain power, distant or hostile relationships.

To determine the best tactics to use in community organization, consider the following **factors**:

- The degree of differences or commonality in the goals between the community group and the target system.
- The relative power of the target system and the community group.
- The relationship of the community group to the target system.

Meeting Needs of Communities Through Community Practice

The conception of a community program should begin with the observation of **a need in the community**, something that may be obvious and publicly discussed or covert and difficult to define. The type of program then determines the level of intervention, its length, cost, participants, and desired goals and outcomes. Weil (1994) identified four **vital processes in community practice**:

- Development
- Organization
- Planning
- Action for progressive social change

The development process can encompass a range of activities affecting small neighborhood groups or may entail major, international efforts. The social or economic development of a particular community may empower members to make changes in the way they work along with their housing, health, safety, and economic future.

Community Organization Practice Models

Model	Foundations
Locality development model	• Involves working in a neighborhood with the goal of improving the quality of community life through broad-spectrum participation at the local level. • Process-oriented with the purpose of helping diverse elements of the community come together to resolve common problems and improve the community. • Tactics include consensus and capacity building. As the organization resolves smaller problems, it facilitates the solving of more complex and difficult problems. • The worker's roles include enabler, coordinator, educator, and broker.
Social planning model	• Involves careful, rational study of a community's social, political, economic, and population characteristics in order to provide a basis for identifying agreed-upon problems and deciding on a range of solutions. Government organizations can be sponsors, participants, and recipients of information from social planners. • Focuses on problem solving through fact gathering, rational action, and needs assessment. • Tactics may be consensus or conflict. • The worker's roles include researcher, reporter, data analyst, program planner, program implementer, and facilitator.
Social action model	• This model requires an easily identifiable target and relatively clear, explainable goals. Typically, the target is a community institution that controls and allocates funds, community resources, and power, and clients are those who lack social and economic power. • Assumption in this model is that different groups in the community have interests that are conflicting and are irreconcilable. In many cases, direct action is the only way to convince those with power to relinquish resources and power. • Tactics include conflict, confrontation, contest, and direct action. • The worker's roles include that of advocate, activist, and negotiator.
Social reform model	• In collaborating with other organizations for the disadvantaged, the worker's role is to develop coalitions of various groups to pressure for change. • This model is a mixture of social action and social planning. • Strategies include fact gathering, publicity, lobbying, and political pressure. • Typically, this approach is pursued by elites on behalf of disadvantaged groups.

Citizen Participation

With American culture becoming more private and individualistic over the past decades, **citizen participation** in social change diminished as racial and multicultural tensions rose. Civic clubs tend to attract or recruit people of similar social backgrounds: however, community study circles, created by Everyday Democracy (formerly the Study Circle Resource Center) have focused on bringing people of diverse cultures together in a deliberative democratic process to discuss and take action on community problems. A community organizing in this fashion meets not only the most pressing community needs, but also builds connections among community members who might not otherwise encounter each other in the course of their daily lives.

Program Development and Service Delivery

Program Planning

Methods of Strategic Planning

Strategic planning involves the overall guidance of an organization in accordance with its stated vision. It includes decision-making, activities, and resource allocation of the organization and is administered by higher-echelon managers. **Four methods of strategic planning** include the following:

1. **Alignment of strategies and outcomes** is used to fine-tune what is working and change what is not working.
2. **Issues-based planning**, which is often used when resources are low, looks at the most important current issues and brainstorms alternatives.
3. **Organic planning** in real time uses a dialogue model to strategize for change.
4. **Vision and goals-based planning** uses the vision, mission, and goals to create an action plan.

Goal-Setting in Program Planning

Goal-setting needs to be part of the planning process, and some goals may also be referred to the clients for their input. The larger the program, the greater the variety of goals, which may range from setting staff training benchmarks to meeting funding application dates as well as marking particular milestones in the program itself. Goals need to be precisely delineated, measurable, and as objective as possible. Goal setting has a recursive element: for example, setting a deadline helps with focus and achievement, whereas having no deadline can cause projects to languish.

Planning Service Delivery

Service delivery is another factor to consider in the planning process. In a community where public transportation is limited, holding a first-aid class necessary for employment in food service at a center on the edge of town may prevent people from participating. Anticipating and resolving such basic and important problems ideally begins in the program planning stage, but when unanticipated issues arise, having the flexibility to create spontaneous solutions can mean the difference between the success and failure of a program.

Process and Program Evaluation

Process Evaluation

The process of a program may evolve as feedback systems return information about how individual elements of the program are faring. Outcomes, identified at the beginning planning stages, can be assessed only at the end of the program. Goals are intermediary steps in the process and may be used as milestones marking progress toward the ultimate desirable outcomes. The purpose of a **process evaluation** is to catch errors or omissions in planning and to provide for changes that occur either in the program environment or due to the program itself.

Process evaluation takes place throughout the program as it runs, ideally identifying and correcting problems. Methods of process evaluation are necessarily primary, including interviews, focus groups, and observation. Outcome, or summative evaluations, will often include posttest measures providing quantitative data as well as qualitative measures.

PROGRAM EVALUATION

Program evaluation is important for several reasons:

- It demonstrates a **belief in and accountability for the program** on the part of the agency and establishes credibility.
- Documenting the progress and changes due to the program enables the administrators to **pass along their findings to communities** seeking to solve similar problems.
- **Funders** are interested in demonstrable success, and the only way to produce such evidence to those outside the program is in documentation. Even a successful program can lose its funding if it fails to demonstrate its success in measurable ways.

STEPS TO PROGRAM EVALUATION

The proper steps to program evaluation are as follows:

1. Determine what will be evaluated
2. Identify who will be the consumer of the research
3. Request the staff's cooperation
4. Indicate what specific program objectives are
5. Outline objectives of evaluation
6. Choose variables
7. Develop design of evaluation
8. Apply evaluation design (conduct the evaluation)
9. Analyze and interpret findings
10. Report results and put them into practice

OUTCOME ASSESSMENT

Different programs will be assessed differently, with some being a fairly straightforward matter of gathering statistics and others a more elaborate process of surveys, interviewing, tracking participants across time, and gathering information from a variety of agencies. **Outcome measures** should be identified early on and assessed for reliability and validity, appropriateness to the program, fitness to the particular outcome to be measured, practicality of use, and cost.

As outcomes are used to justify continuing or enlarging a program and are important measures in requesting additional funding, rigorous and professional reporting becomes even more crucial. Even when there are failures, careful cataloging can assist in later program development efforts. A project may have unintended outcomes, helpful or harmful, which should also be noted, for further research or to provide warnings and prevent those errors from occurring in later work.

OUTCOME EVALUATIONS

Outcome evaluations may be more than a single measure administered once, as programs are often planned to have a reach extending over a long period of time. For example, to see if an after-school program for girls reduces teen pregnancies and increases their educational achievement, outcomes may be measured over years. Ideally, there is also a way to identify and measure unintended outcomes because programs may have more global effects than initially understood. Process evaluations may show up surprise effects along the way, allowing for changes to ameliorate or eradicate the negative or enhance and document the positive. In outcome evaluations, feedback from interviewed participants may also help pinpoint unexpected results.

Formative/Summative Evaluations

Formative evaluations, which are done while the program is in progress, must be considered as part of the design process, and the degree to which the formative evaluations will be utilized to guide or assess the process must be determined. Formative evaluations that are appropriate should be developed for each stage. For example, a policy change may be followed by a brief questionnaire asking about the effectiveness of the policy. If the evaluations are used to guide development of the rest of a program, then strict timelines for completing the evaluations and assessing results should be part of the plan.

Summative evaluations, which are done at the completion of the program, should be planned to assess outcomes. As part of the design process, it's important to determine what exactly needs to be evaluated and how best to carry out the assessment to render the needed data.

Cost-Benefit and Cost-Effective Analysis

A **cost-benefit analysis** uses the average cost of an event and the cost of intervention to demonstrate savings. For example, if an agency pays for 40 hours of overtime costs weekly (1.5 X hourly salary of $27 = $40 per hour), the cost would be $1620 per week or $84,240 per year. If a new hire would cost $56,160 plus benefits of $19,656 the total cost of the new hire would be $75,816 (1.35 X base salary). Cost-benefit analysis reveals the current event cost of $84,240 minus the intervention cost of $75,816 renders a cost benefit of $8424.

A **cost-effective analysis** measures the effectiveness of an intervention rather than the monetary savings. For example, if the rate of pregnancies among female adolescents in a county averages 75 per 1000 and an aggressive program of education and access to birth control decreases the rate to 55 per 1000, the program resulted in 20 fewer adolescent pregnancies per 1000.

Interorganizational Relationships and Social Network Analysis

Healthcare and social welfare fields often remain poorly integrated into larger community networks and systems. Social work agencies need to better coordinate and build partnerships to more fully meet the needs of their individual clients and the community at large. One **barrier to interorganizational relationships** is the allocation of resources, as funds for both health care and social services are limited. A related concern is the interpenetration of organizational boundaries, often established to preserve resources and each organization's client base. Consequently, there is often conflict within and between agencies on how best to proceed to the next level of service and who will be primarily responsible. One way to overcome past divisiveness is to have shared memberships in key planning processes, by which to map the flow of care from one level to the next. Always central to this process is the need to enhance how different agencies communicate with one another to provide cohesiveness and continuity.

Basic Fiscal Management Principles

Understanding basic fiscal management principles is critical in the social work environment, where the work is almost always budget driven.

- The **operating budget** may include various private, local, state, or federal grants or donations and each of those may have specific requirements for use and/or separate budgets.
- **Expenses** must not exceed income, and interventions must be paid for out of the correct budget or budget category, so appropriate record-keeping and coding of services are essential.
- **Return-on-investment** must be considered and calculated for any new proposals, such as hiring of staff.
- With **fee-for-service contracts**, services and payments are usually outlined in detail and the social workers must comply with directives.
- With **performance-based contracts**, in which reimbursement is based on meeting performance measures, measures to cut expenses and improve outcomes are generally central concerns. Every intervention must be assessed accordingly, but there is more freedom in prescribing interventions.

Social Policy and Social Change

Social Policy

Social policy refers to the collection of laws, regulations, customs, traditions, mores, folkways, values, beliefs, ideologies, roles, role expectations, occupations, organizations, and history that all focus on the fulfillment of critical social functions.

Advocating for Policy Change

In advocating for policy change, the social worker engages with institutions, groups, and individuals to bring about changes in procedures, practices, or policies that will benefit clients. The process of advocacy is a combination of education and persuasion, beginning with the assumption that policy makers are unaware of or do not understand the negative effects of their current policies. In such a case, educating and informing policy makers as well as raising their awareness of the problems are the first steps in advocacy.

Aspects of Persuasion

The aspects of persuasion involve using influence to convince policy makers and then the public that the issue is important and needs to be addressed. Networking and coalition building make the best use of resources and get a critical mass behind the push for change. Acquiring funding from private funders and legislators may require grant writing, high-level networking, or social media campaigns as well as carefully documented research on the problem and its possible solutions. Once the change is in effect, evaluation sets the stage for ongoing advocacy efforts.

Social Policy Analysis

Social policy analysis is the research supporting the process of solving problems through policy making or change. Like many other aspects of macro practice, it involves a step-by-step procedure that identifies the problem; creates alternatives focused on efficiency, equity, and liberty; assesses the benefits of alternatives (such as comparing costs and benefits for each); and chooses the best alternative. Designing and implementing the policy is followed by evaluating the outcomes of the change.

Analysis is often both the starting point and the ending point in policy advocacy. Gathering and interpreting the data on conditions is fundamental in convincing people that a particular problem exists (and having a mutual understanding of its scope and duration and the harm it causes) and that the problem stems from particular sources, which can be addressed by the means identified by the research.

Theories of Social Change

Modernization Theory of Social Change

Modernization theory, developed after World War II, focused on the democratization of the Global South, where new countries were emerging after many years of colonialism. More recently, modernization provided the basis for the Republican Party under President Reagan and the UK's Conservatives' Prime Minister Thatcher to come to power. With conservative economic policies in effect, the rich were accorded more benefits (such as lower taxes) under the idea that assets would begin to trickle down to the poor. This strategy has been called the neoliberal development model.

Marxism

Marxism sought to change society by rejecting the concept of market capitalism and by creating a paternalistic father state where, in theory, all people were equal. As social change focused on collectivization, individual freedoms were abolished, creating a system of oppression and tyranny.

The Marxist belief that societal change would and should occur not in increments but in revolution threatened not only Western ideals of market capitalism but the ideal of personal freedom, a combination that proved intolerable and caused immeasurable suffering by way of wars, political reactivity, and the Cold War. Countries once part of the USSR are still finding their way out of the web of economic and social isolation and poverty that trapped them for decades.

Dependency Theory

Dependency theory (or international structuralism) arose in the 1960s and 1970s, combining criticism of modernization with Marxist ideals. Adopting the stance that modernization was Western countries' attempt to economically exploit Latin American countries in an updated version of colonialism, populist leaders attempted to restrain the economic takeover of their countries. Third-world solidarity through economic and social justice would be the means of improving the lives of the people.

Sustainable Development Theory

The sustainable development theory is a recent and popular developmental theory that denies that increased industrialism is the only necessary component of economic growth and that materialism is responsible for many of the world's ills, both socially and environmentally. The fair-trade movement is one expression of sustainability, replacing gigantic corporate interests with small, often family-run local enterprises. Sustainability embraces the importance of community as an extension of the family, work practices that support individual workers, and the belief that education pays off in more than creating a knowledgeable workforce but in developing an empowered community.

Support Programs

Social Services and Social Welfare Services in the US

Social services endeavor to maintain quality of life in society and include social welfare (poverty and poor health prevention via entitlements), along with other government and privately operated programs, services, and resources. **Types of social services** include the following:

- Education
- Employment
- Health and medical services
- Housing
- Minimum income grants
- Nutrition
- Retirement
- Welfare (for children and the elderly)

Benefits include cash grants (e.g., unemployment and supplemental income) and in-kind benefits (e.g., food stamps). **Delivery systems** include the following:

- **Employment-based**, obtained by or through employment, such as health insurance, retirement, and disability (both short- and long-term, including maternity and family leave)
- **Government-based**, consisting of tax relief, such as deductions (e.g., dependents, medical costs) at the local, state, or federal level
- **Philanthropy-based**, comprising programs for needy families, at-risk youth, etc.
- **Personal contributions**, such as child care, private health care, etc.
- **Public-based**, whereby not-for-profit agencies and public agencies provide services, such as shelters, adoption services, and disaster relief, free or at a reduced rate (sliding scale, etc.)

Eligibility Criteria for Social Service Programs

Eligibility for social services can be determined in many different ways. Three common methods include:

- **Universal eligibility**: Open to all applicants
- **Selective eligibility**: Criteria are specified (e.g., age, dependent children) and often means-tested (for income and resources) with sliding scale costs
- **Exceptional eligibility**: Open only to individuals or groups with special needs (e.g., veterans, people with specific disabilities) and usually not means-tested

Social Security Act of 1935

The Social Security Act (SSA) of 1935 provided old-age-survivor benefits, with full coverage beginning at age 65. Full eligibility gradually increases to age 67 for those born in or after 1960. To be fully vested, one must have 40 lifetime credits (earned at 4 credits per year). Reduced compensation may be available for those retiring earlier. Today, the program covers not only retirees, but those with certain permanent disabilities and the minor children of deceased beneficiaries, in certain situations. As an insurance trust fund, the program was intended to be self-sustaining by all those who pay in.

Social Security Disability, Worker's Compensation, and Supplemental Security Income

Individuals with a permanent disability severe enough to prevent them from becoming gainfully employed may qualify for **Social Security Disability (SSD)**. The disabling condition must be expected to last for at least one year or to result in the individual's demise.

Individuals who contract a job-related illness or who are injured in the course of their work are covered by the social insurance program known as **worker's compensation**. Injuries resulting from intoxication, gross negligence, or deliberate misconduct are not covered. Coverage varies from state to state for this federally mandated, state-administered program. Funding is primarily employer based, though some states may supplement operation costs.

Supplemental Security Income (SSI) is a federally funded program supplemented by the state. It ensures baseline cash income to bring means-tested recipients above the poverty line. Poor elderly, disabled, and blind persons are the primary recipients.

Unemployment Insurance and Child Welfare Programs

Unemployment insurance is a benefit to prevent undue economic hardship, providing for individuals who become involuntarily and temporarily unemployed. To be eligible, an individual must be actively seeking gainful employment. Benefits include job-seeking assistance and cash payments in reduced proportion to the lost income. The benefits are time limited and once exhausted they cannot be obtained again unless a new episode of employment and job loss occurs. Originating with the Social Security Act of 1935, the program is federally mandated and state administered. Funding comes from employer taxes, distributed by the states to those needing assistance.

A variety of child welfare services and programs have been created for the safety, care, and support of abused, disabled, homeless, and otherwise vulnerable children. Services include adoption and foster care. Agencies investigating abuse and securing out-of-home placement, if necessary, also exist, along with programs for family maintenance and reunification.

Government Funding and Oversight of Social Service Programs

Government programs are **funded** by income taxes and Social Security taxes. Income taxes are termed *progressive* because they increase as income increases. Taxes such as sales taxes and Social Security taxes are termed *regressive* because they are flat-rate taxes that offer non-proportional relief to those in low-income situations. Flat-rate tax reform efforts have continued to fall short primarily because of the loss of available deductions, in spite of proposals for tax elimination for the very poor. Dependent deductions can be crucial to low-income families, and home mortgage deductions are crucial for some homebuyers. A trend to privatization of government programs has increased in recent years (e.g., government oversight and funding of privately operated agencies). However, concerns about adequacy, availability, and accountability remain.

Available Food and Nutrition Assistance Programs in the US

Available food and nutrition assistance programs in the US include:

- **Supplemental Nutrition Assistance Program (SNAP)**, previously food stamps: SNAP provides funds to purchase approved groceries, issued according to family size and income (selective eligibility, means-tested), state-administered and federally funded.

- **WIC (Women, Infants, and Children)**: WIC is a means-tested, selective eligibility program providing assistance to pregnant women, mothers of infants up to 5 months old, breastfeeding mothers of infants up to 12 months old, and children under 5 years old. Subsidies are provided for specific nutritious foods (infant formula, eggs, etc.). The program is state-administered and federally funded.
- **School lunch programs**: These programs provide federally funded assistance to children in means-tested families.
- **Elderly Nutrition Program**: This program provides food assistance for needy persons over age 60 via local churches and community centers.
- **Meals on Wheels**: This locally funded and administered program delivers meals to means-tested individuals and families.

Public Housing Programs

Public housing consists of government-built residential facilities that provide low-cost to no-cost rent for means-tested poor individuals and families. The **Subsidized Housing Program** offers federal funds to reduce rental costs for the means-tested poor and to aid in maintaining public residential facilities. Additional public housing assistance programs include home loan assistance programs, home maintenance assistance programs, and Section 8 low-income reduced rent programs (rental vouchers).

TANF Program and General Assistance

The **Temporary Assistance for Needy Families (TANF) program** replaced the Aid to Families with Dependent Children (AFDC) program. TANF was created by the 1996 Personal Responsibility and Work Opportunity Reconciliation Act (also known as welfare reform) and is a federally funded, state-administered block grant program. The focus is on moving recipients into the workforce and returning welfare to its intended temporary and transitional role.

General Assistance (GA) refers to a variety of social welfare programs developed by state and local government to aid those unable to meet eligibility for federal assistance programs. Eligibility criteria vary from state to state (even region to region, in some areas). Because there is no mandate for GA programs, they do not exist in all states, though most states have created some form of safety net of this kind.

Medicare

Medicare was established in 1965 and is now run by the Centers for Medicare and Medicaid Services. Coverage was initially instituted solely for those over age 65 but was expanded in 1973 to include the disabled. **Eligibility criteria** include an individual or spouse having worked for at least 10 years in Medicare-covered employment and US citizenship. Coverage options include up to four sections:

Medicare Part	Coverage Offered
Part A	Hospital insurance (hospital care, skilled nursing home care, hospice, and home health care)
Part B	Medical insurance (doctor's services and outpatient hospital services, diagnostic tests, ambulance transport, some preventive care including mammography and Pap tests, and durable medical equipment and supplies)

Medicare Part	Coverage Offered
Part C	Medicare Advantage (MA), run by private companies to provide Part A and Part B benefits and often additional benefits such as vision, hearing, and health and wellness programs
Part D	Medicare Advantage-Prescription Drug plans (MA-PD) that include prescription drug coverage

MEDICAID

1965 Title XIX Social Security Act introduced **Medicaid** as a federal-state matching plan for low-income individuals supervised by the federal government. Funding comes from federal and state taxes, with no less than 50%, but no more than 83%, being funded federally. Each state is able to add optional eligibility criteria on the list, and they may also put restrictions (to a point) on federally directed aid. Patients who receive Medicaid cannot get a bill for the aid, but states are able to require small copayments or deductibles for particular types of help.

Federal regulations require that states support certain individuals or groups of individuals through Medicaid, although not everyone who falls below the federal poverty rate is eligible. **Mandatory eligibility groups** include the following:

- Patients deemed categorically needy by their state and who receive financial support from various federal assistance programs
- Individuals receiving Federal Supplemental Security income (SSI)
- Patients that are older than 65 that are blind or have complete disability
- Pregnant women and children younger than 6 years of age who live in families that are up to 133% of the federal poverty level (some states allow for a higher income to meet eligibility in this class)
- Adults under the age of 65 that make less than or equal to 133% of the federal poverty level and are not receiving Medicare

Review Video: Medicare and Medicaid
Visit mometrix.com/academy and enter code: 507454

FINANCIAL AND ORGANIZATIONAL STATUS OF NOT-FOR-PROFIT AGENCIES

In many ways, not-for-profit (nonprofit) entities operate similarly to for-profit entities. However, there are some key differences:

- Not-for-profit organizations must not be structured to pursue commercial purposes (i.e., profiteering on goods and services sold to the public).
- Members of a not-for-profit organization may not personally benefit as shareholders or investors.
- Certain tax benefits can accrue to not-for-profit organizations, within parameters defined by the Internal Revenue Service, which are not available to for-profit entities.
- Finally, the goals of these organizations tend to be charitable in nature (e.g., caring for vulnerable populations), and they seek and receive funding primarily via government and philanthropic grants, as well as from gifts, donations, and fundraising events.

Leadership

Leadership vs. Management

The definition of various roles and responsibilities differ from leader to manager.

Factor	Leader	Manager
Role	Encourages change and values achievements of self and others	Maintains stability and values end-results
Problem-solving	Facilitates decision-making and encourages innovative approaches	Makes decisions and decides on the course of action, generally with tried-and-true approaches
Power	Derives from personal charisma and the trust of others	Derives from position and authority granted by the organization
Actions	Proactive, anticipating problems and taking action to prevent them	Reactive, looking for solutions to problems after they occur
Risk taking	Willing to take risks to achieve results	Avoids risk taking as a threat to stability
Organizational culture	Shapes the current culture and seeks modifications	Supports and endorses the current culture
Resources (human)	People who follow and provide support	Employees who are hired to serve in subordinate positions
Focus (work)	Leading people to work more effectively	Managing the flow of work and personnel effectively
Goals	Focuses on long-term goals	Focuses on short-term goals

Leadership Styles

Leadership styles often influence the perception of leadership values and commitment to collaboration.

Charismatic	This style depends upon personal charisma to influence people and may be very persuasive, but this type of leader may engage "followers" and relate to one group rather than the organization at large, limiting effectiveness.
Bureaucratic	This leader follows the organization's rules exactly and expects everyone else to do so. This is most effective in handling cash flow or managing work in dangerous work environments. This type of leadership may engender respect but may not be conducive to change.
Autocratic	An autocratic leader makes decisions independently and strictly enforces rules, but team members often feel left out of the process and may not be supportive. This type of leader is most effective in crisis situations, but may have difficulty gaining the commitment of staff
Consultative	A consultative leader presents a decision and welcomes input and questions although decisions rarely change. This type of leadership is most effective when gaining the support of staff is critical to the success of proposed changes.
Participatory	This leader presents a potential decision and then makes a final decision based on input from staff or teams. This type of leadership is time-consuming and may result in compromises that are not wholly satisfactory to management or staff, but this process is motivating to staff who feel their expertise is valued.

Democratic	A democratic leader presents a problem and asks staff or teams to arrive at a solution, although the leader usually makes the final decision. This type of leadership may delay decision-making, but staff and teams are often more committed to the solutions because of their input.
Laissez-faire (free rein)	This leader exerts little direct control but allows employees/teams to make decisions with little interference. This may be effective leadership if teams are highly skilled and motivated, but in many cases, this type of leadership is the product of poor management skills and little is accomplished because of this lack of leadership.

POWER

Power is defined as the ability to influence others in intended ways. **Sources of power** depend on the following:

- Control of resources
- Numbers of people
- Degree of social organization

Power exists in several forms, some conducive in motivating and inspiring long-term change, others effective only in the short term.

- **Coercive power** uses one's ability to instill fear and enforce negative consequences to motivate specific actions or steer away from other actions.
- **Reward power** uses one's ability to provide incentives (bonuses, recognition) to motivate specific actions.
- **Legitimate power** is power resulting from stature, title, or position and is only effective when the position of power is universally respected by those who are subordinate to the position of power.
- **Expert power** comes from having a unique and specific skill set that is essential for growth and change.
- **Referent power** results from gaining the trust and respect of one's followers by leading by example and putting the greater good above the self. This is the most effective power in motivating change.

Supervision and Administration

Administration

Administration can be described as follows:

- Managing organizations and all of their parts in order to maximize goals and have the organization succeed and grow
- Directing all the activities of an agency
- Organizing and bringing together all human and technical resources in order to meet the agency's goals
- Motivating and supervising work performed by individuals and groups in order to meet agency goals

Agency Policies and Procedures

Agencies usually have written statements of values and a mission, and new employees are given copies of the statements in their orientations or induction periods. Mission and value statements disseminate the general goals and attitudes of the agency. **Policies** are more specific documents outlining important **procedures** for areas such as informed consent, documentation, confidentiality, and antidiscrimination. In agencies that value the autonomy of staff, there are policies enabling employees to provide feedback about organizational customs or policies operating contrary to the best interests of clients or employees.

Impact of Agency Policy and Procedures on Social Work Practice

The work environment for social workers is as important as for any professionals. The **agency's policies and culture** should be in alignment with the ethics and values of the profession, supporting the wellbeing and development of the staff. Workload management, appropriate supervision, ongoing professional development opportunities, and fair pay and benefits provide a supportive structure for social workers. Formal or informal policies should never compel social workers to engage in risky behaviors in regard to client confidentiality, informed consent, or health and safety of clients or workers. As in any job, employees should be given access to training and recognition if they are to experience job satisfaction and quality of life.

Agency Administration, Structure, and Bureaucracy

All organizations should have a **mission statement** that sets forth the purpose, goals, and target service population of the organization. An **organizational structure** is then needed to pursue the delivery of services and achievement of the identified goals. An agency typically has three levels of **bureaucratic staff**: institution-wide leaders, management-level staff, and direct service providers. Typical social service agencies follow a classic Weberian bureaucratic model of organization. In a bureaucracy, leadership flows from the "top down," and tasks are rationally delegated to employees and departments best suited to achieve administrative and agency goals.

Key **characteristics of a bureaucracy** (according to Max Weber) include the following:

- Labor is divided by functions and tasks according to specialized skills or a specific focus needed.
- A hierarchical structure of authority is in place.
- Recruitment and hiring are based upon an initial review of key qualifications and technical skills.
- Rigid rules and procedures are generally applied impartially throughout the organization and specify employee benefits, duties, and rights.
- Activities and responsibilities are rationally planned to achieve overarching agency goals.

Administrative Functions in an Agency/Organization

Basic administrative functions include the following:

- **Human resource management**: Recruiting, interviewing, hiring, and firing, as well as orienting and reassigning employees within the organization.
- **Planning and delegation**: Ensuring that the organization's mission, goals, objectives, and policies are in place, appropriate, and effective, and delegating necessary tasks to achieve these ends.
- **Employee evaluations, reviews, and monitoring** to ensure competency and efficiency.
- **Advocacy**: Horizontal interventions (between staff or across a department) and vertical interventions (between departments and hierarchical staff relationships) to resolve conflicts and complaints.
- **Conflict resolution**: Acting as a mediator and a protector of the various parties involved, ensuring equitable outcomes that remain within the scope of the organization and its goals.

Relationships Between Administrators, Supervisors, and Supervisees

While all agency staff are concerned with providing quality services, **administrators** have a more external focus, while supervisors and direct service staff are focused internally. Administrators are charged with broad program planning, policy development, and ensuring agency funding, along with managing the agency's public image and community perceptions. By contrast, **supervisors** are more responsible for the implementation of policy and programs and ensuring staff adherence to those guidelines provided. New employees (during a probationary period) and those seeking licensure may engage in more formal supervision experiences as **supervisees**. In the case of supervision for licensure, a written agreement will outline the goals, purpose, and scope of the supervision, along with meeting frequency and duration (to accrue required licensure hours), evaluations, whether or not sessions will be recorded (videotaped, etc.), and how feedback will be provided. Consultation and supervision differ, as consultation is an episodic, voluntary problem-solving process with someone having special expertise, in contrast to continuous and mandatory oversight with administrative authority.

Boards of Directors

Functions

The power and authority vested in a **board of directors** depends upon whether they are overseeing a private or public agency. Public agencies have board members that are largely advisory or administrative, with less direct authority than those overseeing private entities. In private agencies or voluntary organizations, the board is empowered to define the general path of the agency and to control all systems and programs operating under its auspices. The board is responsible to any sources that provide monetary contributions, to the community, to the government, and to all consumers that use the agency's programs. To be successful, members of a social service agency's board must have knowledge of all operations. The function of the board is to oversee the design of policies, develop short- and long-term planning, confirm the hiring of personnel, oversee general finances and financial expenditures, deal with the public, and be accountable for the actions of the agency.

Selection and Composition

The agency's mission and overall goals must be kept paramount when **choosing board members**. Members must be committed, honest, and able to invest their time and energy in the agency. Responsibilities must be discharged with personal expertise and through meaningful relationships within the community. Interpersonal skills are essential, as board members deal directly with the other members of the board, professionals at the agency, and the general public. Some boards require the representation of certain professions within the community (e.g., a banker), but all members must bring a particular expertise to the board. The agency's mission and the personal responsibilities of each board member should be understood, and a specific orientation experience should be provided to ensure this understanding. Terms are typically limited to three years, with the possibility of a second term for those making unique contributions. The terms should rotate to ensure that seasoned board members are always available.

Relationship of Agency Staff with Board Members

The board of directors oversees the development of policies by agency administrators, and the staff of the agency carries out the policies as approved. The board must hold the staff accountable for the implementation of the policies, because policy operationalization may utilize a variety of potential pathways. Administration evaluates the staff, and the performance of the staff ultimately reflects on the agency, which in turn reflects on the board. Representative staff members have the right to communicate with the board about any problems they face in implementing the policies. Open lines of communication between the board and the staff ensure success in the agency. The board, administration, and staff should have a triangular relationship based on clear job descriptions that state the responsibilities of each party.

Supervision

Aspects of Supervision

There are three aspects of supervision:

- **Supportive supervision** assists the social worker in handling stress and in learning self-care. Both activities are needed to provide the best service to clients.
- **Educational activities** identify needs and teach new skills.
- **Administrative aspects** of supervision are concerned with accountability to the public; for example, numbers of documented supervision hours are required to meet licensing requirements.

Group Supervision

Group supervision has been described as a blending of mediation and mutual aid as supervisor-led and peer groups can provide workers with the four Cs of supervision: confidence, competence, compassion, and creativity. The need for information, balanced with the need for self-care, make supervision a multipurpose activity designed to support the effectiveness and efficiency of workers in their capacity to help clients.

Two primary structures of group supervision are the supervisor-led group and the peer group. In a supervisor-led group, the supervisor holds the group as any group therapist would, creating a safe, nonjudgmental environment and mediating among group members.

SOCIAL WORK SUPERVISORY ROLES

As a middle manager, supervisors oversee direct service staff and report to administrative directors; they provide indirect client services (via direct service staff) and primarily serve the agency.

Supervisory roles include the following:

- **Recruitment and orientation**
- **Management**: Delegating duties, overseeing staff work, and resolving conflicts
- **Education, training, and staff development**: Instructing staff regarding policies and procedures, and ensuring that training is available or pursued via in-service meetings, workshops, and continuing education courses
- **Assessment and review**: Evaluating and providing feedback regarding staff performance
- **Support**: Helping staff resolve issues and cope with stress and promoting a healthy work environment
- **Advocacy**: Resolving complaints and pursuing necessary support for staff
- **Role modeling** of quality practice, values, and ethics
- **Program evaluator**: Ensuring that policies and procedures are effective and that staff adhere to guidelines

SUPERVISION GROUPS

Supervision groups may be theme-centered, case-centered, or worker-centered, with many groups addressing all three as relevant issues arise. Many supervision groups move between an educational stance and a focus on self-reflective practice, allowing for teaching and growth of self-understanding as necessary components of professional development. In group supervision as in individual supervision, the supervisor may be held accountable for the actions of his or her supervisees (*respondeat superior*) in ethical situations that may come to legal action.

PEER SUPERVISION

Supervision should be regularly scheduled, transparent, and open and nonjudgmental, whatever the model used. Three models of peer supervision include the **developmental**, **role-centered**, and the **psychodynamic models**, and peer groups will vary within those models based on the group focus and whether or not case presentation is part of the process.

SOCIAL WORKER'S RESPONSIBILITY TO SEEK OUT AND RECEIVE SUPERVISION

Supervision is important in the care of clients, in continuing learning for social workers, and in ethical competence. If a social worker finds herself or himself in a situation in which supervision is not provided in the workplace, it is that person's ethical duty to find appropriate supervision. With technologic advances, even remotely based social workers can arrange virtual supervision, provided that they take precautions for clients' confidentiality. Social workers have the right to privacy in their supervision sessions.

IDENTIFYING AND FILLING LEARNING NEEDS

Identifying learning needs and developing objectives are important in supervision because client care depends on the skills and understanding of the social worker as well as his or her attentiveness to ethics. Supervision is a vital part of professional development, and the knowledgeable supervisor notes and matches the learning style (visual, auditory, or kinesthetic) of the supervisee to methods of teaching, can explain the reasons for the assigned interventions, and is able to give constructive feedback and evaluate the learning process. With the social worker's value on empowering the individual, the ideal supervision process includes the participation of the supervisee in identifying learning needs and working in concert with the supervisor to meet them.

Positive Work Environment

Creating a positive work environment includes policies and procedures that support employees (good supervision and professional development opportunities), good terms of employment (e.g., salaries and benefits, chances for recognition and advancement), autonomy instead of micromanagement, and good physical working conditions. The culture of the workplace should uphold the values of the social work profession, provide for the health and safety of employees, and have strategies in place to prevent burnout and employee turnover.

Transference and Countertransference in Supervisory Relationships

Transference can be as overt and disturbing as an attempt to create a romantic or sexual relationship with a supervisor or as subtle as wanting to please or compete with a supervisor who reminds the social worker of someone in his or her life outside the profession.

Countertransference is the set of irrational feelings, thoughts, or ideas of the supervisor toward the supervisee that may be acted out, repressed, or addressed in supervision, depending on the appropriateness of the situation. In a parallel process, transferential issues between the social worker and client may arise, as can similar issues between social worker and supervisor. Working with the powerful and sometimes confusing conflicts generated by the various forms of transference bring history, personal feelings, and ethical considerations together, making supervision a rich, challenging, and interesting process.

Professional Relationships, Values, and Ethics

Legal Issues and Client Rights

Liability for Social Workers

Concepts relating to liability for social workers are as follows:

- Clients can sue social workers for malpractice.
- The chain of liability extends from the individual worker to supervisory personnel to the director and then to the board of directors of a nonprofit agency.
- Most agencies carry malpractice insurance, which usually protects individual workers; however, workers may also carry personal liability and malpractice insurance.
- Supervisors can be named as parties in a malpractice suit as they share vicarious liability for the activities of their supervisees.

General Rights for Social Work Clients

General rights for social worker clients include:

- Confidentiality and privacy
- Informed consent
- Access to services (if service requirements cannot be met, a referral should be offered)
- Access to records (adequately protective but not onerously burdensome policies for client access to services should be developed and put in place)
- Participation in the development of treatment plans (client cooperation in the treatment process is essential to success)
- Options for alternative services/referrals (clients should always be offered options whenever they are available)
- Right to refuse services (clients have a right to refuse services that are not court ordered; ethical issues exist when involuntary treatment is provided, but mandates do not allow options other than referrals to other sources of the mandated service)
- Termination by the client (clients have a right to terminate services at any time and for any reason they deem adequate, except in certain court-ordered situations)

Right to Privacy

Every individual has a right to expect that personal information disclosed in a clinical setting, including data such as their address, telephone number, social security number, financial information, and health information will not be disclosed to others, and no preconditions need be fulfilled to claim this right. The 1974 Federal Privacy Act (PL 93-579) also stipulates that clients be informed of the following:

- When records about them are being maintained
- That they can access, correct, and copy these records
- That the records are to be used only for the purpose of obtaining absent written consent otherwise

Exceptions include:

- Need-to-know sharing with other agency employees
- Use for research if identifying information is omitted
- Release to the government for law enforcement purposes
- Responding to a subpoena
- In emergencies, where the health and safety of an individual is at risk

While the law applies only to agencies receiving federal funds, many state and local entities have adopted these standards.

Client's Right to Refuse Services

The right to refuse services rests with adults, so ordinarily an adult (or an emancipated minor who has been granted the rights of adulthood) can refuse any medication, treatment, counseling, or placement, although this is not always true in social work. Court orders override these rights, and if the court has declared a person is incompetent, this person's guardian makes the decisions. Additionally, if the court has ordered specific treatment, therapy, or placement, then the client must comply even against the client's wishes. Children, including adolescents, have no rights to refusal, but they should be consulted as much as possible, and their wishes should be respected and incorporated into the plan of care. For example, if a child does not want to be placed into a group home, then other living arrangements should be explored because forcing a child to do something often results in poor outcomes.

Confidentiality

HIPAA

In 1996 the federal government passed legislation providing privacy protection for personal health information. Known as **HIPAA** (Health Insurance Portability and Accountability Act), this act:

- Places privacy protections on personal health information and specifically limits the purposes for its use and the circumstances for its disclosure.
- Provides individuals with specific rights to access their records.
- Ensures that individuals will be notified about privacy practices. The act applies only to "covered entities," which are defined as health care providers (physicians and allied health care providers), clearinghouses for health care services, and health plans.

Review Video: What is HIPAA?
Visit mometrix.com/academy and enter code: 412009

Review Video: Ethics and Confidentiality in Counseling
Visit mometrix.com/academy and enter code: 250384

Policies Reflecting Expectation of Confidentiality

Organizational policies can reflect the **expectation of confidentiality** through the following:

- Records must be secured and locked.
- Policies should be in place that ensure that records are not left where unauthorized persons are able to read them.
- Computerized records should be secured with the same attention given to written records (hard copies).
- Agencies must provide spaces that permit private conversations so that conversations about clients can be held where they cannot be overheard.

Utilization of Informed Consent

Through **informed consent**, a client may provide consent for the worker to share information with family members, or with other professionals or agencies for purposes of referral. When the client provides this consent, he or she has reason to expect that shared information is in his or her best interest and designed to improve his or her situation.

Confidentiality for Social Workers vs. Lawyers or Clergy

Social work privilege does not have the same force as that of attorneys and clergy. Unlike clergy and attorneys, social workers may be compelled to testify in court under certain circumstances.

A social worker who is sued for malpractice may reveal information discussed by clients. The worker should aim to limit the discussion of the content of clinical discussions to those statements needed to support an effective defense.

NASW Code of Ethics

Ethical Principles

- **Service**: Social workers are responsible for providing help to individuals; finding solutions to social problems; and using their professional knowledge and skills in service of others, including unpaid volunteer efforts.
- **Social justice**: Social workers seek social change and access to information, services, and resources that improve the lives of those who are poor, unemployed, discriminated against, or suffering other social injustices. Social workers seek to provide these individuals with access to opportunities and decision-making, and to promote knowledge about social inequities and ethnic diversity within their profession and to the public.
- **Dignity and worth of the person**: Social workers remain aware of their responsibility to the individual and society as a whole. Social workers comprehend the need to resolve conflicts that arise between the individual and the society, and encourage autonomy in addressing needs and making changes.
- **Importance of human relationships**: Social workers recognize the importance of partnerships in serving others and strengthening relationships in the community.
- **Integrity**: Social workers always strive to maintain ethical standards and practice accordingly, and to apply these same ethical standards to the organizations that they serve.
- **Competence**: Social workers work within their area of competence and continually strive to improve their knowledge and skills and to contribute to the growth of the profession.

Social Workers' Ethical Responsibilities to Clients

1.01 Commitment to Clients

While a social worker's primary responsibility is to the welfare of the client, clients should be advised that the greater needs of society and legal requirements (such as reporting abuse or risks for harm to the self or others) may at times supersede the needs of any single client.

1.02 Self-Determination

Social workers recognize that clients have the right to self-determination and should actively support them as they identify their goals. This right to autonomy is limited only when it presents a risk to the client or others.

1.03 Informed Consent

- Social workers serve clients only in a professional capacity and provide informed consent with language understandable to the clients so that they clearly understand the risks, benefits, costs, durations, limits of service, and their right to ask questions and even refuse consent.
- Social workers provide information in a manner that is comprehensible to the client, using appropriate language and an interpreter/translator if necessary.
- Social workers protect the interests of those unable to provide informed consent and seek consent from appropriate third parties, ensuring that the third parties respect the interests of the clients and that all efforts are made to enhance the clients' abilities to consent.
- Social workers should provide detailed information about involuntary services, including the type of service and any rights the clients have regarding refusal of service.
- Social workers should inform clients about policies regarding the use of technology while providing services.

- Social workers using technology during the provision of services (such as intake screening or interviews) should obtain informed consent at the initial contact and should request identifiers (e.g., name and location) when using technology to communicate.
- Social workers should assess clients' intellectual, emotional, and physical suitability for technology that allows for electronic/remote services and their ability to give informed consent for such use. Social workers should ensure clients understand the right to refuse the use of technology and should be prepared to provide alternative forms of service.
- Social workers must ensure that informed consent is obtained for audio recordings, video recordings, or observations by a third party.
- Social workers should obtain informed consent from a client before carrying out an electronic search for information about the client unless the purpose is to protect the client or others from harm or for other critical professional reasons.

1.04 Competence

- Social workers should provide services only within the limits of their education and level of competence.
- Social workers should only utilize techniques and interventions for which they received training and adequate preparation.
- Social workers should ensure that emerging practices are safe for the client and exercise diligence through research and training even when standards for such practices are not yet established.
- Social workers must be competent in the use of technology and aware of potential challenges.
- Social workers must comply with all applicable laws and regulations regarding technology.

1.05 Cultural Competence

- Social workers should appreciate diverse cultures and understand their effects on behavior and society.
- Social workers must utilize knowledge of diverse cultures to guide practice, empower those who are marginalized, act against racial injustice and discrimination, and recognize personal privilege.
- Social workers must reflect on their own biases, recognize the knowledge clients have about their own cultures, and commit to continuous learning. Social workers must ensure that institutions exhibit cultural humility.
- Social workers must educate themselves about issues of social and cultural diversity and oppression related to race, ethnicity, national origin, color of skin, sexual identification and expression, age, marital status, political and religious affiliations, immigration status, and differences in abilities.
- Social workers must recognize potential cultural and socioeconomic barriers to the use of electronic technology and should assess issues that may impact delivery or access to services.

1.06 Conflicts of Interest

- Social workers must avoid conflicts of interest by remaining alert and exercising impartial judgement; informing clients of the possibility or existence of conflicts of interest; and taking steps to resolve any issues in the best interests of the clients, including terminating a professional relationship if necessary.
- Social workers must not exploit professional relationships for personal gain or interests of any kind.

- Social workers should avoid dual or multiple relationships with current or former clients that could pose a risk of client exploitation or harm, and should make efforts to protect clients and set appropriate boundaries if dual or multiple relationships are unavoidable.
- Social workers must clarify professional obligations when providing services to two or more individuals in a relationship, try to avoid or minimize conflicts of interest, and make the clients aware of any possible conflicts of interest and the role the social worker will take in those instances.
- Social workers should avoid communicating with clients for personal or non-work-related reasons using electronic media (social media, email, telephone, video, text messaging).
- Social workers must remain alert to the possible negative effects (boundary violations, dual relationships, client harm) that can result from posting personal information on social media.
- Social workers must understand that posting information about personal affiliations (race, ethnicity, national origin, color of skin, sexual identification and expression, age, marital status, political and religious affiliations, immigration status, and differences in abilities) on social media may negatively impact their ability to work with some clients.
- Social workers should not establish or accept social media relationships with clients because they could lead to boundary violations, dual relationships, and client harm.

1.07 Privacy and Confidentiality

- Social workers should respect clients' rights to privacy by not asking for unnecessary personal information and not sharing clients' personal information with others.
- Social workers may only divulge confidential information with the consent of the client or someone legally authorized to represent the client.
- Social workers must maintain the confidentiality of information obtained in a professional capacity unless disclosure is necessary to prevent harm to the client or others, and any such disclosure should be the minimum necessary and only that which is directly relevant.
- Social workers should advise clients of any necessary disclosure of confidential information in advance (if possible), whether with or without client consent.
- Social workers should discuss issues related to confidentiality, including limits and legally required disclosures, early in the relationship and as necessary.
- Social workers providing counseling services to families or groups of clients should discuss issues related to confidentiality, including agreements to respect confidentiality and avoid disclosure on social media without consent. Social workers must also advise clients that there is a risk that someone in the family or group may break these agreements and disclose confidential information.
- Social workers providing counseling services should advise clients of any relevant policies concerning the social worker's disclosure of confidential information among the members of the group.
- Social workers must avoid disclosure of confidential information to a third-party payer without consent of the client.
- Social workers should avoid any discussion of confidential information, electronically or personally, in any setting (elevator, hallway, restaurant, etc.) or situation in which privacy is not absolutely ensured.
- Social workers must try to lawfully protect the confidentiality of clients during legal proceedings. If ordered by the courts to disclose confidential information without client consent, and if that information may be harmful to the client, then the social worker should ask the court to withdraw the request for information, limit the order, or keep the records under seal to avoid public exposure.

- Social workers responding to media requests for information should protect the confidentiality of clients.
- Social workers should ensure the confidentiality of written and electronic records, ensure that records are stored securely, and ensure that the records are protected from unauthorized access.
- Social workers should ensure that electronic communications (email, texts, social media, cellphones) to clients or third parties are appropriately safeguarded (encryption, firewalls, and/or passwords).
- Social workers must have policies and procedures in place to notify clients of any breach of confidential information.
- Social workers must follow applicable laws and standards when notifying clients of unauthorized access to clients' records, electronic communication, or storage systems.
- Social workers must communicate to clients the policies regarding the use of electronic technology, including the use of search engines to obtain information about clients.
- Social workers should avoid searching electronically for information about clients unless professionally necessary and should, whenever possible, do so only with client consent.
- Social workers should not post any confidential or identifying information about clients on professional websites or social media.
- Social workers must dispose of client records in accordance with applicable laws and licensure, ensuring that clients' confidentiality is protected.
- Social workers must ensure that clients' confidentiality is protected in the event that a social worker terminates practice, becomes incapacitated, or dies.
- Social workers should avoid sharing any identifying information about clients in the course of teaching or training others.
- Social workers should avoid providing identifying information of clients to consultants unless the clients have given consent.
- Social workers should maintain the confidentiality of clients even after the clients have died.

1.08 Access to Records

- Social workers should allow clients reasonable access to their records, interpret for or consult with the client regarding records that may result in misunderstanding or harm, and limit access only if access may result in serious harm to the clients. If a client requests access to their records, then this request must be documented. If access to the records is not granted, then the rationale for withholding them must also be noted.
- Social workers should disclose policies regarding the use of technology to allow clients to access their records.
- Social workers must protect the confidentiality of individuals who are identified or discussed in clients' records when allowing clients access to those records.

1.09 Sexual Relationships

- Social workers must not engage in sexual activities of any kind with current clients, and they are also prohibited from maintaining sexual communications in person or through technology (consensual or forced) with them.
- Social workers should not engage in any type of sexual activity or sexual contact with relatives of clients or those with whom the clients have close relationships. Such conduct could pose potential harm to the client and negatively affect the social worker-client relationship. Also, the burden for setting appropriate boundaries lies with the social worker, not with the client or anyone else.

- Social workers should avoid engaging in any type of sexual activity or sexual contact with former clients. If the social worker feels that an exception is warranted, it is the social worker's responsibility to demonstrate that the former client has not been intentionally or unintentionally exploited, coerced, or harmed.
- Social workers should avoid providing clinical services to individuals with whom they have previously had a sexual relationship because of the potential for harm to the individuals and the difficulty in maintaining appropriate professional boundaries.

1.10 Physical Contact

Social workers should avoid physical contact with clients that may be misconstrued and/or cause harm to the clients (e.g., cradling, caressing). Social workers must ensure that all physical contact with clients is appropriate and that clear and socially sensitive boundaries are established.

1.11 Sexual Harassment

Social workers should not sexually harass clients by making sexual advances, solicitations, requests for sexual favors, or other forms of contact of a sexual nature (whether physical, electronic, verbal, or written).

1.12 Derogatory Language

Social workers should always communicate with respectful language and avoid any type of communication with derogatory language.

1.13 Payment for Services

- Social workers should set fair and reasonable fees that reflect the services provided and the clients' ability to pay.
- Social workers should avoid accepting bartering in lieu of fees for professional services because it may result in conflicts of interests, exploitation, or other inappropriate boundaries. Bartering is only appropriate if it is an accepted practice in the local community, is at the request of the client, and involves no coercion. The social worker must be able to demonstrate that agreeing to bartering is not detrimental to the clients and does not negatively affect the professional relationship.
- Social workers should not request payment of a private fee for services for which the client is already entitled.

1.14 Clients Who Lack Decision-Making Capacity

Social workers must ensure that the rights and interests of clients are safeguarded, especially with clients who are unable to make informed decisions.

1.15 Interruption of Services

Social workers should ensure that clients will have continuity of services in the event that the social worker becomes unavailable because of an inability to communicate electronically, relocation, disability, or death.

1.16 Referral for Services

- Social workers should refer clients to other professionals if they believe the knowledge and expertise of those professionals will better serve the needs of the clients.
- Social workers referring clients to other professionals should ensure that transfer is orderly and that all pertinent information is disclosed with clients' permission.
- Social workers may not give or receive payment for referring clients to other professionals if the social worker provided no professional services.

1.17 Termination of Services

- Social workers should end services to clients who are no longer in need of such services.
- Social workers should avoid abandoning clients and minimize the effects of doing so if it becomes necessary, ensuring that the clients will continue to receive needed services.
- Social workers who see clients on a fee-for-service basis may end services for nonpayment as long as the clients are not at risk of harm to self or others and the clients are aware of clinical and other consequences of nonpayment.
- Social workers should not end services with a client in order to pursue a different type of relationship with the client (sexual, social, financial).
- Social workers should make clients promptly aware of any future termination or interruption of services and assist them with transfers or referrals so that services can be continued.
- Social workers leaving employment should advise clients of the options for continuing services and discuss the risks and benefits of those options.

Social Workers' Ethical Responsibilities to Colleagues

2.01 Respect

- Social workers must treat colleagues with respect and fairly represent their qualifications, views, and obligations.
- Social workers should avoid unwarranted criticism of colleagues to clients or other professionals in any form, such as by making negative comments about their professional ability, race, ethnicity, national origin, color of skin, sexual identification and expression, age, marital status, political and religious affiliations, or immigration status.
- Social workers should strive to serve clients by cooperating with social work colleagues and other professionals.

2.02 Confidentiality

Social workers must recognize and protect the confidentiality of colleagues regarding information shared during a professional relationship, and should ensure that colleagues understand the social workers' role in safeguarding confidentiality and any possible exceptions.

2.03 Interdisciplinary Collaboration

- Social workers participating in interdisciplinary teams with established ethical obligations should draw on their viewpoints and experience to help make decisions that affect clients' wellbeing.
- Social workers who have ethical concerns about team decisions should try to resolve the conflicts or pursue other means to assure the clients' wellbeing.

2.04 Disputes Involving Colleagues

- Social workers must avoid exploiting the disputes of others, such as those between a colleague and their employer, to further their own careers.
- Social workers should avoid taking advantage of clients during any conflicts with colleagues or discussing such conflicts with clients.

2.05 Consultation

- Social workers should consult with and ask for advice from colleagues when doing so is beneficial to clients.
- Social workers should be knowledgeable about the expertise and competence of colleagues and consult only with those who are qualified to deal with the issue at hand.
- Social workers should avoid disclosing any unnecessary information about clients when consulting with colleagues.

2.06 Sexual Relationships

- Social workers in a position of authority should not engage in sexual activities or sexual contact of any kind with subordinates.
- Social workers who engage in sexual relationships with colleagues should ensure that there are no conflicts of interest and should transfer professional responsibilities as necessary to avoid conflicts of interest.

2.07 Sexual Harassment

Social workers must not sexually harass subordinates by making sexual advances; solicitations; requests for sexual favors; or physical, electronic, verbal, or written communications of a sexual nature.

2.08 Impairment of Colleagues

- Social workers who are aware of the impairment of a colleague related to personal, psychosocial, mental health, or substance abuse problems, and who recognize that the impairment is affecting the colleague's professional practice, should address those concerns directly with the colleague and help them to develop a plan of correction.
- Social workers should take the necessary steps to report a colleague's impairment through the appropriate channels (employer, NASW, licensing bodies, regulatory bodies, professional organizations) if the colleague has failed to address their impairment.

2.09 Incompetence of Colleagues

- Social workers who are aware of incompetence on the part of colleagues should address those concerns directly with the colleagues and assist them in developing a plan of correction.
- Social workers should take the appropriate steps to report a colleague's incompetence through the appropriate channels (employer, NASW, licensing bodies, regulatory bodies, professional organizations) if the colleague has failed to address their impairment.

2.10 Unethical Conduct of Colleagues

- Social workers should take necessary actions to prevent, expose, or correct any type of unethical conduct by colleagues, including technological misconduct.
- Social workers must be aware of policies and procedures (national, state, and local) established to deal with colleagues' unethical behavior, including those of an employer, the NASW, licensing bodies, regulatory bodies, and professional organizations.
- Social workers who are aware of the unethical behavior of colleagues should address this with the colleagues directly (if possible) if doing so may resolve the issue.

- Social workers should take the necessary and appropriate steps to report colleagues that have acted unethically through the appropriate channels (licensing bodies, regulatory bodies, NASW National Ethic Committee, and other professional ethics committees).
- Social workers should defend and help colleagues charged with unethical conduct if the colleagues are innocent.

Social Workers' Ethical Responsibilities in Practice Settings

3.01 Supervision and Consultation

- Social workers who serve as supervisors or consultants should have the necessary knowledge, skills, and competence to do so.
- Social workers who serve as supervisors or consultants should establish clear boundaries that are appropriate and culturally sensitive.
- Social workers who serve as supervisors should avoid dual or multiple relationships (including those involving social media) with those being supervised in order to avoid exploitation or possible harm.
- Social workers who serve as supervisors should evaluate supervisees fairly and respectfully.

3.02 Education and Training

- Social workers, in their roles as educators, field instructors, or trainers, should provide the most current professional information within their own areas of knowledge and competence.
- Social workers, in their roles as educators, field instructors, or trainers, should evaluate students fairly and respectfully.
- Social workers, in their roles as educators, field instructors, or trainers, should ensure clients are aware that services are provided by students.
- Social workers, in their roles as educators, field instructors, or trainers, should avoid dual or multiple relationships (including those involving social media) with students in order to avoid exploitation or possible harm, and should establish clear boundaries that are appropriate and culturally sensitive.

3.03 Performance Evaluation

Social workers responsible for the supervision of others should evaluate their performance fairly based on established, stated criteria.

3.04 Client Records

- Social workers should ensure that all documentation (paper and electronic) accurately describes the services provided.
- Social workers should ensure that documentation is timely and sufficient so that clients receive necessary current and future services.
- Social workers should document events in a manner that protects clients' privacy while providing information that is necessary for the delivery of services.
- Social workers should store records after services are terminated in the manner and for the time period required by laws, agency policies, or contractual agreements.

3.05 Billing

Social workers should have accurate billing practices that identify who provide the services being charged and the extent of those services.

3.06 Client Transfer

- Social workers should carefully consider whether to accept clients who request services but are already receiving services from other providers. They should ascertain the nature of the clients' current relationship with other providers and assess the risks and benefits of changing service providers.
- Social workers providing services to clients who had previous service providers should discuss with the clients whether consultation with the previous provider(s) is warranted.

3.07 Administration

- Social workers should advocate for adequate internal and external resources to best serve the needs of their clients.
- Social workers should advocate for fair and nondiscriminatory resource allocation procedures, applying appropriate and consistent principles even when all clients' needs cannot be met.
- Social workers in administrative positions should develop policies to ensure there are adequate resources for supervision of staff.
- Social workers in administrative positions should develop policies to ensure their working environment is in compliance with the NASW Code of Ethics and should eliminate any conditions that may negatively impact compliance with the Code.

3.08 Continuing Education and Staff Development

Social worker supervisors and administrators should ensure continuing education and staff development to address current and emerging knowledge pertaining to social work and ethics for all of the staff working under them.

3.09 Commitments to Employers

- Social workers should honor the commitments they have made to their employers and employing agencies.
- Social workers should take steps to improve policies and procedures of employing agencies.
- Social workers should make an effort to ensure that employers are aware of the ethical obligations that the social workers have to the NASW Code of Ethics and the implications these obligations have for practice.
- Social workers should not allow any policy, regulation, or orders from an employing organization interfere with their ethical practice of social work. They should ensure that the employing agencies' practices are consistent with the Code of Ethics.
- Social workers should ensure that employing organizations practice nondiscriminatory work assignments, policies, and procedures.
- Social workers should only work or assign students to employing organizations that treat personnel fairly.
- Social workers should exercise care with employing organizations' resources, save funds when possible, and avoid any misuse or misappropriation of funds.

3.10 Labor-Management Disputes

- Social workers may participate in labor unions, including organizing and forming unions, in order to better provide for clients.
- Social workers who are involved in labor-management disputes must ensure their actions are guided by the values, principles, and ethics of the profession and should consider the impact their actions may have on clients.

Social Workers' Ethical Responsibilities as Professionals

4.01 Competence

- Social workers should accept assignment or employment only in areas for which they have competence or plan to acquire competence.
- Social workers should always plan to be proficient in all practice, remain current in emerging knowledge, critically review professional literature, and participate in continuing education regarding social work practice and ethics.
- Social workers should utilize recognized knowledge and ethics in the field of social work as the basis for practice.

4.02 Discrimination

Social workers must not support or practice any type of discrimination based on race, ethnicity, national origin, sexual identification and expression, political and religious affiliations, immigration status, and differences in abilities.

4.03 Private Conduct

Social workers' private conduct should not interfere with their ability to carry out their professional duties.

4.04 Dishonesty, fraud, and deception

Social workers should not engage in or condone any dishonest, fraudulent, or deceptive practices.

4.05 Impairment

- Social workers should avoid letting their personal, legal, psychosocial, mental health, or substance abuse problems interfere with their fulfillment of professional responsibilities.
- Social workers whose personal, legal, psychosocial, mental health, or substance abuse problems interfere with their fulfillment of professional responsibilities should seek professional help and take corrective action (reduce workload, terminate their practice, or take any necessary actions) to protect the interests of clients and other interested parties.

4.06 Misrepresentation

- Social workers should keep statements and actions carried out as private individuals separate from what they do as social workers representing the profession, professional organization, or place of employment.
- Social workers should take care when representing a professional social work organization to reflect the official and authorized positions of the organization.
- Social workers should ensure that any representations to others (clients, agencies, public) regarding professional qualifications, accomplishments, credentials, and services are accurate. Social workers should claim only those professional credentials to which they are entitled and should correct any misunderstandings related to their credentials.

4.07 Solicitations

- Social workers should not attempt to solicit potential clients who may be vulnerable and easily influenced, manipulated, or coerced.
- Social workers should not attempt to solicit testimonials or endorsements from current clients or others who may be vulnerable and easily influenced.

4.08 Acknowledging Credit

- Social workers should take credit (including authorship) only for work they are personally responsible for or that they contributed to.
- Social workers should be open about the work and contributions of others.

Social Workers' Ethical Responsibilities to the Profession

5.01 Integrity of the Profession

- Social workers should strive to maintain, refine, and advocate for high practice standards.
- Social workers should take steps to advance and spread the social work profession and its values, ethics, and knowledge through study, research, discussion, and appropriate criticism.
- Social workers should lend their time and expertise to support activities, such as teaching, researching, consulting, providing testimony, giving presentations, and participating in professional organizations that promote respect for the social work profession.
- Social workers should freely share their knowledge and contribute to social work literature to broaden and spread the knowledge base of the profession.
- Social workers should actively prevent social work practice that is unauthorized or unqualified.

5.02 Evaluation and Research

- Social workers should oversee and evaluate policies, programs, and interventions.
- Social workers should further efforts to contribute to knowledge.
- Social workers should carefully evaluate emerging knowledge and apply evidence derived from evaluation and research to their practice.
- Social workers must consider the ramifications of their evaluation and research, and should ensure guidelines are followed to consult with institutional review boards and protect participants in research.
- Social workers should obtain voluntary and written informed consent that covers specific details about a project, including risk and benefits, from participants for their evaluation and research. They should also avoid any type of coercion or implied penalty for declining to participate.
- Social workers should ensure that participants utilizing technology in evaluation and research give informed consent from any such use, are able to use the technology, and have an alternative available.
- Social workers who engage in evaluation and research with participants who are unable to give informed consent should provide explanations proportional to their understanding and seek informed consent from an appropriate proxy.
- Social workers should avoid carrying out evaluation and research that does not include consent, such as through observations or archival research, unless no acceptable alternative is available and the research can be justified through diligent review.
- Social workers should ensure that any participants in evaluation and research are aware of their right to withdraw at any time without suffering any negative consequences.
- Social workers should ensure that any participants in evaluation and research are provided with appropriate supportive service.
- Social workers should ensure that any participants in evaluation and research have protection from any type of distress or danger.
- Social workers who are evaluating services should share collected information only with those who have a legitimate professional interest.

- Social workers should ensure that the anonymity and confidentiality of any participants in evaluation and research are protected and that participants are aware of limits to confidentiality, measures taken to ensure confidentiality, and plans for destruction of records with research data.
- Social workers should ensure that the identification of participants in evaluation and research is omitted from records unless participants have consented to disclosure.
- Social workers should ensure that all evaluation and research findings are accurately reported in published data, should correct any errors, and should avoid any falsifications or fabrications.
- Social workers who engage in evaluation and research should avoid any conflicts or dual relationships with participants and should alert participants to the possibility of conflicts of interest and strive to resolve any such issues.
- Social workers should strive to educate themselves and others about responsible research practices.

Social Workers' Ethical Responsibilities to the Broader Society

6.01 Social Welfare

Social workers should advocate for society's general welfare through betterment efforts ranging from community to international levels and by encouraging the development of all individuals and environments. Social workers should promote the improvement of living conditions so that people have access to basic needs; values (socioeconomic, political, and cultural); and institutions that support social justice.

6.02 Public Participation

Social workers should encourage public participation in the development of social policies and institutions.

6.03 Public Emergencies

Social workers should, during public emergencies, be prepared to provide any appropriate professional services needed.

6.04 Social and Political Action

- Social workers should actively engage in social and political actions to spread the access that people have to the elements of society that allow them to meet basic needs (resources, jobs, services, opportunities). Social workers should be cognizant of how politics affect practice and should actively promote policies that improve the lives of people, allowing them to meet basic needs and promoting social justice.
- Social workers should take actions to ensure that all people have access to expanded choices and opportunities, especially those who are vulnerable or otherwise disadvantaged or oppressed and easily exploited.
- Social workers should highlight the importance of social and cultural diversity and promote policies and practices that increase respect for this diversity and expand knowledge about culture. Social workers should support policies and programs that demonstrate cultural competence and equality and protect social justice.
- Social workers should take steps to fight against the discrimination and exploitation of any person, group, or class because of personal, legal, psychosocial, mental health, or substance abuse problems.

Record-Keeping and Documentation

Principles of Documentation and Record Management

All records of social work should be considered legal documents and stored in locked cabinets (if paper) or secured electronically (if digital). Records should never be placed so that unauthorized individuals can gain access. Records should be organized according to established guidelines so that information is easily accessible. **Principles of documentation** include the following:

- Avoid the use of jargon and slang
- Ensure that each page of the record contains the client's name to ensure it is in the correct record
- Document all important information so that other case workers could assume care of the client
- Leave no lines blank in documents and mark errors by drawing one line through the text and initialing the entry (in paper documenting)
- Report the source of all information
- Avoid abbreviations that are not approved
- Spell check electronic entries
- Describe observations (flat affect, lethargic, monotone) and avoid judgment and diagnoses (depressed)
- Use appropriate coding and descriptions for billing and reporting purposes

Elements of Social Worker's Client Records

The elements of a social worker's client records include:

- **Face page**: Demographic information
- **Family tree**: Information about members, such as profession and history of drug abuse
- **Eco map**: Diagram of resources, such as neighbors, community, friends, extended family
- **Psychological report**
- **Court orders**: Such as termination of parental rights (TPR)
- **Education records**: Schools attended, grades, disciplinary actions, attendance
- List of **goals** and **plan of care**
- **Monthly progress reports**: From meetings with child and foster parent or caregiver
- **Family support team (FST) reports**: From meeting with interested parties to evaluate child's progress in meeting goals (usually submitted to the court)
- **Permanency plan review team reports**: From meeting (usually every 6 months) with all interested parties (parents, foster parents, CASA workers, social workers, supervisor etc.) to determine progress and the need for any modification in the plan (usually submitted to court)
- Additional reports, such as **CASA (court appointed special advocate) reports**
- **Financial records**: Such as social security or death benefits
- **Discharge summary**

Formal Records

Formal records created by social workers may include the following:

Type of Record	Details Included
Proposals	A proposal is a formal request to develop a project, buy equipment, or suggest a course of action, such as a solution to a problem. An informal proposal may be in the form of a letter. A grant proposal usually requires a specific format explaining the need and the plan for use of the grant and may be quite detailed.
Letters	A letter is a formal written or typed form of communication that is sent by mail to another individual, such as letters requesting information or letters of recommendation.
Brochures and pamphlets	Social workers may develop educational brochures and pamphlets about services or areas of concern (such as drug abuse).
Reports	Social workers may do various types of reports, including the assessment report, reports to the court, summary reports, and discharge reports. The reports often follow a prescribed format.
Evaluations	Social workers may carry out evaluations as part of progress reports for clients and may evaluate programs for effectiveness. Social workers may also carry out supervisory evaluations of other staff members.

Case Recording and Documentation Practices

Different agencies have different requirements and processes for **case recordings** used in supervision and evaluation. The traditional method was audio recordings, but with technological advances, video recording has become completely accessible. Clients should sign informed consent and confidentiality forms allowing supervisors to view their sessions for training purposes, and there should be policies in place for video storage methods, the length of time videos are kept, how and when they will be destroyed, and other considerations affecting confidentiality.

Importance of Filing in Record-Keeping

Keeping correspondence in paper or digital files is another important part of record-keeping and can impact clients' lives as well as the credibility of the agency. **Files** also serve an important purpose in the current employment environment where social workers may change agencies and need to come rapidly to a general overview of a client's past, perhaps receiving service through several social workers over a period of years. Letters communicating with other agencies can help the new social worker on the scene form an impression of the kind of help clients have received from that agency, even when case workers have come and gone.

Record-Keeping Requirements

Each agency has its own particular **reporting and record-keeping requirements**, which will vary by location, population served, funding bodies, governmental oversight, boards of committees, and even technological considerations. In general, issues of confidentiality and informed consent will be similar across agencies, and the age and intellectual capacity of clients will also influence reporting requirements. Social workers whose schedules take them out into communities may keep a work journal during the day, reporting their activities to their agency upon returning to the office. In the case of journaling, the social worker should protect the client's confidentiality by omitting identifying information.

Professional Development and the Use of Self

Core Social Work Values

According to the NASW, the core social work values are as follows:

- Service
- Social justice
- Dignity and worth of the person
- Importance of human relationships
- Integrity
- Competence

Core Social Work Goals

Core social work goals held by the major social work theorists are to help clients:

- Improve social functioning
- Resolve problems
- Achieve desired change
- Meet self-defined goals

Social Work Roles

Social workers may serve in many roles, including the following:

Role	Responsibilities
Administrator	Evaluating and developing policies and managing programs
Advocate	Defending, representing, and supporting vulnerable clients
Broker	Providing resource and service linkages to individuals in need
Case manager	Connecting, coordinating, and monitoring client services
Counselor	Exploring, treating, and resolving client, family, or group issues and problems
Educator and teacher	Researching and providing educational information, organizing and leading classes, teaching knowledge, skills, and behaviors that facilitate successful coping, growth, and relationships
Policy maker or lobbyist	Working to identify, understand, and resolve problems in local communities or in society as a whole by garnering support from key interest groups to marshal and wield influence for positive and necessary change

Stages of Professional Development

Professional development is supported by education, conferences, and practice that help increase and refine skills and knowledge of the field. Activities of professional development include mentoring and coaching, supervision, consultation, assistance with technical matters, and interdisciplinary collaboration with other communities of care.

The **steps of professional development** begin with the orientation process. Social workers tend to work autonomously but with regular supervision. Teamwork follows, with workers moving from independent operations to working as part of a group. Later career development includes specialization and then acting as a mentor or supervisor oneself.

Performance Appraisal of Professional Social Workers

Performance appraisals may vary from self-assessment, to narrative assessment, to checklists, and assessments based on outcomes related to a list of goals. Despite the varied forms of appraisal, basic skills are almost always evaluated:

Skill Evaluated	Focuses of Evaluation
Work-associated skills	The ability to carry out the processes and procedures of social work, including applying appropriate interventions and dealing effectively with client problems and concerns.
Organizational skills	The ability to manage time effectively and carry out job responsibilities in a timely and efficient manner.
Leadership and management skills	The ability to serve as a model for others, to influence other professionals, and to lead and supervise effectively.
Cultural competence	An awareness of different cultures (including customs and religions) and understanding of cultural sensitivity when dealing with others.
Communication skills	The ability to document and code correctly, and to communicate effectively with co-workers and clients. Ability to use conflict resolution strategies and to accommodate various points of view.

Time Management Approaches

Approaches that the social worker can utilize for time management include the following:

- **Planning ahead**: Maintaining a master schedule that lists visits and meetings
- Keeping **schedule** up to date on a daily basis
- **Utilizing color coding**: Using colored stickers or pens to indicate different needs, such as red stickers for those things that require urgent attention
- **Scheduling a time to return calls**: Making calls first thing in the morning so that any alterations needed in the schedule can be made promptly
- Utilizing time management or case management **software**
- Making appropriate **referrals**
- Preparing **reports** (such as those submitted to the court) in advance, avoiding last minute rush
- Making **to-do lists** or **action plans**
- Creating **templates** for frequently used forms and letters
- **Filing** immediately and throwing out unnecessary paperwork
- Utilizing **GPS and mapping software** to plan routes of visits
- **Prioritizing** work
- Avoiding all **procrastination**

Social Worker Self-Care

Burnout and Secondary Trauma

Burnout, a response to ongoing stress, is a problem pervasive in social work. Social workers often have excessive workloads and work long hours, often including unwanted overtime because of inadequate staffing. Social workers may feel that they have little control over their work and do not receive sufficient reward or support. They may also feel that social workers are often treated unfairly or are victims of bullying in the workplace. Stress tends to build up over time, interfering with the individual's ability to concentrate and to carry out duties effectively. Additionally, dealing with clients' trauma may lead to **secondary trauma** with signs similar to PTSD: nightmares, insomnia, or anxiety, which increase the risk of burnout. Stages of stress leading to burnout include:

1. Fight or flight response: Withdrawal, discord
2. Emotional reaction: Anger, shock, surprise
3. Negative thinking: Despair, anger, depression, anxiety
4. Physical reaction: Headaches, GI upset, backache
5. No change in stressor or person: Increased stress
6. Burnout

Social workers may need to negotiate a smaller workload, utilize time management strategies, take small periodic breaks, and participate in stress management programs.

Compassion Fatigue

Compassion fatigue can occur when people overly identify with the pain and suffering of others and begin to exhibit signs of stress as a result. These people are often empathetic, tend to place the needs of others above their own, and are motivated by the need to help others. Indications include:

- Blaming others and complaining excessively
- Isolating oneself from others and having trouble concentrating
- Exhibiting compulsive activities (gambling, drinking)
- Having nightmares, sleeping poorly, and exhibiting a change in appetite
- Exhibiting sadness or apathy
- Denying any problems and having high expectations of self and others
- Having trouble concentrating
- Questioning spiritual beliefs, losing faith
- Exhibiting stress disorders: tachycardia, headaches, insomnia, pain

Social workers who exhibit compassion fatigue may need to take a break from work in order to recover some sense of self and may benefit from stress management programs, cognitive behavioral therapy, relaxation and visualization exercises, and physical exercise.

Masters Practice Test #1

Want to take this practice test in an online interactive format?
Check out the bonus page, which includes interactive practice questions and much more: **https://www.mometrix.com/bonus948/swmasters**

SCAN HERE

1. A social worker has been called to conduct a mental status exam (MSE) with an 86-year-old elderly man who is suspected of having early symptoms of dementia. At one point the social worker asks him to interpret the idiom, "People who live in glass houses shouldn't throw stones." He responds, "Someone living in a glass house has to be careful, because stones can break glass." This response represents an example of:

a. formal operational thought.
b. pre-operational thought.
c. sensorimotor interpretation.
d. concrete operational thought.

2. The human and development and behavior theorist most closely associated with Functionalism is:

a. John B. Watson
b. William James
c. Alfred Adler
d. Lev Vygotsky

3. The theorist in human development and behavior who is most focused on moral development is:

a. Lawrence Kohlberg.
b. Margaret Mahler.
c. Carol Gilligan.
d. John Bowlby.

4. A key difference between the theorists Wilhelm Wundt and William James regarding cognitive and emotional responses to experiences is:

a. James felt cognitive processing precedes emotions, while Wundt felt that emotions emerge prior to cognitive understanding.
b. James felt emotional reactions precede cognitive processing, while Wundt felt that cognitive processing precedes emotional reactions.
c. James felt that cognitive processing and emotions occur simultaneously, while Wundt felt emotions emerge before cognitive processing.
d. James felt that cognitive processing precedes emotions, while Wundt felt that cognitive processing and emotions occur simultaneously.

5. Sigmund Freud proposed the concepts of *preconscious* and *unconscious* to describe thoughts, feelings and ideas that are outside of conscious awareness but that nevertheless influence behavior and thinking. The primary difference between preconscious and unconscious thought is:

a. unconscious thoughts can never be brought to conscious awareness, while preconscious thoughts can only be brought to awareness with great difficulty.
b. preconscious thoughts can never be brought to conscious awareness, while unconscious thoughts can be brought to awareness only with great difficulty.
c. unconscious thoughts can be brought to awareness relatively easily, while preconscious thoughts are much more difficult to bring to awareness.
d. preconscious thoughts can be brought to awareness relatively easily, while unconscious thoughts are much more difficult to bring to awareness.

6. An 11-year-old boy is seen in clinic for multiple episodes of stealing behavior, exclusively involving the theft of inexpensive toys from a local store. From the perspective of Freud's structure of personality, describe the driving personality force in this behavior and the MOST immediately effective intervention.

a. The driving force is the Superego, and the most effective intervention would be an appeal to the child's sense of empathy for the needs of the store's owner
b. The driving force is the Ego, and the most effective intervention would be to discuss acceptable ways to meet the desire for toys
c. The driving force is the Id, and the most effective intervention would be to cite the negative consequences of the behavior
d. The driving force is the Life Instinct, and the most effective intervention would be to examine the role of altruism in proper behavior

7. A 46-year-old woman is referred for treatment for nicotine and alcohol addiction. She is also some 150 pounds overweight. The client claims to "like smoking" with no desire to quit, denies the extent of her alcoholism, and suggests that she doesn't "really eat very much." From a Freudian perspective, the client may have a fixation in which of the following stages of Freud's five stages of psychosexual development?

a. Latency Period
b. Phallic Stage
c. Anal Stage
d. Oral Stage

8. A couple comes to see a social worker. Married just two years, they're having difficulty adjusting. He's the youngest in his family and she's the oldest, which seems at the root of some of their problems. For example, she feels he's being irresponsible, and he feels she's being harsh and uncaring of his situation. Specifically, he has been out of work for several months, and she's working a marginal, late-night waitressing job just to make ends meet. She's tired and upset, and wants him to take any of a number of jobs he has passed up. He's pushing for something even better than any in his past. To make matters worse, he's been making troubling purchases "just for fun," which have caused more financial burden. From an Adlerian perspective, which of the following would BEST explain their situation?

a. Needs hierarchy and separation-individuation
b. Ego vs Superego conflicts
c. Birth order and guiding fiction
d. Inferiority vs superiority

9. An 8-year-old girl is brought in by referral from a school counselor. The referral indicates the child is inordinately afraid of being outdoors, refusing recess periods and other normal play experiences. Accompanied by her mother, she seems quite shy and reserved. During the child's intake interview, the mother repeatedly interrupts questions about the child's various fears. Comments such as, "Well, of course she won't want to be on the playground! It's a dangerous place!" frequently emerge, along with voiced concerns about physical activity ("she could fall"), being outside on the sidewalk with friends ("a car could come by and hit them"), etc. Noting the mother's marked overprotective posture, the social worker draws upon which of the following theorists in considering a possible etiology of the problem?

a. B. F. Skinner
b. Ivan Pavlov
c. Jean Piaget
d. John B. Watson

10. A man comes in to see a social worker about a compulsion that is troubling him. Whenever someone brings up something very serious (a family death, grave illness, loss of a crucial job, or other major misfortune) he finds himself compelled to resort to humor to minimize the intense feelings involved. This has offended many people. During exploration of the problem, it is learned that his father was violently intolerant of any expression or display of negative emotion. Drawing upon Pavlovian theory, the client's compulsion can best be described as a/an:

a. unconditioned stimulus.
b. unconditioned response.
c. conditioned stimulus.
d. conditioned response.

11. When evaluating a 16-year-old girl's depression a social worker discovers that she's distressed, in part, because she has never learned to drive. Consequently, she's passed up occasional babysitting jobs, social events, and other activities. She feels inferior to others. Pointing this out to the parents, her father states, "She just can't learn. I've taken her driving and shown her what to do many times, but she isn't able to cut it." The social worker recommends enrollment in a professional driving class, but the father resists, saying, "There's nothing some driving instructor knows that I can't teach her." To overcome his resistance the social worker notes the unique driving tools available to an instructor and explain the concept of:

a. behavior modification.
b. interactive scaffolding.
c. defense mechanisms.
d. anaclitic depression.

12. An older woman who has recently lost her husband and been placed in a long-term nursing care facility because of impaired mobility is oppositional and refuses to participate in activities or eat scheduled meals, complaining that the staff members are "incompetent and rude" and that no one cares about what she wants. The woman is increasingly demanding to the point that staff members are avoiding her. Which action is most appropriate for the social worker to do FIRST?

a. Counsel the staff members on methods of dealing with the woman
b. Listen actively to the woman's complaints
c. Advise the woman that her behavior is inappropriate
d. Help the patient to devise a personal schedule of activities

13. A hospital social worker is assigned to work with families in an intensive care unit. A husband was recently told that his wife is terminally ill. In speaking with him, the social worker attempt to discuss his feelings about the impending loss of his wife and how he and his family are coping. However, the social worker finds the conversation persistently returning to recent medical tests, current physical indicators, and potential changes in her medications. This is an example of which of the following defense mechanisms?

a. Projection
b. Compensation
c. Intellectualization
d. Rationalization

14. A 32-year-old single woman comes to see a social worker about depression. The worker notices that she wears an excessive amount of makeup, dresses in teen-style attire, wears her hair in a faddish fashion, and uses a mixture of old and new era teen terms and language. As they talk, she narrates activities dominated by associations at teen and young adult clubs and haunts, and describes attempted relationships with individuals much younger than herself. When the social worker asks about peer relationships, she indicates that she avoids those her age as she does not want to become "old before her time," and sees herself as much more youthful that others her age. The defense mechanism she employs is BEST described as:

a. avoidance.
b. fixation.
c. devaluation.
d. affiliation.

15. A social worker is counseling a man at a walk-in community clinic. He had moved in with his girlfriend, but was recently evicted from her home. His way to work was by riding with her, and he now is unsure how to keep his job given the loss of transportation. This has left him with no stable living situation and in danger of unemployment. He has no family or close friends in the area. Emotionally, however, he is preoccupied with the loss of his relationship and the security and affection he found through it, which is all he wants to talk about. According to the theorist Abraham Maslow, the BEST response to this situation is to:

a. go where the client wants to be, and work on his feelings about the relationship loss.
b. refuse to talk about relationship issues until immediate needs regarding housing, transportation, and employment are met.
c. permit some discussion on feelings of loss, but keep the focus on his immediate housing, transportation, and employment needs.
d. explain to him that his needs are beyond what can be offered and refer him to a shelter program.

16. A 38-year-old man is being seen in an STI (sexually transmitted infections) clinic for treatment of chlamydia. The social worker has been called to discuss his sexual history with a focus on safe-sex practices, particularly while being treated. The social worker learns that he has a history of short-term sexual relationships with women, with many involving "one-night" encounters. He also admits to occasionally paying for sexual favors. According to the ego psychology theorist Erik Erikson, this client is struggling with mastery of which of the following stages of personality development?

a. Stage 1: Trust vs. Mistrust
b. Stage 5: Identity vs. Identify Diffusion
c. Stage 6: Intimacy vs. Isolation
d. Stage 8: Integrity vs. Despair

17. A 28-year-old woman comes to see you with complaints about rejection by her new boyfriend. They've been dating for about 6 weeks, and she notes that he's just no longer being as attentive as he was. She wants to know what to do to "win him back." Upon further inquiry the social worker learn that she's experienced this in all her prior dating relationships. The social worker further learn that she calls, texts, drops by, and otherwise attempts to stay in contact throughout every day. She voices great fear that he will soon leave her "like the others." As she talks, high lability is noted in her emotions, ranging from fear and anxiety to intense anger. She also uses frequent criticism of herself, suggesting she is "not worth" having a relationship with, etc. The social worker quickly recognizes symptoms of likely borderline personality disorder. In considering a treatment approach, the social worker draws upon Margaret Mahler's work, which posits that this disorder likely occurs from problematic experiences during:

a. normal autism phase.
b. symbiosis phase.
c. differentiation (hatching) phase.
d. rapprochement phase.

18. A normally well-behaved 15-year-old girl is being seen for her recent onset of conflict and behavior problems. The parents are overwhelmed and in need of direction. They have used a variety of behavioral modification techniques (e.g., lectures, restrictions, grounding, loss of privileges) without success. The behavior has become so problematic that it has impeded the father's normal overseas travel for work. With further inquiry, the social worker learns that the father's employment has taken him away for extensive periods in the child's life, but that she now has his nearly undivided attention. Drawing upon the operant conditioning work of B.F. Skinner, the social worker identifies the problem as one of:

a. positive reinforcement.
b. negative reinforcement.
c. punishment.
d. extinction.

19. The difference between Ivan Pavlov's conditioning and B.F. Skinner's operant conditioning is:

a. Pavlovian conditioning deals with the modification of voluntary behavior via consequences, while Skinner's operant conditioning produces behavior under new antecedent conditions.
b. Skinner's operant conditioning deals with the modification of voluntary behavior via consequences, while Pavlovian conditioning produces behavior under new antecedent conditions.
c. Pavlovian conditioning deals exclusively with involuntary bodily functions, while Skinner's operant conditioning deals solely with voluntary behaviors.
d. Skinner's operant conditioning deals exclusively with involuntary bodily functions, while Pavlovian conditioning deals solely with voluntary behaviors.

20. A couple is receiving counseling to overcome identified obstacles and increase marital satisfaction. In the course of several visits, the social worker becomes aware that the husband often speaks of his "duty" to his family and his obligation to "do right by them." Using Lawrence Kohlberg's multistage model of moral development, the social worker identifies the husband's level to be:

a. Level 1: Stage 2.
b. Level 2: Stage 4.
c. Level 3: Stage 5.
d. Level 3: Stage 6.

21. When the social worker is assessing a one-year-old's attachment to the child's mother, the mother and child are placed in a room with a one-way mirror so the interactions can be observed. The mother plays with the child for a few minutes and then leaves the room, and the child responds by crying, a typical reaction. When the mother then returns to the room, which FIRST action by the child suggests the child is securely attached to the mother?

a. The child continues crying and resists contact with the mother
b. The child hugs the mother and then calms
c. The child acts ambivalently toward the mother
d. The child clings to the mother and resists letting go

22. The social worker is working with a group of women who are substance abusers. The women come from a variety of ethnic and social groups and have little interaction. During sessions with the group, if the social worker is applying feminist theory, which of the following would the social worker stress?

a. The differences among the women
b. The individual functional abilities
c. The women's position in patriarchal society
d. The commonalities among the women

23. During what period of child development would evidence of childhood psychopathology most likely become apparent?

a. Physical development
b. Cognitive/intellectual development
c. Sexual development
d. Language development

24. Failure of an infant to crawl by which of the following ages would be cause for concern?

a. 6 months
b. 9 months
c. 12 months
d. None of the above

25. A 10-year-old girl is brought in by her parents for evaluation because she has unexpectedly experienced menarche. They are concerned about possible sexual abuse, though they acknowledge that no other symptoms are present. The FIRST and most appropriate social work response would be to:

a. refer the child to a qualified pediatrician for examination.
b. contact local child abuse authorities and make a suspected abuse referral.
c. interview the child immediately for risks of sexual abuse.
d. reassure the parents that this is not unexpected for the child's age.

26. The term *sandwich generation* refers to:

a. the prevalence of fast-food consumption in the current era.
b. the loss of whole family–present dinner time meals in the home.
c. the pressure of couples still rearing children while being required to care for aging parents.
d. the pressure between health problems of aging and rising retirement age requirements.

27. A school counselor is seeing an 8-year-old girl who has symptoms suggestive of reactive attachment disorder (aversion to accepting comfort and affection, even from familiar adults, particularly when distressed), which is strongly correlated with severe abuse and/or neglect. There is no evidence of sexual abuse, but ample evidence of excessive punishment, emotional abuse, and significant neglect. From social work training, the social worker is aware that the MOST likely perpetrator of such abuse of a child this age would be:

a. the father.
b. the mother.
c. older siblings.
d. another adult relative.

28. A home health referral indicates that an elderly client's caregiving needs are not fully met by the live-in caregiving son and daughter-in-law. The client is constantly left in a windowless back bedroom with no television or radio, and virtually never brought out. There are also signs of skin breakdown, isolation-induced depression, and questionable nourishment, all of which were addressed by the referring nurse. The caregivers now openly acknowledge they are not able (or willing) to meet the client's needs, so they openly support placement. However, they emphasize that they have given up employment to provide care, are living on the client's retirement funds, and note that the home (which could be sold to pay for care) has been left to them in a will. Consequently, they are unwilling to make the changes required for placement. The FIRST social work response should be to:

a. accept that the caregiver's situation cannot be changed at this time.
b. refer them to a caregiver education seminar coming up in 2 months.
c. arrange a prompt extended family meeting to explore options.
d. contact the local Adult Protective Services to report suspected abuse.

29. The social worker is conducting a home evaluation of a client with two children. One child is 8 years old and doing well in school, but the other child is 6 years old and has autism spectrum disorder. This child is nonverbal and cognitively impaired, and needs almost constant attention. The client admits to being overwhelmed at times and feeling like running away. Based on role theory, how would the social worker describe the client's situation?

a. Role set
b. Role strain
c. Role conflict
d. Role exit

30. A husband finds his wife is drinking too much. She often apologizes and indicates she'd like to get help, though she refuses to call and make an appointment. Eventually he calls for her, and sets up an appointment with the social worker. In exploring her drinking, the social worker learns that he does most of the shopping for groceries, and for the alcoholic beverages brought into the home. He reveals that he purchases the alcohol to keep peace, and because he knows she would suffer with symptoms of delirium tremens if she was left without any access to alcohol. Worried for the children, he would at times call into work claiming to be sick when he knew she was having a particularly bad drinking binge. His behavior is BEST described as:

a. addictive.
b. codependent.
c. manipulative.
d. maladaptive.

31. A hospital social worker has been called to evaluate a patient who has been dealing with a diagnosis of terminal cancer. Recently he came to his physician and offered him a considerable sum of money to pursue an unorthodox, unproven treatment. The physician tried to explain the problems with such treatment, but the patient remained insistent, and even accused the physician of being unwilling to seek a cure in deference to continuing to bill his insurance for other fruitless procedures and treatments. Deeply disturbed, the physician referred the patient to the social worker. After speaking with the client and confirming the above, the social worker recognized the symptoms as characteristic of:

a. a psychotic break.
b. chemotherapy toxicity.
c. grief bargaining.
d. acute denial.

32. The social worker has two 10-year-old clients from similar traumatic and abusive backgrounds, but one client seems resilient and functions well, getting good grades in school and interacting well with friends, while the other client has become depressed and withdrawn, is failing most classes, and has no friends. Which of the following is the FIRST step to building resilience in the withdrawn 10-year-old?

a. Providing positive reinforcement
b. Providing opportunities for the child to be successful
c. Facilitating an attachment to a nurturing adult
d. Encouraging the child to try different strategies

33. The social worker wants to conduct research on social change and is considering a number of different theories as the basis for study. If the social worker is interested in how resources and power are distributed and determines that the conflict theory is the most appropriate, what is the FIRST question that the social worker would pose?

a. Who is oppressed?
b. What is the meaning?
c. What is the function?
d. Who most benefits?

34. A social worker is interviewing a client from a different culture. The client is encouraged to tell stories about his life from a cultural perspective, stories about traditions, history, and culture-specific experiences. Even though the client speaks English, a skilled interpreter is present to capture and elucidate unique idioms, phrases, and terms that have a unique meaning from within the client's cultural context. Listening carefully for underlying feelings and cultural meanings, the social worker restates important concepts, and incorporates the unique terms into the overall narrative. This form of engagement is referred to as:

a. conceptual reframing.
b. ethnographic paraphrasing.
c. ethnographic interviewing.
d. conceptual exploration.

35. The difference between the *nurturing system* and the *sustaining system* is:

a. the nurturing system refers to family and intimate supports, while the sustaining system refers to institutional supports and society as a whole.
b. the sustaining system refers to family and intimate supports, while the nurturing system refers to institutional supports and society as a whole.
c. the nurturing system refers to educational opportunities and support, while the sustaining system refers to employment opportunities and support.
d. the sustaining system refers to educational opportunities and support, while the nurturing system refers to employment opportunities and support.

36. Working at a bicultural community counseling center for Southeast Asian families, a social worker encounters a family troubled by sharp divisions between older family members and their young children. In particular, from the parent's viewpoint, the children seem to have lost respect for their elders, often treating their parents and even their grandparents in dismissive ways. According to Robbins, Chatterjee, and Canada (1998) this is evidence of:

a. traditional adaptation.
b. marginal adaptation.
c. assimilation.
d. bicultural adaptation.

37. A study attempts to measure the efficacy of a new antidepressant medication. A "control" group of depression sufferers will receive only a placebo, while an "intervention" group will receive the new medication. In this study, the "null hypothesis" would state the following:

a. the intervention group will report fewer symptoms of depression than the control group.
b. the control group will report fewer symptoms of depression than the intervention group.
c. both the control group and the intervention group will report fewer numbers of depressive symptoms.
d. there shall be no measurable difference in depression symptom reporting between the control group and the intervention group.

38. A 32-year-old client living with two adolescent children (13 and 15) in a temporary shelter for battered women and their children did not graduate from high school and has never held a job because her ex-partner believed women should stay in the home and care for children. The social worker has assisted the client to apply for welfare benefits. Which of the following is likely the best additional intervention to lift the client and her family from poverty?

a. Assist the client in finding a job
b. Encourage the client to return to school and attend college
c. Advise the client to continue to depend on welfare benefits
d. Enroll the client in a job training program

39. A social worker is working with a 22-year-old woman who is grappling with her emerging sexual identity as a lesbian. She expresses comfortable acceptance of her lesbianism, and indicates meaningful support from an extended circle of friends in the LGBT community. Even so, she has yet to reveal her sexuality to her heterosexual friends and family, citing fears of rejection and stating that she is embarrassed to take this very difficult step. According to Robins, Chatterjee, and Canada (1998), this client is in which of the following stages of the Coming Out Process?

a. Stage 2: Identity recognition
b. Stage 4: Disclosure
c. Stage 7: Pride in identity
d. Stage 8: Increased disclosure

40. In the LGBT community, the term *intersex* refers to:

a. ambiguous sexual anatomy (hermaphrodite).
b. heterosexual orientation.
c. sexual encounters outside of preference.
d. sexual attraction to both men and women.

41. A 46-year-old woman has come in with complaints of depression. Attempts at exploration of the underlying issues reveal numerous long-standing challenges (work, marriage, children), but no clear precipitating event(s). Along with dysphoria, the client has clear vegetative symptoms as well (anorexia, insomnia, fatigue, anhedonia, and impaired attention). Other than ventilation and support, what should be the social worker's FIRST response in this situation?

a. Press the client further in seeking a precipitating depressive event
b. Refer the client to a psychiatrist for antidepressant evaluation
c. Begin working with the client's denial about depressive issues in her life
d. Refer the client to a primary care physician for a health evaluation

42. A 72-year-old Caucasian man comes in to see the social worker with symptoms of depression. Although widowed, he has a supportive extended family, is well educated, generally financially solvent, and has only typical age-related health concerns (moderate arthritis, borderline high blood pressure, and a pacemaker). Successful throughout his life, he has a very stable history. During the conversation he makes a passing comment about "wondering if life is worth it anymore." The BEST response to this somewhat offhand comment would be to:

a. ignore it as a common phrase that shouldn't be troubling.
b. note it, but wait to see of similar feelings arise again.
c. reassure him that life is always worth living, even if challenging.
d. key in on the phrase and inquire directly about suicidal thoughts.

43. The social worker has a special interest in assisting clients who are attempting to move from welfare benefits to the world of work. Which of the following would best indicate that the social worker is activity promoting economic justice?

a. Establishing partnerships with industry to train and employ clients
b. Explaining to clients that they have the right to equal pay for equal work
c. Serving on an economic justice committee with a professional organization
d. Conducting in-service training for other social workers on economic justice

44. A social worker is seeing a recently returned 26-year-old male military veteran who had been deployed on active duty in the Middle East. He has obvious symptoms of posttraumatic stress disorder (PTSD) (intrusive memories, flashbacks, hypervigilance, angry outbursts, etc.). The social worker should explore the possibility of all of the following as potential causes of these symptoms EXCEPT:

a. combat stress.
b. disciplinary issues.
c. mild traumatic brain injury (MTBI).
d. sexual assault trauma.

45. The National Association of Social Workers (NASW) has established a clear position with regard to undocumented (illegal) immigrants. The position includes all of the following EXCEPT:

a. advocating for rights and services for undocumented residents.
b. transitioning undocumented immigrants back to their homeland.
c. opposing any mandatory immigration reporting by social workers.
d. facilitating documentation and benefits for undocumented residents.

46. During an intake interview, key areas of data collection include all of the following categories EXCEPT:

a. problem areas, strengths, and support systems.
b. attitude and motivation.
c. insurance and ability to pay.
d. relationships, resources, and safety.

47. The social worker has increasing numbers of clients who are refugees from third world countries, such as Somalia, and notes that many exhibit signs of depression (withdrawal, crying, insomnia, sadness) but are very resistant to any type of referral to mental health services, denying that they have a problem. What is the most likely reason for this response?

a. Different attitude toward mental illness
b. Lack of education
c. Fear of medical interventions
d. Resentment toward healthcare providers

48. In the clinical setting a social worker is asked to assess clients based upon their complaints, deficits, and identified problems. This method of assessment draws upon which of the following assessment models?

a. Strengths perspective
b. Medical model
c. Biopsychosocial model
d. None of the above

49. An adolescent client in foster care repeatedly complains of various ailments, but symptoms usually subside shortly after the client is allowed to stay home from school, suggesting the client is feigning illness. Which of the following is the most appropriate response?

a. "It's clear that you are not really ill, so you need to explain why you are pretending."
b. "You can't continue to pretend to be sick morning after morning because school is important."
c. "I can see that you are avoiding school because of something that may be difficult for you to talk about."
d. "Pretending to be sick is very dishonest, and you have to stop."

50. A client arrives for services at a community counseling clinic. He is pleasant, easily engaged, and discusses the need to work on "some interpersonal problems." When asked about any prior treatment, he notes that he has been seen by another social worker for the past 8 months. However, he now needs to seek services closer to home due to a change in his work schedule. When presented with an information release for contact with his prior social worker he becomes agitated and upset, and refuses to allow the contact. The BEST response in this situation would be to:

a. accept the client's need to keep his therapeutic past private.
b. discuss his concerns and support him, but require the collateral contacts.
c. refuse services to the client based on his refusal to permit collateral contacts.
d. do none of the above.

51. During a Friday afternoon counseling visit, a client voices thoughts about suicide. She does not appear to be emotionally overwrought, but rather seems peaceful and calm. She discusses that she feels she has accomplished all she can in life, particularly given the poor relationship she has with her husband and the fact that the last of their children recently left home. She notes having read some online information about a cardiac medication she takes (Digoxin), and believes that an overdose of this medication would precipitate rapid cardiac arrest. She just had the prescription refilled, and is just considering when to act—perhaps when her husband is out golfing the next Sunday morning. The FIRST appropriate response to this information should be to:

a. call 911 to ensure the client receives immediate help for her suicidal intent.
b. call local law enforcement to involuntarily escort the client for further suicide evaluation and hospitalization.
c. complete a suicide risk evaluation, and then arrange voluntary hospitalization if the client will accept it.
d. create a very detailed suicide prevention contract with the client, and plan several sessions to address her suicidality.

52. A social worker is seeing a married couple, at times individually. During an individual session the husband reveals that he is bisexual. He also reveals a lengthy history of sexual liaisons with other men and discloses that he recently learned he is HIV positive (via confirmatory tests through his primary care physician). Inquiring, the social worker discovers that he has not disclosed his HIV status to his spouse and that he does not use any barrier protection when with her. Upon explaining the life-and-death risk to his wife, he still maintains that he won't change this behavior. He first minimizes the risk, and then claims she would "suspect something" if he started using protection. After lengthy counseling he remains unwilling to either reveal his HIV status or to use protection. According to recent interpretations of the Tarasoff Case the social worker's duty now is to:

a. contact the client's wife to inform her of the danger.
b. contact the client's physician to inform him/her of the problem.
c. report the case to the department of public health.
d. continue this as a priority counseling topic.

53. A mental status exam (MSE) covers all the following domains EXCEPT:

a. addictions and compulsions.
b. appearance and attitude.
c. mood and affect.
d. insight and judgment.

54. An 8-year-old child has an out-of-home placement in a temporary foster home because of severe neglect and abandonment by her parents. The child had been found after living alone in a filthy apartment for a week. The child reports that she has one younger sibling but does not know the location of the child. What should be the FIRST consideration of the social worker?

a. Locating the parents
b. Locating kin
c. Locating permanent foster parents
d. Locating the sibling

55. While the use of the multiaxial system in *DSM-IV* has been removed from *DSM-5*, the use of specifiers continues. The purpose of diagnostic specifiers is to:

a. offer clinical justification.
b. delineate subtypes and severity.
c. differentiate between related diagnoses.
d. indicate uncertainty.

56. In determining the degree of severity of an intellectual disability, the most important determinant is:

a. IQ score.
b. adaptive functioning.
c. intellectual functioning.
d. deficits in person responsibility.

57. In working with an 11-year-old girl, it is noted that she seems to have limited verbal skills, including problems in word selection and use. Intelligence testing indicates normal cognitive capacity. Other testing has not shown any sensory impairments or other medical conditions. These early indicators are BEST suggestive of which of the following tentative diagnoses?

a. Speech sound disorder
b. Childhood-onset fluency disorder
c. Autism spectrum disorder
d. Language disorder

58. An 8-year-old boy presents with a number of complex developmental deficits. In particular, the child seems to isolate himself as evidenced by an apparent disinterest (or perhaps inability) in communicating with others, an idiosyncratic use of words and language, little imaginative play or social imitation, poor peer relationships, limited responses to others in his presence even if engaged, and odd, repetitive motions, routines, and rituals. The most likely tentative diagnosis would be:

a. social (pragmatic) communication disorder.
b. intellectual disability.
c. autism spectrum disorder.
d. language disorder.

59. A homeless client was a victim of an assault, resulting in a broken nose and multiple bruises, and is being treated in an emergency department. The social worker urges the client to file a complaint with the police because he is the fourth homeless person to be assaulted recently and recognized the perpetrator, but the client refuses to file a complaint because of distrust of the police. Which of the following is the best response?

a. "If you receive medical care, you must report the incident to the police."
b. "Let the doctor treat you and then you can decide later about filing a complaint."
c. "I understand. You don't have to report the incident."
d. "If you don't file a complaint, more people will be assaulted."

60. A social worker in a medical clinic is called to evaluate a 15-year-old girl who admits to persistent eating of paper products. The problem has persisted for some 6 months, and has led to minor weight loss and some level of poor nutrition. The preferred paper for ingestion is tissue paper, either toilet roll paper or facial tissues. The parents first noted the problem when tissue products continually disappeared in the home. There has also been some evidence of her ingesting other nonfood materials, such as clay, and sand, and obvious evidence of her consuming an inordinate amount of ice chips. The parents report that the patient is eating meals normally otherwise. The patient is reluctant to talk about any of this, just saying things such as "I don't know" and "maybe" and "I guess" to most any inquiry, and/or growing silent. The MOST LIKELY tentative diagnosis would be:

a. pica.
b. bulimia nervosa.
c. anorexia nervosa.
d. rumination disorder.

61. When used in reference to an individual who is chronologically at least 4 years old (or, mentally, at least 4 years old), the term *encopresis* refers to:

a. the voluntary expelling of fecal matter in an inappropriate place.
b. the involuntary expelling of fecal matter in an inappropriate place.
c. the expelling of fecal matter in response to symptoms of stress or anxiety.
d. all of the above.

62. A mother brings in her 8-year-old daughter due to her inability to sleep in her own bed at night. The mother has a history of sleeping with her daughter since about age 2, when she became divorced. She has, however, recently remarried and the daughter's insistence to sleep in the bed with her mother has become extremely problematic. When efforts are made to send the daughter to her own bed (in a room alone) the daughter becomes extremely stressed, tearful, and eventually displays tantrum-like behavior that fully disrupts sleep for the household until she is allowed to sleep with her mother. The MOST LIKELY diagnosis for this behavior would be:

a. Oppositional-Defiant Disorder.
b. Separation Anxiety Disorder.
c. Agoraphobia.
d. Panic Disorder.

63. Delirium differs from encephalopathy in which of the following ways?

a. Delirium has a sudden onset, while encephalopathy is gradual
b. Delirium involves sepsis, while encephalopathy involves toxins
c. Delirium has a gradual onset, while encephalopathy is sudden
d. None of the above

64. A social worker is called to evaluate a 78-year-old man (per his driver's license) found wandering by police, who was seen in the emergency department for "altered mental status." Staff suggest he appears "senile" and is probably in need of placement in a residential care setting. Upon meeting the patient, the social worker screens him using the Folstein Mini-Mental State Exam (MMSE). He is indeed confused, disoriented, forgetful, and otherwise cognitively impaired. Medical staff note he has no emergent condition. He is not febrile (no fever) or septic (only slightly elevated white blood cell count), no respiratory distress (breathes easily), and no cardiac compromise (age-expected elevated blood pressure and heart rate, with normal cardiac sounds and ECG tracing). No family can be reached; no information about prescription medication is available. The BEST social work response in this situation is to:

a. record "probable dementia" and arrange out-of-home placement.
b. arrange patient transportation back home with a home health referral.
c. delay any response until family or other collateral contact can be made.
d. advocate for the patient to be admitted for further medical evaluation.

65. The social worker is interviewing a 48-year-old male after receiving a referral from adult protective services. The man appears unkempt, and his apartment is dirty and garbage-filled. The man exhibits confusion, disorganized speech, and flat affect. The social worker notes a number of medication bottles on a nearby table and asks to review them: hydrochlorothiazide, clozapine, acetaminophen, simvastatin, and lisinopril. The social worker recognizes that clozapine is a psychotropic medication. What should the social worker's FIRST action be?

a. Ask the man why he is taking clozapine
b. Check the date on the clozapine and other medication bottles and the numbers of pills remaining
c. Contact the physician listed on the medication bottle
d. Recommend a 72-hour psychiatric hold

66. A chemical dependency counselor is counseling a 38-year-old married man regarding his ongoing use of alcohol. The client consumes alcohol on weekends and at parties, and tends to drink heavily about twice each month. At times, recovery from significant inebriation has resulted in his being unable to go to work on a Monday, and on one occasion he was given a DUI citation, resulting in this court-ordered counseling. The pattern of the client's alcohol use is best described as:

a. alcohol intoxication.
b. alcohol use disorder.
c. recreational alcohol use.
d. alcohol withdrawal.

67. In a county psychiatric emergency clinic, a social worker is asked to evaluate a 19-year-old woman for unspecified psychotic behavior. She is accompanied by her parents, who brought her to the clinic. Upon contact it is noted that she is disheveled and unkempt in grooming and hygiene. In talking with the social worker, she often pauses inexplicably, rambles about something unrelated, laughs to herself, and then turns her face away. Episodically attending to the social worker, she spontaneously claims that the worker is controlling her mind, and indicates that she sees odd objects floating around the social worker. There is no recent history of substance abuse (though remotely positive for amphetamines), and her symptoms have been prominent for most of the past year, though particularly acute this evening when she attacked her mother claiming that she was a clone and trying to pull her "real mom" out of the clone's body. The most likely diagnosis for this presentation is:

a. bipolar disorder.
b. schizoaffective disorder.
c. schizophrenia.
d. substance-induced psychosis.

68. A 34-year-old man makes an appointment to see a social worker for help coping with a difficult relationship in his life. At intake the social worker learns that he feels a famous movie actress has hidden affection for him. He has written her many times through her fan club, and has received letters from club personnel—never from the actress herself. But, he explains, this is just because she's "not currently free to express her feelings openly" due to a waning relationship with a wealthy businessman. When talking about the businessman, there are clear feelings of competition. When asked for greater detail or information to buttress his beliefs he avoids the questions. The MOST appropriate early diagnostic impression would be Delusional Disorder, with the following subtype:

a. grandiose type.
b. jealous type.
c. persecutory type.
d. erotomanic type.

69. A call is received from a family member about an adult male loved one who is "behaving in an extremely bizarre way." Specifically, he is racing from home to home, claiming that he is being followed by some sort of assault team (SWAT) intent on arresting him. He claims that people are hiding in cars all around him, even going so far as to claim entire parking lots are filled with cars hiding his assailants. He insists on pulling drapes and hiding out in the home for his safety. No evidence corroborates his story. He does have a history of deployment in Middle East combat, as well as a history of substance abuse, though neither presents as proximal to this event. By the next morning he appears fine, and becomes angry if the incident is brought up, suggesting it is all an exaggeration by others. The MOST appropriate diagnostic impression would be:

a. posttraumatic stress disorder, acute episode.
b. brief psychotic disorder.
c. drug-induced psychosis.
d. bipolar disorder, manic episode.

70. A social worker has been called to evaluate a 28-year-old female client described as "very depressed." Upon assessment the worker discovers that she has been struggling with depression since her late teens. She also admits to periods when she's entirely free of depression, even to the extent of thinking the problem is solved. Further questioning reveals that her depressions are quite deep, though not entirely anhedonic or debilitating, nor are her "up" periods marked by extremes in mood, grandiosity, insomnia, etc. Even so, her up and down phases are significant enough to disrupt relationships, work, and school (e.g., feeling unable to get out of bed when down, and pressured speech and euphoria to the extent to make others uncomfortable). Given this presentation, the MOST appropriate diagnostic impression would be:

a. bipolar disorder.
b. dysthymia.
c. cyclothymia.
d. mood disorder NOS.

71. A 72-year-old widow comes to see a social worker for help with feelings of bereavement. Her spouse died of a sudden heart attack just over a year ago. There was no prior history of a heart condition, so the loss came as a substantial shock and without forewarning. Since that time the client feels she has been unable to recover emotionally. She notes remaining intensely preoccupied with thinking about her husband, cries more days than not, feels estranged from others in many ways without him (e.g., other friends and couples seem distant), and describes her emotions as generally numb, when not overwhelming. Sometimes she yearns to die so that she can "be with him" again. There is no overt suicidality, but there is a feeling that life without him is meaningless in many ways. The MOST appropriate early diagnostic impression would be:

a. major depressive disorder.
b. posttraumatic stress.
c. uncomplicated bereavement.
d. persistent complex bereavement disorder.

72. The key difference between Bipolar I and Bipolar II is:

a. Bipolar I involves mania and Bipolar II involves primarily depression.
b. Bipolar I involves primarily depression and Bipolar II involves mania.
c. Bipolar I involves hypomania and Bipolar II involves dysthymia.
d. None of the above.

73. A social worker has been called to evaluate a 23-year-old man in a hospital emergency room. He presented with fear that he was having a heart attack, but medical staff have ruled this out following laboratory and clinical testing. He notes that his symptoms have subsided, but that when he arrived his heart was pounding, he was tremulous, gasping for breath, and had significant tightness in his chest. He recognized the symptoms as being cardiac in nature, as his father died recently from a heart attack when similar symptoms were present. After lengthy discussion he revealed that the symptoms had been coming and going rapidly over the last month, and that he had actually been sleeping in his car outside the hospital for the last several days to ensure he could get help when needed. The symptoms struck and peaked quickly (within minutes), leaving him fearful that help would not be available if he didn't remain close. These symptoms MOST closely resemble:

a. anxiety disorder due to a medical condition.
b. generalized anxiety disorder.
c. acute stress disorder.
d. panic disorder.

74. A social worker is called to a medical clinic to evaluate a 56-year-old woman who presents with persistent fears of a new diagnosis of melanoma. She had a small skin lesion removed from her nose approximately 2 years ago, which had precancerous tissue changes upon evaluation by pathology. Since that time, she has become intensely preoccupied with the status of her skin, and tends to check and recheck every blemish that occurs. Frequent visits to her dermatologist have not resulted in the identification of any new dermatological problems, and despite reassurances her worries continue unabated. The problem has grown to the point that she regularly asks her spouse to help her monitor her skin and examine her back to ensure no new problems. He has grown increasingly frustrated. She also refuses to go outdoors unless overly swathed to ward off any exposure to the sun. This has resulted in her increasingly avoiding the outdoors altogether. The MOST likely diagnosis for her presentation is:

a. Malingering Disorder.
b. Factitious Disorder.
c. Illness Anxiety Disorder.
d. Somatic Symptom Disorder.

75. A client is brought into a county mental health clinic by law enforcement. He has no personal identification, and cannot recall any personally identifying information. This forgetfulness appears to be genuine, not due to any threat or allegation of any kind. He does have receipts and other papers on his person that indicate he was recently many hundreds of miles away, but he cannot confirm or deny this. There is no history of head trauma, substance abuse, or prior mental illness that can be ascertained. The MOST appropriate initial working diagnosis would be:

a. dissociative identity disorder.
b. dissociative amnesia with dissociative fugue.
c. depersonalization/derealization disorder.
d. dissociative trance.

76. A newly married 23-year-old woman has been referred for counseling due to her experiences of painful intercourse. She was not sexually active prior to marriage, and so there is no history to draw upon for past experiences. The problem is painful penetration, not involving spasms of the vagina but characterized by marked vaginal dryness. The proper term for her condition is:

a. female sexual interest/arousal disorder.
b. genito-pelvic pain disorder.
c. substance/medication induced sexual dysfunction.
d. female orgasmic disorder.

77. A 26-year-old woman is seeing a social worker regarding her persistent desire to leave her bedroom window blinds open so that she might be seen disrobing by her male neighbor, who participates voyeuristically in an open way. She is aware that the activity is fraught with problems—he is a married man, and potentially other passersby might see in her window from the street. To this point, however, she finds these risks somewhat exciting and stimulating. She also finds herself compulsively thinking about the activity and planning ways to be "caught" by the man in compromising moments. Diagnostically, her behavior is best described as:

a. frotteurism.
b. voyeurism.
c. exhibitionism.
d. other specified paraphilia.

78. During an interview with a 15-year-old client, the client persists in making suggestive remarks about the social worker's appearance and asks if the social worker is married or has a partner. Which of the following is the most appropriate response?

a. "Stop making those comments and asking questions."
b. "It's not appropriate for us to discuss personal information, and I feel uncomfortable with your comments."
c. "Why are you talking like this?"
d. "If you continue making these types of comments, you will need to work with another social worker."

79. A social worker has been seeing a 26-year-old female client for about 6 months. She originally came to see the social worker about distress over a recent romantic relationship breakup. Over time the worker has learned that she tends to have serial relationships of short duration, which inevitably end badly. A common theme in the relationships is a pattern of over-idealizing, rejecting, and then clinging and trying to avoid perceived abandonment. Her mood is often labile, and she frequently follows a similar pattern in the counseling relationship: praising the social worker effusively and then later accusing him of neglect, professional incompetence, and bias, etc. The social worker has learned that she had poor childhood attachment with her parents, with a substantial history of physical abuse by them both. It now appears that the early primary diagnosis of adjustment disorder would now be coupled with:

a. Histrionic Personality Disorder.
b. Narcissistic Personality Disorder.
c. Borderline Personality Disorder.
d. Antisocial Personality Disorder.

80. Face-to-face work with clients is often described as:

a. direct practice.
b. clinical practice.
c. micro practice.
d. all of the above.

81. The social worker is utilizing role playing in group therapy with a client who has problems with interpersonal relationships and anger management. The first technique involved identifying a problem and the client enacting his role in the situation with a partner. The social worker then suggests they practice mirroring. What would this involve?

a. The partner reflects the behavior displayed by the client
b. The client enacts the role of the partner
c. The client acts out an imaginary future interaction
d. The client reenacts the role in an idealized manner

82. A crisis is an event that threatens or upends a state of equilibrium in ways that breach the coping capacity of the participants involved—usually a threat or obstacle to important relationships or goals. All of the following are major types of crises that may need to be addressed EXCEPT:

a. cultural/societal.
b. transitional.
c. maturational.
d. situational.

83. The social worker's client is a single mother with few resources and many issues: three young children, unemployed, homeless, victim of intimate partner abuse, and a long history of alcohol abuse. The client and her children are currently living in a temporary shelter. If utilizing the principle of partialization, which of the following would the social worker do FIRST?

a. Make a list of resources
b. Ask the client what she wants to deal with first
c. Choose one-half of problems to focus on
d. Make a list of problems

84. The *Premack Principle* refers to:

a. a guideline for crisis intervention.
b. a tool for managing intra-family conflicts.
c. a process for improving client rapport.
d. a method for increasing desired behaviors.

85. A contingency contract is used in behavior modification to:

a. ensure a specific response for a specific behavior.
b. provide a reward for specific behavior.
c. provide a punishment for a specific behavior.
d. all of the above.

86. There is strong empirical evidence that the therapeutic approach and treatment of choice for depression should be:

a. cognitive-behavioral therapy.
b. reality therapy.
c. behavior modification.
d. Critical Incident Stress Management.

87. A client comes to see a social worker, citing problems with choosing a career. Working collaboratively the social worker assists in clarifying the problem and identifying outcome goals, with specific steps to engage and achieve the goals and concluded by feedback and evaluation of client progress. From this process it is clear that the model of intervention being used is BEST described as:

a. dialectical behavioral therapy.
b. reality therapy.
c. solution-focused therapy.
d. none of the above.

88. The Neo-Freudian psychotherapist that differed from Freud's views primarily on the root origins of anxiety was:

a. Erich Fromm.
b. Karen Horney.
c. Harry Stack Sullivan.
d. None of the above.

89. A 32-year-old male veteran has come to see a social worker over troubling dreams that have persisted long after his return to the United States. The dreams involve reliving combat experiences in which he sees the deaths of important colleagues. Together, they work to relieve and psychologically reconcile these events, allowing the client to discharge the pent-up emotions associated with them. This psychotherapeutic approach is known as:

a. reorientation.
b. catharsis.
c. purging.
d. abreaction.

90. The term introjection is used differently between psychoanalysis and Gestalt therapy. Specifically, in Gestalt therapy the term refers to:

a. failing to produce a boundary that defines a unique sense of self.
b. modeling oneself after relationally important caregiving adults.
c. living into the labels that others place on us.
d. gradually defining oneself, by rejection or integration of outside ideas.

91. A social worker has been asked to facilitate an ongoing group experience for young married couples. The goals are relationship enrichment, with a particular focus on marital success after the birth of their children and in the press of career development. The group meets weekly, with no set termination date. This group is best described as:

a. an open-ended socialization group.
b. an ongoing support group.
c. an open educational group.
d. an ongoing growth group.

92. The social worker is working on a project with a coworker who persists in berating the social worker for missing a meeting scheduled when the social worker had to deal with a client emergency. The social worker needs to ask for information but realizes this will give the coworker another opportunity to complain. Which of the following exemplifies the most effective assertive communication?

a. "Can you review the data with me so I can get up-to-date."
b. "I'm so sorry that I missed the meeting, but can you review the data with me."
c. "I realize I missed the meeting and that was inconvenient for you, but what did the data show?"
d. "I'll try to review the data before we meet again."

93. In seeing a couple with significant conflict issues, a number of hot-point issues begin to emerge. In avoiding taking sides, the social worker is seeking to prevent:

a. coaching.
b. triangulation.
c. identity fusion.
d. emotional cutoff.

94. In Communications/Experimental Therapy, the idea that the same results can be secured in different ways is referred to as:

a. circular causality.
b. relational symmetry.
c. equifinality.
d. complementary conclusion.

95. A 4-year-old child has been placed into foster care because his father is unknown and his mother has been charged with child endangerment after leaving the child unattended while she engaged in prostitution. The child is otherwise healthy and appears to have been well cared for, but this is the second foster care placement for the child for the same reason. When engaging in permanency planning for the child, which of the following should be the FIRST goal?

a. Family reunification with mother
b. Kinship placement with family
c. Long-term foster care
d. Adoption by unrelated family

96. A couple in their 40s have come in to manage conflict issues in their marriage and family. In particular, neither can agree on basic roles as a couple. Both work outside the home; both tend to retain their income independently; each feels the other should be paying a greater portion of the bills; neither wants to be responsible for cooking, shopping, or housecleaning. According to Salvador Minuchin's Structural Family Theory, the couple is struggling with:

a. complementarity.
b. alignments.
c. power hierarchies.
d. disengagement.

97. A 16-year-old boy is acting out in ways that are regularly disruptive of the family's home life and social relationships. It soon becomes clear to the social worker that he feels misunderstood, unappreciated, and isolated from much of the family. To encounter this, the social worker asks each of the other family members, "Why do you think he is behaving in these ways?" This is an example of Mara Selvini Palazzoli's Milan Systemic Therapy known as:

a. hypothesizing.
b. counter-paradox.
c. positive connotation.
d. circular questioning.

98. In community organizing, the fundamental client is:

a. individual community members.
b. institutional community members.
c. the community itself.
d. informal community organizations.

99. A community member approaches a social worker/community organizer and reveals that a Latino factory owner has been hiring illegal immigrants and then denying them basic breaks and overtime benefits while threatening them with reporting and deportation. In seeking change, the FIRST step the citizen is encouraged to take is as a:

a. negotiator.
b. whistleblower.
c. litigant.
d. protestor.

100. In pursuing change for individuals or a community, potential social work roles include of the following EXCEPT:

a. client advocate.
b. legal advisor.
c. mediator.
d. broker.

101. Given that social workers are generally trained to work with voluntary clients (e.g., those who come seeking help), it can be difficult to work with involuntary (e.g., court or employment ordered) clients. Common mechanisms of resistance by involuntary clients include all of the following EXCEPT:

a. aggression.
b. diversion.
c. humor.
d. withdrawal.

102. The primary objective of supervision is:

a. keeping the agency running.
b. meeting the clients' individual needs.
c. developing the supervisee's skills.
d. making sure that work is completed.

103. The purpose of clinical/professional consultation in an agency is to:

a. share expertise.
b. obtain alternate leadership.
c. receive direction.
d. defer to an expert.

104. The concept of productive conflict management is drawn from which of the following types of management theories?

a. Bureaucratic
b. Administrative
c. Participative
d. Structuralist

105. A method of program evaluation that examines the extent to which goals are achieved and how well the outcomes can be generalized to other settings and populations is known as:

a. cost-benefit analysis.
b. formative program evaluation.
c. summative program evaluation.
d. peer review.

106. A client is being treated for anxiety but reports having difficulty concentrating on schoolwork and tasks because of being unable to stop worrying. The client has been sleeping poorly and has lost weight. Which complementary therapeutic approach should the social worker advise FIRST?

a. Music therapy
b. Yoga
c. Relaxation exercises
d. Meditation

107. Each state's Division of Child and Family Services (DCFS) commonly provides all of the following services EXCEPT:

a. Child Protective Services.
b. domestic violence shelters.
c. employment training.
d. education referrals.

108. At a transitional family shelter, a newly arrived mother and her three children are being reviewed during an interdisciplinary team consultation. The team consists of the social worker, a housing specialist, and an education and employment specialist. The mother lost her job in another city and was attempting to find work in a larger city. They were living in her car when it was burgled of all possessions. All seem unwell and congested. The oldest child, a 4-year-old boy, has severe asthma and needs a sheltered setting. The 3-year-old girl seems expressively vacant and emotionally detached. The 9-month-old female infant is clearly hungry and lacks diapers and other basic necessities. Food is being obtained for them all. Prior to presenting to the agency director, the FIRST social work step should be to:

a. complete a psychosocial assessment for mental health issues.
b. inquire about the availability of extended family support.
c. obtain clean, warmer clothing from a local clothes closet.
d. promptly refer the asthmatic boy to a medical doctor.

109. The case recording/progress record acronym SOAP stands for:

a. Subjective, Overview, Analysis, Prognosis.
b. Subjective, Observation, Acuity, Proposal.
c. Subjective, Objective, Assessment, Plan.
d. Subjective, Orientation, Acceptance, Posits.

110. The service delivery model used by the social worker focuses on helping the client to deal with current behavior in social interactions with a goal of the client's exhibiting behavior that is more acceptable to others so that the client receives positive feedback, further encouraging a change in behavior. Which of the following service delivery models does this exemplify?

a. Learning/Education
b. Ecological
c. Medico-clinical
d. Social functioning

111. The social worker is on the committee to update the policy and procedure manual for the healthcare organization based on a negative accreditation finding. Other members of the committee have suggested a number of different policies, but the social worker is concerned that the development of policies is not being adequately considered. Which should be the FIRST step in policy development?

a. Brainstorming different policies
b. Reviewing other policy and procedure manuals
c. Identifying problems
d. Asking for guidance from the board of directors

112. The social worker is in charge of an outreach program that is its own cost center. The organization utilizes a zero-based approach to departmental budgets, and the budget period is coming to an end. Which of the following is the most appropriate action for the social worker?

a. Wait to see if a budget for the program is allocated
b. Request that budget be provided based on previous needs
c. Prepare a report on the benefits of the program and projected budget needs
d. Expect that the same budget will be provided for the upcoming year

113. Social work ethics may best be defined as:

a. standards of nonmaleficence.
b. key professional values.
c. conduct standards based on values.
d. standards of beneficence.

114. The ethical concept of Self-Determination refers to:

a. the right to do anything one wants to do.
b. the right to require others to help one achieve goals.
c. the right to make choices dangerous to others.
d. the right to personal autonomy and decision making.

115. All of the following relate to the concept of confidentiality EXCEPT:

a. the lack of signage on a substance abuse treatment facility.
b. installing password protections on clinical computers.
c. sharing client information only with written permission.
d. guarding against discussing a client in a public place.

116. In treating a client, the social worker discovers that she had been sexually involved with her last licensed social work therapist. Further questioning revealed that the therapeutic relationship was terminated specifically to allow a relationship, and that sexual contact did not occur until a full year had elapsed after the termination. The client seems fine with how things were handled, and cites her right to confidentiality in an effort to ensure the social worker will not report the issue, even adding that she would deny the information if asked. The BEST response to the information would be to:

a. ignore it as they are consenting adults, she's no longer his client, and the client has cited confidentiality and intent to deny it.
b. double-check state laws to see how much time must elapse after termination of a client status before a relationship is possible.
c. consult with the supervisor or legal counsel to ensure a proper response to the situation.
d. note the NASW ban on all relationships with clients, current and former, and report, but keep the client's name confidential.

117. A client approaches his social work therapist and asks to see his case files. However, the therapist is concerned that exposure to some sensitive parts of the case record would be harmful to the client. Therefore, the MOST appropriate response to this request would be to:

a. Refuse, as the case records are the property of the social worker or the agency
b. Refuse, as the case records are the property of the agency
c. Allow the review, but with assistance to understand sensitive notes
d. Allow only a partial review, withholding portions deemed too sensitive

118. During a couple's therapy session they approach a social worker about their 3-year-old daughter's intensely frightening dreams at night. At first it sounds like they are discussing nightmares, but then the social worker recognizes the symptoms as *sleep terrors* (also known as *night terrors* or *pavor nocturnus*). They ask for advice on how to manage the symptoms. As a fully licensed social worker, but with no significant pediatric sleep disorder experience, the BEST response would be to:

a. refer the child to a counselor with experience in pediatric sleep disorders.
b. tell the family you will get back with them after doing some research.
c. complete a quick Internet search and offer a printout of reputable material.
d. set up an appointment to see the child, and consult a colleague on the issue.

119. The social worker who works in a program for homeless youth is concerned that the need for assistance is much greater than the resources available and is interested in engaging in fundraising to provide an increased budget for the program. What is the FIRST step in fundraising?

a. Develop budget for fundraising
b. Establish a goal for fundraising
c. Determine the target population for fundraising
d. Define the purpose of the fundraising

120. A client has a concern that warrants consultation. A consulting therapist has expertise in the required area. The BEST way to secure the consult is to:

a. share the problem and leave the file with the coworker for review.
b. ask the coworker to review the file, especially recent notes, and offer direction.
c. set up a formal consultation appointment to discuss the issue(s) in the office.
d. discuss the concern with the coworker in the cafeteria over lunch.

121. A social worker becomes aware that her colleague has a substance abuse problem. It has become increasingly severe over time, to the extent that the colleague occasionally shows up after lunch breaks clearly compromised and under the influence. The FIRST responsibility of the social worker in this situation is to:

a. contact a supervisor and report the problem internally.
b. contact the licensing board and report the problem.
c. contact the colleague and discuss treatment options.
d. contact local law enforcement to have them intervene.

122. A social worker discovers that his agency is not following the NASW Code of Ethics as related to secure record-keeping. In particular, file cabinets are not kept locked, laptop computers used in the field are not password protected, and local university students are regularly permitted to sit in on group therapy sessions without the agreement of group participants and without securing commitments of confidentiality from them. The BEST social work response would be to:

a. tender a resignation rather than work outside the NASW's standards.
b. seek to bring the agency's policies and procedures into compliance.
c. refuse to work with those resources and conditions outside compliance.
d. none of the above.

123. In the shared governance model used by an organization, each department has autonomous decision- making regarding issues that directly apply to that department, and the leader of each department is also a member on the administrative council. The social worker is interested in making a major change in procedures that involve more than one department. What should be the social worker's FIRST step?

a. Make a formal proposal to all departments involved regarding the change
b. Make a formal proposal to the social work department regarding the change
c. Make a formal proposal to the administrative council, which represents all departments
d. Discuss the proposal with members of the different departments to build consensus

124. A social worker has been working with homeless clients for many months and has begun to feel mentally and physically exhausted and overwhelmed by encountering the same problems over and over again. The social worker doubts his ability to continue to care for his clients. If these feelings are consistent with compassion fatigue, how is the social worker likely to respond to clients?

a. With numbness toward their suffering and blaming them for their problems
b. With compassion and empathy toward their problems
c. With anger and contempt toward their problems and life choices
d. With increasing disinterest and apathy toward their problems

125. The presence of a strong therapeutic relationship is fundamental to making positive life changes. Among the most important features of a meaningful therapeutic bond is:

a. compassion.
b. empathy.
c. sympathy.
d. condolence.

126. In a conversation with a case manager she describes some of her caseload as consisting of "numerous schizophrenics, several bipolars, and some borderlines," after which she proceeds to discuss some of the unique challenges the caseload presents. A primary problem with describing a caseload in this way is that it:

a. depersonalizes the clients.
b. stereotypes the clients.
c. diminishes the clients.
d. all of the above.

127. In situations of long-term case management, clients should be encouraged to openly share their emotions and feelings. All of the following are benefits to this sharing EXCEPT:

a. allowing judgment of how acceptable or not the feelings are.
b. reducing the emotional burdens the client feels.
c. offering insights into the client's emotional state and coping.
d. helping the client and worker to see problems more clearly.

128. A social worker is a case manager for a 26-year-old man with a diagnosis of paranoid schizophrenia. In seeking to allow him to ventilate feelings, the client taps into a reservoir of anger about the board and care facility where he resides, and about the operator and his co-residents. His emotions begin to escalate quickly, and a marked sense of lability is present. The BEST response is to:

a. confront him about his anger and label it as inappropriate.
b. join him in expressing anger and frustration about his situation.
c. evaluate him for homicidality and the possible need for intervention.
d. seek to understand his feelings while soothing/deescalating them.

129. When offering a client short-term and/or very narrow services, the best way to handle client's expression of feelings is to:

a. encourage the deep expression of feelings.
b. limit the expression of intense or deep feelings.
c. refuse to communicate about feelings in any way.
d. none of the above.

130. The social worker can only make one more visit during the workday but has four clients in need of visits, so some visits will have to be made the following day:

- A 2-year-old girl who was placed with a foster parent 5 months previously
- A 12-year-old boy who has repeatedly run away from his foster home
- A 16-year-old girl who is in an emergency room after being raped
- A 14-year-old boy who is hospitalized after a recent suicide attempt

Which client should the social worker visit FIRST?

a. 2-year-old girl in foster care
b. 12-year-old-boy who repeatedly runs away
c. 16-year-old girl who was raped
d. 14-year-old boy who recently attempted suicide

131. There are circumstances in which clients reveal a significant role in producing the situation they find themselves in (e.g., addiction, criminal behavior, violence). In such circumstances the FIRST role of the social worker is to:

a. point out important societal standards and expectations.
b. cite relevant legal and moral standards and expectations.
c. ensure a nonjudgmental attitude, regardless of the client's past.
d. discuss the consequences of choices and the need for change.

132. A social worker is contracted to work in a probation-sponsored drug rehabilitation setting with court-mandated clients. The program has an information release form that specifies the release of "any relevant information" to "any interested party" for "any requested purpose" without termination date. Staff explain that, given the clientele, information must at times be released to legal authorities or others on an urgent basis, making this broad form necessary. The safety of the public or others could be at stake. The proper social work response would be to:

a. use the form as directed, given the circumstances.
b. use the form, but note concerns with administration.
c. meet with administration to address the use of the form.
d. refuse to use the form on grounds that it is unethical.

133. Exceptions to Confidentiality and Release of Information requirements include all of the following EXCEPT:

a. in situations of actively expressed suicidal ideation.
b. when a law enforcement official formally requests information.
c. where a client leads a social worker to suspect harm to others.
d. where a client discloses abuse to a minor or dependent adult.

134. Confidentiality is BEST managed in group counseling sessions by:

a. telling participants that confidentiality cannot be assured.
b. committing group members to keep confidentiality.
c. having group members sign confidentiality agreements.
d. all of the above.

135. A social worker at a community counseling agency receives a subpoena to testify in court about one of her clients. The information outlined in the subpoena includes information that could easily be psychologically damaging to her client. The BEST response to this subpoena would be to:

a. comply with the subpoena, as no other options exist.
b. refuse to testify, even if contempt of court charges could result.
c. request the court withdraw the order, or limit its scope.
d. none of the above.

136. In situations of the death of either the client or the social worker, confidentiality agreements:

a. remain in full force and effect.
b. become null and void.
c. pass on to family members and/or the holder of the client's records.
d. remain in effect for the client, but not for but not the social worker's records.

137. In working with a client, the social worker discovers him to be manipulative, confrontational, at times deceptive, and otherwise very difficult to work with. Over time the social worker finds it increasingly difficult to work with him, and struggling to contain anger and even expressions of contempt. Concerned that she may not be able to maintain therapeutic clarity and requisite positive regard to support the change process, the social workers FIRST step should be to:

a. refer him to another social worker.
b. share these feelings with the client.
c. seek supervision and/or consultation.
d. ignore the problem, as it may improve.

138. A social worker is providing counseling services to a Southeast Asian family. After several sessions, the family presents her with a gift of a carefully crafted piece of folk art that they produced themselves. Although the materials involved are of little value, the overall value of the handcrafted item is unclear. In this situation, the social worker should FIRST:

a. explore the meaning of the gift with the family.
b. accept the gift graciously, but cite ethical standards for the future.
c. reluctantly accept the gift, expressing ethical uncertainty.
d. decline the gift while citing ethical standards as the reason.

139. A social worker provides services to an auto mechanic. At one point the social worker required auto repair work, and the client offered to perform the work in lieu of direct payment for services. The BEST response to this would be to:

a. accept the request, as it offers mutual advantages.
b. accept the offer, but set clear boundaries.
c. decline the offer, suggesting the need for boundaries.
d. decline the offer, citing professional ethics.

140. The social worker realizes that few staff members are able to leave work on time because of the need for extensive paperwork, and a quality assurance review finds that paperwork is often incomplete. In reviewing the documents required, the social worker notes a number of redundancies and believes that changing the document formats to eliminate redundancies would save considerable time. What should the social worker do FIRST?

a. Ask the other staff members to help design new documents
b. Suggest the supervisor consider revising documents
c. Do a mockup of revised documents and take to the supervisor
d. Complain to the supervisor that documentation is inefficient

141. A hospice social worker has had an extended relationship with a terminally ill client and his family. After the client's death, the family extends an invitation to attend the funeral and a family-only luncheon following the service. In this situation the BEST response by the social worker would be to:

a. decline to attend either the funeral or the luncheon.
b. decline the funeral invitation, but attend the luncheon.
c. attend the funeral, but decline the luncheon invitation.
d. attend both the funeral and the luncheon as invited.

142. The social worker has a 16-year-old client who is morbidly obese and expresses shame and anxiety about the weight and her body shape. The client is able to lose a few pounds but invariably then engages in binge-eating and regains the weight that is lost plus additional weight. This causes the client to feel increasingly worthless. Which of the following should the social worker focus on FIRST?

a. The triggers that result in binge-eating
b. The client's feelings about body image
c. Dieting strategies for weight loss
d. The client's goal for weight loss

143. Social work communication is facilitated through meaningful client questioning. Questions that possess the underlying goal of securing client agreement are known as:

a. leading questions.
b. stacked questions.
c. open-ended questions.
d. close-ended questions.

144. A social worker is seeing a client under mandatory court orders following conviction for a protracted period of sexual offenses with a minor. In the dialogue process, the client repeatedly refers to her offenses as "a mistake I made" and "when that happened," as well as, "he said he wanted it" and "he kept coming back for more," even after repeatedly being redirected. Recognizing that planned behavior does not just "happen mistakenly" and that a minor can never consent to such behavior, the MOST appropriate therapeutic response would be:

a. empathic responding.
b. reflective listening.
c. confrontation.
d. none of the above.

145. The concept of *transference* is BEST defined as:

a. an effort to shift blame for one's own wrongdoing from oneself to another individual.
b. an emotional reaction toward another, drawn from prior experiences with someone else.
c. the awareness of how an individual's appearance, mannerisms, language, or behaviors is a reminder of someone difficult from one's past.
d. a social worker's feeling about a client based upon prior experiences from the social worker's own background.

146. A parent appears to have good communication with his child and shows much warmth and affection but imposes few limits and very little guidance, believing that children should develop "naturally." As a result, the child tends to run wild and has been expelled from two different preschools because of refusal to cooperate. What type of behavior in childhood commonly results from this type of parenting?

a. Bullying, aggressive, and rebellious behavior
b. Destructive and delinquent behavior
c. Passive and needy or aggressive behavior
d. Independent and capable behavior

147. There are two forms of counseling records that can be kept by a social worker. They are generally referred to by three different titles (two common titles for one, and one for the other). All of the following titles may be used EXCEPT:

a. the primary client record.
b. the clinical/medical record.
c. journal notes.
d. psychotherapy notes.

148. A client has annual major depression events briefly accompanied by psychotic features. This has resulted in a misdiagnosis of bipolar disorder with psychotic features. The case manager notes that decompensation always occurs in the same month (the anniversary date of the death of her children in a car she was driving), and eventually discovers the misdiagnosis. In attempting to correct the problem, she is coached to leave it unchanged as the client's insurance will not cover the agency's services for a major depression diagnosis. The BEST social work response to this dilemma is to:

a. leave the diagnosis unchanged, as it was made by a psychiatrist.
b. leave the diagnosis unchanged to preserve client services.
c. seek supervision and/or consultation to explore the issue further.
d. change the diagnosis to properly reflect the client's condition.

149. A social worker has been working with a client for 18 months and the client's problem has been fully addressed and resolved. An appropriate process of termination has been concluded and all services have been discontinued. The state has no prevailing statute for a period of retention for social work records. The client's record should now NEXT be:

a. destroyed.
b. thinned and only essential information retained.
c. kept intact for another 3 years.
d. retained in accordance with state medical record statutes.

150. A social worker in a genetics clinic is employed to help families given difficult news about their own genetic makeup, or that of their children or unborn children. Part of the counseling process involves the discussion of abortion for fetuses that might otherwise be born with a variety of impairments, ranging from relatively mild to severe. The social worker at times feels distressed by offering the option of abortion in cases of only mild fetal defects. Her BEST response in such situations would be to:

a. help the family explore their feelings about the defects, their family circumstances, and the meaning of available options.
b. present all options to the family in a dispassionate and officious manner.
c. discuss the sanctity of life and how essential it is to preserve it.
d. help the family understand how manageable it would be to raise a child with only mild defects.

Answer Key and Explanations

1. D: This response represents an example of concrete operational thought. The client is demonstrating a very "concrete" and tangible-focused interpretation of the concept presented. Other key features of concrete operations include decentration (moving from an egocentric perspective to a view centered within a larger world view), reversibility, and manipulation of the steps of a process to achieve determined ends. Sensorimotor interpretation refers to the limited use of physical senses and movement to evaluate the world. Preoperational thought allows for the use of objects in representation (a stick as a sword, etc.), without the ability to logically reason or interpret with insight. Formal operations reflect the ability to reason through hypothetical and abstract concepts. Jean Piaget proposed four stages of cognitive development, noting specifically that some people do not develop past the concrete operational stage even in adulthood. Whether this client has regressed from formal operational thinking to concrete operational thinking, as a symptom of dementia, can be assessed by obtaining a history of his prior cognitive functioning. If so, such regression could represent an early symptom of cognitive impairment.

2. B: William James (1875) researched the function of consciousness as opposed to structure. Other early theorists, in order of theory construction, include the following: Wilhelm Wundt (1873): Structuralism (term coined by his student, Edward Titchener: examining the structure, not the function, of the conscious mind; Wundt is considered the "father of Experimental Psychology"); Sigmund Freud (1900) – Psychoanalytic Theory of Personality; Alfred Adler (1917) – Individual Psychology (birth order, personality development, self-image, etc.); John B. Watson (1920) – Behaviorism (conducted the "Little Albert" experiment, and focused on observable behavior as opposed to mental or emotional states); Ivan Pavlov (1927) – Classical or Respondent Conditioning (experimenting with dogs); Jean Piaget (1928) – Cognitive Development (producing a four-stage developmental model); Lev Vygotsky (1934) – Child Development and Social Development Theory (focused on language in learning processes); Kurt Lewin (1935) – Social Psychology (as well as applied psychology and organizational management); and Anna Freud (1936) – Ego Defense Mechanisms.

3. A: Lawrence Kohlberg (1958) researched the moral reasoning development and produced a six-stage moral judgment model. Other later theorists who focused on human development and behavior include Abraham Maslow (1943) – Hierarchy of Needs (producing a pyramid model of human needs, founded on those most basic and progressing to higher-order needs); Rene Spits (1945) – Ego Development (focused on maternal-child relationships, and identified a form of "hospitalism" called "anaclitic depression"); Erik Erikson (1950) – Ego Psychology (produced a psychosocial developmental model encompassing birth to death); Margaret Mahler (1950) – Separation-Individuation (studied maternal-infant interaction, and created a model of developmental stages from birth through 4 years); B.F. Skinner (1953) – Operant Conditioning (modifying behavior through consequences); John Bowlby and Mary Ainsworth (1969) – Attachment Theory (the psychological impact of losing important attachment figures—typically the mother); Elisabeth Kübler-Ross (1969) – Death and Dying (identified five grief stages when confronting death); Carol Gilligan (1982) – Feminist Social Psychology (studied gender differences); and, James Karl and Karen Wandrei (1990s) – Person in Environment System (PIE) Theory.

4. A: James felt cognitive processing precedes emotions, while Wundt felt that emotions emerge prior to cognitive understanding. Wilhelm Wundt, *the father of experimental psychology*, posited a *structural* view of human consciousness. He focused on exploring the basic structures of the mind, and the subsequent elements of feeling and sensation that constitute consciousness. From this structural perspective, his research experiments in Liepzig, Germany, utilized a technique called *Introspection*, wherein research subjects were provided an experience and then asked to report their feelings and emotional responses. He did not foresee subconscious or unconscious elements in the mind, and thus his experiments were centered on exploration of the conscious mind. William James, *the American father of experimental psychology*, believed that the *functions* of consciousness were more significant and adaptive than the involved *structures*. Consequently, his work at Harvard University focused on how thoughts and behaviors (mental states) serve a functional role in individual adaptation to the environment.

5. D: Preconscious thoughts can be brought to awareness relatively easily, while unconscious thoughts are much more difficult to bring to awareness. Both forms of thought, feeling and ideas, however, actively influence emotions and behaviors and thus must be accounted for in exploring human thinking and behavioral dynamics. Distressing ideas and experiences (i.e., that produce negative feelings and/or responses from others) may be *repressed* and pushed out of the conscious mind into the unconscious realm. Repressed experiences, thoughts, and ideas can exert considerable influence on human behavior. Substantial levels of distress from repression can produce psychological or even physiological dysfunction (e.g., emotional and somatic complaints). Treatment focuses on delving into and bringing repressed thoughts and ideas back to awareness, tracing the associated symptoms, and re-living the troubling experiences and situations in such a way as to produce constructive resolution. Freud's *Psychoanalytic Theory of Personality* addressed: structure of personality, psychosexual stages of child development, and levels of consciousness. Treatment techniques include *free association* and *dream analysis*.

6. C: The driving force is the Id, and the most effective intervention would be to cite the negative consequences of the behavior (arrest, punishment, etc.). Freud postulated three personality structures: 1) the *Id* (pleasure-seeking without regard to others needs or wants); 2) the *Ego* (reality-based, seeking needs in socially appropriate ways); and, 3) the *Superego* (morality based and conscience-driven, replacing the role of parents). This client is still living through the Id, and thus will respond most immediately to the threat or imposition of consequences. While most immediately effective, this has poor long-term influence. Next steps will involve teaching prosocial rules through logical cause-and-effect analysis and understanding (Ego development), ultimately followed by Superego development (teaching empathy and insight into the needs of others, the role of community solidarity and collective contributions to the shared social good, etc.). The Superego includes: a) the *conscience* (the "should nots" of behaviors) and b) the *ego ideal* (the "shoulds" that lead to rewards such as personal esteem and self-dignity and pride). *Life instinct* (Eros) refers to energy (libido) driving basic survival, pleasure, and reproductive needs.

7. D: This client may have a fixation in the Oral Stage. Freud suggested that fixation in the oral stage (the first year) might emerge in cases of infant neglect (inadequate feeding) or overprotection (excessive feeding). The mother's breast (or a substitute) becomes an early object of cathexis (emotional attachment). Thus, a neglected child may become a manipulative adult, seeking to compensate for the neglect, and an overprotected child may regress to untoward dependence upon others. In theory, oral-stage fixations become evident in various oral stimulus needs (eating, chewing on things, garrulousness, alcoholism, smoking, etc.). The Anal Stage (2-3 years of age) is not relevant, as it manifests in preoccupation with bowel and bladder functions. The Phallic Stage (3-6 years of age) involves genital discovery and pleasure, as well as mastery of Oedipal or Electra Complexes, which are unrelated to this situation. The Latency Period (6-11 years of age) is not relevant as it focuses on work and play with same-sex friends, with fixation here resulting in later untoward discomfort with opposite-sex relationships. Finally, the Genital Stage (age 12 to adulthood) would not apply as it occurs with puberty, and a return to opposite sex interests.

8. C: Birth order and guiding fiction would best explain their situation, according to the Adlerian perspective. While opposites may attract, mismatching can be complicated. Adler characterized the youngest as potentially dependent and spoiled, and potentially willing to manipulate others into caregiving and support. An oldest, by contrast, tends to be focused on responsibility and control. Both are evident in their conflicts. Further, the spouse's need for a superordinate work position suggests Adler's *guiding fiction* (an internally created self-image, never fully congruent with reality) is dysfunctionally present, where childhood feelings of inferiority compel him to find success beyond immediate experience or capacity and to shun any perceived menial work. *Needs hierarchy* is not Adlerian, as it was developed by Maslow, nor is it applicable here. Ego and superego are not relevant, as Adler did not accept these Freudian constructs. Inferiority and superiority issues are evident, but these concepts do not provide an optimal paradigm from which to pursue treatment.

9. D: John B. Watson, an American psychologist, developed the concept of *Behaviorism*, which consisted of an objective method of analyzing the cause and effect of identified behaviors. In exploring behavior, he conducted the "Little Albert" experiment in which a child was taught to fear a white rabbit—not because of anything the rabbit did, but because of overprotective parental anxiety and chastisement. The initial target of Little Albert's fear was a white rat, but it was readily generalized to a white rabbit. In like manner, this child's fear of going outdoors and certain home situations gradually expanded to a great many other social situations. Both Skinner and Pavlov were behavioral theorists, but both also focused primarily on direct stimulus-response conditioning (action-consequence links), as opposed to the expanded generalized conditioning that was the focus of Watson's Behaviorism. Jean Piaget studied cognitive development as opposed to behavioral conditioning. Thus, Piaget could better describe the cognitive threshold required for such complex associations to be made, as opposed to the behavioral conditioning that could produce it.

10. D: This compulsion would be described as a conditioned response. The word "Pavlovian" refers to the theoretical work of Ivan Pavlov. An unconditioned stimulus is one that evokes an innate unconditioned response (i.e., a startle reflex at a loud noise). A conditioned stimulus is one that produces a learned response, because it has been paired with an unconditioned stimulus in the past (e.g., a rush of elation when your football team scores a touchdown—two experiences that would have no real meaning or response until they were paired and learned). The classic example is that of Ivan Pavlov's research with dogs. Presented with meat powder, the dogs would salivate. Eventually, a bell was added at the point of presentation of the meat powder. Ultimately the dogs would salivate at the sound of the bell alone, without any meat powder. Thus, an unconditioned stimulus and response, when paired with another stimulus, eventually became a learned stimulus with a learned response.

11. B: The human development theorist Lev Vygotsky focused his research primarily on child development, and introduced a concept later known as *scaffolding*. His original concept, called the *Zone of Proximal Development* (ZPD), explains how a child functions at a lower limit if all help is withheld, and moves to a higher level with skilled assistance. *Scaffolding* is an extension of ZPD. It refers to a teaching pattern where an adult provides more intensive assistance to a child at the outset of learning a difficult task, and then tapers back as greater skill is acquired. A professional driving instructor uses a teaching vehicle with two steering wheels and two brake pedals, which allows for a measured transition between teaching and allowing the new driver to gradually assume full control. Scaffolding is not possible in a vehicle lacking these tools. Behavior modification may be helpful in extinguishing a persistent bad driving habit, but not in optimizing initial training. Defense mechanisms may explain the daughter's inability to learn from dad, but not the path to learning. Anaclitic depression is a concept from attachment theory with no bearing on this situation.

12. B: This older adult has suffered multiple losses and may feel she has lost control of her life, so exhibiting oppositional behavior is her way of reasserting control. The social worker should listen actively to the woman's complaints in a non-judgmental manner, encouraging her to express her feelings. Then, the social worker should suggest they collaborate to devise a personal schedule of activities, explaining why some things can't be changed (meal times, scheduled activities) and encouraging choice in other things (bathing, room cleaning). After this, the social worker should counsel the staff but should avoid telling the woman that her behavior is inappropriate.

13. C: This is an example of intellectualization. Specifically, *intellectualization* occurs when an individual attempts to use logic and reasoning to avoid facing difficult feelings. As with many other defense mechanisms, this coping effort is not necessarily problematic as it may offer the spouse a place of refuge until he is psychologically ready to encounter the devastating feelings that it is covering. Thus, this need should be recognized and accommodated unless it becomes unduly protracted and/or exclusive of gradual exploration of the underlying emotional concerns. *Projection* addresses the denial of one's own negative characteristics while attributing them to someone else (e.g., "I'm not a racist! You should see what my mom says about foreigners!"). *Compensation* refers to success seeking in one life area to substitute for barriers in another that cannot or have not been overcome. Rationalization involves hiding one's actual motivations under an appeal to more socially acceptable reasoning and logic (e.g., saying "I can't make the trip because the kids are sick," instead of admitting you don't enjoy the people or activity).

14. B: The defense mechanism known as *fixation* refers to arrested personality development at a stage short of normative maturation. This client clearly identifies with individuals and activities that fall short of her age and maturity level. While enjoying youthful associations is not in itself problematic, seeking to live in those associations to the exclusion of normal relationships and activities is problematic. Identifying, addressing, and overcoming the reasons behind this will likely be a major therapeutic endeavor. *Avoidance* is characterized by a refusal to become involved with objects, situations, and/or activities that are related to underlying impulses to avoid potential punishment (e.g., staying away from casinos to cope with a predilection for gambling instead of discovering and overcoming the underlying reasons for the compulsion). *Devaluation* involves the attribution of negative qualities to oneself or others to cope with stress or internal emotional conflicts (e.g., coping with being fired from a job by speaking negatively of the job and work colleagues). *Affiliation* involves seeking emotional support and advice from others instead of "going it alone," yet without trying to make others responsible to step in and fix the problem.

15. C: The best response is to permit some discussion on feelings of loss, but keep the focus on his immediate housing, transportation, and employment needs. Abraham Maslow's Needs Hierarchy posits that more essential and basic physiological needs must be met before higher order needs. Thus, needs regarding food, clothing, and shelter are more important than needs for safety (security, protection, predictability, and structure), belonging (friendships, affection, intimacy), esteem (recognition, respect, and appreciation), and self-actualization (meeting one's full potential). Thus, while it is important to acknowledge and make some room for the client's feelings of grief and loss, it is crucial that more basic survival needs be met first. Just "going where the client wants to be" is clinically irresponsible. Rejecting all talk about relationships and loss would be alienating, and referring him away would be abandoning him without the support that is available through the agency.

16. C: This client is struggling with the mastery of Erikson's Stage 6: intimacy vs. isolation. This stage is typically mastered during young adulthood (ages 19-30). Indicators of successful resolution include establishing a committed, intimate, nonexploitive sexual relationship, with meaningful tolerance for the burdens and risks that accompany the relationship. The client has not been able to establish a reciprocal, loving, intimate relationship with another individual. The sexual relationships that he has produced are transient, noncommittal, and often exploitive. Failure to negotiate this stage results in increasing isolation and narcissism. A, Stage 1 (trust vs. mistrust), is not correct as the issue of failures in trust has not been identified. B, Stage 5 (identity vs. identify diffusion), is not correct, as the client does not present with issues related to roles and self-identity. D, Stage 8 (integrity vs. despair) is not correct, as this is an end-of-life construct dealing with self-assessment in retrospect and the client is not at this point in life.

17. D: This disorder likely occurs from problematic experiences in Mahler's Stage 3: Rapprochement. *Rapprochement* is one of four substages in Stage 3 of Mahler's child development model. During this substage, an infant (15-24 months of age) begins to strive for autonomy. Success requires maternal support, as the infant ventures away from immediate contact, and frequently returns for encouragement and assurances of security. Where these are not forthcoming, an infant can develop anxiety and fears of abandonment. This can evolve into a dysfunctional *mood predisposition* that, Mahler felt, could later produce Borderline and/or Narcissistic Personality traits or the full disorder. Answer A (normal autism phase) is not correct, as it refers to a natural obliviousness to the external world common from birth to 1 month. Answer B (symbiosis phase) refers to high levels of attachment between mother and infant from 1-4 months of age, with deprivation/disruption potentially resulting in later symbiotic psychosis and disconnection from reality. Answer C (differentiation [hatching] phase) refers to an infant's realization of being separate from its mother. As an awakening, rather than a process, it is does not produce psychological failure.

18. A: The problem would be identified as one of positive reinforcement. The teenager's acting out led to a variety of responses and punishments. However, it is revealed that the teenager's underlying goal is time and attention from her father. As negative attention is better than no attention at all (i.e., *positive reinforcement*), the teenager continued to act out to receive and extend attention from her father. Answer B (*negative reinforcement*) is incorrect, as it refers to the repetition of a desired behavior to avoid negative stimuli (consequences). The parents were supplying negative stimuli (stern lectures) to produce and strengthen positive (cooperative) behaviors. Answer C (*punishment*) was also being used to weaken the teen's use of negative behaviors. Answer D (*extinction*) refers to the weakening of a conditioned response in one of two ways: 1) in *classical (Pavlovian) conditioning*, it involves interrupting the pairing of a conditioned stimulus and an unconditioned stimulus; 2) in *operant conditioning*, it occurs when a trained behavior ceases to be reinforced (or when the reinforcement is no longer considered rewarding). Ignoring bad behavior is one (operant conditioning) way of bringing it to extinction.

19. B: Skinner's *operant conditioning* deals with the modification of voluntary behavior via consequences, while *Pavlovian conditioning* produces behavior under new antecedent conditions. Ivan Pavlov's classical (or respondent) conditioning utilized the identification of an unconditioned (natural) stimulus that evokes an unconditioned response (e.g., food inducing salivation). A conditioned stimulus is created when an unconditioned stimulus is repeatedly paired with a stimulus to be conditioned (e.g., ringing a bell with the presentation of food), which evokes the unconditioned response (salivation), which is gradually transitioned into a conditioned response (salivation at the sound of the bell). Skinner identified an antecedent (stimulus) that could be used to produce a response (behavior) that could be controlled or modified by means of a consequence (positive or negative). Positive and negative reinforcements strengthen targeted behaviors, while punishment and extinction weaken targeted behaviors.

20. B: The husband's level, according to Kohlberg's multisystem model of moral development, would be at Level 2: Stage 4. This stage embodies a law-and-order perspective, focused on adherence to concrete perceptions of correct behavior and duty. Clearly, the husband is intent on ensuring he does not fail in his role as husband and father. To increase marital satisfaction, however, the husband needs to progress beyond Levels 1 and 2, and past Level 3: Stage 5 (societal expectations and agreements) into Stage 6, which is conscience- and ethics-driven according to principles of goodness and morality. Answer A (Level 1: Stage 2) is incorrect as Level 1 (Pre-Conventional Morality) is focused first on a punishment avoidance orientation (Stage 1) and next on a reciprocity, instrumental orientation (Stage 2: "you scratch my back and I'll scratch yours). The husband is beyond these stages. He is also beyond Level 2 (Conventional Morality), which deals with approval seeking (Stage 3: being "good" for praise). Answer C (Level 3: Stage 5) is incorrect, as it refers to behavior that has been carefully examined via a social-contract perspective. Finally, answer D (Level 3: Stage 6, ethics and morality driven) is the desired goal, which has yet to be pursued.

21. B: When assessing a one-year-old child's attachment to her mother, the mother plays with the child and then leaves the room, and the child typically begins to cry. When the mother then returns to the room, the first action by the child that suggests the child is securely attached to the mother is if the child hugs the mother and then calms and usually resumes playing. If the child is not securely attached, the child may act ambivalently toward the mother, may continue to cry and even resist comforting, or may cling fearfully to the mother.

22. D: If the social worker is applying feminist theory to a group of women who are substance abusers and come from a variety of ethnic and social backgrounds, the social worker would stress the commonalities among the women. Feminist theory intends to cast light on issues of discrimination inequality, oppression, objectification, and stereotyping faced by women, regardless of their background. Feminist theory considers not only the individual's ability to function in a situation or deal with a problem but also the social circumstances associated with the situation or problem.

23. D: Childhood psychopathology would most likely become apparent during language development. This developmental period requires mastery of *phonology* (making sounds correctly); *semantics* (the encoding of messages); *syntax* (proper combining of words); and *pragmatics* (proper use of word context). Because of the complexity of language development, some forms of psychopathology (e.g., autism) are more readily apparent in this developmental phase. Irregularities in physical developmental milestones are more likely to identify congenital defects, while poor cognitive development may more readily reveal genetic and drug exposure issues. Sexual development requires careful parenting, to ensure sexual curiosities are properly directed in socially appropriate manners, while also ensuring that emerging sexuality is not "shamed" or otherwise impaired or distorted.

24. C: Failure of an infant to crawl by 12 months would be a cause for concern. On average, from birth to 2 months infants respond to faces and bright objects; by 2 months, most visually track moving objects and exhibit social smiling; by 4 months, cooing sounds are evident as well as enjoyment of important people and familiar objects; by 5 months, grasping and holding skills are observed; by 6 months, babies can turn over and teething begins; around 7 months objects can be picked up; by 8 months sitting independently occurs, and stranger anxiety begins; at 9 months crawling is usually seen; at 10 months active play and paying attention are evident; at 11 months standing can be achieved with help; at 12 months a baby can turn pages to see pictures; from 10-12 months the range of emotional expression broadens, and walking with help begins; by 15 months independent walking starts and naming of familiar objects is evident; by 18 months running is observed; at 24 months speech in short sentences is possible; and by age 6 years speech and imagination are both well demonstrated.

25. D: The most appropriate response would be to reassure the parents that this is not itself a symptom of sexual abuse. Approximately 10% of girls will experience menarche before age 11, most at 12.5 years of age, and 90% by 13.75 years of age. Adolescence is typically identified as the period from 12 to 18 years of age. Sexual maturation may begin as young as age 10. Interest in the opposite gender becomes increasingly prominent as maturation progresses. Adolescent development broadens into areas such as emotional and spiritual awareness and capacity. The period is markedly influenced by factors such as gender, socioeconomic status, culture, genetics, and disabilities. Friends and institutional influences become more significant, and adolescents experiment with a variety of "personality styles" as their self-image is formed. Gender identity and potential confusion may occur and require careful response to avoid psychological distress and accompanying increases in depression, abuse, and suicide. Of all developmental periods, this transitional time is typically the most turbulent and traumatic.

26. C: Sandwich generation refers to the pressure of couples still rearing children while being required to care for aging parents. Other significant pressures in adulthood include: 1) caring for disabled children (whether due to health, substance abuse, or other disability); 2) rearing grandchildren for divorced or otherwise unavailable children; 3) economic challenges and poverty, including difficulties accompanying retirement; and 4) personal health changes related to aging. Early to-mid-adulthood is characterized by a focus on dating, marriage, home establishment, and childbearing and rearing. Early family structure can be particularly compromised by physical and/or mental illness, divorce or widowhood (with the accompanying financial, emotional, and social changes), and poor parenting skills (often derived from family of origin). The availability of social work resources can help mitigate the impact of these stressors and challenges. Late-life stressors also include mobility and cognitive changes (e.g., inevitable declines in short-term memory, and the possibility of dementia due to Alzheimer disease, Parkinson disease, stroke).

27. B: The most likely perpetrator in this situation would be the mother. While sexual abuse and/or physical abuse in a child older than 14 years is more likely to be perpetrated by a father or other male father figure in the home, for nonsexual abuse of a child younger than 14 years, the most common perpetrator is the female parent. Common signs of physical abuse include bruising, welts, burns, fractures, and internal injuries. Routine signs of sexual abuse include trouble sitting or walking, inordinate shyness in changing clothes around others, sexual acting out, running away from home, and sexually transmitted diseases. Emotional abuse signs include delays in language skills, distrust, overeagerness to please, insecurity, anxiousness, poor self-esteem, relationship issues, substance abuse, and criminal behavior. Signs of abusive neglect include emotional problems (particularly depression), malnourishment (seen in inhibited development), cognitive delays (due to inadequate stimulation), medical problems and illnesses (especially when left untreated), poor social skills, impaired school performance, poor parental supervision, chronic tardiness or truancy, poor hygiene, and inappropriate clothing.

28. D: The first social worker response should be to contact the local Adult Protective Services (APS) to report suspected abuse. With continued nursing visits, it might be possible to defer a referral if the sole issue is marginal care, while an extended family conference is arranged (option C). However, the withholding of financial resources (the house), as well as isolating and neglecting the client's emotional and nutritional needs, meets clear standards of abuse. Most states have mandatory reporting guidelines when abuse is clear, and the social worker could not ethically or legally withhold the APS referral. Option A is clearly incorrect as it allows the abuse to continue. Option B is not acceptable as it defers any change in the ongoing abuse for at least 2 additional months. Elder abuse includes physical abuse, financial exploitation, and neglect, as well as verbal and emotional abuse, with family being the most common perpetrators. Neglect is the most commonly reported abuse. Living on the client's income and in the client's home are particular risk factors, as are: 1) a difficult to manage client (violent, demented, argumentative, etc.); 2) compromised caregivers (finances, substance abuse, mental illness, etc.); and 3) poor housing (crowded, inadequate, etc.).

29. B: If the social worker is conducting a home evaluation for a client with two children, one neurotypical and the other severely disabled with autism spectrum disorder, and the client admits to being overwhelmed at times and feeling like running away, based on role theory the social worker would describe the client's situation as role strain because the client's stress is related to different aspects of the same status—that of mother. Role conflict arises when conflict arises between different statuses, such as between the role of mother and the role of wife (parts of the client's role set). In some cases, both role conflict and role strain may be present.

30. B: This behavior would best be defined as codependent. Addiction is frequently a family disorder, as it affects all members in the household. Codependent behavior can include making excuses for the addiction, minimizing the extension of the addiction, covering for (or hiding) the addict's behavior, providing access to the substance to keep peace and minimize discord, and bypassing important obligations and responsibilities to compensate for the addict's behaviors and to ensure the safety of the addict or others. Addictions tend to persist because they engage the brain's pleasure center, releasing neurotransmitters that reinforce the addiction. While many addictions involve the use of psychoactive substances, other areas of addiction include eating, shopping, gambling, hoarding, pornography, and the excessive use of electronic devices (computer games, etc.). While most treatment tends to be cognitive behavioral in nature, there are numerous treatment approaches; no one treatment will meet the personality and needs of all addicted individuals.

31. C: These are symptoms of grief bargaining. Drawing upon the work of Kübler-Ross, the social worker recognizes the symptoms of the *bargaining* stage of coping with profound loss. The stages of anticipatory dying were first outlined by the psychiatrist Elisabeth Kübler-Ross. She identified five stages associated with anticipatory grief: *Stage 1: Denial* (rejection of the diagnosis; often a feature of emotional shock). *Stage 2: Anger* (rage, resentment, and frustration with God and others). *Stage 3: Bargaining* (attempting to make a deal with God or others). *Stage 4: Depression* (profound sadness as reality sinks in). *Stage 5: Acceptance* (ceasing to struggle against impending death). Answer A (psychotic break) is not correct, as a psychotic break is symptomatic of a complete detachment from reality, rather than just one deeply distressing element of life. Answer B (chemotherapy toxicity) is inaccurate, as it suggests a chemically driven psychological stage that would be very poorly integrated and lack goal-directed intent. Answer D (acute denial) is not correct, as it would manifest more as a total rejection of the diagnosis, rather than an effort to bargain around it.

32. C: If the social worker has a 10-year-old client who does not appear to be resilient after surviving a traumatic and abusive background, the first step to building resilience in the child is to facilitate a nurturing relationship with an adult. Children who lack resilience are often very fearful and feel unsafe in the world, so they need to identify with an adult who can provide a safe haven, and that can be a parent, family member, or other caring adult. The next step is to provide the child with opportunities to be successful in order to begin to build the child's sense of self-esteem.

33. D: If the social worker wants to conduct research and decides to utilize the conflict theory as the basis for research, the first question that the social worker would pose is "Who most benefits?" Conflict theory is based on the survival of the fittest and the competition for resources and power, resulting in winners and losers, or elite and others. Conflict theory developed from the ideas of Karl Marx and often focuses on issues of inequality.

34. C: Ethnographic interviewing allows for deeper cultural insights to be winnowed out of a client's narratives. Attending to both feelings and cultural meanings, the interviewer is better able to delve into and understand narratives and circumstances from the client's unique perspective. Common listening techniques such as *reframing* and *paraphrasing* are avoided, as they tend to suffuse the narrative with meanings and understandings that reflect the culture and history of the interviewer rather than that of the interviewee. Instead, *restating* and *incorporating* are used to retain the client's unique meanings. The use of an interpreter is important to ensure that unique expressions, such as idioms, or borrowed native-language terms, are not misunderstood or overlooked. Other culturally responsive assessment tools may be helpful. For example, 1) A *Culturagram* can be used to examine family relationships, cultural ties, and offer some perspective about the role and depth of culture in the client's life. 2) A *Cultural Evaluation* may also be used, as it explores a variety of cultural beliefs, values, behaviors, and support systems during the assessment process.

35. A: The *nurturing system* refers to family and intimate supports, while the *sustaining system* refers to institutional supports and society as a whole. As theorists such as Leon Chestang posit, everyone is a part of and in need of both systems of support. Thus, it is essential to understand the roles that culture and diversity play in either furthering or hindering the efficacy and balance of both of these systems in the lives of individuals. In particular is a "dual perspective," which may arise in the lives of culturally diverse clients, wherein they must constantly reposition themselves between nurturing family supports and a broader social construct that may not be in support of the nurturing family's culturally unique ways of living and supporting family members. Discrimination and cultural norms that are incongruent with the broader sustaining system may significantly impede the utilization of important social services in particular.

36. C: In developing a bicultural identity, *assimilation* occurs when the norms and values of the sustaining system (institutions and society) are learned and followed to the exclusion of the norms and values of the nurturing system (family and cultural roots). This division can be particularly problematic among new immigrants and their young offspring. The parents, especially those from highly divergent cultures with markedly different languages and traditions, often find themselves unable to function well in mainstream society. Consequently, they become significantly dysfunctional in the eyes of the children, who far more quickly learn the dominant language and ways. As the parents turn to their young children for help in interpreting and guiding them through systems and technologies, traditional values of respect and reverence for adults can be significantly diminished. *Traditional adaptation* exists where adherence to the nurturing system (family and culture) remains dominant. *Marginal adaptation* occurs when neither the nurturing nor the sustaining systems' values and norms are followed. *Bicultural adaptation* exists when the norms and values of both systems become functionally integrated.

37. D: The null hypothesis for this study would state that there shall be no measurable difference in depression symptom reporting between the control group and the intervention group. The null hypothesis (often designated as "H_0") proposes that no relationship exists between two variables (often designated "x" and "y") other than that arising from chance alone. If a study's results demonstrate no difference, then the null hypothesis is "accepted." If differences emerge, then the study "failed to reject the null hypothesis." Statistical testing does not prove any hypotheses, but instead disproves them via rejection.

38. D: If a 32-year-old client living with two adolescent children in a temporary shelter for battered women and their children did not graduate from high school and has never had a job, the client is likely to only qualify for low-paying jobs, which may provide less income than welfare benefits. Realistically, returning to school and attending college would take years, so the best approach to lifting the client from poverty is to enroll the client in a job training program so the client will qualify for a higher paying job.

39. C: This client is still lingering in Stage 6 (withdrawal from the heterosexual world) and Stage 7, as pride and assertiveness about her sexual orientation is still only in its formative processes. The *Coming Out Process* involves 10 Stages: Stage 1: Confusion over sexual identity. Stage 2: Recognition of sexual identity. Stage 3: Exploration relative to sexuality identity (seeking to understand, define, and express sexual identity internally and with others). Stage 4: Disclosure to others. Stage 5: Acceptance of sexual identity. Stage 6: Avoidance of the heterosexual world. Stage 7: Pride in sexual identity. Stage 8: Extending disclosure (to all others). Stage 9: Re-entering the heterosexual world. Stage 10: Moving past sexual orientation (in identity and life focus).

40. A: The term *intersex* refers to ambiguous sexual anatomy (hermaphrodite). Heterosexual orientation is most commonly referred to as being *straight*. There is no specific term for sexual encounters outside of orientation preference. Sexual attraction to both men and women is known as *bisexuality*. Homosexual men are most often referred to as *gay*, while homosexual women are referred to by the term *lesbian*. *Pansexuality* refers to an attraction to and association with any partner regardless of sexual identity. *Transgender* (also called bi-gender) refers to an identity different from birth sex type, with a focus on gender. Transgender individuals may live a heterosexual, homosexual, bisexual, or asexual lifestyle. *Transsexual* individuals have identified themselves as transgender with a focus on sexual orientation. Further, they have an added desire to live an opposite sex lifestyle and desire hormonal and/or sexual surgery to achieve physiological congruence. *Genderqueer* and *Intergender* are catch-all terms for those who feel they are both male and female, neither male nor female, or entirely all binary gender identity.

41. D: The first response should be to refer the client to a primary care physician for a health evaluation. Women are far more likely than men to be diagnosed with a psychiatric disorder, especially a psychogenic disorder of mood, when an underlying medical condition (such as hormone imbalance) is the cause. Seeking parity with men in many areas, including psychiatry, remains a challenge. Culturally, women continue in subordinate positions in society, specifically in medical, legal, and institutional arenas. Problems include 1) psychiatric and medical studies run by men and for men, with findings normed to men (especially in pharmaceutical findings where doses are normed to men's larger size and faster metabolic patterns, and in psychiatric studies that tend to either ignore or pathologize women's unique nature); 2) being uninsured or underinsured (double the rate of men); 3) lower pay for similar work (even worse for female minorities); and 4) poverty (women represent 66% of all Medicaid recipients). Women also fare poorly in intimacy, being far more often abused and more prone to sexual infections (such as HIV). All are also contributors to depression, beyond simple endogenous factors.

42. D: The best response is to key in on the phrase and inquire directly about suicidal thoughts. Elderly people face many challenges, among which is Erikson's *Integrity vs. Despair* resolution process becoming profoundly acute in older years. Among elderly people, losses accumulate, health is fading, children have left, options are narrowing greatly, and the future can easily seem dim. Health and medication problems can further complicate the scenario. Of particular note, while the highest rate of completed suicide is among middle-aged Caucasian men (45 to 64 years old), the second highest rate is among elderly Caucasian men. While women attempt suicide three times as often as men, men are four times more likely to succeed, primarily because they often use more lethal means (firearms, suffocation, etc.). Of all completed suicides, 78.5% are male and 21.5% female. On average, 12 people attempt to harm themselves for every reported death by suicide. Many of these represent gestures rather than real attempts. Elderly persons, however, are decidedly lethal. While the ratio of attempts to completed suicides is 25:1 among youth, it is 4:1 among the elderly. Certainly, it is always important to ask if concerning words are used.

43. A: If the social worker has a special interest in assisting clients who are attempting to move from welfare benefits to the world of work, establishing partnerships with industry to train and employ clients would best indicate that the social worker is actively promoting economic justice. This type of program can help lift clients out of poverty and allow them to earn a living wage. The goal of economic justice is to allow each individual to engage in a productive life.

44. B: Military discipline (assignment changes, rank changes, sanctions, etc.) would not normally contribute to a diagnosis of *Posttraumatic Stress Disorder* (PTSD). Combat stress (battle fatigue) is a primary contributor to PTSD. It includes exposure to experiences of violence and mayhem, and the psychological trauma associated with killing and living under the constant stress of being killed. *Military Sexual Trauma* (MST) is often overlooked in recovering veterans (rates of MST are 22% and 1.2%, respectively), especially if the veteran is male. *Mild traumatic brain injury* (MTBI) is also an often-overlooked contributor. Of note, MTBI does not require loss of consciousness or even a diagnosable concussion to be an issue. Any substantial blow to the head or even close proximity to certain kinds of explosive blasts can bring it on, sometimes immediately and sometimes in a delayed form. They key symptoms are unexplained episodes of confusion, disorientation, loss of concentration, feeling dazed, etc. Neuropsychiatric consultation is important in such situations.

45. B: The NASW position on undocumented immigrants, most recently updated in 2018, is to assist these individuals and families in obtaining rights, services, benefits, education, health care, mental health, and other services whenever possible. Not only does the NASW Code of Ethics direct members to oppose any mandatory reporting by social workers, but to also oppose such requirements by members in other professions such as health, education, mental health, policy makers, and among public service providers. Further, undocumented immigrants are to be recognized as particularly vulnerable to exploitation and abuse, and thus they are to receive advocacy services and all available protections from violence (especially as perpetrated upon women) and other forms of abuse and exploitation. All these services are to be provided in a culturally competent manner.

46. C: Insurance and ability to pay is obviously important, but it is not part of an *Intake Interview*. Rather it is a part of screening for services. Key areas of an intake interview include the following: 1) Problem areas (presenting problem, or chief complaint); common areas include relationships, finances, and psychosocial functioning. 2) Strengths: coping skills, resources, capacities, etc. 3) Support systems: significant others, family, friends, organizations, and affiliations, and their scope of involvement and availability. 3) Attitude: positive and progressive versus defeatist and negative, which may influence treatment. 4) Motivation: direct and clear, or for secondary gain or manipulation (e.g., to placate others, meet legal or employment requirements). 5) Relationships: nature, significance and role in life. 6) Resources: those used previously and others currently available, as well as personal resources (faith, values, cognitive capacity, problem-solving skills, etc.). 7) Danger to self or others: suicidality and homicidality must always be explored if there is any indication of relevance. Important risk factors that might contribute to dangerousness should also be noted.

47. A: If the social worker has increasing numbers of clients who are refugees from third world countries and notes that many exhibit signs of depression but are very resistant to any type of referral to mental health services, denying that they have a problem, the most likely reason for this response is a different attitude toward mental illness. Because there is often a stigma attached to a diagnosis of mental illness, people may consider indications, such as withdrawal, crying, insomnia, and sadness, as simply part of life and not something that requires intervention.

48. B: The *medical model* in health care is focused on the *presenting problem* or *chief complaint*. Thus, when used in mental health, it is focused on clients' complaints, deficits, and identified problems. However, this assessment approach tends to miss identification of a client's positive life features, strengths, resiliency, and motivation. The *strengths perspective* views a client's capacities, internal motivations, and dedication to be essential elements of successful problem resolution, healing, and overcoming. A focus on problems can often disempower a client, leaving them feeling mired and overwhelmed in their challenges. In contrast, the strengths perspective focuses on competencies, capacities, resources, confidence, and alternatives—all of which are empowering, positive, and success focused. The *biopsychosocial model* explores the biological (physical), psychological, and social features that may be contributing to a client's concerns and challenges. It readily accounts for issues of environment, culture, poverty, social status, and health as a relevant constellation in which problems and challenges are embedded. Each model has something valuable to offer, and one or another may be preferable depending upon the clinical purpose, therapeutic goals, and environment (crisis vs. long-term contacts, etc.).

49. C: If an adolescent client in foster care repeatedly complains of various ailments but symptoms usually subside shortly after the client is allowed to stay home from school, suggesting the client is feigning illness, the most appropriate response is, "I can see that you are avoiding school because of something that may be difficult for you to talk about." Directly challenging an adolescent or demanding an explanation is likely to result only in withdrawal, but the social worker should acknowledge the client's feelings and allow the opportunity for sharing.

50. B: The best response is to discuss his concerns and support him, but require the collateral contact. It is important to create a therapeutic bond with the client, but not to the exclusion of collateral contacts that are reasonable. The client should be given every opportunity to discuss his concerns, particularly if the therapy ended badly, and he should feel well heard and supported. Further, some collateral contacts (such as with a bitter ex-spouse) can very understandably be refused, but an extended therapeutic relationship should not be circumscribed by a client, as crucial information could be lost and the therapeutic work be thwarted.

51. C: The first response should be to complete a suicide risk evaluation, and then arrange voluntary hospitalization if the client will accept it. As the client's social worker, it is important to complete a suicide risk evaluation, recognizing that it may be more complete, candid, and factual than what the client might reveal during assessment by an unfamiliar clinician. Given the client's emotional state (deliberate calm), detailed plans, and summary rationale, the client is at very high risk for acting on her suicidal thoughts. Further, she has not only motivation and rationale, but the means and anticipated timing for carrying out her plans. Therefore, even if the client were to recant, hospitalization would still be essential to ensure client safety. Calling 911 immediately would be premature and overly reactive. Calling local law enforcement is also overly reactive, and prevents the client from accepting voluntary hospitalization (as involuntary confinement is traumatic, and may produce unintended legal, social, and emotional consequences). Finally, research suggests that suicide prevention contracting alone tends to be ineffective, though potentially meaningful in early suicidal ideation situations.

52. A: The social worker's duty now is to contact the client's wife to inform her of the danger. According to recent interpretations of the case Tarasoff v. Regents of the University of California

(1976, California Supreme Court ruling) confidentiality, in this situation, may be breeched if 1) the HIV infection is known; 2) unprotected sex (or sharing of needles) is occurring; 3) the behavior is actually unsafe; 4) the client refuses to modify his behavior even after being counseled regarding the harm; and 5) if HIV transmission will likely occur.

53. A: The MSE does NOT cover addictions and compulsions. The domains examined in a Mental Status Examination (MSE) are: alertness (attending) and orientation (to person, place, and time = A&Ox3) appearance (physical presentation, dress, hygiene, grooming, etc.), attitude (e.g., cooperative, hostile, guarded, suspicious), behavior (activity, eye contact, movements, gait, mannerisms, psychomotor agitation or retardation, etc.), mood and affect (euphoric, euthymic, dysphoric, anxious, apathetic, anhedonic, etc.), thought processes (rate, quantity, and form [logical or illogical, rapid, or pressured "flights of ideas," perseveration], etc.), thought content (delusions [with or without ideas of reference], grandiosity, paranoia, erotomanic, insertions, broadcasting, etc.), speech (rate and rhythm, poverty or loquacious, pitch, articulation, etc.), perception (hallucinations [visual, auditory, tactile, gustatory, or olfactory], depersonalization, derealization, time distortion [déjà vu], etc.), cognition (alertness, orientation, attention, fund of information, short- and long-term memory and recall, language, executive functions [tested via interpretations], etc.), insight (understanding of problems and options) and judgment (logically reasoned decisions).

54. D: If an 8-year-old child has an out-of-home placement in a temporary foster home because of severe neglect and abandonment by her parents and reports that she has one younger sibling but does not know the child's location, the first consideration of the social worker should be to locate the sibling. It's possible that the other child is in grave danger. The social worker may begin the search by trying to contact other family members, neighbors, or associates of the parents but may need the assistance of the police department.

55. B: Diagnostic *specifiers* in the *Diagnostic and Statistical Manual of Mental Disorders* (*DSM*), currently in its fifth edition, are used almost exclusively to indicate a diagnostic subtype or to rank the status or severity of a diagnostic condition. Many old specifiers and numerous new specifiers are now in use. Common specifiers include "generalized," "with mixed features," "with (or without) insight," "in controlled environment," "on maintenance therapy," "in partial remission," "in full remission," and "by prior history." Other specifiers are used to rank symptom severity (e.g., mild, moderate, and severe). While the NOS (not otherwise specified) acronym has been omitted, the NEC (not elsewhere classified) option has been continue or updated in some diagnostic categories, allowing for idiosyncratic presentations and/or early diagnostic ambiguity.

56. B: Although the criteria for a diagnosis of intellectual disability includes both cognitive capacity and adaptive functioning, the degree of severity (mild, moderate, severe or profound) is determined by adaptive functioning. Cognitive capacity is often measured by IQ scores. Intelligence quotient (IQ) scores include a margin for measurement error of five points. In the *DSM-5*, the term *Mental Retardation* has been replaced with *Intellectual Disability (intellectual developmental disorder)* or ID, to better conform to terms in medical and educational fields. While IQ scores have been removed from the diagnostic criteria, placing greater emphasis on *adaptive functioning*, testing is still necessary. Deficits must now exist in three domains: 1) intellectual functioning (e.g., reasoning, judgment, abstract thinking, and academic and experiential learning); 2) in personal independence and social responsibility (e.g., communication, self-care, home living, social/interpersonal skills, use of community resources, self-direction, functional academic skills, work, leisure, health, and safety); and 3) with onset during the "developmental period" (less rigid than "before age 18"). Supporting associated features include poor social judgment, gullibility, an inability to assess risk, etc.

57. D: *Language Disorder* is characterized by substantial impairment in speaking, as seen in lower scores on standardized tests of language use in the presence of otherwise normal cognitive capacity. Speech sound disorder (formerly called *Phonological Disorder)* presents as substantial impairment in making appropriate speech sounds, sufficient to impede success in academic, occupational, or interpersonal communication. Childhood-onset fluency disorder (*Stuttering)* involves a disturbance in the timing and fluency of speech, unrelated to age and normal development.

58. C: *Autism spectrum disorder* (ASD) presents with virtually all classic symptoms. Some with autism spectrum disorder tend to experience delays in language development and have below average IQ, while others tend to have an average or above average IQ and speak at their expected age range. Children with ASD often become obsessed with a single object or topic, and tend to talk about it nonstop. Social skills are significantly impaired, and they are frequently uncoordinated and awkward. ASD encompasses four disorders that previously under DSM-IV were separate, but are now all believed to be the same disease, with differing severity levels: autistic disorder (autism), Asperger's disorder, childhood disintegrative disorder, and pervasive developmental disorder. *Social communication disorder* cannot be diagnosed if the client presents with restricted repetitive behaviors. As most of these behaviors deal with social issues, and there is no mention of changed IQ, difficulty reasoning/thinking, or failures to be personally independent, *intellectual disability* would not be appropriate.

59. B: If a homeless client was a victim of assault and is being treated in the emergency room but refuses to file a complaint with the police even though the client recognized the perpetrator and he was the fourth homeless person to be attacked, the best response is: "Let the doctor treat you and then you can decide later about filing a complaint." The social worker should avoid trying to put undue pressure on the client but can discuss the reasons for filing a complaint after the client's immediate needs are attended to and may offer to accompany the client to file a complaint.

60. A: The most likely tentative diagnosis for this client is *pica*, which is characterized by the persistent ingestion of nonfood items and materials, demonstrated in her ingestion of paper, clay, and sand. Key features include compulsive craving for nonfood material (for some, ice; rarely, caused by mineral deficiency), and an otherwise normal use of normal foods. The classic symptoms of *Anorexia* center around a poor body image (e.g., seeing oneself as fat) and the avoidance of food to control weight. This may be accompanied by the use of laxatives and exercise to further manage body weight. *Bulimia nervosa* involves binging followed by purging (e.g., vomiting and/or laxative use). *Rumination disorder* involves regurgitating food and re-chewing it. In deriving a tentative diagnosis, note that this adolescent is not drastically losing weight, nor is she avoiding regular food, both which may indicate anorexia if such actions were present. There is no binge-purge cycle and no re-chewing of swallowed and regurgitated food which remove bulimia nervosa and rumination disorder as possible diagnoses.

61. D: *Encopresis* refers to incontinence of bowel in an individual who is at least 4 years of age, chronologically or mentally. It may occur due to stress, anxiety, or constipation, as oppositional or retaliatory behavior, and it may be either voluntary or involuntary. It must occur at least monthly for 3 consecutive months. It must not, however, be due to a neurological, medical, chemical-, or substance-induced disorder or stimulant. The term for similar problems with bladder incontinence is *enuresis*, which has similar diagnostic features, with the exception that bladder incontinence must occur at least twice a week over 3 consecutive months.

62. B: *Separation Anxiety Disorder* involves profound distress when an individual separated from the presence of a primary attachment figure. Onset must be before the age of 18, and the symptoms must be present for at least 4 weeks prior to diagnosis. Symptoms frequently include undue anxiety, irrational fears or worries about safety, inability to fall asleep alone, nightmares, and exaggerated homesickness. These symptoms may also be accompanied by somatic symptoms such as stomachache, dizziness, palpitations, or vomiting, which may lead to medical evaluation when the underlying disorder is psychological in nature. Symptoms during attachment figure separation are developmentally expected until a child reaches 3 to 5 years of age. Clinicians must first rule out agoraphobia before making this diagnosis, especially in older children. *Oppositional Defiant Disorder* requires rebelliousness; *Panic Disorder* involves intense generalized fear that something bad is about to happen; *Agoraphobia* (a type of Panic Disorder) involves severe anxiety in situations deemed uncomfortable, dangerous, or remote from help. None of these are relevant in this situation.

63. D: Both delirium (ICD-10 code of F05) and encephalopathy (G93.40), whether metabolic or toxic, are clinically virtually the same condition. Toxic encephalopathy/delirium occurs secondary to drugs (including alcohol), while metabolic refers to all other inducing mechanisms (sepsis, renal or hepatic failure, etc.). The term delirium tends to be used in psychiatry, while encephalopathy tends to be used in medicine, especially by neurologists. Of note, delirium is a nonspecific ICD (International Classification of Disease) code by Medicare (and thus, by most other payers). Some medical insurers will not reimburse for F05 (see ICD-10), as it falls into a "mental disorder" definition (within the ICD F code range). However, both terms refer to sudden-onset altered mental status conditions, most of which are reversible if the underlying cause is resolved. In elderly persons, medication toxicity and underlying infections with fever are typical causes of delirium/encephalopathy.

64. D: The best response is to advocate for the patient to be admitted for further medical evaluation. There is too much unknown about this seriously compromised elderly patient. He may be malnourished, toxic from overmedication, mildly septic without pyrexia (fever) or elevated WBC, particularly if a urinary tract infection is involved. Sending him back home, from where he apparently wandered away, would be unethical and inhumane. Placing him outside his home, even on a short-term basis, could further compromise his mental status and traumatize him. Delaying discharge until collateral contacts can be made is an option, but family cannot provide an adequate medical explanation for his condition and his safety is clearly at risk. Living alone and wandering suggests delirium (a sudden onset, likely reversible condition) rather than insidious dementia (slow onset, with irreversible impairment) With hospitalization, it can be seen if his condition clears or worsens, collateral contacts can be ensured, and underlying health problems can be explored and potentially resolved. Advocacy in such a situation is a key social work role.

65. B: If the social worker is interviewing a 48-year-old male and notes that the man has a prescription for clozapine, a psychotropic medicine, and other medications, the first action of the social worker should be to note the date on the bottles and count the numbers of pills remaining to try to determine if the man has likely been taking his medications. The social worker should gather as much information as possible before taking further action, such as contacting the man's physician or recommending a 72-hour psychiatric hold.

66. B: The client has at least two of the possible eleven criteria for alcohol use disorder. Most important are the ones that could change the course of his life (missing work and legal issues). Symptoms of withdrawal (delirium tremens, etc.) arise with the cessation of drinking but are not mentioned in this scenario, and may not occur as the client is said to just drink on the weekends. Symptoms of alcohol intoxication (slurred speech, impaired gait, attention and memory impairment, etc.) is not mentioned in this scenario. Recreational use involves sporadic ingestion at such times and in such a way as to avoid negative family, employment, and social consequences, but used heavily enough to produce a pleasurable (recreational) effect.

67. C: The client is clearly displaying both hallucinations (seeing things not there, objects floating) and delusions (believing things that are not true, thought control), as well as the rambling and disorganized speech characteristic of *Schizophrenia*. The condition has existed longer than 6 months, though it is currently in an acute phase. No subtype specifier is required, as the *DSM-5* no longer uses the prior specifiers (paranoid, disorganized, undifferentiated, etc.), with the exception of catatonic type. A diagnosis of *Bipolar Disorder* would not be correct, as there is no evidence of mood cycling and this is not an exacerbated manic phase with psychotic features. *Schizoaffective Disorder* would not be correct, as it requires the presence of a clear affective component (mania or depression), which is not in evidence either by history or presentation. *Substance-Induced Psychosis* requires the proximate use of a mind-altering substance (such as methamphetamine), which is also not in evidence. While there is a remote history (and one cannot entirely rule out more recent ingestion), the parents indicate the symptoms have been consistently present for the greater part of a year, which precludes the episodic presentation of Substance-Induced Psychosis.

68. D: The most appropriate early diagnosis would be Delusional Disorder, erotomanic type. The client openly indicates that this famous person has loving feelings for him, in spite of the fact they've never met or directly communicated in any way. Classic features of *erotomania* (sometimes also called de Clérambault syndrome) include identification with someone in higher status (famous, wealthy, etc.), and is more common among women than men. The symptoms are not infrequently manifest in either schizophrenia or bipolar mania, at which point either would be the proper primary diagnosis (e.g., bipolar, acute manic phase, with erotomanic features). *Grandiose type* is not correct as it focuses on a client's belief that he or she has special talents, unique understandings, or an unrecognized or unreported extraordinary accomplishment. *Jealous type* is not correct, as the inordinate jealousy must be centered in faulty perceptions of infidelity in a real relationship. *Persecutory type* is not correct, as it focuses on a fear of a conspiracy by others to do him harm.

69. B: The diagnosis of *Brief Psychotic Disorder* requires schizophrenic-like symptoms for at least 1 day and no longer than 1 month (e.g., such as hallucinations and/or delusions, both of which this client claimed). It cannot be due to drug-induced psychosis (illicit or licit drugs), or another medical condition. *Posttraumatic Stress Disorder* would not be appropriate as it is not characterized by schizophrenic-like symptoms, but rather flashbacks and trauma-linked stressors that are not indicated here. *Drug-induced psychosis* would not be appropriate, as the vignette specifically disclaims drug use. *Bipolar disorder* would not be correct, as there is no evidence of cycling (manic depression). Thus, Brief Psychotic Disorder is the diagnosis that best fits the available information.

70. C: To be diagnosed with cyclothymia, the moodiness must have been present for at least 2 years (at least 1 year in children and adolescents) and there must have been multiple periods with hypomanic symptoms that do not meet criteria for a manic episode and numerous periods with depressive symptoms that fall short of a major depressive episode. Additionally, the hypomanic and depressive periods must have been present at least half the time and never without the symptoms for more than 2 months at a time. Bipolar disorder involves more dramatic mood swings, with extreme mania and depression. Dysthymia is a form of depression that does not meet Major Depression criteria and does not have hypomanic or manic features. Mood Disorder NOS is not a DSM-5 disorder.

71. D: Persistent complex bereavement disorder is diagnosed when intense and compromising grief extends at least beyond the first year. Key features with the client is her sense of meaninglessness without her spouse, estrangement from others, emotional numbness, and preoccupying thoughts about dying to be with him again. The diagnosis of Major Depression would not be correct due to the fact that the focus is on the loss, rather than a generalized meaninglessness, hopelessness, and helplessness. Posttraumatic stress would not be correct because it centers on key features associated with experiencing an overwhelming and traumatic event (such as combat), with flashbacks and other emotions tied directly to the event itself, rather than to a loss. Uncomplicated bereavement would not be correct, as the intensity and compromising features of the loss are not resolving over time, but rather becoming overly protracted. Of note, *DSM-5* has removed the "bereavement exclusion." It is possible to be diagnosed both with bereavement and major depression, if the circumstances warrant.

72. A: Bipolar I involves mania and Bipolar II involves primarily depression. Bipolar I Disorder requires a minimum of one manic episode (or mixed episode), as well as episodes with features typical of Major Depression. In contrast to this, Bipolar II requires at least one Major Depression episode, and a minimum of at least one Hypomanic episode. Adequate control requires medications. Preferred treatment medications more commonly focus on atypical antipsychotics (Abilify, Geodon, Risperdal, Seroquel, or Zyprexa), which provide greater symptom relief than the older mood stabilizing medications such as lithium, Depakote, or Tegretol. These are now more commonly used only as adjuncts. An extended depressive episode may also be treated with antidepressants. Education about the condition, as well as therapy (e.g., cognitive-behavior, interpersonal, social rhythm, family therapy), greatly enhances successful management.

73. D: These symptoms most closely resemble panic disorder. The symptoms of a panic attack appear very quickly and generally peak within 10 minutes. Typical symptoms include rapid heart rate, shortness of breath, light-headedness, trembling, derealization and depersonalization (feeling surreal and detached from self), nausea, dizziness, numb and tingling feelings, etc. These are typically accompanied by feelings of impending doom and/or death. Many of the symptoms are a direct result of hyperventilation during the acute panic phase. Anxiety disorder due to a medical condition is not correct, as there is no underlying medical condition. Generalized anxiety disorder is not correct, as it does not have sudden onset but rather is an accumulation of worry and anxiety that persists for 6 or more months (without an underlying medical condition or substance use precipitant). Acute stress disorder is not correct, as it involves a precipitating PTSD-like traumatic event that induces the symptoms of stress.

74. C: The key features of Illness Anxiety Disorder (care-seeking type) include an intense preoccupation with the acquisition of a serious health problem, an absence of actual somatic symptoms (or only very mild symptoms), an honest belief and fear of an illness (e.g., not manipulative in any way), a high level of health anxiety, and excessive health-preoccupied behaviors that have continued for more than 6 months. Care-seeking type can be specified, as the client continues to seek help and support from a medical provider on a regular basis, even after adequate reassurances have been provided. Malingering Disorder is not correct, as it involves exaggerating or falsely claiming symptoms for secondary gain (e.g., insurance claims, to be relieved of unpleasant work). Factitious Disorder is not correct, as it involves the deliberate fabrication of symptoms without the intent to receive tangible or concrete rewards, but rather for the nurturance or attention thereby derived. Somatic Symptom Disorder is not correct, as it requires the presence of actual somatic (physical) symptoms. Note: Somatization Disorder, Hypochondriasis, Pain Disorder, and Undifferentiated Somatoform Disorder have been removed from *DSM-5* and replaced with Somatic Symptom Disorder.

75. B: Key features of dissociative amnesia with dissociative fugue are localized or selective amnesia surrounding certain events, or generalized amnesia involving identity and life history, along with some sort of purposeful travel or simply aimless wandering. The amnesia must produce significant distress, and/or impairment in social, occupational, or other significant areas of personal function. It must not be a result of substance ingestion or a medical (especially neurological) condition. Dissociative Identity Disorder (in the past known as Multiple Personality Disorder) would not be correct as it involves the development to one or more separate identities.

76. B: Genito-pelvic pain disorder refers to any form of pain during sexual intercourse that persistently recurs. Causes can include involuntary contractions of the outer third of the vagina (involving the pubococcygeus muscles), vaginal dryness, inflammation, infection, skin conditions, sexually transmitted infections (STIs), or any other underlying medical condition. Female sexual interest/arousal disorder would not be correct because it involves a psychological aversion to or avoidance of sexual activity, rather than physical pain. Female Orgasmic Disorder is incorrect because it involves a failure to reach orgasm, even with appropriate stimulation, excluding an underlying medical condition.

77. D: The most likely diagnosis to describe this behavior would be other specified paraphilia. Exhibitionism involves a minimum of 6 months of recurrent urges, fantasies, and/or behaviors involving the exposure of one's genitals to an unsuspecting person, or where clinically significant distress or impairment in social, occupational, or other meaningful areas of functioning occurs. In this case, however, the recipient of the client's disrobing behaviors is not an unsuspecting stranger, nor does the vignette specify that she exposes her genitals or if she fully or only partially disrobes. Thus, this is more an act of consensual sex-play, rather than exhibitionism. Voyeurism is not correct, as it involves watching an unsuspecting person disrobing. Frotteurism is inaccurate as it involves intense sexual arousal from the urge, fantasy, or act of touching or rubbing against a nonconsenting person.

78. B: If a 15-year-old client persists in making suggestive remarks about the social worker's appearance and asks if the social worker is married or has a partner, the most appropriate response is one that not only clearly sets limits but also gives the reason: "It's not appropriate for us to discuss personal information, and I feel uncomfortable with your comments." The social worker should focus on "I" rather than "you" and should speak clearly and directly but avoid any indications of anger.

79. C: Borderline Personality Disorder is characterized by, among other features, a pervasive pattern of unstable relationships, chronic feelings of emptiness, poorly controlled chronic anger, and alternating devaluing and overvaluing relationships, followed by frantic efforts to avoid abandonment. Histrionic Personality Disorder would not be appropriate, as the client's high emotions and attention-seeking behaviors are just a subset of other problematic issues, beliefs, and behaviors. Narcissistic Personality Disorder is also not correct, as the client's problems are not centered on grandiosity, absence of empathy, arrogance, or entitlement, etc. Antisocial Personality Disorder would be incorrect, as features of aggression, violations of the law, or absence of remorse are not central to the client's presentation. The presence of a personality disorder, however, is clear, as the issues involve a pattern of interacting with the world that guides her life and shapes her experiences.

80. D: All of the listed terms are all used interchangeably. Common guidelines for direct practice include: 1) Start with client-identified issues. 2) Use positive goal setting. 3) Overcome difficulties by modeling honest and direct communication. 4) Ensure culturally competent service by careful assessment. 5) Use a client's native language, if possible, or obtain an interpreter. 6) Avoid reality testing a delusional client's thoughts, and instead seek to calm and support pending further assessment and/or medications. 7) Carefully watch for transference and countertransference processes. If a client requires hospitalization, seek a voluntary placement where possible, and carefully follow involuntary hospitalization and evaluation guidelines when necessary.

81. A: If the social worker is utilizing role playing in group therapy and the client has enacted his role in a problem situation with a partner and then the social workers suggests they practice mirroring, this would involve the partner reflecting the behavior displayed by the client. Thus, if the client paces back and forth and frowns, the partner would also pace and frown. The purpose of mirroring is to allow the client to see how his behavior is observed and perceived by others.

82. B: While life transitions can be stressful, these transitions tend to be gradual and thus lack the short-term and overwhelming qualities that properly define a crisis. Cultural-Societal crises are those where fundamental worldviews collide in traumatic ways, for example, immigrating to a foreign country, or revealing homosexuality in a heterosexual community. Maturational crises involve developmental events, such as beginning school, leaving home, or marriage. Situational crises involve a sudden traumatic event, such as a car accident, witnessing violence, or being assaulted. To help individuals re-establish their coping skills and equilibrium, Crisis Intervention has three primary goals: 1) reducing the impact and symptoms that accompany a crisis (e.g., normalizing, calming, empowering); 2) mobilizing resources, both internal (psychological) and external (e.g., social, financial); and 3) restoring the precrisis level of function.

83. D: If the social worker's client has few resources and many issues and the social worker is utilizing the principle of partialization, the first actions should be to collaborate with the client in creating a list of problems and them to group them and identify the highest priority. The principle of partialization aims to help manage complex situations by focusing on one problem at a time and setting priorities with initial focus on the problem that is most critical.

84. D: The Premack Principle is a method for increasing desired behaviors. The *Premack Principle* is applied by pairing a low-probability behavior with a high-probability behavior in order to increase the frequency that the low-probability behavior will be engaged. For example, a child will be permitted to play sports, watch television, or play video games only after he or she has completed all daily assigned homework. In this way, the motivation and desire to complete assigned homework is increased. This is a form of *Operant Conditioning*. Other Operant Conditioning tools include: 1) The use of *Reinforcers* (positive consequences following a desired behavior). Reinforcers may be *primary* (naturally reinforcing, such as needs for food, water, and sleep), or *secondary* (a stimulus that an organism learns to value). *Positive reinforcement* involves a stimulus reward following a desired behavior, and *negative reinforcement* involves the withdrawal of an unpleasant consequence when desired behavior occurs.

85. D: A *Contingency Contract* is used in treatment to specify a particular consequence, either positive or negative, contingent upon whether or not a specific behavior or behaviors occur as agreed upon. It is a meaningful tool for modifying individual behavior. Another commonly used *Operant Conditioning* tool to reinforce desirable behavior is called the *Token Economy*. It involves the delivery of representative tokens that can be redeemed for desirable reinforcers by the individual. It is most commonly used with children to modify behavior. Other concurrently used strategies include the use of *verbal prompts* and *clarifications*. As reminders (prompts) are provided and clarifications are supplied to increase understanding and focus, behaviors can be more rapidly modified and solidified.

86. A: Three forms of cognitive-behavioral therapy (CBT) predominate: 1) Aaron Beck's *Cognitive Therapy* views depression and mental illness as a bias toward negative thinking via thinking errors (all-or-nothing and black-and-white/dichotomous thinking, emotional reasoning, overgeneralization, magnification and minimization, catastrophizing, and mind reading). Relief is found through collaborative empiricism, Socratic dialogue, guided discovery, decatastrophizing, reattribution training, and decentering. 2) Albert Ellis' *Rational Emotive Therapy* identifies common irrational beliefs (demands and absolutes), which are rationally challenged, evaluated, clarified, and resolved. 3) Donald Meichenbaum's *Self-Instruction Training* focuses on maladaptive self-statements that frequently underlie negative thinking patterns, negativity, and self-defeating thoughts and behaviors. Therapy involves thought assessments, situational self-statement exploration, and developing new self-statements that better reflect truth and mental health.

87. C: The key components of *Solution-Focused Therapy* include the following: 1) problem description; 2) formulating goals; 3) collaboratively identifying solutions; 4) feedback at close of session; and 5) evaluation of progress. *Dialectical Behavioral Therapy* is most often used in the treatment of Borderline Personality Disorder, and consists of four modules: 1) mindfulness (observe, describe, and then participate); 2) interpersonal effectiveness (learning to assertively ask for change and say no when needed); 3) distress tolerance (identifying and tolerating things that cannot be changed); and 4) emotion regulation (becoming emotionally aware and able to direct emotions). *Reality Therapy* focuses on meeting four psychological needs (belonging, freedom, fun, and power) through internally oriented, purposeful behaviors. It rejects the medical model of mental illness, and side-steps past attitudes, behaviors, and feelings in favor of current perspectives on whether any given behavior can responsibly meet one's needs without damaging others. Reality testing is used to reject unsuccessful behaviors and identify those that will truly succeed.

88. B: Karen Horney concurred with Freud that anxiety underlies most neuroses. However, she disagreed that conflicts between instinctual drives and the superego produced this anxiety. Rather, anxiety arises through problematic parental behaviors: rejection, over-protectiveness, and/or indifference. Children cope by: 1) over-compliance (moving toward people), 2) detachment (moving away from people), or 3) aggression (moving against people). Resolution requires: 1) meeting biological needs, and 2) protection from danger, fear, and pain. *Erich Fromm* also moved past Freud and Marx, believing that individuals can transcend biological and societal barriers through pursuit of internal freedom. Efforts to escape freedom (responsibility) produce self-alienation and "unproductive" families that favor symbiosis (enmeshment) or withdrawal (indifference). He identified four problematic personality orientations: 1) receptive, 2) exploitative, 3) hoarding, and 4) marketing, and one healthy orientation, 5) productive (rational responsibility). Harry Stack Sullivan emphasized relationships over lifespan issues, focusing on three modes of cognitive experience in personality development: 1) Prototaxic (momentary perceptions in early life); 2) Parataxic (misperceptions or distortions of early important events); and 3) Syntaxic (the emergence of logical, sequential, modifiable, and internally consistent thinking).

89. D: Carl Jung developed the concept of *abreaction*, which involves relieving, retelling, and reorienting an experience to discharge the negative psychological burdens that accompany the experience. Abreaction is a form of *catharsis*, where abreaction involves dealing with specific biographical experiences and catharsis involves the release of more generalized emotional and physical tension. Jung felt that behavior is derived from past experiences in the context of future goals and aspirations. Personality is two-fold: the *conscious*, oriented toward the external world, and the *unconscious*. The unconscious is composed of personal and collective elements. *Personal unconscious* consists of repressed or forgotten experiences, and the *collective unconscious* consists of inherited memory traces and primordial images (*archetypes*) that produce commonly shared understandings in societies. Key archetypes include the *self* (producing unity in the personality), the *persona* (a public mask), the *shadow* (or dark side) of personality, and the *anima* (feminine) or *animus* (masculine). Personality consists of attitudes (introversion and extroversion) and four basic functions (feeling, intuiting, sensing, and thinking).

90. D: Introjection refers to gradually defining oneself by thoughtful rejection or integration of outside ideas. Gestalt Therapy differs from Freudian Psychoanalysis on introjection primarily in its definition of a gradual rather than immediate construct. Psychoanalysis posits a prompt and full acceptance by the client of the analyst's conclusions, whereas Gestalt suggests a gradual integration of only that information that the client deems accurate following due reflection. Four key boundary disturbances defined in Gestalt Therapy are: 1) introjection: differentiating between "me, and not me," lacking which a client is overly compliant and attempts to please others at the loss of true self; 2) projection: assigning uncomfortable aspects of the self to others (e.g., "he never liked me," when it is you who dislikes him); 3) retroflection: directing inward the feelings one has for another (seen as expressions of self-blame when addressing such feelings with another); and 4) confluence: an absence of boundaries between self and others, resulting in feelings of both guilt and resentment over actual differences. The therapeutic goal is to create healthy boundaries and self-integration (integrity).

91. D: This group is best described as an ongoing growth group. Generally, groups are defined as either task or treatment oriented. Open-ended groups have no termination date. Task groups are formed solely to accomplish a specific goal (preparing a New Year's dance, etc.). Treatment groups serve to enhance members' social and/or emotional needs and/or skills. Types of treatment groups include: 1) educational groups: formed to enhance learning about specific issues or problems, providing needed information and skills; 2) growth groups: focus on personal enrichment and progress, as opposed to remediating past problems and concerns; 3) socialization groups: aid members in accommodating role and environmental challenges (e.g., a new immigrants group); 4) support groups: bring together people with common issues or circumstances to help them in coping with their shared concerns (e.g., a bereavement group); and 5) therapy groups: serve to offer remediation and/or rehabilitation of a specific concern or problem (e.g., a gambling problem group).

92. C: If the social worker is working on a project with a coworker who persists in berating the social worker for missing a meeting scheduled when the social worker had to deal with a client emergency and must ask for information but realizes this will give the coworker another opportunity to complain, the most effective assertive communication is: "I realize I missed the meeting and that was inconvenient for you, but what did the data show?" This response begins with an "I" statement and defuses the possible complaints by stating them upfront and then asks directly for information needed.

93. B: Triangulation is the introduction of a third party into a conflict between two individuals. The goal is to produce a power asymmetry in order to turn events to one's favor. Family problems typically involve triangulation. Therapeutic triangulation occurs when a social worker is drawn into taking sides. The eight interlocking concepts of Family Systems Theory include: 1) *Self-Differentiation* (vs. fused identities); 2) *Nuclear Family Emotional System* (formerly the *Undifferentiated Family Ego Mass*) of fused identity; 3) *Triangles* (drawing a third party into conflicts); 4) *Societal Emotional Process* (emotional processes in societal interactions, similar to family); 5) *Emotional Cutoff* (severing intergenerational ties); 6) *Sibling Position* (drives some personality characteristics); 7) *Family Projection Process* (parents transmitting patterns to offspring); and 8) *Multigenerational Transmission Process* (patterns transmitted intergenerationally).

94. C: Equifinality refers to the idea that the same results can be secured in different ways. The *Circular Model of Causality*, however, notes that the behaviors of different subsystems can nevertheless reciprocally influence each other. Responses B and D are not formal Communications/Experimental Therapy terms. Other forms of dysfunctional communication include criticizing, blaming, mind-reading, implying events that can be modified or improved are unalterable, overgeneralizations, double-bind expressions (contradictory demands that functionally allow only one of two required consequences to be achieved), denying that one is communicating (which can never be true), and disqualifying other's communications.

95. A: If a 4-year-old child has been placed into foster care for the second time because his mother was charged with child endangerment after leaving the child unattended while she engaged in prostitution, the first goal for permanency planning should be family reunification with the mother. While the child appears healthy and well cared for, the child must also be safe, so the social worker must work with the parent to develop plans for childcare. Being a sex-worker does not preclude a person from being a good parent.

96. A: The concept of *complementarity* addresses the harmony and disharmony that arises when family roles cannot be reconciled. *Alignments* are coalitions that are produced between various family subsystems to achieve specific goals, the nature of which may or may not be dysfunctional. *Power hierarchies* reveal the distribution of power within the family as a whole. *Disengagement* occurs when family members and subsystems become emotionally and/or interactively isolated. Of further note: *subsystems* are separate functional family units (e.g., parents) that operate within the larger family structure. *Enmeshment* results from over-involvement or concern with family members to the point that individual recognition and autonomy are lost. *Inflexibility* addresses situations in which the family structure becomes so rigid that adaptation cannot occur when required.

97. D: *Circular questions* are used to enhance relational perspectives by helping family members to take the standpoint of another, particularly with a family member who may otherwise be misunderstood. *Hypothesizing* is something done by the therapy team, wherein they attempt to understand the presenting problem and formulate a successful intervention, refining throughout the therapeutic process. *Counter-paradox* is an extension of *paradoxical prescription* (wherein problem behaviors are actually prescribed) by which a problem behavior and all related interactions around it are prescribed. *Positive connotation* reframes problematic symptoms as efforts to preserve the family and promote solidarity. Other techniques include *neutrality* (in which social worker-family member alliances are avoided to prevent triangulation}, and *rituals* (repetitive behaviors used to counter dysfunctional family rules).

98. C: The community itself. Community organization involves work with larger entities, citizen groups, and organization directors for the purpose of: 1) solving social problems; 2) developing collaborative and proactive qualities in community members; and 3) redistributing decision-making power through community relationships. Community organizers assist communities to learn how to meet their needs, eradicate social problems, and enrich lives, as well as balancing resources and social welfare needs. To accomplish this, the community must first be accepted as it is, and then learn of the interdependence of its constituent members and intra-community entities.

99. B: Social workers often serve as community organizers, and may readily be approached with problems in the community. In this situation, the first and best step for the citizen to take is as a whistleblower. This step draws attention to the problem, activates oversight agencies, and begins to bring a problem out into the open. Next steps may include: 2) negotiation with the factory leadership; 3) community education, to help others understand the problem; 4) social protesting (picketing, demonstrations, boycotting); 5) lobbying entities responsible to intervene; 6) conducting action research to further explore the problems; 7) forming self-help groups to assist the oppressed to better understand resources and their rights; and 8) legal efforts such as mediation and/or lawsuits to compel change.

100. B: Only an attorney can offer legal counsel and advice. A social worker can, however, point out options and refer a client or community to appropriate resources for legal counsel and advice. Other intervention roles that may be assumed by a social worker include: 1) broker: identifying and referring clients to needed resources within a community; 2) case manager: assisting clients lacking the capacity to take independent action and/or follow through with resource referrals; 3) client advocate: working on behalf or in conjunction with clients seeking access to needed resources; and 4) mediator: collaborating with both the client and resource provider(s) to overcome conflicts and obstacles in identifying a path to receive needed services and resources.

101. C: Involuntary clients may utilize humor in their interactions, but not as a primary mechanism for resisting the treatment process. More commonly, resistance comes in the forms of: 1) aggression: becoming either verbally or even physically assaultive, or producing a pseudo-cooperative passive-aggressive response that needs to be mitigated before meaningful progress can be made; 2) diversion: commonly seen through blaming ("someone else made this happen"), seeking to turn attention to others ("he did something way worse"), shifting the focus back to the social worker ("you think you're better than the rest of us"), or simply guiding the discussion in another direction; and 3) withdrawal: seen as a refusal to talk, avoiding discussions about feelings, or minimizing relevant issues, etc. Each of these forms of resistance must be overcome before treatment can properly proceed.

102. B: The primary objective of supervision is meeting the clients' individual needs. It is important to recognize the difference in purpose between supervision and supervising tasks. The primary purpose of supervision is to ensure that clients' needs are fully, ethically, and competently addressed and met. To accomplish this, the supervisor must also ensure that staff have adequate training and necessary access to resources and services. The supervisor must also establish and conduct quality control reviews to regularly monitor the work of agency staff and outside providers. The primary task of the supervisor is to ensure that essential work is completed. This is necessary to keep the agency functioning and to ensure that an appropriate number of clients can be served. This requires both administrative and clinical expertise on the part of the supervisor and his or her designated leaders within the agency.

103. A: The purpose of consultation is to share expertise, seek options, consider recommendations, and otherwise collaborate and explore clinical and/or operational needs and resources and optimal options. Consultation is not designed to serve as alternate leadership, to be directive or determinative, or to serve as a deferral opportunity such that leaders or staff relinquish their obligation to continue to carry out their professional responsibilities. Consultation may be considered in six stages: 1) entry (early contracting, orientation, and overcoming resistance; 2) identifying consultation goals (which requires adequate problem exploration and understanding); 3) defining goals (which must be a collaborative venture); 4) providing intervention(s) (supported by brainstorming and Delphi methods to obtain participation from all); 5) assessment (of progress and continuing or new problems); 6) concluding the relationship (involves fostering independence, determining continuing availability, etc.).

104. D: The structuralist management style views organizations as deeply impacted by environmental factors, with conflict as inevitable but not necessarily negative if handled properly. Bureaucratic theories (Max Weber) espouse vertical hierarchy, policy-driven, merit rewards, and a careful division of labor that maximizes efficiency and control. Scientific theories utilize an economic and rational perspective to maximize productivity. Contingency theories focus on flexibility and responsiveness. Participative theories conclude that democratic leadership and participant buy-in make for greater loyalty and productivity. Quality Circles are based on self-governance and evaluation. Total Quality Management (TQM) focuses on service delivery processes and a broader view than Quality Assurance models. Maslow's Hierarchy of Needs theory allows management to ensure greater participant fulfillment and thus job satisfaction and productivity. Job Enrichment theory (Herzberg) posits that good job "hygiene" (benefits, conditions, salary, etc.) plus motivators (freedom, challenges, growth, etc.) optimized management outcomes. Needs Theory (McClelland) views the paramount needs as power, affiliation, and achievement as the path to optimal management and staff success.

105. C: *Summative Program Evaluation* examines the degree to which goals and objectives are realized, as well as how generalizable the outcomes may be to other settings and populations, in determining program efficacy and value. *Cost-Benefit Analysis* produces a ratio of direct costs to outcome benefits in determining program effectiveness. *Cost Effectiveness* evaluation focuses on a program's operational costs as compared with final output (unit) costs, requiring a favorable ratio to deem a program effective. *Formative Program Evaluation* is conducted longitudinally (from program inception through implementation) to determine its final efficacy and value. *Peer Review* involves collegial evaluations using professional standards to determine the quality of work and the resultant outcomes.

106. C: If a client is being treated for anxiety but reports having difficulty concentrating on schoolwork and tasks because of being unable to stop worrying and has been sleeping poorly and has lost weight, the complementary therapeutic approach that the social worker should advise first is relaxation exercises, such as deep breathing and visual imagery. These exercises are easy to teach and to learn and can be mastered very quickly, so the client can utilize the exercises immediately.

107. B: A given state's Division of Child and Family Services (DCFS, though sometimes called by other titles in various states) would not typically provide safe shelters for victims of domestic violence. They would, however, provide referrals and linkages for services of this nature to ensure the safety of individuals who are in an unsafe home environment. Services commonly provided directly include therapy services, educational referrals, employment training, family counseling and intervention, and other services designed to mitigate family problems and restore successful family functioning. Within most DCFS programs are Child Protective Services (CPS) programs that offer services such as investigations of abuse, shelter care, family therapy, juvenile court linkages, foster care, and other services and resources to help stabilize difficult home situations.

108. D: The first step should be to promptly refer the asthmatic boy to a medical doctor. Asthma can be life-threatening, and the child is also described as congested and unwell. Given that "all" possessions were lost, it is reasonable to conclude that the child has little or no remaining inhaler medicines for an asthma crisis. While all may attend the medical visit, the boy needs to be seen urgently. Following or concurrently, a complete psychosocial evaluation needs to be completed. After further evaluation, the key elements of a case presentation for the director should include: 1) psychosocial history: mental health issues and social history such as living situation, finances, education, etc.; 2) individual issues: substance abuse history, legal history, physical abuse and neglect history, as well as resources, strengths, and resiliency, etc.; 3) family history, family dynamics, and extended family resources; 4) potential community resources and supports; 5) diversity issues: culture, language, race/ethnicity, orientation, etc.; 6) potential ethical issues and presenting issues in self-determination; and 7) intervention recommendations, including requisite resources.

109. C: SOAP stands for Subjective, Objective, Assessment, Plan. This method of documentation or charting is frequently used by health care providers to structure their clinical notes. An entry typically includes some or all of the following information: 1) Subjective information: information reported by the client and others closely involved. 2) Objective information: such as laboratory results, test scores, examination data, and scores from screenings. 3) Assessment: the summary review and ultimate conclusions derived from the subjective reports and objective tests, evaluations, examinations, screenings, etc., concluding in an overall impression of the presenting problem(s). 4) Plan: the steps that need to be taken to resolve the presenting problem(s), as derived from all prior information and conclusions drawn.

110. D: Social functioning is the service delivery model used by the social worker who focuses on helping the client to deal with current behavior in social interactions with a goal of the client's exhibiting behavior that is more acceptable to others. This often results in positive reinforcement, further encouraging socially behavior modification. The social functioning model is concerned less with issues that arose in the past and more with those in the present.

111. C: If the social worker in on the committee to update the policy and procedure manual, the social worker should recognize the first step in developing policies is to identify problems. Each problem should be assessed to determine how it has arisen, the conditions under which it is evident, and the stakeholders involved in or affected by the problem. Next, issues related to the problem, such as whether it is localized or generalized, should be identified and potential solutions brainstormed and then rank-ordered in order to choose the most appropriate solution from which to develop the policy.

112. C: If the social worker is in charge of an outreach program that is its own cost center and the organization utilizes a zero-based approach to departmental budgets and the budget period is coming to an end, the most appropriate action for the social worker is to prepare a report on the benefits of the program and the projected budget needs. With zero-based budgets, all cost centers are re-evaluated each budget period to determine if they should be funded or eliminated, partially or completely.

113. C: Social work ethics may best be defined as conduct standards based on values. A belief system is defined by core values, and ethics operationalize the values-defined belief system into standard of conduct. The core values of the social work profession are as follows (NASW, 2008): 1) dignity and worth of the individual; 2) the importance of human relationships; 3) the pursuit of social justice; 4) competence in professional knowledge and practice; 5) personal and professional integrity; and 6) service. The NASW Code of Social Work Ethics applies to all who practice social work, whether or not they belong to the NASW. There are six ethical areas: 1) responsibilities to clients; 2) responsibilities to colleagues; 3) responsibilities in practice settings; 4) responsibilities as professionals; 5) responsibilities to the profession; and 6) responsibilities to society.

114. D: Self-determination refers to the right to personal autonomy and decision making. Social workers are charged with helping their clients choose their own life's direction and destiny. An exception is when a client's choices are suicidal, homicidal, or abusive of others' rights. True self-determination requires: 1) the internal capacity for autonomy, 2) freedom from external constraints, and 3) information to make well-informed choices. Social workers should primarily assist clients in identifying and clarifying their own goals, rather than goals others might choose for them. Involuntary hospitalization or other mandated limits placed on self-determination do not allow professionals to fully ignore this ethical principle. Thus, the concepts of "least restrictive" and "least intrusive" come into play. Involuntary or mandated courses of action should be used only as a last result as is possible, without unduly risking the client's life or intruding upon or abusing other individuals.

115. A: The lack of signage on a substance abuse treatment facility is not an element of confidentiality. *Confidentiality* refers to an individual's right to control how identifiable information the client has divulged, or data about that individual, is handled, managed, and disseminated. Through confidentiality, individuals can retain control over the circumstances, timing, and extent to which personally sensitive information is shared with others. *Privacy* does not relate to information or data, but rather to the person themselves. Thus, privacy involves control over the circumstances, timing, and extent to which one wishes to share oneself physically, intellectually, and/or behaviorally with others. It is practiced by interviews in closed areas (not for information or data reasons, but for allowing expressions of emotion, sharing of thought processes, etc.), proper changing areas, and excusing others (including family, at times) from sharing experiences, etc. Confidentiality and privacy may be compromised for serious safety concerns, for the client or others.

116. C: The best response is to consult with a supervisor or legal counsel to ensure a proper response to the situation. It is significant to note that the NASW Code of Ethics (2008), Standard 1.09, bans all sexual involvement with both current and former clients and offers no time or circumstances limitation. Violation of this standard will thus result in prompt termination of any NASW membership. It is also important to note, however, that state licensing statutes vary on the topic (e.g., some states do not prohibit former client relationships at all, or may cite a 1 to 2 year prohibition only, after which such relationships are possible) and confidentiality requirements in such situations may also be complex; indeed, reporting may circumvent confidentiality in many ways. Therefore, it is important to know relevant state laws, and to seek competent consultation from a skilled supervisor or legal advisor.

117. D: The most appropriate response is to allow only a partial review, withholding portions deemed too sensitive. Clients have the right to reasonable access to records kept about them personally. However, social workers also have an obligation to prevent a client from reading case notes deemed potentially harmful to the client, or that could breach confidentiality of others (e.g., a party reporting suspected abuse). In situations where appropriate explanations would suffice to mitigate any concern of harm, the social worker has the right to review the case record with the client to offer explanatory insights and understandings. Where harm cannot be otherwise avoided, the social worker must restrict the client from viewing any harmful portion. For such portions, summary notes can be produced for the client, if desired. Regardless, it should be noted in the file the date and time of the client's review, and the rationale for any restrictions on review should be fully explained and documented in the case record.

118. A: The best response is to refer the child to a social worker with experience in pediatric sleep disorders. Obtaining licensure is only a first step in establishing a competent clinical practice. Remaining in areas of clear clinical expertise is ethically important, and not leading families to believe that one possesses skills that have not yet been developed is essential. When a new issue arises that is very closely related a social worker's primary scope of practice, it is reasonable to broaden skills through collateral research and consultation. However, if a treatment area (e.g., pediatric sleep disorders) is entirely beyond the scope of practice, it would be inappropriate to try to produce requisite skills through brief reading or consultation, when the skills actually require extended training and experience to develop. In such situations it is essential that the client be referred to another clinician for proper evaluation of the presenting problem.

119. D: If the social worker works in a program for homeless youth and is interested in engaging in fundraising to provide an increased budget for the program, the first step should be to define the purpose of the fundraising so that potential donors have a very clear understanding. Then, the goal for fundraising should be established and should be realistic because further support is more likely if the initial goal is reached. The social worker must also establish a budget for fundraising as there are almost always costs involved. Last, the target population must be determined as this will influence the fundraising approach.

120. C: The best way to secure the consult is to set up a formal consultation appointment to discuss the issue(s) in the office. It is tempting to discuss client cases over a meal or after hours, as it saves work time and allows for more informal sharing. However, discussing clients in a public setting produces a substantial likelihood that client confidentiality will be breached with others seated or walking nearby. It may also seem easier to leave a client's file with a consultant for review, as the consultant can then thoroughly review the case and more closely examine all specifically relevant issues. However, it is unethical for a primary social worker to disclose more client information to a consultant than is essential for the consulting issue to be properly addressed. Leaving a client file with the consultant offers no confidentiality boundaries at all. Consequently, consultation in an office setting, during a formal appointment, and by direct confidentiality-focused dialogue is the proper way to obtain an ethically structured consultation.

121. C: The first responsibility of the social worker is to contact the colleague and discuss treatment options. As with any client, the most appropriate intervention is one that occurs voluntarily and openly, with adequate support and caring concern offered. If the colleague refuses to seek immediate help in this situation, then further steps are necessary, including reporting the problem to a supervisor who can the address the issue further in accordance with agency policy and guidelines. Certainly, the safety and well-being of the colleague's clients must be preserved, and no delay in addressing the issue can be afforded. Similar guidelines apply to colleagues who unethically practice outside the scope of their area of competence, or who behave unethically with clients, coworkers, or other outside programs and staff.

122. B: The best response is to seek to bring the agency's policies and procedures into compliance. Simply quitting does nothing to resolve this underlying problem with ethics and standards of conduct. Neither does a blanket refusal to work with materials, resources, and conditions that are outside NASW Code of Ethics standards. Optimally, a social worker should utilize his or her professional skills to seek to bring about change. Explaining the applicable ethical standards, and pointing out the protections they afford both staff and clients, provides a compelling case for change. If no progress is subsequently made, it may become necessary for the social worker to resign and leave the work setting, and/or to report the ethical issues to any proper oversight entity. In this way, ethical standards can be provided to all clients in any agency setting.

123. D: If the shared governance model used by the organization allows each department autonomous decision-making regarding issues that directly apply to that department, the leader of each department is a member of the administrative council, and the social worker is interested in make a major change in procedure that involves multiple departments, the social worker should first discuss the proposal with members of the different departments to build consensus.

124. A: If the social worker has been working with homeless clients for many months and has developed compassion fatigue from encountering the same problems over and over again, the social worker is likely to respond to clients with numbness toward their suffering and may begin to blame them for their problems rather than feeling empathy toward them. The social worker may need to take a break or rotate assignments in order to gain some perspective. Otherwise, other departments may feel that the social work department is imposing changes to which they have had no input.

125. B: Empathy is the most important feature of a meaningful therapeutic bond. Compassion involves concern for the misfortunes and welfare of another. Condolence involves expressions of compassion and sympathy. Sympathy literally means to feel with, or have a resonate feeling for another. Feelings of compassion and sympathy are expressed in carefully chosen words of condolence. *Empathy*, however, is deeper. It literally means to "feel into" the heart and mind of another, projecting oneself into their situation, feelings, and experiences. The term originated in psychology, drawn as a translation from a German term. It is an important tool in creating a therapeutic bond, as it involves a shared emotional state most fully realized when one has "been there," whereas sympathy is the natural state when one has not. Other important components of a strong therapeutic relationship include: 1) *warmth* (a show of genuine care and acceptance); 2) *authenticity/genuineness* (open and natural sharing in a meaningful way); and 3) *trust* (which involves a certainty of safety and predictability, and is maintained by practices such as confidentiality and privacy).

126. D: It can become easy to use short-hand descriptors to refer to one's caseload. However, doing so can subtly but powerfully alter the way a case manager feels and even interacts with clients. Far better to describe a caseload as "numerous people with schizophrenia, several people with bipolar disorder, and some other clients struggling with borderline personality disorder." The use of the words *people* and *clients* lets them retain their humanity. Everyone needs to be seen as an individual with unique qualities and contributions. Casually categorizing and stereotyping clients can lead to losing sight of their humanity, individuality, and uniqueness. Casework is and must remain client-focused, respectful, and understanding of clients' unique circumstances, needs, and potential. Using care in the verbiage chosen to speak about clients can help social work case managers avoid the biases, prejudices, and cultural insensitivities that can otherwise enter the case management process.

127. A: Allowing judgment of how acceptable or not the feelings are is not going to aid in the process of sharing. Feelings should not be appraised judgmentally. Rather, they should be evaluated for how they are affecting the client and how functional they are in the processes of living and interacting with others. Expressions of feelings offer an important window into understanding how a client perceives his or her life situation, as well as their sense of hopefulness, security, and safety. If feelings and emotions become too negative and burdensome, it may become important to incorporate the management of the client's feelings into the ongoing evaluation and treatment plan. Finally, if received and handled well, the sharing of deep feelings in a long-term case management or treatment processes further strengthens the therapeutic bond, which in turn enhances the effectiveness of the case manager/social worker in addressing the client's challenges and problems.

128. D: The best response is to seek to understand his feelings while soothing/deescalating them. Acknowledging and being sensitive to his feelings, even while reassuring, soothing, and comforting the client would produce the best result. This would allow him to feel heard, and yet not advance his expression of negative emotions. Confronting a client with a diagnosis of paranoid schizophrenia could easily cause an overreaction and escalation of emotion. Further, feelings of heightened anxiety and/or paranoia could easily grow to the extent that greater intervention could be required. Joining him in his anger could have a similar escalating result. Unless intense anger is coupled with threats, there would be no immediate need to evaluate the client for issues of homicidality or to involve law enforcement.

129. B: The best way to handle the client's expressions of feelings in this type of service is to limit the expression of intense or deep feelings. It should be noted that a client revealing highly personal or sensitive feelings too early on in the therapeutic process can produce a wedge of embarrassment and/or guilt, which can inhibit the therapeutic process and reduce the ability to provide needed services. This can be particularly problematic when: 1) the services are already of a very short-term nature; and 2) where the services provided are very narrow and do not allow for extensive emotional support. Further, if a client precipitously discharges considerable emotion, it can have the effect of over-burdening the social worker/case manager. Thus, the expression of feelings in the therapeutic relationship should: 1) be metered and managed to not outstrip the bonds and ties of the growing relationship; and 2) should be maintained within the scope and mission of the services being provided so as to not leave the client feeling abandoned when services are necessarily terminated.

130. C: If the social worker only has time for one visit, the most critical visit is the 16-year-old girl who was raped because she requires immediate emotional support and assistance. The next visit should be to 14-year-old the boy who attempted suicide because he is at risk for repeat attempts and being hospitalized may be frightening for the adolescent. The third visit should be to the 12-year-old boy who repeatedly runs away to try to determine the reason and to try to mitigate issues if possible. The last visit is to the 2-year-old girl because this is a routine visit.

131. C: The first role of the social worker in these circumstances is to ensure a nonjudgmental attitude, regardless of the client's past. Typically, clients are aware of longstanding societal mores, standards, expectations, and morality. While not always fully aware of the entire scope of the legal ramifications of their choices, most clients know when they are participating in illicit activities. Where an understanding of the consequences of their choices was lacking, by the time they have sought help (or have been mandated to seek it), they are typically well aware of many of the consequences involved. Thus, clients will usually feel averse to the social worker offering a roster of such things in response to their disclosures. Rather, clients are looking to be understood and accepted. Where their behavior is obviously unacceptable, the person should nevertheless be accepted and understood for the pain they are experiencing. Thus, blame, judgment, critique, and other such responses should be withheld and a nonjudgmental attitude should prevail. Where this is not forthcoming, the client will typically sense it, even if not verbalized, and it will hamper the development of a therapeutic bond and the ability to work together positively.

132. C: The proper response would be to meet with administration to address the use of the form. The release of information, particularly information about substance abuse, mental health, and HIV status, is governed by both federal and state laws. Federal HIPAA regulations always apply, and these regulations are not dependent upon an individual's legal standing (incarcerated, on parole or probation, etc.). Minimum standards for a release of information are: 1) the individual's identifying information; 2) identifying information for the recipient of information; 3) the purpose of the release; 4) the specific information to be released (with the client having the right to review the release of specific mental health information prior to authorizing it); and 5) the duration of validity of the signed release (i.e., an expiration date). Other regulations apply in circumstances of imminent danger to the client or others, thus removing the need to circumvent an appropriate form. Both ethics and confidentiality laws are relevant in any release of information.

133. B: Law enforcement personnel are not entitled to confidential client information without a court order, unless there are imminent circumstances of life-threatening danger to the client or others. Valid exclusions to confidentiality include: 1) situations of actively expressed suicidal ideation by the client; 2) when a client leads a social worker to genuinely suspect a client may harm to others (if homicidality is suspected, Tarasoff regulations apply); 3) if a client discloses abuse (physical injury or gross neglect, sexual abuse, etc.) to a minor or a dependent adult; and 4) in situations of grave disability, where a client lacks the mental capacity to secure (or direct others to secure) essential food, clothing, shelter, essential medical care, etc. In all exceptions, the information to be released should be limited to that requisite to resolve the immediate circumstance involved.

134. D: Confidentiality cannot be entirely assured in a group counseling setting; it is no longer just the social worker who is privy to confidential information. Even so, group participants can and should be put under commitment to keep confidential all information shared in group. This should extend to not discussing information about other participants outside group in any way, even among themselves. Further emphasis on confidentiality can be provided by including a confidentiality clause in written treatment consent paperwork. In spite of this, some participants may not manage confidentiality well and all group participants should be apprised of this when entering the group counseling agreement. In this way, participants can be particularly careful about sharing unnecessarily personal information in an open group setting.

135. C: The best response is to request the court withdraw the order, or limit its scope. When possible, psychologically damaging information should be protected from an open court setting. While a social worker may be compelled to testify in certain situations, it is always appropriate to petition the court to withdraw the order by providing a rationale for the concerns involved. Failing this, it remains appropriate to petition the court to limit the scope of the testimony being sought to information that would not be psychologically damaging to the client. While a prosecutor or plaintiff's attorney may attempt to exact as much testimony as possible to press the case more readily to a favorable conclusion, the judge will have no such bias and may agree to withdraw or revise a subpoena if given adequate rationale and insight. The client's mental health should always remain the social worker's first priority, along with honest efforts to maintain agreed upon confidentiality.

136. A: In situations of death, confidentiality agreements remain in full force and effect. Confidentiality agreements are entered into between a client and his or her social worker. They remain legally binding for the two parties involved, even in the event of demise or incapacity. They also remain ethically binding for any new social worker who receives the records of a previous client, and upon the original social worker should his or her client die. To ensure continuity of confidentiality, it is important for social workers to make provisions for their records in the event they die or become cognitively incapacitated. This may involve reciprocal agreements with trusted colleagues or an attorney, or some other appropriate means. Regardless of the provisions made, they should adequately protect a client's confidential information and privacy as fully as possible. Failing to make such provisions constitutes a failure to look after the welfare and well-being of the social worker's clients, and legal action can be taken against a social worker's estate if this is neglected.

137. C: The first step should be to seek supervision and/or consultation. Referring the client to another social worker is a profound disservice to the client. He will be difficult for anyone to work with, and reestablishing with another social worker will be time-consuming and costly. Sharing these feelings with the client will damage the relationship, and will certainly escalate the problem behaviors that have been so troublesome in the first place. Ignoring the problem will not improve it in any way. Clearly these behaviors are very entrenched in the client's interactive repertoire, and thus will continue unless properly addressed and redirected. Engaging in supervision and/or consultation is therefore essential, both for the client's well-being and to produce a therapeutic engagement plan that can be successful. Ongoing consultation and revision of any plan produced will almost certainly be required over time.

138. A: The social worker should first explore the meaning of the gift with the family. Small tokens of appreciation can be graciously accepted, but gifts suffused with deeper meaning (assuming bonding, or symbolizing something that obligates the client to the clinician) should be avoided. When accepting even a small token gift, a clinician should cite ethical standards for the client's future reference. An open and gracious expression of appreciation should always be the response to a small gift. Adding information about ethical standards, however, is important to set the idea of boundaries. It is best, however, to preempt the issue during an intake session, explaining that professional standards prohibit receiving or exchanging gifts. In this way the family becomes aware of guidelines, without encountering a subsequent rejection of a modest gift. If cash or a check in a modest amount is received in the mail from a client or family of ample means, it may be donated to a cause important to the family and in their name (typically a notice of recognition and appreciation is then sent to the family by the organization). Always document any gift situation and resolution in the clinical record so that the outcome is clear.

139. D: The best response is to decline the offer, citing professional ethics. At issue is the creation of a dual relationship, one that extends beyond the clinical setting into other areas of work and life. The social work *Code of Ethics* specifically addresses exploitive relationships, where the social worker holds an undue power advantage. Such relationships should be avoided. For non-exploitive exchanges, there are two views on the matter: the deontological (categorical), calling for total avoidance, and the utilitarian (situational), suggesting a reasoning process. With past clients, the following questions may help: 1) is it exploitive; 2) how much time has passed; 3) the nature (length and intensity) of the relationship; 4) events at termination; 5) the client's vulnerability; 6) the likelihood of a negative impact on the client. A boundary crossing occurs when one bends the code situationally, and boundary violations involve breaking the code. A crossing becomes a clear violation when the dual relationship has negative consequences for the client.

140. C: If the social worker is aware of a quality assurance problem, such as redundant documentation, it is the responsibility of the social worker to take action in a way that is most effective. In this case, the social worker should do a mockup of revised documents and take them to the supervisor because simply complaining or asking the supervisor or other staff to consider revising the documents puts the burden on someone else. When suggesting changes to policies or procedures, it is best to come well-prepared with supporting evidence/samples.

141. C: The most appropriate response would be to attend the funeral, but decline the luncheon invitation. In this situation it is entirely appropriate to accept an invitation to the funeral, demonstrating a show of care and respect for the deceased client and family. For many, it offers an important sense of closure to a loss that the social worker has also experienced. However, the family-only luncheon serves to place the social worker in a more intimate family-like relationship. It can also be a difficult situation for all involved, as gauging appropriate comments and conversation may be challenging among extended family members—a great many of whom will have no relationship with the social worker. Exploring the meaning of the invitation with the family at the time it is extended will allow the social worker to better reassure them and help them understand the important ethical issues involved in stepping out of a preexisting formal role of a counseling nature.

142. A: If the social worker has a 16-year-old morbidly obese client who engages in binge-eating and regains lost weight and feels increasingly worthless because of her failure to lose weight, the first thing the social worker should focus on is the triggers that result in binge eating. The social worker might begin by asking the client to think back to the last episode and discuss what the client was feeling when the client began binging and what might have happened to trigger the desire to binge.

143. A: An example of a leading question would be, "You really do want to go back to school, don't you?" In this way, the client is prompted to agree to something important. However, caution must be used with such questions, as it does not allow for a client's true feelings to necessarily find expression. *Stacked questions* are produced by asking questions in rapid succession, leaving no time for a response and thus shaping the course of the conversation. *Open-ended questions* are constructed to as to elude a "yes" or "no" response, and elicit greater meaning and interpretation (e.g., "How did that make you feel?"). *Close-ended questions* are intended to elicit short and specific answers (e.g., "When were you born?").

144. C: In this situation, the most appropriate therapeutic response would be through confrontation. Empathic Responding refers to accurate perception of a client's feelings followed by accurate restating and sharing. While empathic responding can lead to better therapeutic outcomes, it is not the first-choice technique when a client persists in deluding herself into thinking violating behaviors were simple mistakes or happenings that were sought out by a victim with clear understanding. Reflective (Active) Listening is a useful tool for establishing mutual understandings between individuals. However, it is not designed to identify illicit behavior and directly prompt change. Confrontation can prompt change, though in a rather emotionally traumatic way. Because of this, confrontation must be: 1) carefully timed, usually immediately after the problematic expression or event; 2) with enough time remaining in session to reground the relationship; 3) specific to the issue being addressed; 4) client-focused (as opposed to allowing the social worker to vent at the client's expense); and 5) culturally centered: recognizing how the client will receive the experience, and using an interpreter of there is a language barrier.

145. B: Transference is an emotional reaction toward another, drawn from prior experiences with someone else. For example, feeling resentment toward an employer who seems to treat you in ways reminiscent of how your father treated you. Transference is typically something one remains unaware of without careful thought. It can be a substantial barrier to a therapeutic relationship unless it is addressed and resolved. When a social worker has reactions toward a client based upon the social worker's own background, it is called counter-transference. Other client-based communication barriers include the use of problem minimization or outright denial; reluctance to be honest about something for fear of rejection; limits on open sharing due a fear of losing emotional control; and limits on sharing due to mistrust. Social worker barriers to communication include excessive passivity, leaving the client feeling unsupported; over-aggression, causing the client to feel threatened and unsafe; premature assurance, limiting full disclosure; too much self-disclosure, focusing away from the client; as well as, sarcasm, guilt, judgment, interrupting, and inappropriate humor.

146. A: If a parent appears to have good communication with his child and shows much warmth and affection but imposes few limits, this is typical of permissive parenting. This often results in a child who is creative but has difficulty cooperating with others and may be self-centered and impulsive. The child often has difficulty making friends and may engage in bullying, aggressive, and rebellious behavior. During adolescence, the child may be less mature and less responsible than peers.

147. C: The term journal notes is never used to refer to a social worker's case notes in any way. The *primary client record* is sometimes referred to as the clinical or medical record. The second kind of case notes are referred to as *psychotherapy notes.* In this record the social worker records private notes for subsequent clinical analysis of social worker-client communications. All social worker notes may be more readily subject to subpoena or court-ordered disclosure if they are kept together. However, if kept separately, the private therapy notes are much more difficult to obtain. The primary client record includes information such as assessment, clinical tests, diagnosis, medical information, the treatment plan and treatment modalities used, progress notes, collateral information, billing records, dates and times of sessions, etc. If a subpoena is received requesting the "complete medical record," it need not include the separate psychotherapy notes without further legal stipulation.

148. C: The best response is to seek supervision and/or consultation to explore the issue further. The diagnosis problem cannot be ignored for two important reasons: 1) it leaves the underlying condition untreated, as the client currently receives medications for bipolar disorder and no treatment for the depression and grief issues; and 2) billing under a known erroneous diagnosis can constitute fraud, if it continues. Correcting a diagnosis made by a psychiatrist, however, would not typically be undertaken independently by a social work case manager. Instead, supervision and/or consultation should be obtained to ensure that any attempted corrective steps are not inappropriate, and to ensure that essential services for the client are not terminated without alternative support in place in advance.

149. D: The clients records should next be retained in accordance with state medical record statutes. Not all states have statutes governing the retention period for social work clinical notes. Of those states that do have statutes, the minimum retention period was 3 years and the maximum as much as 10 years. Other standards may apply for clients under the age of majority, who may have further need of the records during their minor years. Where no statutes exist, it has been advised that clinicians retain records in accordance with statutes governing the management of medical records. Regardless, clinicians should be sensitive to the fact that clients may return for further services at a future date, whereupon a prior record could be of considerable assistance in exploring, understanding, and resolving any subsequent problems.

150. A: The best response is to help the family explore their feelings about the defects, their family circumstances, and the meaning of available options. It is essential that the family be permitted to find their own answers in a way that meets their own values and allows them all their rights under the law. Merely offering a dispassionate review of options does not assist the family in discerning their personal and unique feelings about the circumstances. Providing a review of the sanctity of life serves to pressure them into a life-prolonging decision, and emphasizing the reasonable nature of raising a child with even mild defects again pressures them to bear a child in an absence of information that could help them fully understand the meaning and significance of raising that child. If the social worker does not feel able to assist them in fully and personally coming to a decision based on their own values and beliefs, then she should defer to a colleague to provide these important services.

Masters Practice Test #2

1. Executive functioning broadly refers to:

a. the skill and capacity of a leader to lead.
b. higher order cognitive functions and capacity.
c. administrative policy and guidelines.
d. a bureaucratic leadership style.

2. A patient who is described as "oriented times four" (or "oriented x4") is able to demonstrate awareness of which of the following four features?

a. Name, date, city, and season
b. Age, current year, location, and situation
c. Name, gender, ethnicity, and marital status
d. Person, place, time, and situation

3. A supervisor in a counseling clinic is approached by clerical staff asking how long they should retain patient counseling records. The BEST answer to could give is:

a. until the client is no longer being seen.
b. until the patient dies.
c. until the statute of limitations expires.
d. as long as possible, preferably indefinitely.

4. A social worker is called to evaluate a 64-year-old male with chronic obstructive pulmonary disease. He lives in an assisted living facility, and was brought to the emergency room by his daughter. She had taken him to lunch, and became distressed when he refused to return to the facility. He states he wants to live in his motor home, as he resents the loss of privacy at the facility. His daughter confirms he owns a working, fully self-contained motor home (i.e., stove, shower, refrigerator, etc.). He has adequate funds. He plans to park the motor home in a nearby Kampgrounds of America (KOA) campground, where all utilities can be hooked up. He can have food and other supplies delivered. However, it is November and it is unseasonably cold. The doctor confirms that the patient is prone to pneumonia, and the daughter states "he will die if he doesn't return to the facility." The patient refuses to consider any other living situation. In this situation, the social worker should:

a. call the police and have them take the patient back to the facility.
b. call adult protective services for further intervention.
c. allow the patient to move into his motor home.
d. place the patient on an involuntary hold for suicidal behavior.

5. A social worker is called to evaluate the 4-year-old child of a Southeast Asian family. The child has been ill for some days, and was brought to the emergency room with a temperature of 102° and symptoms of a pulmonary viral infection. During the medical examination, the physician noted numerous long, reddened welts on the child's skin, with superficial ecchymosis (bruising) and petechiae (minute hemorrhages) across the child's chest, suggestive of some form of abuse. Through an interpreter, he learned that a healing "shaman" had repeatedly performed a "coin rubbing" procedure in an attempt to draw out "bad wind" or "bad blood." The social worker views the child's back, and also see these marks. A nurse notes that "coin rubbing" to induce healing is common among traditional Vietnamese, Chinese, Hmong, Cambodians, and Laotians. She suggests that there is no need to report it as abuse. The social worker doesn't want to alienate the family or cause them to avoid seeking health care. As a social worker, the best response would be to:

a. concur with the nurse, and close the case.
b. call a local Southeast Asian cultural center to learn more.
c. call child protective services and let them decide.
d. call the police and request an investigation.

6. Define the terms reliability and validity in evaluative testing.

a. A test is reliable if it is easy to use, and valid if it is commonly used.
b. A test is reliable if it produces consistent results, and valid if it measures what it claims to measure.
c. A test is reliable if it includes Likert scale response options, and valid if it has been endorsed by major research institutions.
d. A test is reliable if it measures what it reports to measure, and valid if it produces consistent results.

7. A social worker has been seeing a significantly depressed client for some months and have been carefully keeping records following each session. Recently the client became upset, as he felt the social worker has been critical of his life and past decisions. During the last session, the client seemed overly suspicious and even a bit paranoid, despite efforts to reassure him and regain rapport. The next day, the client shows up without an appointment and demands to see the clinical notes. The social worker's BEST response would be to:

a. tell the client to make an appointment to review his records.
b. tell the client his is not permitted to see private notes.
c. immediately give the client a photocopy of his records.
d. give the client the original record, after making a copy.

8. A social worker has been called to see the family caregiver of a 32-year-old developmentally delayed dependent adult with a handprint bruise on his arm. The caregiver reports having to restrain the patient forcibly when the patient tried to leave the facility and run into busy traffic. The physician reports that the patient has no other old bruises, and no evidence of fear on the part of the patient when interacting with the caregiver is observed. The social worker realizes, however, that a report must be filed, due to the nature and circumstances surrounding the injury. After interviewing the caregiver and consulting with the physician, the physician tells the social worker that his nurse will be calling Adult Protective Services, so the social worker need not bother. The proper response is:

a. to thank the physician and nurse for taking on this burden.
b. to call APS later and make sure that they received the nurse's report.
c. to call the care facility's licensing board and make a report there.
d. to call Adult Protective Services yourself.

9. In Erikson's eight-stage model of psychosocial development, which stage could be negatively affected by inappropriate toilet training, leading to an "anal-retentive" or "anal-expressive" personality type later in life?

a. Trust versus mistrust
b. Autonomy versus shame
c. Initiation versus guilt
d. Industry versus inferiority

10. A social worker has just had his first session with a 24-year-old college student. She is seeing him following the break-up of a two-year relationship, which occurred without warning about six weeks prior to this visit. As she explained it, "He met someone else and just moved on." She has been having trouble sleeping and concentrating on her studies since that time. Today she presents as dysphoric and tearful, but is affectively expressive and responsive to humor and other interactive stimuli. The university she attends is a considerable distance from her family and friends, leaving her with limited support during this difficult time. The most appropriate diagnosis would be:

a. primary insomnia.
b. major depression.
c. adjustment disorder with depressed mood.
d. acute stress disorder.

11. Identify the difference between psychotherapy and counseling.

a. Psychotherapy is generally considered to be long-term in nature, and counseling to be more short-term.
b. Psychotherapy uses a specific systems approach, while counseling is less bound by theory.
c. There is no difference between the two terms.
d. The term psychotherapy may only be used properly when referring to psychoanalysis.

12. In Erikson's psychosocial model of development, which stage is typical of those entering young adulthood?

a. Identify vs role confusion
b. Initiative vs guilt
c. Ego integrity vs despair
d. Intimacy vs isolation

13. Measuring the effectiveness of an intervention rather than the monetary savings is:

a. a cost-benefit analysis.
b. an efficacy study.
c. a product evaluation.
d. a cost-effective analysis.

14. What primary condition is treated by monoamine oxidase inhibitors (MAOIs), serotonin-norepinephrine reuptake inhibitors (SNRIs), and selective serotonin reuptake inhibitors (SSRIs)?

a. Attention deficit disorders
b. Eating disorders
c. Sleep disorders
d. Depressive disorders

15. A social worker works for a major corporation as a counselor. The available services are broad, and include family therapy and couples counseling. The social worker as sought out by a husband, experiencing significant marital discord. He is employed by the corporation, and he took the first steps to enter couples counseling. After a few sessions, it becomes clear that the wife has traits of a serious mental health disorder, and over time the social worker begins seeing her exclusively. It has been two months since the last contact with the husband. The primary client is:

a. the husband.
b. the wife.
c. the corporation.
d. the couple.

16. There is a high co-morbidity rate between substance abuse and:

a. other disorders.
b. yearly income.
c. IQ.
d. none of the above.

17. All of the following are National Association of Social Workers (NASW) standards for cultural competence EXCEPT:

a. social workers should endeavor to seek out, employ, and retain employees who provide diversity in the profession.
b. social workers shall endeavor to resources and services in the native language of those they serve, including the use of translated materials and interpreters.
c. social workers should develop the skills to work with clients in culturally competent ways, and with respect for diversity.
d. social workers should work with diverse clients only if they have had specific training in that client's unique cultural background.

18. The Health Insurance Portability and Accountability Act (HIPAA) regulates:

a. the transfer of patients from one facility to another.
b. the rights of the individual related to privacy of health information.
c. medical trials.
d. workplace safety.

19. A social worker is working with a 42-year-old executive who is coping with the after-effects of a business failure and subsequent personal bankruptcy. He is generally coping well, but he reveals a past history of alcoholism and indicates that he is struggling with a desire to resume drinking. The social worker encourages him to follow with an Alcoholics Anonymous group, but he responds that he thinks he can manage without such help. The social worker has a personal drinking history herself, and she recognizes the warning signs. She then considers revealing her personal story to bolster her recommendation that he seek help, and to demonstrate the level of her personal understanding and empathy, and to motivate him to take further action. The BEST course of action would be:

a. to withhold this information, because it involves personal disclosure by a social worker in a professional counseling relationship.
b. to share the personal story, because it is entirely relevant to the client's specific situation.
c. to share the personal story, because the consequences if the client returns to drinking are potentially severe.
d. to disclose limited information, being careful not to reveal too much about one's own history, in order to motivate the client.

20. The core features of borderline personality disorder are often disagreed upon. However, two factors are common to the disorder—highly variable mood and:

a. delusions
b. impulsive behavior
c. hallucinations
d. psychotic ideology

21. Cultural competence in individual social work practice is best defined as:

a. the ability to work well with diverse groups.
b. receiving excellent training in diversity.
c. the possession of a wide-ranging knowledge of many diverse groups.
d. the ability to recognize stereotypes, prejudiced views, and biases.

22. A retrospective attempt to determine the cause of an event is:

a. root cause analysis.
b. external benchmarking.
c. internal trending.
d. tracer methodology.

23. A study attempts to measure the efficacy of a new antidepressant medication. A "control" group of depression sufferers will receive only a placebo, while an "intervention" group will receive the new medication. In this study, the "null hypothesis" would state the following:

a. the intervention group will report fewer symptoms of depression than the control group.
b. the control group will report fewer symptoms of depression than the intervention group.
c. both the control group and the intervention group will report fewer numbers of depressive symptoms.
d. there shall be no measurable difference in depression symptom reporting between the control group and the intervention group.

24. In adults, manic episodes last for how long?

a. A few hours
b. At least 2 days
c. At least one week
d. At least 3 months

25. A manic episode first experienced after the age of 40 is:

a. common.
b. highly unusual.
c. unlikely to be due to substance abuse.
d. unlikely to be due to a medical condition.

26. Which chemical is known as the one that accompanies bonding behavior between mothers and children and between lovers?

a. Serotonin
b. Dopamine
c. Oxytocin
d. Oxycontin

27. Clinical pathways should be based on:

a. a survey of current practices in the area.
b. committee recommendations.
c. evidence-based research.
d. staff preferences.

28. In statistical research, a "Type I Error" (also called an "alpha error," or a "false positive") refers to:

a. failing to reject the null hypothesis when the null hypothesis is false.
b. a failure to randomize research participants, thereby potentially introducing bias.
c. rejecting the null hypothesis when the null hypothesis is true.
d. assuming a normal statistical distribution when it is skewed.

29. An 80-year-old patient is dying of cancer and has been in and out of consciousness. The family should be encouraged to:

a. go home, as the patient does not know they are present.
b. talk to the patient, as hearing is usually the last sense to fail.
c. offer the patient frequent sips of water to avoid dehydration.
d. raise the head of the patient's bed if respirations become rattling to help the patient clear secretions.

30. Bipolar disorder can easily be confused with which of the following disorders?

a. Borderline personality disorder
b. Clinical depression
c. Anxiety disorder
d. Conduct disorder

31. Categories of risk for early-onset intellectual disability include which of the following?

a. Problems at birth
b. Poverty
c. Age of verbal acquisition
d. Problems at birth and poverty

32. In statistical research, a "Type II Error" (also called a "beta error" or "false negative") refers to:

a. a failure to reject the null hypothesis when the null hypothesis is false.
b. erroneously selecting a statistical analysis model based upon invalid assumptions.
c. rejecting the null hypothesis when the null hypothesis is true.
d. making an error in mathematical calculations, upon which a finding is based.

33. _______________ is a disorder of thought, unlike _______________ which is a disorder of mood.

a. Borderline; conduct disorder
b. Conduct disorder; depression
c. Bipolar disorder; schizophrenia
d. Schizophrenia; bipolar disorder

34. Basing the opportunities, options, and benefits available to a specific group of people based upon preconceptions and assumptions is BEST defined as:

a. bigotry.
b. discrimination.
c. prejudice.
d. misogyny.

35. Failure mode and effects analysis (FMEA) is done:

a. retrospectively.
b. upon utilization of a new process.
c. during the trial of a new process.
d. prior to utilization of a new process.

36. How do team members usually deal with issues of power?

a. By observing and emulating the leader
b. By arguing
c. By following strict rules of discourse
d. By rotating leadership roles

37. A social worker is hired by a private practice therapist who operates a court-supervised violent offender treatment program. One of the social worker's responsibilities is to screen new client referrals, to ensure that only low-risk, first-time offenders are accepted into the program. In this process, the social worker is to have each client sign a treatment consent form, which also includes a detailed consent for release of information. The worker notes that instead of the usual time and target limits, the form allows information to be released at any time to "any law enforcement agency," "any spouse, ex-spouse, or significant other," "any welfare or abuse protection agency," etc. When asking about the ethics of having clients sign this form, the social worker is told, "It's a hassle to try and get specific information releases, and the safety of the public is at stake. Use the form." The BEST response is to:

a. use the form as directed.
b. refuse to use the form.
c. call the licensing board and discuss the form.
d. call law enforcement and discuss the form.

38. Which assessment tool for dementia involves remembering and repeating the names of 3 common objects and drawing the face of a clock with all 12 numbers and hands indicating the time specified by the examiner?

a. Mini-mental state exam (MMSE)
b. Mini-cog
c. Digit Repetition Test
d. Confusion Assessment Method

39. Identify the four most common minority classifications:

a. ethnicity, gender, sexual orientation, culture.
b. religion, race, gender, sexual orientation.
c. age, appearance, social standing, gender.
d. age, gender, race, sexual orientation.

40. A client reports his fear of the local television station and his belief that it is transmitting harmful sound waves. What he's likely experiencing would be called a:

a. hallucination.
b. delusion.
c. somatic hallucination.
d. gustatory delusion.

41. The term "deinstitutionalization" refers to:

a. helping a client accommodate to a community living environment after having been institutionalized for an extended period (usually, years).
b. creating a treatment program that serves the needs of the client, as opposed to the needs of the institution.
c. changes in policy and law that led to the release of many mental health patients who would have otherwise remained in institutional settings.
d. a philosophy of client- social worker collaboration in treatment, as opposed to hierarchical social worker-driven treatment.

42. Thought insertion/withdrawal refers to what?

a. A psychoanalytic therapy technique
b. The belief that thoughts are being put into or taken out of one's head
c. A behavior therapy technique related to operant conditioning
d. A type of hallucination

43. The Occupational Safety and Health Administration (OSHA) regulates:

a. patient right to privacy.
b. disposal methods for sharps, such as needles.
c. reimbursement for services.
d. patient surveys.

44. A disease characterized by a diffuse atrophy of the brain is:

a. bipolar disorder.
b. Alzheimer's disease.
c. schizoaffective disorder.
d. obsessive compulsive disorder.

45. According to Bush et al (2003), what percentage of people who successfully commit suicide have made a prior unsuccessful attempt?

a. 76%
b. 23%
c. 49%
d. less than 10%

46. Which scale is used to assess and predict the risk of a patient developing pressure sores based upon sensory perception, moisture, activity, mobility, nutrition pattern, and friction and sheer?

a. Norton Scale
b. Pressure Ulcer Scale for Healing (PUSH)
c. The Braden Scale
d. Diabetic Foot Ulcer Scale (DFS)

47. A primary purpose of interdisciplinary teams is:

a. sharing ideas and perspectives to solve problems.
b. cost-savings.
c. improved patient satisfaction.
d. time saving.

48. A family therapist asks the daughter to place other members of her family in positions that she feels demonstrates their current relationships to each other. The daughter places the mother and son very close together, with the teenage son's hand leaning on his mother's shoulder. She places her father at the door, with his hand on the doorknob, but facing his wife. Finally, she puts herself in a chair at the far end of the room, as if she is observing the others, but not part of the group. In this sculpting technique, what is the client MOST likely saying about her family?

a. She is demonstrating a family secret
b. She is showing enmeshment between mother and son
c. She is showing this family's low cohesion
d. She is showing her lack of attachment

49. A 60-year-old male is being treated for a myocardial infarction. While he is progressing well physically, he becomes upset when asked to make independent decisions and he rings the call bell constantly asking for reassurance that he will get well. This psychological response to stress is an example of:

a. dependence.
b. passivity.
c. depression.
d. confusion.

50. In terms of quality assurance in social work practice, what does the acronym "CQI" represent?

a. Certification of Quality Institute
b. Communication Quality Index
c. Command of Quality Indicators
d. Continuous Quality Improvement

51. Which members of the healthcare institution are responsible for identifying performance improvement projects?

a. Administrative staff
b. Nursing team leaders
c. Physicians
d. All staff

52. Identify the five classifications of race most commonly used.

a. Asian, Black, Hispanic, Native American, White.
b. Asian, Black, Native American, Spanish, White.
c. African, Asian, Indian, Spanish, White.
d. Asian, Black, Mexican, Native American, White.

53. Which type of sexual disorder is most likely to come to the attention of a social worker?

a. Gender dysphoria
b. Voyeurism
c. Paraphilia
d. Sexual function disorders

54. Which of the following is part of 23 leading health indicators (determinants of health) outlined in Healthy People 2030?

a. Pregnancy
b. Chronic disease
c. New cases of diabetes
d. Family support

55. Identify the missing step in Albert R. Roberts seven-stage crisis intervention model: 1) assess lethality; 2) establish rapport; 3) ________; 4) deal with feelings; 5) explore alternatives; 6) develop an action plan; 7) follow-up. The third step is:

a. evaluate resources.
b. identify problems.
c. environmental control.
d. collateral contacts.

56. Which of the following provides research and funding for the development of evidence-based practice guidelines?

a. Occupational Health and Safety Association (OSHA)
b. Food and Drug Administration (FDA)
c. Health Insurance Portability and Accountability Act (HIPAA)
d. Agency for Healthcare Research and Quality (AHRQ)

57. Frotteuristic disorder refers to a:

a. personality disorder.
b. symptom of schizophrenia.
c. sexual disorder.
d. common bipolar symptom.

58. Presenting symptoms that may appear to reflect from mental illness, but which actually arise from specific cultural practices, beliefs, or values, are referred to as:

a. belief-based symptoms.
b. iatrogenic symptoms.
c. factitious syndromes.
d. culture-bound syndromes.

59. According to principles of adult learning, adult learners tend to be:

a. unmotivated.
b. lacking in self-direction.
c. practical and goal-oriented.
d. insecure.

60. The Instrumental Activities of Daily Living (IADL) tool includes an assessment of:

a. bathing.
b. toileting.
c. ascending or descending stairs.
d. financial responsibility.

61. Which of the following has criteria for diagnosis that it occurs for at least two years, more days than not, making it not very episodic?

a. Bipolar disorder
b. Disruptive mood dysregulation disorder
c. Major depressive disorder
d. Dysthymic disorder

62. Which is the most common lifetime disorder?

a. Conduct disorder
b. Depression
c. Borderline personality disorder
d. Schizophrenia

63. In obtaining an interpreter for a non–English-speaking client, the best option would be to select:

a. another staff person at the facility or agency.
b. a professional interpreter.
c. a friend of the client.
d. a relative of the client.

64. The best time to initiate conflict resolution is:

a. when those in conflict have had time to resolve their differences.
b. when conflict first emerges.
c. when conflict interferes with function.
d. when those involved ask for conflict resolution.

65. The psychological theory that characterizes a hierarchy of needs culminating in self-actualization was developed by:

a. Jung.
b. Havighurst.
c. Maslow.
d. Freud.

66. According to J.W. Drisko (2009), the five key factors required for a quality therapeutic relationship between client and clinician are: 1) affective attunement; 2) mutual affirmation; 3) joint efforts to resolve missteps; 4) ________; and 5) using varying types of empathy. The fourth key factor is:

a. use of humor.
b. accepting criticism.
c. capacity to trust.
d. goal congruence.

67. Certain exceptions to confidentiality exist. These include: 1) mandated reporting issues; 2) subpoenas or other court orders; 3) treatment continuity (cross-coverage by other agency staff); and all of the following EXCEPT:

a. disclosures for insurance coverage purposes.
b. disclosures at a client's written request.
c. disclosures to an employer providing insurance coverage.
d. disclosures regarding a child (e.g., mandated reporting, violations of the law, etc.).

68. Upon first meeting a client, a social worker should begin by taking the following steps (in the order listed):

a. summarize legal and ethical obligations, complete a counseling contract, explore the client's presenting problem, and assess the client.
b. complete a service contract, summarize legal and ethical obligations.
c. establish rapport, summarize legal and ethical obligations, complete a service contract, and assess the client.
d. assess the client, summarize legal and ethical obligations, complete a service contract, and establish a rapport.

69. Which of the following theories is characterized by the contention that life is an unending process of changes and transitions?

a. Life course/Life span
b. Modernization
c. Geo-transcendence
d. Exchange

70. An organization that is arranged hierarchically, with numerous departments and units through which segments of specialized services are provided, moving toward the achievement of a common goal, is referred to as a(n):

a. complex organization.
b. hierarchical organization.
c. bureaucracy.
d. institution.

71. Harry's mother is extremely concerned that her son is not crawling at 7 months of age, because "all the other children in his playgroup are." She wants to have him evaluated for a disability, despite the fact that in every other way, his development is quite normal. What is the FIRST thing the caseworker should suggest?

a. A medical evaluation
b. Play therapy
c. Waiting another 90 days to see what happens
d. Therapy for his anxious mother

72. When considering outcome measures, striving for patient satisfaction is:

a. a long-term outcome.
b. a short-term outcome.
c. both a long-term and a short-term outcome.
d. a process.

73. A form of client assessment that focuses on a client's social and relational functioning is known as:

a. a genogram.
b. a social status examination.
c. a social resource review.
d. a social assessment report.

74. Which of the following can increase one's risk of attempting suicide in the future?

a. Prior suicide ideation
b. Past suicidal behavior in one's family
c. History of frequent mobility
d. All of the above

75. Assessing a client by means of a checklist or questionnaire is particularly useful when:

a. the client doesn't want to see the social worker.
b. the client is unsure how to describe the situation, or if it is complex or risk laden and the social worker needs to be thorough.
c. the social worker is too busy to see the client personally.
d. the social worker wishes to avoid a client interview.

76. When considering the use of an interpreter for a patient who does not speak English, which consideration is most important?

a. The interpreter has training in medical vocabulary for both languages
b. The interpreter speaks both languages well
c. The interpreter knows the patient's history
d. The interpreter is available onsite

77. Freud described the concept of pain (whether physical or emotional) as arising through the psychic process of:

a. repression.
b. introjection.
c. cathexis.
d. fixation.

78. The basic functions of administrators include: 1) monitoring, reviewing, advising, and evaluating employees; 2) planning and delegation; and all of the following EXCEPT:

a. frontline organizational services.
b. advocacy (both horizontally with departmental staff, and vertically between other departments and staff).
c. conflict resolution and mediation.
d. planning and delegation.

79. A diagram that helps individual and families to visually depict the quality of individual and/or family relationships with others, within a community, and with important resources in their lives (e.g., food, shelter, work, school, health care, etc.) is called:

a. an eco-map.
b. a family diagram.
c. a genomap.
d. a relational diagram.

80. A 40-year-old client presents with complaints regarding not feeling comfortable socially. He states that after gaining weight he now finds social situations to be overwhelming. He has stopped attending church and recreational activities, and does not engage in new activities, although before he was known for being adventurous. A likely diagnosis would be:

a. borderline personality disorder.
b. avoidant personality disorder.
c. schizotypal personality disorder.
d. depressive disorder.

81. The DSM-5 provides for the diagnosis of specific personality disorders and one category for indeterminate behaviors that appear to be characteristic of a personality disorder. These disorders are grouped into clusters. Identify the cluster that does not properly describe a personality disorder group:

a. Cluster A: paranoid, schizoid, and schizotypal disorders (also referred to as "odd or eccentric behavior disorders").
b. Cluster B: impulsivity and/or affective dysregulation disorders (also referred to as "dramatic, emotional, or erratic disorders").
c. Cluster C: anxiety and compulsive disorders (also referred to as "anxious or fearful disorders").
d. Cluster D: violent and/or explosive disorders (also referred to as "aggressive and intrusive conduct disorders").

82. A social worker meets with a client who has been struggling financially. It becomes apparent that he must reduce his standard of living in order to maintain financial solvency. He therefore sells his large luxury automobile and purchases a small but reliable economy vehicle, realizing considerable savings. According to Heinz Hartmann's "Ego Psychology" this kind of accommodation is an example of:

a. defensive functioning.
b. alloplastic behavior.
c. integrative functioning.
d. autoplastic behavior.

83. Which of the following professional communication skills is used to facilitate communication with intra- and inter-disciplinary teams?

a. Interpreting the statements of others to facilitate the flow of ideas
b. Reacting and responding to facts rather than feelings
c. Providing advice when it appears needed
d. Asking questions to challenge other people's ideas

84. Identify the most commonly used intelligence measurement scale:

a. Wechsler-Bellevue Intelligence Scale.
b. Stanford-Binet Intelligence Scale.
c. Binet-Simon Intelligence Scale.
d. Wechsler Adult Intelligence Scale.

85. A supervisor's role involves: 1) being a role model; 2) recruitment and orientation; 3) day-to-day management; 4) staff training, education, and development; 5) staff assessments and reviews; and all of the following EXCEPT:

a. advocating for staff and program needs.
b. allocating interdepartmental operating funds.
c. evaluating the program for ongoing improvement.
d. providing support and counsel to staff.

86. Certain codes in DSM-5 are used to identify conditions that are a focus of clinical attention, but for which insufficient information exists to determine if the issues can be attributed to a mental disorder (or which may, in fact, not be due to a mental disorder but still require clinical attention). These codes are called:

a. DSM-5 Codes.
b. GAF Codes.
c. V Codes.
d. ICD Codes.

87. According to "Object Relations Theory," an infant's separation and individuation from its mother should largely be complete by the time the infant is aged:

a. 24 months.
b. Five months.
c. 14 months.
d. Nine months.

88. All of the following are methods of program evaluation EXCEPT:

a. outcome evaluation.
b. participatory evaluation.
c. reciprocal evaluation.
d. process-oriented evaluation.

89. The update to the Diagnostic and Statistical Manual of Mental Disorders (DSM)-5 included major changes to categories and classifications. Which of the following is not a DSM-5 category?

a. Sleep-wake disorders
b. Sexual dysfunctions
c. Pervasive developmental disorders
d. Gender dysphoria

90. A client comes to see a social worker with numerous personal issues of varying severity. The decision regarding the issue(s) that should be addressed first should be made:

a. by the client alone.
b. by the client, in exploration with the social worker.
c. by the social worker alone.
d. based upon severity of life impact.

91. The following are all approaches to program "outcome evaluation" EXCEPT:

a. the aggregate evaluation approach.
b. the decision-oriented approach.
c. the experimental evaluation approach.
d. the performance audit approach.

92. Self-Psychology, as postulated by Heinz Kohut, acknowledges that personality is partly formed by social structure. A cohesive self is achieved by incorporating the perceptions and functions of healthy significant others and objects into an internalized self-structure through a process called:

a. empathic mirroring.
b. rapprochement.
c. differentiation.
d. transmuting internalization.

93. A social worker has been seeing a client for several weeks, with considerable progress having been made. As a mutually agreed upon date for termination approaches, the client expresses considerable anxiety and even some anger regarding the impending termination. The social worker's best initial response would be to do which of the following?

a. Offer a follow-up appointment some weeks away
b. Assure the client that services can again be sought at any time
c. Cancel the termination date and continue services
d. Explore and discuss the client's feelings about termination

94. A client verbalizes discontent regarding the progress of his treatment plan. The social worker asks, "Are you saying you're not pleased with your progress up to this point?" The social worker then adds, "You sound upset" and reassures the client that "things will get better soon." This communication involves several errors. Which of the following is one of them?

a. A lack of demonstrated warmth and empathy on the part of the social worker
b. A response that isn't confrontational enough
c. Inappropriate reassurance
d. A focus on conscious thoughts

95. The following are all approaches to program "participatory evaluation" EXCEPT:

a. cluster evaluations.
b. action research.
c. self-evaluations.
d. peer reviews.

96. According the DSM-5 criteria, a client that has previously met the criteria for stimulant use disorder but now has not met the criteria for stimulant use in 10 months (except for craving) would be termed to be in _____ remission.

a. Full
b. Partial
c. Early
d. Sustained

97. The following are all comparisons between consultation and supervision EXCEPT:

a. consultation is provided by an outside expert, while supervision is provided by an internal staff leader.
b. consultants have broad administrative authority, while supervisors have only interdepartmental authority.
c. consultants provide advice and recommendations, while supervisors tend to provide binding directives and procedures.
d. consultation is episodic (as sought) and voluntary, while supervision is ongoing and mandatory.

98. The primary focus of Gestalt Psychology, as founded by Frederick Perls, is on:

a. the developmental issues and the past, as they influence the present.
b. the "here and now."
c. adaptation and the future.
d. moral development.

99. A 19-year-old college student sustains a severe head injury in an accident. Post-rehab testing reveals a subsequent IQ of 62. Which diagnosis would be the most likely?

a. Dementia, mild, due to head trauma
b. Mild neurocognitive disorder due to traumatic brain injury
c. Borderline intellectual functioning
d. Intellectual disability, mild, due to head trauma

100. The process by which a client and social worker review past goals, summarize progress made, and finalize plans to maintain and continue past progress is called:

a. closure.
b. wrap-up.
c. finalization.
d. termination.

101. A type of record-keeping that consolidates and reports all information (including progress, interventions, and conclusions) in an ongoing story form is called:

a. descriptive recording.
b. journaling.
c. narrative recording.
d. summary recording.

102. A single mother and a teenage son present for relationship problems. The son is actively defiant of instructions, argues regularly over minor requests, and can be spiteful and resentful over normal parenting efforts. School performance is marginal, but only one unexcused absence has occurred during the current school year, which is nearing its end. The most appropriate diagnosis would be:

a. oppositional defiant disorder
b. conduct disorder
c. intermittent explosive disorder
d. parent-child relational problem

103. Simon is 66 years old and was recently ordered by the court to attend counseling for an outburst in a grocery store, where he threw a can of pop at the clerk for being too slow in ringing up his purchases. His wife attends the first session as well, and although he insists his memory is "as good as it ever was," she shakes her head. He seems distracted and angry; she placates him, but he lashes out verbally. When the caseworker asks her if anything has changed recently, she tells him that Simon has always been a good-natured, easygoing man, but that lately he has been "difficult." As they are leaving, Simon, looking puzzled, says, "I don't even know why we're here."

What is the FIRST possible diagnosis a caseworker would consider in this case?

a. Alcoholism
b. Alzheimer's disease
c. Bipolar disorder
d. Impulse-control disorder

104. A type of record-keeping that chronologically and systematically records client information (usually beginning with a fact-laden face sheet, a statement of the presenting problem, goals, and current obstacles) is called:

a. outline recording.
b. summary recording.
c. contiguous recording.
d. process recording.

105. According to the DSM-5, a client with an intelligence quotient (IQ) of 59, who lives alone but requires support to do grocery shopping and manage money, is unable to read and is very gullible should be considered to have:

a. severe intellectual disability
b. borderline intellectual functioning
c. moderate intellectual disability
d. mild intellectual disability

106. An elderly female client presents with marked disorientation, word-finding problems, memory impairment, and a high degree of distractibility. Her daughter states that the patient was "just fine" until two days prior to this contact, and that she seems better in the mornings. There have been no external or environmental changes. The most likely diagnosis would be:

a. medication-induced cognitive changes
b. senile dementia, rapid onset
c. delirium
d. neurocognitive disorder, not otherwise specified

107. Another type of record-keeping focuses on goals, and is segmented into four sections: 1) factual information (a face sheet or database section); 2) the assessment and expected treatment plan; 3) the progress notes; and 4) progress review entries (usually at 6-12 week intervals). It is called:

a. person-oriented recording.
b. goal-oriented recording.
c. manifold recording.
d. continuous review recording.

108. The capacity to understand death is a developmental process. From ages 2-5, death is not understood as permanent and may be viewed as sleep. From ages 5-9, death's permanence may be recognized, but some children may not understand it will happen to them (external symbols such as angels and skeletons predominate). By age ten (but more often around age seven, especially if loss of a pet or loved one has occurred), death is understood as permanent, irreversible, and inevitable. The two developmental stages that encompass these increasingly elaborate understandings (in ascending order), as identified by Piaget, are:

a. formal operational, concrete operational.
b. pre-operational, formal operational.
c. pre-operational, concrete operational.
d. sensorimotor, pre-operational.

109. A husband and wife present for help with her substance use. She had been recreationally using cocaine on some weekends, and indicates that she has a strong desire to stop, but has been unsuccessful in stopping before. The precipitating incident was an episode of driving under the influence on a weeknight that resulted in her arrest, impounding of the family car, and considerable fines, charges, and increases in automobile insurance. This is the second driving incident in the last two years. The most appropriate diagnosis for the wife, given the relevant details would be:

a. stimulant intoxication.
b. stimulant dependence.
c. stimulant use disorder.
d. stimulant use withdrawal.

110. A social worker is seeing a 16-year-old youth who has, for the past year, been losing his temper frequently, is regularly argumentative with adults, often refuses to follow direct requests, is easily annoyed, and routinely uses blaming to escape responsibility. Approximately four months ago he was caught in a single episode of shoplifting. The most appropriate diagnosis for this youth is:

a. oppositional defiant disorder.
b. conduct disorder.
c. intermittent explosive disorder
d. antisocial personality disorder

111. An additional type of record-keeping focuses largely on a client's ongoing issues. It contains four components: 1) factual information (a face sheet or database section); 2) a checklist section providing a rank-order roster of client issues; 3) a resolution plan (steps for resolving the primary issues); and 4) progress notes summarizing actions taken and results achieved. This method of record-keeping was borrowed from the medical arena, and is modeled after the "SOAP" format (subjective, objective, assessment, and plan). In social work it is called:

a. transactional recording.
b. problem-oriented recording.
c. summary recording.
d. SOAP recording.

112. An early cognitive theorist, who worked directly with Freud, established a theoretical orientation that differed from Freud's in three key features: 1) an individual's personality is best perceived as a whole, rather than as having hierarchical segments or parts; 2) social relationships drive behavior more than sexual motivations; and 3) current beliefs and thoughts play a far greater role in human behavior than is suggested via psychoanalytic theory, which is based largely in the unconscious and in past experiences and beliefs. The name of this theorist is:

a. Lawrence Kohlberg.
b. Anna Freud.
c. Albert Ellis.
d. Alfred Adler.

113. A 20-year-old male college student has been referred for evaluation by his family. They note that over the last six to seven months he has increasingly avoided contact and/or talking with family members and friends, that he often seems intensely preoccupied, and that his hygiene and grooming have become very poor. In speaking with him, the social worker notes that he seems very guarded, that his affect is virtually expressionless, and that he resists talking. After he is coaxed to speak, his speech is very tangential, disorganized, and even incoherent at times. He seems to be responding to internal stimuli (hallucinations and/or intrusive thoughts). The family and he deny substance abuse. Which would be the MOST likely diagnosis?

a. Schizophrenia
b. Somatization disorder
c. Bipolar disorder
d. Major depression with psychotic features

114. A young man with autism shows swift improvement when he is paired with a horse and starts learning to ride. His parents remove him from the program, citing an inability to drive him to the stables, and they refuse to allow the social worker to provide alternative transportation. The man speedily reverts to his self-harming behaviors and has to be hospitalized. From a systems standpoint, what is the MOST likely explanation for his parents' decision?

a. They simply could not provide the needed transportation
b. Systems cannot tolerate change
c. The parents were protecting their son from outside influences
d. The parents were unconsciously reestablishing the homeostasis of their system

115. Encopresis is defined as:

a. the voluntary or involuntary passage of stool in an inappropriate place by a child over the age of four.
b. the voluntary or involuntary passage of stool in an inappropriate place by a competent adult.
c. deliberate fecal incontinence only in a child over age four.
d. involuntary fecal incontinence only in a developmentally delayed adult.

116. Critical components of universal precaution practice standards of the Occupational Safety and Health Administration include which of the following?

a. Use of personal protective barriers
b. Proper hand washing
c. Precautions in handling sharps
d. All of the above

117. Common forms of research designs include all of the following EXCEPT:

a. descriptive studies.
b. experimental studies.
c. exploratory studies.
d. statistical studies.

118. Which cognitive-behavior approach incorporates a theory of emotion known as the "ABC Theory of Emotion"?

a. mindfulness-based cognitive therapy.
b. rational emotive therapy.
c. functional analytic psychotherapy.
d. cognitive analytic therapy.

119. Following a recent remarriage, a blended family has sought help from a social worker. They are struggling to develop workable family roles, standards, and cohesion. Following considerable effort, the family begins to work together better and conflicts have been largely minimized. According to eco-systems theory, the changes would best be referred to as:

a. socialization
b. adaptation
c. role reorganization
d. social accommodation

120. The following criteria are all used to distinguish delirium from dementia, except one. Select the pair that is not used to distinguish delirium from dementia:

a. acute onset vs slow onset.
b. diagnosis in patients under age 65 vs patients over age 65.
c. consciousness fluctuates broadly vs relatively stable symptoms.
d. global cognitive impairments vs idiosyncratic cognitive impairments.

121. Problem identification, background information, hypothesis formulation, operationalization (selecting a study model and data collection), evaluation (data analysis), and further theorization can be referred to as:

a. study design.
b. the research process.
c. scientific investigation.
d. knowledge generation.

122. A 22-year-old college student comes to a hospital emergency room complaining of chest pain. The medical work-up is negative. The social worker learns that his father recently died of a heart attack (a few weeks ago) while he was away at school, and that he is now experiencing episodes of sudden-onset fear accompanied by symptoms such as a rapid heart rate, sweating, tremors, chest pain, and shortness of breath, and feelings that he is about to die. After a short time, the symptoms subside. In recent days he has been sleeping outside the hospital, fearful that he may not otherwise arrive in time when the symptoms strike. Which is the most likely diagnosis?

a. Generalized anxiety disorder
b. Panic disorder
c. Somatization disorder
d. Post-traumatic stress disorder

123. In working with a client, the social worker becomes aware that she persistently behaves in ways to please or gain the approval of others. While this is not always problematic, the social worker discovers that she is obsessed with wearing the "right" clothes, living in the "right" neighborhood, and marrying the "right" person. At present, her finances are in a shambles as she tries desperately to "keep up with the Joneses," and her romantic life is suffering, as she only pursues relations that she believes others think are optimum, rather than judging relationships on more personally relevant values, such as her feelings for them, baseline compatibility, etc. Utilizing Kohlberg's Theory of Moral Development, specify the Level and Stage of moral development that applies to this individual:

a. conventional Level, Stage 3.
b. pre-conventional Level, Stage 1.
c. post-conventional Level, Stage 6.
d. conventional Level, Stage 4.

124. "Single system" research designs involve observing one client or system only (n=1) before, during, and after an intervention. Because of their flexibility and capacity to measure change over time, single system designs are frequently used by practitioners to evaluate:

a. their practice.
b. difficult clients.
c. conformation to policy.
d. regulation adherence.

125. A social worker is seeing a client who has previously been diagnosed with heroin use disorder. He has not met the criteria for substance use disorder, except for craving, for 5 months. He lives at his mother's home and is using a methadone treatment program. He would be classified as:

a. early remission.
b. sustained remission.
c. not in remission.
d. early remission, controlled environment.

126. Bipolar disorder is most commonly treated with which of the following medication?

a. lithium
b. haloperidol
c. Librium
d. Prozac

127. Name the four kinds of reinforcement used in Operant Conditioning Theory, as established by B.F. Skinner:

a. positive reinforcement, conditioned stimulus, consequence responses, and negative reinforcement.
b. negative reinforcement, punishment, conditioned responses, and antecedent events.
c. consequence responses, deprivation responses, rewards, time-out responses.
d. positive reinforcement, negative reinforcement, punishment, and extinction.

128. There are three types of single system research "case studies" or "pre-designs." Identify the answer below that is ERRONEOUSLY described.

a. Changes in case study (Design B-C).
b. Intervention only (Design B).
c. Observation only (Design A).
d. Time series only (Design A-B).

129. To meet criteria for diagnosis of schizophrenia a client must have at least two out of three major symptoms for a significant amount of time during a one-month interval. Which of the following is NOT one of the three major symptoms <u>necessary</u> to diagnosis schizophrenia?

a. Delusions
b. Hallucinations
c. Disorganized speech
d. Blunted affect

130. A 48-year-old woman is seen in clinic for personal problems. Upon interview she describes having quit her grocery clerk job because of fear that something might happen that she can't cope with at the work site. When pressed, she is vague but finally states that she's fearful she could have gas (burping or flatulence), bowel or bladder incontinence, or be badly embarrassed by others on the job. She acknowledges that she has no current gaseous or incontinence issues, and that she's never been humiliated by anyone in the past. However, she insists that she cannot tolerate the possibility it might occur. The most likely diagnosis is:

a. Panic disorder.
b. Agoraphobia.
c. Social anxiety disorder.
d. General anxiety disorder.

131. Identify the four steps (in the proper order) that Albert Bandura formulated to operationalize Social Learning Theory:

a. Attention, retention, reproduction, motivation.
b. Attention, motivation, retention, reproduction.
c. Motivation, retention, reproduction, attention.
d. Reproduction, motivation, attention, retention.

132. In an "A-B" single system research design, "A" indicates an initial phase without any intervention, and "B" refers to the intervention phase and requisite data collection. This design is called:

a. The "intervention" single system design.
b. The "planned" single system design.
c. The "basic" single system design.
d. The "descriptive" single system design.

133. As part of a pending disability application, a social worker meets with the client. The client voices complaints about significant chronic back and shoulder pain, which is the basis of the claim. During the course of the in-home assessment the social worker notes that the individual is able to bend down to move and pick things up, and is able to reach over her head into an upper cabinet—all without apparent difficulty or complaints of pain. The most appropriate determination would be:

a. Illness anxiety disorder.
b. Malingering.
c. Factitious disorder.
d. Somatic symptom disorder.

134. A couple presenting for counseling evaluation reveals that the wife comes from a dysfunctional, neglectful, alcoholic home and has little trust or tolerance for relationships. Consequently, their marriage is marred by constant arguing and distrust, frequent demands that he leave, episodes of impulsive violence, alternating with brief periods of excessive over-valuation (stating that he is the "best thing that ever happened" to her, "too good" for her, et cetera. Which is the most likely diagnosis?

a. Anti-social personality disorder
b. Histrionic personality disorder
c. Borderline personality disorder
d. Narcissistic personality disorder

135. A social worker has a client experiencing significant cognitive dissonance. She considers herself as a very principled person, and holds herself to very high standards of conduct. She very openly condemns drinking, gambling, and other "vices," yet she reveals that she has long struggled with a desire to gamble. Her very vigorous denunciations of gambling, even while harboring a desire herself, constitute the application of what defense mechanism?

a. Projection
b. Rationalization
c. Reaction formation
d. Substitution

136. A social worker should choose a practice framework based upon any of the following criteria EXCEPT:

a. an accepted psychological theoretical base.
b. treatment goals and treatment type (individual, family, group, etc.).
c. the model most commonly used by other social workers.
d. the client's problem and/or time and resources available.

137. There are four categories of measurement. One is called the "nominal" category. Nominal measurements are used when two or more "named" variables exist (e.g., male/female, high/medium/low, etc.). All of the following are also categories of measurement, EXCEPT:

a. the "interval" category.
b. the "additive" category.
c. the "ordinal" category.
d. the "ratio" category.

138. Which one of the following does NOT represent common practice frameworks?

a. Ethnic-sensitive and feminist frameworks
b. Systems and eco-system frameworks
c. Generalist and strengths frameworks
d. Behavioral and cognitive frameworks

139. A social worker has been contacted by a couple to assist them with issues of marital discord. They have been married about six months. The wife presents as vulnerable, tearful, and anxious, and the husband presents as angry and overwhelmed. The wife openly claims that "he has never loved me," and expresses anger that he married her without "the proper feelings." The husband responds that he has "done everything possible" to "prove" his love (to the point of near bankruptcy and jeopardizing his employment with frequent absences), but nothing is sufficient. During the interview, the social worker discovers that she has had many short-term relationships in the past, that she has a history of suicide gestures and "fits of rage." Further, she frequently demands a divorce and then begs him to stay, is routinely physically assaultive, etc. The most likely diagnosis is:

a. intermittent explosive disorder.
b. histrionic personality disorder.
c. paranoid personality disorder.
d. borderline personality disorder.

140. A newly divorced client has been working on numerous past marital issues, and was readily disclosing many feelings and concerns. However, when episodes of her infidelity arose, the client became reluctant to reveal her feelings about what had occurred, when, and its specific impact on her life. The psychoanalytic approach would refer to this as resistance and the proper response would be to:

a. ignore the resistance in deference to the client's feelings.
b. mention the resistance, but make no effort to move the client forward on the matter.
c. confront the issue of resistance and make a point of addressing and exploring it with the client.
d. require the client to continue disclosing her feelings and coping with her pain as related to this highly sensitive matter.

141. A 52-year-old man has been referred to see a social worker for "family and work problems." Two months ago, he lost his job as an executive in a major corporation, and has not found new work. On intake the social worker discovers his drinking has increased, and he reports feeling depressed most days. He can't seem to enjoy doing anything, not even golf, which he used to love. Rather, all he can seem to do is sleep and "sit around the house." He feels useless, empty, and helpless to change his situation. He has tried reading the want-ads, but he just can't seem to focus. He's gained over 18 lbs. He then adds, "Sometimes I seem to hear voices, telling me I'm just 'no good,' and that things will never get better. When that happens, I try to plug my ears, but it doesn't help. Only booze seems to get the voices to stop. Do you think I'm going crazy?" What is the client's probable primary diagnosis?

a. Major depressive disorder
b. Major depressive disorder with psychotic features
c. Alcohol use disorder
d. Alcohol-induced depressive disorder

142. A social worker begins to feel an unexpected affinity toward a client who reminds her of her father. This is a classic example of:

a. direct influence.
b. free association.
c. transference.
d. countertransference.

143. Key principles and concepts of the psychoanalytic approach include all of the following EXCEPT:

a. individuals are best understood through their social environment.
b. treatment is, by design, a short-term process, not to exceed six to twelve months.
c. behavior derives from unconscious motives and drives, and problematic experiences in the unconscious mind produce dysfunction and disorders.
d. resolution of problems is achieved by drawing out repressed information to produce greater understanding and behavioral change.

144. After identifying a specific behavior that a client wishes to change, the next priority for a social worker using a behavioral (behavior modification) approach is to:

a. identify and evaluate the antecedents and consequences of the behavior.
b. search for any related unconscious motivations or drives.
c. examine the emotions associated with the target behavior.
d. operationally define the behavior.

145. A hospital emergency room social worker is asked to see a client who was treated for traumatic assault injuries following a robbery. The client is clearly fearful, vulnerable, and overwhelmed. At the time of discharge the client expresses a reluctance to leave, voicing unrealistic fears of possible further assault. The most effective intervention approach in this situation would be which of the following?

a. Grief therapy
b. Crisis intervention
c. A psychoanalytic approach
d. A task-centered approach

146. A social worker is called to a hospital emergency room to see a 26-year-old university student. He came in claiming he was having a heart attack, but the medical work-up was entirely negative. He notes that at night his chest begins to tighten, his heart starts racing, his mouth goes dry, and his breathing becomes difficult. Next, his palms become sweaty and his hands start to tremble and tingle. Then he feels dizzy, nauseous, and worries that he's about to die. This is been going on for about six weeks. His studies have suffered, and he's becoming depressed and overwhelmed. He has no substance abuse history. Finally, he notes that his dad died of a heart attack at about his same age. His most likely diagnosis is:

a. panic disorder.
b. specific phobia.
c. acute stress disorder.
d. obsessive-compulsive disorder.

147. A social worker sees a newly married client who is having marital problems. The client discloses that her prior spouse was repeatedly unfaithful. She acknowledges a tendency to be overly suspicious and accusatory of her current spouse due to the persistent fears from her prior marriage. The social worker suggests that the client mentally construct a new or alternate scenario that applies to her new marriage in order to free herself from the old persistent fears. This approach would best be referred to as:

a. complementary therapy
b. collaborative therapy
c. narrative approach
d. social learning approach

148. The gender and typical age when the "Electra Complex" occurs is which of the following?

a. Females, 3-7 years of age
b. Males, 3-6 years of age
c. Females, 8-12 years of age
d. Males, 6-12 years of age

149. Strategic family therapy focuses on:

a. family communication.
b. family structure.
c. family rules and behavioral patterns.
d. family subsystems.

150. A group of individuals with one or more characteristics (social, physical, religious, or cultural) identified as being subordinately distinct in a larger societal context is referred to as a:

a. heterogeneous group.
b. minority group.
c. target group.
d. homogenous group.

Answer Key and Explanations

1. B: Executive functioning refers to higher order cognitive functioning. Specific examples include: organization (attention, decision-making, planning, sequencing, and problem solving), and regulation (initiation of action, self-control, and self-regulation). Lower order cognitive measures include: orientation to place, registration (recall of new learning immediately or within seconds, such as repeating words or numbers provided), recall (short-term and long-term memory), attention, and calculation.

2. D: A patient who is "oriented times four" is able to adequately identify: 1) himself (person); 2) his immediate location (place); 3) general features of time (day, month, year, etc.); and 4) his general circumstances (situation; i.e., in a counseling office seeking help, etc.).

3. D: The records should be retained as long as possible, preferably indefinitely. Records serve two purposes: 1) to maintain continuity between clinician-patient contacts; and 2) to document quality care. At a minimum, records must be kept in accordance with the state's statute of limitations. However, the social worker may not be legally protected even then, and certainly not after a patient's death (which could be construed, in some cases such as suicide, as a failure in quality care). Therefore, counseling records should be maintained as long as possible, and the longer the better.

4. C: In this situation the social worker should allow the patient to move into his motor home. The patient has a plan sufficient to meet his needs for food, clothing, and shelter. He has the legal right to choose where he wishes to live, even if others are not comfortable with his choice. Calling the police will not help, as they cannot force him to return to the facility. Adult protective services may have a subsequent role, if the patient begins to exhibit marked self-neglect or cognitive changes, but they cannot force the patient either. Finally, the patient is not eligible for an involuntary hold, as he is not placing himself or others in danger based upon a diagnosable mental illness, intoxication, or other substance abuse. Careful collateral planning, however, will be important (ensuring the daughter visits and checks in on him, etc.) to try and maximize his potential for success. After coping with the hardships of independent living, he may willingly return to assisted living.

5. C: Social workers are mandated to report even "suspicions" of child abuse. Therefore, the social worker should always call Child Protective Services and allow them to decide whether or not a formal investigation should be undertaken. It would be important, however, to also inform them of the nurse's prior experience, so that they may seek appropriate direction and avoid undue intervention that could otherwise damage an immigrant family's willingness to seek health care for a child in the future.

6. B: An evaluative test is reliable if it produces consistent results (i.e., if the same test was administered to the same subjects twice [i.e., "test-retest"], or to two similar groups with similar results [i.e., "split half"], it would produce similar results), and it is valid if it measures what is claims to measure. Consequently, a test may be reliable (consistently producing similar results in test-retest experiments) and yet invalid (failing to measure what it claims to measure. However, a truly valid test will always be reliable. Inter-rater reliability indicates whether the scoring process can be accurately carried out by different individuals using the same scoring procedure.

7. A: The best response is to tell the client to make an appointment to review his records. Although laws governing patient access to psychiatric records vary widely, most states do allow patients to view these records—although some limits are allowed in certain jurisdictions if the clinician has a compelling concern regarding the welfare of the patient. Regardless, all states allow these records to be obtained by a patient's attorney under subpoena. While the clinician owns the psychiatric record, the information held within that record is generally viewed as belonging to the patient. Past research indicates that patients typically cope well with this information. Even so, some information may have a deleterious iatrogenic effect. At a minimum, the clinician should view the record in company with the patient, to explain, clarify, reassure, and otherwise guide the review process to a wholesome outcome. Become thoroughly informed of the laws in the area governing patient records access.

8. D: In most (but not all) states the social worker is a mandated reporter if Dependent Adult abuse is suspected. Where reporting laws exist, the social worker should call Adult Protective Services directly, and submit the necessary written report unless they indicate specifically that they do not wish to receive a duplicate report. While health care providers may occasionally offer help of this nature, it is not possible to discharge this mandated reporting requirement in this manner. Where no laws for Dependent Adult reporting exist, care should be taken not to violate confidentiality, and appropriate consultation should be obtained.

9. B: Autonomy versus shame takes place between the ages of 1 and 3, the time in life when children are being toilet trained. Erikson theorized that harsh toilet training methods would create withholding or "anal-retentive" personality traits, and that permissive toilet training would lead to "anal-expressive" traits.

10. C: The most appropriate diagnosis would be adjustment disorder with depressed mood. Criteria for this disorder includes a time-limited nature, usually beginning within three months of the stressful event, and lessening within six months—either with removal of the stressor or through new adaptation skills. Adjustment disorder is a "sub-threshold disorder," allowing for early classification of a temporary condition when the clinical picture remains vague. While the patient does have insomnia, it arises from the stressful loss and not as an independent condition. Many of the essential criteria for a major depression are absent (weight loss, psychomotor agitation, blunted affect, etc.), although without successful treatment this condition could emerge. The diagnosis of acute stress disorder is not appropriate as the precipitating event did not involve threatened or actual serious injury or death.

11. A: Psychotherapy is generally considered to be more long-term (and complex) in nature, and potentially depending more on a specific theoretical orientation, while counseling is often seen as shorter in duration and oriented more toward immediate problem-solving. However, these terms are often used interchangeably. The term "counseling" has been attributed to Frank Parsons, who used it in his writings in 1908. The renowned psychologist Carl Rogers adopted the term when the psychiatric profession refused to allow him to call himself a psychotherapist. Some in the psychoanalytic field still feel the term should be reserved to those providing formal psychoanalysis, but this is not a widely shared view.

12. D: Erikson's psychosocial development model focuses on conflicts at each stage of the lifespan and the virtue that results from finding balance in the conflict. The first 5 stages refer to infancy and childhood and the last 3 stages to adulthood:

- Intimacy vs. isolation (Young adulthood): Love/intimacy or lack of close relationships.
- Generativity vs. stagnation (Middle age): Caring and achievements or stagnation.
- Ego integrity vs. despair (Older adulthood): Acceptance and wisdom or failure to accept changes of aging/despair.

13. D: A cost-effective analysis measures the effectiveness of an intervention rather than the monetary savings. For example, annually 2 million nosocomial infections result in 90,000 deaths and an estimated $6.7 billion in additional health costs. From that perspective, decreasing infections should reduce costs, but there are human savings in suffering as well, and it can be difficult to place a dollar value on that. If each infection adds about 12 days to hospitalization, then a reduction of 5 infections (5 X 12 = 60) would result in a cost-effective savings of 60 fewer patient infection days.

14. D: Monoamine oxidase inhibitors (MAOIs), serotonin-norepinephrine reuptake inhibitors (SNRIs), and selective serotonin reuptake inhibitors (SSRIs) are three classes of medications that are used primarily to treat depressive disorders.

15. B: Initially, the identified client would be the husband. Upon entry of the wife into the picture, the identified client would be the couple, given that the social worker was working with them both and seeing them only jointly. After the passage of time, however, and upon identification of issues requiring primary work with the wife, the identified client would be the wife. Ideally, the social worker would have come to closure with the husband more formally, identifying specifically that the focus had shifted from them as a couple to a primary endeavor with the wife. Regardless, the information now being entered in the clinical record is exclusively that related to the wife, and the husband should no longer be privy to that content. In keeping with this, the identified client has become the wife.

16. A: Because of the high co-morbidity rate between substance abuse and other disorders, the social worker needs to look at any patterns of substance use by individuals who suffer from other disorders. Conversely, substance abuse may mask symptoms of other disorders.

17. D: Although it is ideal for social workers to receive specific training regarding each of the individual minority populations they typically serve, they should still ensure that someone from an unfamiliar background receives needed services even where no staff with special training in that background is available.

18. B: The Health Insurance Portability and Accountability Act (HIPAA) addresses the rights of the individual related to privacy of health information. Health care workers must not release any information or documentation about a patient's condition or treatment without consent. The individual has the right to determine who may be given access to information considered "protected health information" (PHI). This includes all "individually identifiable health information" such as health history, condition, treatments in any form, and any related documentation. Personal information can be shared with a spouse, legal guardians, and those with durable power of attorney only if: 1) the patient agrees (or at least does not object), or 2) when it is professionally determined to be in the patient's "best interest" for certain specific and essential information to be provided (i.e., "directly relevant to the involvement of a spouse, family members, friends, or other persons identified by a patient, in the patient's care or payment for health care").

19. D: The best course of action is to disclose limited information. Personal revelations are normally discouraged in a therapeutic relationship. They can turn the counseling experience into a mutual sharing process, robbing the client of proper attention. They can also cause the client to devalue the social worker if any revelation comes as an unwanted surprise. An exception to this rule exists when the therapeutic context is entirely centered in the information to be revealed—such as in a drug and alcohol rehabilitation program, where the sole purpose of the counseling is to address the issue being revealed (usually a group setting, where self-disclosure is essential to the process). Disclosures must not occur early, before trust is in place, and the group leader should always clearly understand his or her full intent and goals before revealing any personal information.

20. B: People with borderline personality disorder exhibit variable moods and impulsive behavior along with a tendency to view others negatively. People with this disorder are very social yet have significant difficulty maintaining relationships.

21. A: Cultural competences is best defined as the ability to work well with diverse groups. Quality training, wide-ranging knowledge, and the ability to recognize stereotypes, prejudices, and biases are all important contributors to cultural competence; however, only when a social worker also possesses the capacity to properly apply this information, can he or she work well with diverse populations.

22. A: Root cause analysis (RCA) is a retrospective attempt to determine the cause of an event, such as a death or other sentinel event. RCA involves interviews, observations, and review of medical records. External benchmarking monitors data from outside an institution, such as national rates of infections, and compares them to internal data. Internal trending compares internal rates of one area or population with another. Tracer methodology looks at the continuum of care a patient receives from admission to post-discharge, using a selected patient's medical record as a guide.

23. D: The null hypothesis for this study would state that there shall be no measurable difference in depression symptom reporting between the control group and the intervention group. The null hypothesis (often designated as "H_0") proposes that no relationship exists between two variables (often designated "x" and "y") other than that arising from chance alone. If a study's results demonstrate no difference, then the null hypothesis is "accepted." If differences emerge, then the study "failed to reject the null hypothesis." Statistical testing does not prove any hypotheses, but instead disproves them via rejection.

24. C: Manic episodes are commonly seen in bipolar disorder and are characterized by such factors as a decreased need for sleep, racing thoughts and unrealistic ideation. Criteria for a manic episode in adults are that the episode lasts most of the day for at least one week.

25. B: A first manic episode experienced after age forty is highly unlikely with bipolar disorder and more likely would be due to a medical condition or, perhaps, a substance abuse issue. The average age for the first manic episode is the early 20's.

26. C: Oxytocin is known as the "love hormone." It is present during labor, breastfeeding, lovemaking, cuddling, and other bonding experiences such as playing with pets. As a drug, it has been used to precipitate labor.

27. C: Clinical pathways should be based on evidence-based research, which refers to the use of current research and patient values in practice to establish an idealized plan of care. Research may be the result of large studies of best practices, or it may arise from individual research efforts using observations in practice about the effectiveness of a particular treatment. Evidence-based research requires a commitment to ongoing research and outcomes evaluation. Evidence-based research requires a thorough understanding of research methods, including internal and external validity.

28. C: A type I error refers to rejecting the null hypothesis when the null hypothesis is true. A failure to randomize research participants will potentially introduce bias, and may provide grounds upon which to invalidate a study, but it is not a type I error. Assuming a normal statistical distribution when it is skewed will violate the assumptions necessary to apply a proper statistical model to the analysis of data.

29. B: The family should be encouraged to stay and talk to the patient, as hearing is usually the last of the senses to fail. Typical physical changes associated with death include:

- Sensory: Reduced sensations of pain and touch. Decreased vision and hearing.
- Cardiovascular: Tachycardia followed by bradycardia, dysrhythmia, and hypotension.
- Respiratory: Tachypnea, progressing to Cheyne-Stokes respiration.
- Muscular: Muscles relax, the jaw sags, and the ability to swallow and talk is lost.
- Urinary: Output decreases (accompanied by incontinence), and anuria follows.
- Integumentary: Skin becomes cold, clammy, cyanotic, and waxy. Skin in the coccygeal area often tears.

30. A: There is significant overlap between the symptoms of bipolar disorder and borderline personality disorder, and the social worker must take care to differentiate between the two. Borderline personality disorder is characterized by interpersonal issues, while bipolar disorder is more likely to have a biological etiology.

31. D: The causes of many cases of early-onset intellectual disability are difficult to determine. However, major categories of risk include genetic conditions, problems during pregnancy (including at and after birth), poverty and cultural deprivation.

32. A: A type II error refers to the failure to reject the null hypothesis when the null hypothesis is false. Invalid assumptions regarding raw data (i.e., skewed data that was assumed to follow a normal, or "bell shaped" distribution) can lead to the selection of a statistical analysis model that will produce inaccurate output. Rejecting the null hypothesis when the null hypothesis is true is a type I error. Making an error in mathematical calculations is one way to introduce error, but it is not a type II error. This is less common in the computer age, where most calculations have been automated.

33. D: Bipolar disorder is primarily a mood disorder, while schizophrenia is characterized more by disordered thought patterns.

34. B: Discrimination is basing the opportunities, options, and benefits available to a specific group of people based upon preconceptions and assumptions. Bigotry is an intolerance of other ideas and beliefs. Prejudice is accepting unconfirmed information that may be situationally or individually unique, and assuming them to be valid for an entire group or class people. Misogyny refers to a hatred or distrust of women.

35. D: Failure mode and effects analysis (FMEA) is a team-based prospective analysis method that attempts to identify and correct failures in a process before utilization to ensure positive outcomes. Steps include definition, team creation, description (flow chart), brainstorming, identification of potential causes of failures, listing potential adverse outcomes, assignment of a failure severity rating (1 is slight and 10 is death), assignment of a frequency/occurrence rating, assignment of a detection rating, calculation of a risk priority number, and the reduction of potential failures and identification of performance measures.

36. A: Team members usually observe the leader and determine who controls the meeting and how control is exercised, while beginning to form alliances. Arguing is counterproductive, and following strict rules of discourse may not solve power issues and may be too restrictive for small collaborative groups. Group interactions often become less formal as members develop rapport and are more willing to help and support each other to achieve goals. Rotating leadership roles can lead to a lack of focus as styles may vary widely. The leader is responsible for organizing the group, clarifying methods to achieve work, and the means of working together toward a common goal.

37. B: The best response is to refuse to use the form. No client or client population is beneath the ethical standards of the field. An appropriate information release form stipulates a limited period of time beyond which the form expires, the specific kind of information to be released, the specific purpose for which the information is to be provided, and a specific individual or entity to whom/which the information will be provided. While obtaining an information release is indeed a "hassle" it is the ethical standard of care in the field, and deviation from it can open a practitioner to legal liability. The fact that a given client, or client population, may be unaware of this does not excuse the social worker from using an ethically appropriate form in keeping with expected standards of care. Any limitations to confidentiality—such as mandatory reporting if a client expresses intent to commit a crime or harm another—belong on a treatment consent form, rather than on an information release form.

38. B: The Mini-cog test assesses dementia by having patients remember and repeat 3 common objects and draw a clock face indicating a particular time. The MMSE assesses dementia through a series of tests, including remembering the names of 3 common objects, counting backward, naming, providing location, copying shapes, and following directions. The Digit Repetition Test assesses attention by asking the patient to repeat the 2 number, then 3, then 4 and so on. The Confusion Assessment Method is used to assess delirium, not dementia.

39. D: The four most common minority classifications are age, gender, race (ethnicity), sexual orientation.

40. B: This client is most likely experiencing a delusion. Delusions are inaccurate beliefs held by an individual. These delusional beliefs are overwhelmingly contraindicated by known reality.

41. C: Deinstitutionalization refers to changes in policy and law that led to the release of many mental health patients who would have otherwise remained in institutional settings. Involuntary hospital commitment (i.e., in an asylum) became increasingly common up to the 1950s. However, the Community Mental Health Act of 1963 began to reverse this trend, as did the 1999 US Supreme Court ruling in Olmstead vs. LC. In 1970 there were 413,066 beds in state and county mental hospitals, which fell to 119,033 by 1988, and to 63,526 by 1998. This era has since come to be called the era of "deinstitutionalization." Sometimes overdone, issues of homelessness among the mentally ill, and "re-institutionalization" in the prison system have been noted.

42. B: Thought insertion/withdrawal is a type of delusion characterized by the belief that others are putting thoughts into or taking thoughts out of one's mind.

43. B: The Occupational Safety and Health Administration (OSHA) regulates workplace safety, including disposal methods for sharps, such as needles. OSHA requires that standard precautions be used at all times and that staff be trained to use precautions. OSHA requires procedures for post-exposure evaluation and treatment, and the availability of the hepatitis B vaccine for healthcare workers. OSHA regulates occupational exposure to infections, and establishes standards to prevent the spread of blood-borne pathogens, as well as regulating the fitting and use of respirators.

44. B: Alzheimer's disease causes atrophy of the brain tissue and is the most common form of dementia. Cognitive deficits are a common result of this disease.

45. C: Of successful suicides, 49% of those studied had a prior suicide attempt history. Of those previously seen by a mental health professional, 78% had denied having any suicidal ideation at their last contact.

46. C: The Braden scale is used to assess and predict the risk of a patient developing pressure sores. The Norton Scale is also used to predict pressure sores, and is based on scores in 5 categories (physical, mental, activity, mobility, and incontinence). The Pressure Ulcer Scale for Healing (PUSH) is used to assess improvement or deterioration of existing ulcers based on measurements, exudate, and tissue type. The Diabetic Foot Ulcer Scale assesses the quality of life of those with diabetic foot ulcers.

47. A: The primary purpose of interdisciplinary teams is the sharing of ideas and perspectives to solve problems. Collaboration requires open sharing and respect for the expertise of other professionals. Interdisciplinary teams may include doctors, nurses, and other members of the allied health professions as well. While cost-saving, timesaving, and improved patient satisfaction may (and often do) result from innovative approaches to problem solving, these are secondary benefits from effective interdisciplinary collaboration.

48. C: By removing the man from his wife and removing herself from the rest of the group, the daughter is showing that, although the mother and son have a close relationship, the family as a whole has split apart. This displays a sense of low cohesion.

49. A: This patient is exhibiting dependence in response to stress. Typical psychological responses to stress include:

- Dependence: The patient has an inability to make decisions, requires constant reassurance, and calls nurses/families frequently.
- Depression: The patient is withdrawn and sad, fails to take treatments and/or misses appointments, and may be at risk for suicide.
- Anger: The patient is belligerent, uncooperative, and blames others.
- Confusion: The patient is forgetful, disoriented, and bewildered.
- Passivity: The patient defers to others, feeling he/she has no control.

50. D: CQI stands for "continuous quality improvement." This is an outgrowth of the quality assurance (QA) programs of the 1980s, and is intended to symbolize the fact that quality improvement is a never-ending process. Continuing education, problem resolution brainstorming, cause and effect "fishbone diagramming," process flowcharts, improvement storyboards, and implementation of the "plan, do, check, act" method of problem-solving and process improvement are all examples of CQI.

51. D: All staff members are responsible for identifying performance improvement projects. Performance improvement must be a continuous process. Continuous Quality Improvement (CQI) is a management philosophy that emphasizes the effectiveness of an organization and the systems and processes within that organization, rather than focusing on specific individuals. Total Quality Management (TQM) is a management philosophy that espouses a commitment to meeting the needs of the customers (patients and staff) at all levels within an organization. Both management philosophies recognize that change can be made in small steps and should involve staff at all levels.

52. A: The five most common classifications of race include Asian, Black, Hispanic, Native American, and White.

53. C: The paraphilia category of sexual disorders includes pedophilia, and it is the type of sexual disorder most likely to be brought to a social worker's attention.

54. C: Healthy People 2030 outlines leading health indicators (LHIs) to improve health and reduce the risks of disease in order to improve life expectancy and quality of life. Leading health indicators are divided across four categories: (1) All Ages, (2) Infants, (3) Children and Adolescents, and (4) Adults and Older Adults. Within the Adults and Older Adults category, leading health indicators address various conditions including hypertension, cigarette smoking, maternal deaths and new cases of diabetes, amongst others. The leading health indicators are core objectives for HP 2030.

55. B: The steps of the Roberts crisis intervention model are as follows:

1. Assess lethality
2. Establish rapport
3. Identify problems
4. Deal with feelings
5. Explore alternatives
6. Develop an action plan
7. Follow-up

56. D: The Agency for Healthcare Research and Quality (AHRQ) of the US Department of Health and Human Services provides research and funding for the development of evidence-based practice guidelines. The AHRQ has sponsored the development of surveys for assessment of patient safety and is actively involved in outcomes research. The AHRQ research centers specialize in research related to patient safety, quality improvement, outcomes, assessment of clinical practices and technology, healthcare delivery systems, primary and preventive care, and heath care costs.

57. C: Frotteurism is a type of paraphilia, or sexual disorder, in which an individual gains sexual enjoyment by touching genitalia to a non-consenting or unsuspecting individual.

58. D: Some apparent mental health symptoms may arise from certain culture-specific dictates of behavior, mood, or thought processes. For example, talking with ghosts or other spirits, seeing hallucinations or visions, hearing voices, etc., can all be attributed to certain cultural and/or religious groups. In such situations, the individual should not receive a mental illness diagnosis.

59. C: Adult learners tend to be practical and goal-oriented, so they tend to remain organized and keep their educational goals in mind while learning. Other characteristics include:

- Self-directed: Adults prefer active involvement and responsibility.
- Knowledgeable: Adults can relate new material to information with which they are familiar by life experience or education.
- Relevancy-oriented: Adults like to know how they will use information.
- Motivated: Adults like to see evidence of their own achievement, such as gaining a certificate.

60. D: The Instrumental Activities of Daily Living (IADL) tool assesses financial ability (ability to pay bills, budget, and keep track of finances), telephone use, shopping, food preparation, housekeeping, laundry, transportation availability (ability to drive or use public transportation), and medications (ability to manage prescriptions and take medications). The Barthel Index of Activities of Daily Living assesses 10 categories, usually including bathing, toileting, ascending or descending stairs, feeding, mobility, personal grooming, urinary and fecal control, transferring, and ambulatory/wheelchair status.

61. D: Unlike major depressive disorder, which includes severe symptoms and lasts at least two weeks, dysthymic disorder has less intense symptoms and continues for two years or more.

62. B: Depression is the most common lifetime disorder. Some people may have one major episode, while others experience it as a recurring problem throughout their life.

63. B: A professional interpreter is the most appropriate option. Selecting a relative or friend risks violating client confidentiality, as does asking another staff person to become involved. Further, non-professional persons may not have an adequate grasp of special terminology needed to properly address medical, legal, or psychiatric concerns. Of note: written words are "translated," while spoken words are "interpreted."

64. B: The best time to initiate conflict resolution is when conflict first emerges, but before open conflict and hardening of positions. Resolution steps include:

1. Allowing both parties to present their side without bias.
2. Encouraging cooperation through negotiation and compromise.
3. Maintaining focus and avoiding arguments.
4. Evaluating the need for renegotiation, a formal resolution process, or a 3rd party mediator.
5. Utilizing humor and empathy to diffuse tension.
6. Summarizing and outlining key arguments.

65. C: Maslow stated that human behavior is motivated by various needs, and posited that there is a hierarchy of need beginning with basic needs and progressing to personal needs. Maslow theorized that working toward self-actualization is a lifelong process that may involve progress in multiple directions rather than in one direction. Failure results in depression and diminished feelings of value:

- 1st Level (the base): Physiological needs.
- 2nd Level: Safety and security.
- 3rd Level: Love/Belonging.
- 4th Level: Self-esteem.
- 5th level (the apex): Self-actualization.

66. D: Goal congruence, which, according to Drisko (2009), is the fourth of five key factors required for a quality therapeutic relationship between client and clinician. The five key factors are as follows:

- Affective attunement
- Mutual affirmation
- Joint efforts to resolve missteps
- Goal congruence
- Using varying types of empathy

67. C: There is no requirement that information be disclosed to an employer providing coverage, unless the employee has previously stipulated information to be released in consenting to coverage and services. Payment for coverage by an employer does not, in and of itself, entitle the employer to any private client information. Even under conditions of subpoena, social workers may be able to limit the scope of information shared, or even claim "privileged communication" status in response to orders to testify.

68. C: The appropriate steps are as follows: Establish a rapport, summarize legal and ethical obligations, complete a service contract, and assess the client. Establishing a rapport usually includes a review of the client's presenting problem, though it also includes fostering trust, showing empathy and concern, and demonstrating a willingness to be non-judgmental about the presenting issue. Summarizing legal and ethical obligations includes addressing mandatory reporting issues and client confidentiality. A service contract covers mutual roles and expectations, major goals, the anticipated course of treatment, and how to handle issues of non-performance. Assessment should cover the client's personal mental health history, medical history (including substance abuse), family history, work history, and social history. It may also include an evaluation of the client's mood, safety, intellectual functioning, and emotional stability.

69. A: The life course theory of aging is a sociological model that views aging as a lifelong process of social, psychological, and biological changes. The process of change begins in infancy and continues through older adulthood, and is viewed within cultural, economic, social, and historic contexts. Key concepts include:

- The social and historical contexts and environmental location.
- Individual, generational, and historical time.
- Degrees of heterogeneity or variability.
- Social connections.
- Personal agency and control, and control cycles.
- The past as related to future.

70. C: Bureaucracy refers to an organization that is arranged hierarchically, with numerous departments and units through which segments of specialized services are provided, moving toward achievement of a common goal.

71. C: Although Harry's mother may think that his development is abnormally slow, most children start crawling between ages 7 and 10 months, and some even skip crawling and go straight to toddling. The mother seems to be comparing her son unfavorably (and maybe unrealistically) to the children in his playgroup, hoping to use his development to bolster the needs of her ego. The caseworker would do best to reassure the mother that Harry will crawl soon and to recommend patience with the natural process of his growth.

72. A: Striving for patient satisfaction is a long-term outcome. Process is important, but both short-term and long-term outcome measures should be established based upon clinical efficacy, rather than patient satisfaction (e.g., patients may not always appreciate essential treatments and interventions). Short-term outcomes show results directly related to process and allow modification of the process, but long-term outcomes (such as patient satisfaction) often relate to general quality of care and may be used retrospectively to evaluate the process or plan for future care. Three types of outcome measures should be identified: clinical, patient functioning, and patient satisfaction.

73. D: A social assessment report focuses on a client's social and relational functioning. This form of client assessment may also be called a "social history."

74. D: Several factors can cause a person to be at a higher risk of attempting suicide, including having had thoughts about suicide in the past, a history of the behavior in one's family and a history of high mobility.

75. B: A structured questionnaire or checklist can be particularly helpful if a client is having difficulty exploring, formulating, or discussing his situation or concerns. The document provides information that prompts the client, and thereby aids in opening up the problem and specific concerns. Questionnaires and checklists can also be particularly helpful if the situation being evaluated is complex or risk laden and the social worker needs to be particularly thorough (e.g., a suicide assessment, etc.).

76. A: The interpreter should have training in medical vocabulary for both languages. Just speaking the languages well does not mean that the translator will adequately interpret specialized vocabulary. It is not necessary for the interpreter to know the patient's history, as the interpreter's job is only to interpret what is said, not add to it or augment it based on prior knowledge. While onsite interpreters are ideal, interpretation can be provided through a speakerphone at a distance.

77. C: Cathexis refers to the attachment (whether conscious or unconscious), of mental or emotional ("psychosexual") energy (i.e., feelings and significance) to an idea, object, image, or, most commonly, a person. Psychically, pain arises from loss. Cathexes are "objective" when they are directed at the external world, and "narcissistic" when they have meaning only for the subject. Significant pain imposes a substantial narcissistic cathexis that tends to "empty the ego." The result of prolonged pain is often "regression," as the ego becomes less able to serve its "anti-cathexis" role of imposing rationality and executive functioning on a situation characterized by severe pain (whether physical or emotional).

78. A: Frontline organizational services are not one of the basic functions of administrators. Services "in the trenches" are provided by employee staff, instead. Administrative functions do include advocacy, conflict resolution/mediation, and planning/delegation.

79. A: An eco-map (also called an "ecological map" or an ecogram, especially if it includes a genogram) helps individuals and families visually depict the quality of relationships with others, within the community and with important resources in their lives. While a genogram is limited to "family tree" depictions, the eco-map is broadly constructed to include multiple other important relationships to people, systems, communities, extended family, resources, services, etc. It can explore a range of things, from relationships to finances. Lines connecting the "client" (an individual or a family, at the center of the diagram) have direction arrows to depict influence flow (which may be bidirectional), strength of the relationship, and quality of the relationship (i.e., dominant, powerful, and angry would be depicted by the direction of the power, a thick line would indicate a strong connection, and the line would be drawn wavy or red if the relationship is stressful).

80. B: The client is describing the features of avoidant personality disorder. Criteria includes being worried about social situations, unwillingness to try new activities, avoiding activities once found enjoyable if they are social.

81. D: There is no Cluster D – only A, B, and C. These cluster descriptions have been provided by authors in various academic sources, although they only loosely describe each cluster's content. Cluster A includes: paranoid, schizoid, and schizotypal personality disorders. Cluster B includes: antisocial, borderline, histrionic, and narcissistic personality disorders. Finally, Cluster C includes: obsessive/compulsive, avoidant, and dependent personality disorders. Clusters tend to run in families.

82. B: This accommodation is an example of alloplastic behavior. This is a form of adaptation in which an individual changes aspects of his environment in order to better accommodate competing needs or demands. Changes in oneself or one's behavior (as opposed to the environment), in order to better accommodate competing needs or demands is called "autoplastic behavior."

83. B: Reacting and responding to facts instead of feelings to avoid confrontations and diffuse anger helps facilitate communications with intra- and interdisciplinary teams. Professional communication skills to facilitate team communication also include:

- Avoiding interpreting others statements, interrupting, giving unsolicited advice, or jumping to conclusions -- all of which may interfere with the free flow of ideas.
- Listening actively and asking questions for clarification rather than challenging other people's ideas.
- Clarifying information or opinions to help avoid misunderstandings.
- Communicating openly and respecting others' opinions.

84. D: The Wechsler Adult Intelligence Scale (WAIS) was introduced in 1955 as a revised update of the Wechsler-Bellevue Intelligence Scale of 1939. Perhaps the next most common scale used is the Stanford-Binet Intelligence Scale, first released in 1916, which was derived from the French Binet-Simon Intelligence Scale of 1905. The median score for the WAIS is 100, with a standard deviation of 15 (i.e., scores between 85 and 115), which encompasses about 68% of all adults. It is administered to individuals over the age of 16. Individuals between the ages of 6-16 may be given the Wechsler Intelligence Scale for Children (WISC).

85. B: Interdepartmental funding allocation is something done at the administrative level, rather than by supervisory staff. A supervisor's role involves being a role model, recruitment and orientation, day-to-day management, staff training/education/development, staff assessments and reviews, advocating for staff and program needs, evaluating the program for ongoing improvement, and providing support and counsel to staff.

86. C: V Codes are problems or conditions not due to a mental disorder, but that require clinical attention (e.g., noncompliance with treatment or parent-child relational problem). Most of these codes, borrowed from the International Classification of Disease (ICD) manual provide for severity and treatment course specifiers such as mild, moderate, and severe, as well as by prior history, in partial remission, or full remission. Where a specific diagnosis is expected, but has not been finalized, a code may be qualified as a provisional diagnosis. A diagnosis should also be accompanied by a diagnostic differential or formulation, in which the criteria in support of the diagnosis (and against other options) are summarized.

87. A: This should occur at or around 24 months. Margaret Mahler's three stages of development are: 1) the autistic stage; 2) the symbiotic stage; and 3) the separation-individuation stage. The separation-individuation stage consists of four sub-stages, the third of which (the rapprochement substage) is completed sometime between 14-24 months of age. Then, the infant enters the last substage (the "object constancy substage"), which is completed by the infant sometime after 24 months of age.

88. C: Reciprocal evaluation is not a program evaluation method. Outcome evaluation focuses on end-results after the program is completed. Participatory evaluation is an inductive, community-centered evaluative approach. Process-oriented evaluation (also called "formative evaluation") analyzes a certain point in time under specifically selected conditions (e.g., at planning or implementation point, etc.) in order to determine if the segment being evaluated is functioning properly, which allows both strengths and weaknesses to be identified.

89. C: Pervasive developmental disorders is NOT a DSM-5 category. The DSM-5 classifications are:

- Neurodevelopmental disorders:
- Schizophrenia spectrum and other psychotic disorders
- Bipolar and related disorders
- Depressive disorders
- Anxiety disorders
- Obsessive-compulsive and related disorders
- Trauma- and stressor-related disorders
- Dissociative disorders
- Somatic symptom and related disorders
- Feeding and eating disorders
- Elimination disorders
- Sleep-wake disorders
- Sexual dysfunctions
- Gender dysphoria
- Disruptive, impulse-control, and conduct disorders
- Substance-related and addictive disorders
- Neurocognitive disorders
- Personality disorders
- Paraphilic disorders
- Other mental disorders
- Medication-induced movement disorders
- Other conditions that may be a focus of clinical attention

Most disorders that were classified as pervasive developmental disorders under the DSM-IV will now fall under the classification neurodevelopmental disorders and more specifically communication disorders or autism spectrum disorder.

90. B: The decision regarding the issue(s) that should be addressed first should be made by the client, in exploration with the social worker. The client's right of self-determination must control the treatment process (except in situations of specific court-ordered treatment). While the social worker may suggest priorities, the broad goals and specific objectives of the treatment plan must be decided by the client, even if the social worker does not entirely agree. During the course of treatment, revisions to the focus and/or process of treatment (i.e., the treatment plan's goals and objectives) may become necessary and proper, but any such changes must ultimately be decided by the client and not imposed by the social worker.

91. A: The "aggregate evaluation" approach is not a method of program "outcome evaluation." The "decision-oriented" approach utilizes agency data, surveys, interviews, and observations to identify which elements in a program are functioning well and which need improvement. The "experimental evaluation" approach is a very formal endeavor, wherein requisite independent variables and a dependent variable are defined and then testing is undertaken to examine causality. The "performance audits" approach uses an independent, third-party evaluator to examine program performance standards and outcomes.

92. D: Transmuting internalization is the process through which a cohesive self is achieved by incorporating the perceptions and functions of healthy significant others and objects into internalized self-structure. Empathic mirroring is the process by which the mother demonstrates ("reflects") care and understanding of the child, in turn helping the child to develop a self-identity.

Rapprochement is a term from object relations theory, indicating the need for an infant to seek independence while still retaining security. Differentiation is a substage in object relations theory, where an infant begins to look at the outside world, as opposed to the inward focus common to infants younger than five months of age.

93. D: First the social worker should explore and discuss the client's feelings about termination. It may be possible to ameliorate the client's distress by exploring the feelings related to termination. This may well involve assuring the client that he or she can always return for further contact at any time, or even schedule a follow-up appointment in the near future. Revising the termination plan should not occur unless other reasonable options have been explored and attempted. Where early discussion about termination is incorporated in the initial treatment plan, and where accomplishment of client goals is tracked, noted, and discussed, healthy accommodation to termination is enhanced.

94. C: This client/ social worker interaction could be improved in several ways. The first comment is shallow and does not address the feelings presented. The second comment would have better included a more descriptive word, such as "frustrated" or "furious." The final statement gives inappropriate reassurance of what will happen in the course of therapy, which the social worker has no right to ensure.

95. D: Peer reviews are not a form of participatory evaluation. Cluster evaluations are used to examine several program facets at one time. Based on pluralism, they allow multiple programs to determine how to solve joint problems. Action research is an informal method of review conducted by individuals directly affected by the issue being examined. Self-evaluations are a method by which involved staff members evaluate a program.

96. C: Early remission is no stimulant use criteria being met (except for craving) for at least 3 but less than 12 months. Sustained remission is no stimulant use criteria being met (except for cravings) for 12 months or longer. The terms full and partial are no longer used to describe remission.

97. B: Consultants do not have "administrative authority," but function only in an advisory capacity.

98. B: The primary focus of Gestalt psychology is on the "here and now." Gestalt psychology seeks to unify and integrate the personality, and to create "wholeness." It sees individuals as empowered agents able to control and regulate their future by personal choice. A focus on the past and its influence on the present and future is minimized (as compared with psychoanalytic theory).

99. B: The most likely diagnosis would be mild neurocognitive disorder due to traumatic brain injury. A diagnosis of intellectual disability requires both cognitive impairment (an IQ of 70 or lower) and an onset before the age of 18. The condition would be identified as a neurocognitive disorder due to traumatic brain injury, given the history. Dementia is no longer used as a DSM-5 diagnosis- it has been subsumed under neurocognitive disorder.

100. D: Termination can be undertaken for many reasons: 1) when mutually agreed upon goals have been met; 2) when a client must move; 3) following client- social worker conflicts; 4) upon referral to a specialist; and 5) because of finance/insurance changes. Efforts should be made for this to be a positive experience.

101. C: Narrative recording consolidates and reports all information (including progress, interventions, and conclusions) in an ongoing story form.

102. A: The most appropriate diagnosis would be oppositional defiant disorder. The degree of discord is substantial, and the level of verbal conflict is high, thus oppositional defiant disorder would be the most appropriate diagnosis. A parent-child relational problem tends to be less severe in nature, while conduct disorder is much more severe (i.e., involves violations of the rights of others, physical aggression, or property damage, persistent truancy, etc.). Intermittent explosive disorder addresses impulsive acts of aggression or violence (as opposed to premeditated or planned behaviors). Persistent conduct disorder carried into adulthood may meet criteria for antisocial personality disorder.

103. B: Simon's age, change of personality, aggressive behavior, and confusion point to senile dementia and possibly Alzheimer's disease.

104. D: Process recording is the type of record-keeping that chronologically and systematically records client information. Fact sheet information is obtained at the time of client intake, and subsequent entries are made after telephone conversations, face-to-face contacts, etc. This method of record-keeping is time consuming, but it provides a particularly complete summary of interactions, goals, and current issues.

105. D: This child should be considered to have mild intellectual disability. The term mental retardation has been replaced with intellectual disability after the federal statute named Rosa's law. While criteria for intellectual disability include having a deficit in intellectual capacity, which can be determined by IQ, the degree of severity is determined by adaptive functioning. The client being able to live alone while only needing support for specific activities indicates a severity level of mild.

106. C: The key feature to delirium is a rapid onset and fluctuating course throughout the day. Dementia has been encompassed by the term neurocognitive disorder which is characterized by a slow and persistent escalation of symptoms over an extended period of time. Diagnostically, the term senile is only an indicator of age (pre-senile refers to an onset prior to age 65; senile refers to an onset at age 65 or older). While overmedication is a possibility, there was not information provided to suggest this diagnosis, and thus the most likely diagnosis would be delirium due to a rapid onset medical condition (fever, bladder infection, early pneumonia, etc.) in an elderly individual.

107. A: Person-oriented recording focuses on goals, and is segmented into four sections:

- Factual information (a face sheet or database section)
- The assessment and expected treatment plan
- The progress notes
- The progress review entries (usually at 6-12 week intervals)

108. C: The pre-operational and concrete operational stages encompass these increasing elaborate understanding of death from ages 2-5 and 5-9. The sensorimotor stage encompasses birth to two years of age, and children in this stage have only a "here and not here" understanding of loss, at most. The formal operational stage extends from age 11 to age 15, and a child in this stage is capable of hypothetical thinking, and is thus readily able to understand the essential aspects death and many of its more philosophical and existential concepts, as well.

109. C: The most appropriate diagnosis for the wife, given the relevant details, would be stimulant use disorder. The DSM-5 no longer separates substances abuse and dependence but now places all disorders under substance use disorder, substance intoxication, and substance withdrawal. Stimulant use disorder involves the need for escalating amounts of a substance to achieve intoxication, withdrawal symptoms, compulsive use in spite of a desire to stop, compromised social, occupational/educational, familial, and/or other important role compromise due to the use of an intoxicating substance, and includes severe physiological or compulsive use features. Severity is decided by the number of symptoms, and can be classified as mild, moderate, or severe.

110. A: The most appropriate diagnosis for this youth is Oppositional Defiant Disorder. Intermittent explosive disorder is only appropriate when a behavior is compulsive in nature. While anger may be a part of that picture, it tends to be an overreaction to a provocation; other relevant compulsions include gambling, skin-picking, kleptomania, etc. The hallmark of Conduct Disorder is deliberate cruelty, and wanton disregard for others rights and property. This client lacks any pervasive and long-standing evidence in this regard. Antisocial personality disorder is only diagnosed after the age of 18 when there was a history of conduct disorder prior to the age of 15.

111. B: Problem-oriented recording focuses largely on a client's ongoing issues and contains four components:

- Factual information
- A checklist section providing a rank-order roster of client issues
- A resolution plan
- Progress notes summarizing actions taken and results achieved

112. D: Alfred Adler's Adlerian theory also includes a biological view, largely absent in Psychoanalytic Theory, recognizing that hormonal changes, physical illness, chemical imbalances, and neurological disorders can dramatically influence capacity and behavior. It is important to note, however, that Alder still locates false beliefs, irrational thoughts, and misconceptions in the unconscious mind.

113. A: Typical symptoms of schizophrenia include: grossly disorganized or catatonic behavior and/or speech, delusions and/or hallucinations, blunted affect (poor or inappropriate expressive responses to external stimuli), autism (intense self-preoccupation). Continuous signs of symptoms must be present (allowing for waxing and waning fluctuations) for six or more months. There are five types: 1) paranoid; 2) disorganized; 3) catatonic; 4) undifferentiated; and, 5) residual. Early mild symptoms are sometimes referred to as prodromal schizophrenia. Common medications for treatment: Clozaril (clozapine), Haldol (haloperidol), Loxitane (loxapine), Mellaril (thioridazine), Prolixin (fluphenazine), Risperdal (risperidone), Stelazine (trifluoperazine), Thorazine (chlorpromazine), and Zyprexa (olanzapine).

114. D: Systems theory notes that even a positive change in one family member—especially that of the identified patient—disrupts the system, so that other family members attempt to get the family member to change back. Preventing change in one family member means the rest of the family can avoid change, even when it also means certain suffering.

115. A: Encopresis is the voluntary or involuntary passage of stool in an inappropriate place by a child over the age of four (i.e., past toilet training). This is a frequently misused term. It is most frequently applied to children and developmentally delayed adults. Adults with psychosis may warrant use of the term, although the term "fecal incontinence" is more commonly used for adults. A British literature review found only one use of the term in an adult that was not either psychotic or intellectually disabled—a 1932 case of a 36-year-old diagnosed with "infantile neurosis." The most typical etiology is stool impaction (constipation) compromising sphincter control and allowing leakage into the underclothing. However, emotional disorders, anxiety, or oppositional defiant disorder can sometimes underlie the behavior. Incidence of the condition drops steadily after age six.

116. D: Standard precautions were designed by the Occupational Safety and Health Administration to protect patients and employees of health care facilities (or anyone) who come in contact with bodily fluids (e.g., blood, saliva, vomit, feces). They mandate that protective barriers are used (e.g., gloves, eye coverings, gowns, aprons, masks); proper hand washing is performed before and after handling a patient, using soap and water, but also alcohol-based hand sanitizer; and the proper disposal of needles and other items that come in contact with patients in designated containers.

117. D: Statistical studies are not a separate form or category of study design. Statistics can be used in virtually any form of study, and thus it cannot be defined as a category of its own. Descriptive studies build upon known information in an attempt to further extend understandings and to provide new qualitative facts for further theorization. These studies require moderate rigor and control. Experimental studies use dependent variables (the variables of interest) and the manipulation of various independent variables to evaluate the resulting effects on the dependent variables. They require controlled conditions and the reduction or elimination of extraneous and intervening variables. These kinds of studies require the highest rigor and control. Exploratory studies are used in areas and subjects where little or nothing on the topic is known, or to expand existing knowledge. These studies require low levels of rigor and control, allowing for maximum flexibility in the exploration process.

118. B: Founded by Albert Ellis, rational emotive therapy utilizes the "ABC Theory of Emotion." It states that an event ("A"), elicits thoughts and beliefs ("B"), which directly result in specific behavioral consequences ("C"). Therefore, analyzing one's relevant thoughts and beliefs, and restructuring those that are dysfunctional or disturbed, will lead to increasingly healthy and functional responses.

119. B: Eco-systems theory (also known as life model theory) postulates that all individuals experience adaptation by which they attempt to achieve a "goodness of fit" to their physical and social environment. Thus, this blended family adapted by revising roles, rearranging the home as needed, and altering schedules and activities to accommodate each other.

120. B: Delirium is more frequently present in dementia patients than in patients without dementia. This is because patients with dementia are more tenuously balanced cognitively than those without dementia, and thus they succumb more readily to the condition. In elderly dementia patients, a low-grade fever or bladder infection may be sufficient for them to lapse into delirium. Because health care providers often do not know the patient's baseline level of cognition, dementia frequently masks delirium. Indeed, a diagnosis of delirium is missed more than 50% of the time. Rapid global deterioration in cognition (often, in hours to days) is the hallmark. Fever, electrolyte imbalances (usually due to dehydration), and medication toxicity are precipitating factors. A medical exam is therefore necessary for a proper diagnosis to be made.

121. B: The research process includes problem identification, background information, hypothesis formulation, operationalization, evaluation, and further theorization.

122. B: The most likely diagnosis is panic disorder. Criteria for generalized anxiety disorder specifies excessive worry about a number of events or activities as opposed to an isolated fear or concern. Further, it tends to persist for long periods rather than having an abrupt onset. Somatization disorder is characterized by complaints regarding several organ systems involving different body sites and functions, rather a single body organ. Post-traumatic stress disorder requires confronting an event or events that involve actual or threatened death or serious injury. The client was away at school, did not witness his father's death, and it didn't pose any direct threat to him. Panic attacks involve sudden onset, profound fear of death, and other symptoms such as those the client has described. Common treatment medications: Paxil, Klonopin, Tofranil, Celexa, Librium, Valium, Xanax.

123. A: This client is on the Conventional Level, Stage 3. The Theory of Moral Development was created by Lawrence Kohlberg, to extend and enhance Jean Piaget's theory. Overall, Kohlberg felt that the process of moral development was more complex and extended than that put forth by Piaget.

124. A: Single system designs are common to use by practitioners to evaluate their practice. The evaluation process involves: 1) problem identification (called the "target" of the research); 2) operationalization (selecting indices that represent the problem that can be measured; 3) determining the "phase" (the time over which measurement will occur), including a "baseline phase" (without intervention) and an "intervention phase." This may also include a "time series design," where data is collected at discrete intervals over the course of the study.

125. A: In early remission the criteria for a substance use disorder have previously been met, but none of those criteria are fulfilled (except for the criteria for craving) for at least three months but not more than 1 year. In sustained remission, none of those criteria are fulfilled (except for the criteria for craving) for 1 year or longer. If the client is in remission in a controlled environment, this should be specified. Some clients may be on maintenance therapy which is a replacement medication that can be taken to avoid withdrawal symptoms. The client could still be considered in remission from a substance use disorder if while using maintenance therapy, they do not meet any criteria for that substance use disorder except for craving. This client does not live in a controlled environment, such as a sober house, and can be considered in remission despite being in maintenance therapy as long as he has not met criteria for use disorder except craving.

126. A: Although lithium carbonate has been used for many years in the treatment of bipolar disorder, it is by no means the only medication used to treat the condition. In more recent years bipolar disorder has been treated with: 1) anticonvulsants (i.e., certain anti-seizure medications); 2) antidepressants, such as selective serotonin reuptake inhibitors (SSRIs), monoamine oxidase inhibitors (MAOIs), and, less commonly, tricyclic antidepressants; 3) antipsychotics, such as Haldol and Zyprexa; 4) calcium channel blockers (including blood pressure medications such as Nifedipine and Verapamil); and 5) Benzodiazepines, such as Xanax and Valium. Even electroconvulsive therapy has been successfully utilized.

127. D: Positive reinforcement, negative reinforcement, punishment, and extinction are the four kinds of reinforcement used in the Operant Conditioning Theory. Positive reinforcement (the most powerful of all) is the *addition* of something pleasurable following a desirable behavior. Negative reinforcement involves taking something away to support the behavior (i.e., taking a break from an unpleasant task). Punishment involves adding something burdensome when an undesirable behavior occurs. Extinction is the gradual withdrawal of a reinforcement until the target behavior has been fully modified (i.e., reducing the break period from a difficult task if the classroom gets noisy).

128. D: Time series only (Design A-B) is not one of the three. Design A consists of observation only, without any intervention. Design B is an intervention only, without any baseline measurement. Design B-C refers to an initial intervention with data recorded (B), followed by a revised intervention and renewed data recording (C).

129. D: Blunted affect is not a necessary element to diagnose schizophrenia. While a client with schizophrenia may present with a blunted affect, it is not necessary to make a diagnosis of schizophrenia. According to the DSM-5, criteria A of diagnosing schizophrenia includes that the client must present with 2 out the 3 following symptoms: delusions, hallucinations, or disorganized speech.

130. C: The most likely diagnosis is social anxiety disorder. The typical symptoms of panic disorder (dizziness, shortness of breath, palpitations, profuse sweating, tingling, hyperventilation, etc.) are absent. General anxiety disorder is focused more on excessive worry and stress about a variety of issues, and it persists in spite of any specific location or activity. Social phobia involves fears about being in social situations involving performance and scrutiny. While bodily function fears lend to a diagnosis involving agoraphobia, the site-specific nature of this situation validates the greater likelihood of a social phobia.

131. A: The four steps, in order, are attention, retention, reproduction, motivation. Bandura and his colleagues demonstrated that consequences (reinforcement, punishment, etc.) were not always necessary for behavioral change or other learning to take place. Simply observing someone else's activity could be sufficient. The four-step pattern was as follows:

1. Attention -- the individual notices something in the environment.
2. Retention – he remembers what was noticed.
3. Reproduction – he copies what was noticed.
4. Motivation – the environment delivers a consequence (reinforcement or punishment), that affects the probability that the behavior will be repeated.

Most advertising uses these principles: a product is presented as socially desirable (attention). The ad is remembered (retained), the purchase is made (reproducing the ad's direction to buy), and if social approval is forthcoming then further purchases will be made.

132. C: This is the "basic" single system design. This fundamental single system design is more complex than single system case study designs, as it includes a planned intervention and formal evaluation. Although it is flexible, easily operationalized, and easily produces clear evidence of change, etc., the primary drawback of this design is that it cannot demonstrate causation.

133. B: Malingering (though it is a V code (other conditions that may be a focus of clinical attention, it is not a diagnosis). Malingering involves feigning symptoms primarily to derive an external reward (lawsuit settlement, disability benefits, etc.). Illness anxiety disorder involves a misapprehension or misinterpretation of bodily symptoms. Factitious disorder involves a feigning of symptoms primarily in order to receive the attention offered when one assumes a sick role, even in the absence of external reward. Somatic symptom disorder is characterized by complaints regarding several organ systems involving different body sites and functions rather than a single body organ or situation.

134. C: The most likely diagnosis is borderline personality disorder. The key features of BPD involved instability in relationships and affect, poor self-image, and high impulsivity. Violations of personal rights and apathy common to antisocial personality disorder are insufficiently pronounced. While evidence of histrionic behavior exists, the devaluation/over-valuation pattern common to BPD is not accounted for via histrionic personality disorder. Nor is the need for admiration, pervasive with narcissism, not otherwise addressed.

135. C: A reaction formation is a defense mechanism in which unacceptable emotions and impulses are controlled (or by which control is at least attempted) by exaggeration of the directly opposing tendency. Another example would be treating someone you very much dislike in an overly friendly manner. Or a woman professes profound hatred for a man who left her in order to cope with the pain he caused when he dismissed her deep love for him. In this way, one attempts to both hide and cope with their true feelings.

136. C: The model most commonly used by other social workers should not dictate framework selection. Various factors may constrain the practice framework chosen, but it should never be a matter of "popularity" alone. It may become necessary to utilize more than one framework, based upon a clientele's needs, the course of treatment, demands of an agency or an insurer. Regardless, when utilizing a practice framework, it should guide the social worker's approach with the client, and the treatment process.

137. B: The "additive" category is not a category of measurement. The ordinal category is used when a hierarchical arrangement exists, but the distance between each position is not necessarily equal (e.g., first, second, third runners in a race). The interval category can only be used when both a hierarchical and an equal-distant relationship between positions exists (e.g., a 1-10 scale). The ratio category is an interval scale with an absolute zero (a score of five is exactly one-half of ten, etc.).

138. D: Behavioral and cognitive approaches are practice approaches based on theoretical orientations, not frameworks. The ethnic-sensitive framework requires the social worker to view and engage issues from an ethnic and cultural perspective, and the feminist framework orients engagement from the perspective of gender and feminism. The systems framework focuses on behavioral issues as related to biological and social systems. The eco-system framework views behavior from an environmental adaptation perspective. The strengths framework focuses on issues from the vantage point of a client's strengths and the capacity to achieve goals. Finally, the generalist framework provides for an eclectic approach, utilizing a variety of frameworks and approaches as necessary.

139. D: The most likely diagnosis is borderline personality disorder. Individuals with this diagnosis will exhibit: frantic efforts to avoid real or imagined abandonment; unstable and intense interpersonal relationships (especially extremes of idealization and devaluation); an unstable sense of self; extreme impulsivity (e.g., spending, sex, drug use, reckless driving, binge eating, etc.); recurring suicidal behavior (gestures or threats, or self-mutilating behavior); affective instability due to reactivity of mood; chronic feelings of emptiness; intense anger (e.g., frequent displays of temper, recurrent physical fights); transient, stress-related paranoid ideation; or severe dissociative symptoms.

140. C: Confronting the issue of resistance and making a point of addressing and exploring it with the client is the proper response. The psychoanalytic (or psychodynamic) approach provides for direct confrontational address in situations of resistance. Drawing from psychoanalytic theory, ego psychology theory, object relations theory, and psychosocial theory, this theoretical orientation sees resistance as a way to avoid bringing up repressed memories, and unconscious/subconscious information necessary to growth, understanding, and overcoming.

141. B: The probable primary diagnosis is major depressive disorder with psychotic features. The precipitating event was his job loss, which led to depression. When the depression deepened, he started "hearing voices," and he drank to cope with the negative messages (and to cope with his depression). Therefore, while the alcohol use must be included in his diagnostic formulation, it would not be his primary diagnosis. Of note, the diagnosis of major depression with psychotic features is missed about 25% of the time in an emergency room, with only the depression typically identified.

142. D: Countertransference refers to the unconscious feelings, desires, defenses, and reactions to a client. Transference refers to the unconscious feelings and reactions of the client toward the social worker. Free association is a technique wherein the client is directed to express any thought that comes to mind to explore unconscious mind and desires. Direct influence refers to suggestions and advice given a client to enhance understanding and behavioral change.

143. B: The psychoanalytic approach is generally a long-term therapeutic orientation, as time is required to identify, expose, and resolve repressed and unconscious information, experiences, drives and motivations that produce distortions and dysfunctions.

144. A: The next priority is to identify and evaluate the antecedents and consequences of the behavior. In this way the social worker and client will be able to revise the antecedents and consequences in such a way as to induce change. In setting goals and measuring progress, the behavior will be need to be operationally defined (i.e., a vague problem, such as aggression, must be made explicit and measurable--frequency of hitting, throwing things, yelling, etc.), thus allowing for the identification of targets for change, quantified goal setting, and setting positive and negative reinforcers. In general, unconscious motivations, drives, and emotions are not seen as relevant to the goal of behavioral change, from a modification standpoint.

145. B: Crisis intervention recognizes the need for immediate, effective intervention, and a five-stage crisis sequence: 1) acknowledgement of the catastrophic/overwhelming event; 2) a sense of profound vulnerability that overmasters the client's usual coping skills; 3) a last straw precipitating event causing the individual to seek help; 4) emotional turmoil and imbalance; and 5) the application of new and/or more effective coping skills leading to adequate adjustment and acceptance.

146. A: His most likely diagnosis is panic disorder. The symptoms of panic are clear, and there is a specific fear (i.e., he is not suffering for a generalized, nonspecific fear). Specific phobia would lead to avoidance and there is no noted compulsion to go with an obsession noted in the prompt. Common treatment medications: Celexa (citalopram), Haldol (haloperidol), Klonopin (clonazepam), Librium (chlordiazepoxide), Paxil (paroxetine), Valium (diazepam), Tofranil (imipramine), and Xanax (alprazolam).

147. C: This approach would be best referred to as the narrative approach. This family therapy approach suggests that behavior change occurs when family members produce alternate narratives, stories, or scenarios with improved endings by which to focus their energies and beliefs in a more positive way. Complementary therapy refers to supplemental intervention(s) that a social worker may use in addition to individual therapy. Collaborative therapy refers to family therapy provided by two or more social workers pursuing the same cooperative goals. The social learning approach seeks to teach family members added skills (conflict resolution, negotiation, communication, etc.) to address and resolve family dysfunction.

148. A: The "Electra Complex" is the female counterpart to the "Oedipus Complex" and typically occurs between the ages of three and seven.

149. C: Strategic family therapy focuses on family rules and behavioral patterns. This approach suggests that persistent behavioral dysfunction and faulty family rules are at the heart of most family problems. Intervention is supplied by the social worker actively choosing to engage the family in ways that will highlight problematic behavioral patterns. In this way the family becomes more aware of problematic patterns of interaction, after which the social worker can assist the family in choosing more functional behaviors and interactive patterns.

150. B: Minority group is a group of individuals with one or more characteristics identified as being subordinately distinct in a larger societal context. Of significance, in the social sciences, a minority group need not be smaller (in terms of population) than a dominant group. Rather it is identified as such because the distinct identifying characteristic(s) put the group in a position of subordinate status in a societal context.

Masters Practice Test #3

1. A social worker has been asked to see a 15-year-old girl for problems with body image and eating. After speaking with her, the social worker discovers that she suffers with an intense desire to lose weight, feeling that this will help her be more attractive to the opposite sex and more popular in her social circle. She is by no means obese or even "chubby" although she is not overly slender. Her parents recently noted an increase in grocery costs, and that food seemed to be disappearing around the house inordinately quickly—often "junk" food and other quick snacks. Finally, late one night, her mother passed the bathroom and heard the daughter "purge" her food. She confronted her and discovered that the daughter had been "binge" eating and inducing vomiting for some months. She estimates that she purges about 10 times per week. Some modest weight loss had occurred. The most appropriate diagnosis would be:

a. Anorexia nervosa, purging type.
b. Bulimia nervosa, severe.
c. Bulimia nervosa, moderate.
d. Eating disorder, not otherwise specified.

2. A social worker sees a mother with a child recently diagnosed with juvenile onset diabetes. She is stressed and feels overwhelmed with and uncertain of the requirements of caring for this child's new special needs. This parent would best be served by joining which type of group?

a. An educational group
b. A support group
c. A self-help group
d. A task group

3. A social worker is called to see a young black man in his mid-twenties. Two adult sisters brought him for an urgent appointment. The young man is clean, neatly dressed in slacks, dress shoes, and a tweed sport coat. He is also calm, relaxed, and without any signs of agitation. The two sisters, however, appear disheveled, frazzled, and almost histrionic. They blurt out the he "has problems" and urge the social worker to talk with him. Privately, he tells the social worker that he is fine. Later, however, the ladies tell the social worker he left home abruptly and traveled cross-country with no destination. He didn't sleep for three days (with them pursuing him), was spending money excessively and writing checks he couldn't cover. He ended up in a nationally famous amusement park at 3:00 a.m. (having scaled a fence), sitting on an empty rollercoaster "waiting for the ride to start." When confronted, he admits all of this, but says he's now rested, and doing better. The most likely diagnosis would be:

a. Brief psychotic disorder.
b. Bipolar I, manic episode, with psychotic features, in full remission.
c. Bipolar I, hypomanic episode, in full remission.
d. Cyclothymic disorder.

4. Bloom's taxonomy outlines behaviors necessary for learning. Which 3 kinds of learning does the theory describe?

a. Cognitive, affective, and psychomotor
b. Auditory, visual, and kinesthetic
c. Formal and informal
d. Attitudes, subjective norms, and behavioral intention

5. Personality disorders are pervasive and enduring patterns of dysfunction. The DSM provides for the diagnosis of ten specific personality disorders, and one category for indeterminate behaviors that appear to characteristic of a personality disorder. These disorders are grouped into three clusters. Which of the following clusters does not properly describe a personality disorder group?

a. Cluster B: Paranoid, Schizoid, and Schizotypal Disorders (also referred to as "odd or eccentric behavior disorders")
b. Cluster B: Impulsivity and/or Affective Dysregulation Disorders (also referred to as "dramatic, emotional, or erratic disorders")
c. Cluster B: Violent and/or Explosive Disorders (also referred to as "aggressive and intrusive conduct disorders")
d. Cluster C: Anxiety and Compulsive Disorders (also referred to as "anxious or fearful disorders")

6. The term operating revenue refers to:

a. the funds derived through the provision of services and/ or goods.
b. the gains or losses resulting from normal business operations.
c. the bottom line of the organization's financial operations.
d. the net assets of a business at the time of an audit.

7. A school counselor is scheduled to see a 9-year-old boy regarding disruptive behavior in the classroom. Rather than begin with an office visit, the counselor directly observes his behavior in the classroom. There the counselor noted the following: he seemed to constantly fidget and squirm in his seat; he talked nonstop; he was frequently out of his seat, running, touching, and playing with anything and everything he could reach. The teacher's efforts to quiet him appeared to be forgotten almost instantly. When an art period was begun, which engaged most children, he still had difficulty as he was easily distracted and seemed to switch constantly from one activity to another. He appeared unable to slow down long enough to receive even simple and clear instructions. The few moments he was quiet, he seemed lost in daydreaming, staring out the classroom windows. The most likely diagnosis for this youngster is:

a. Attention deficit hyperactivity disorder (AD/HD).
b. Conduct disorder.
c. Obsessive compulsive disorder.
d. Oppositional defiant disorder.

8. Jane's husband expects her to create fabulous dinner parties for his boss, to be the perfectly available mother to their children, and to be ready for sex several nights a week. He also expects her to continue working the 12-hour shifts of a registered nurse. What problem is Jane MOST likely experiencing?

a. Role complementarity
b. Role discomplementarity
c. Role ambiguity
d. Role overload

9. The perspective from which a social worker approaches client interactions should be based upon a blend of: 1) time and resources available; 2) the treatment modality required (individual, family, group); 3) the issues to be addressed; 4) the outcomes (goals) sought; and 5) an appropriate theoretical framework. Taken together, this defines the social worker's:

a. theoretical orientation.
b. practice framework.
c. clinical approach.
d. model of interaction.

10. A social worker notices that the waiting area outside the pediatric intensive care unit is frequently filled with parents talking and sharing together. Over time it becomes apparent that there is an informal structure to the group, and considerable information is being exchanged (some accurate, some not). The social worker recognizes this group structure as a:

a. formed group.
b. natural group.
c. closed group.
d. structured group.

11. A practice framework that acknowledges and accounts for a client's overall context in: 1) social setting (family, peers, neighborhood, etc.); 2) social relations quality (e.g., with other family members, friends, coworkers, etc.); 3) external pressures (work, organizations, etc.); 4) culture; and 5) life-course events (marriage, births, retirement, etc.) is called a(n):

a. ecosystems framework.
b. cultural framework.
c. strengths framework.
d. generalist framework.

12. Rose often becomes frustrated in school, makes loud noises in public, and doesn't understand what people are saying to her. She often seems rude. To her trusted teacher, she fluently describes a life of loneliness and confusion, but even in her family, no one understands her. She cannot read as well as most adolescents in her age group, but her IQ is quite high. However, she is considering not going to college because she thinks it would be too difficult. What is MOST likely Rose's problem?

a. Rose has elective mutism
b. Rose has autism
c. Rose is hearing impaired
d. Rose is visually impaired

13. A practice framework that approaches a client's issue or presenting problem from the perspective of gender, sex roles, and related stereotyping and discrimination, along with the influence that these elements may bring to bear on the issue or presenting problem, is called a:

a. gender framework.
b. roles framework.
c. strengths framework.
d. feminist framework.

14. Providing professional guidance and being someone to whom other staff can bring questions or concerns may be described as:

a. mentoring.
b. role modeling.
c. supervising.
d. coaching.

15. A social worker has her first counseling session with a young Native American man, and she finds it nearly impossible to get him to look her in the eye, much less to talk at any level beyond answering intake questions about his age and address. She is worried that he may be schizoid, although the school counselor who referred him gave a preliminary diagnosis of an adjustment disorder. What accounts for the difference in the counselors' opinions of the young man's problem?

a. Inappropriate affect
b. Cultural confusion
c. Cultural competence
d. Discrimination

16. The best determinant of the effectiveness of patient education is:

a. patient satisfaction.
b. a patient's ability to demonstrate a procedure.
c. a patient's ability to explain a procedure and demonstrate understanding.
d. a patient's behavior modification and compliance rates.

17. A therapeutic approach that views the client from a social context, that sees behavior as derived from unconscious drives and motivations, that views disorders and dysfunction as emerging from internal conflicts and anxiety, and that seeks to facilitate the conscious awareness of previously repressed information is called a:

a. cognitive approach.
b. psychoanalytic approach.
c. Gestalt approach.
d. behavior approach.

18. Which right is included in the Patients' Bill of Rights?

a. Affordable healthcare
b. Pain control
c. Right to sue
d. Access to latest medical technology

19. If a client has difficulty working with a particular social worker because the social worker reminds her of her father, and the social worker is struggling to work well with the client because she has strong traits reminiscent of those of his ex-spouse, the client and the social worker (respectively) are experiencing issues known as:

a. individuation/separation conflicts.
b. separation/individuation conflicts.
c. transference/countertransference conflicts.
d. countertransference/transference conflicts.

20. Jamie is being counseled to aid in dealing with her fear of intimacy. During a session, the social worker notes that whenever her mother's name is mentioned, Jamie's responses become shorter and she quickly changes the subject. What should the social worker do?

a. Increase Jamie's comfort level by avoiding the subject of her mother
b. Focus attention on the issue of Jamie's mother
c. Ignore the mother issue, as it's not significant
d. Use the mother issue to springboard into gaining more information about other family members

21. A recently retired middle-aged couple find themselves sharing their downsized home with their daughter, son-in-law, and two grandchildren. Although the situation is temporary, no one can predict when the younger couple will find work after losing their business to bankruptcy. The older couple find themselves stressed, and the time they had looked forward to spending in a second honeymoon is being spent with crying children and an overfilled house. They come to counseling to address their recently started, constant bickering. What is the FIRST thing their social worker should do?

a. Bring in the younger couple for family counseling
b. Provide job assistance to the younger couple
c. Help the older couple find ways to support each other and their marriage
d. Analyze the bickering and suggest alternative ways to communicate

22. Which of these efforts is NOT integral in effective group leadership?

a. Consciously using body language to facilitate communication and openness
b. Preserving an effective, safe, and nurturing group environment (ensuring quality information is shared, dispelling myths, deflecting ganging up, pairing, scapegoating, and clique [subgroup] development by some members, etc.)
c. Unconditional positive regard for and non-judgmental acceptance of group members
d. Recruiting membership to ensure a large and diverse population, ideally consisting of more than 20 group members

23. A therapeutic approach that views issues of dysfunction from the perspective of behavior (as opposed to emotional and mental problems), and that discounts delving into past history and unconscious motivations in favor of conditioning, reinforcement, consequences, and conscious choice would best be referred to as a:

a. Gestalt approach.
b. cognitive approach.
c. behavioral approach.
d. task-centered approach.

24. A legal document that specifically designates someone to make decisions regarding medical and end-of-life care if a patient is mentally incompetent is a(n):

a. advance directive.
b. Do-not-resuscitate order.
c. Durable Power of Attorney for Health Care.
d. general power of attorney.

25. An unmarried middle-aged client of Italian descent presents at a feminist therapy center with generalized anxiety and strongly conflicted feelings about her father. While she admits he "may be a little pushy," the examples she gives of her father's behavior toward her strike her counselor as being frankly domineering, sexist, and on the edge of abusive. But the client loves her father, describes him also as kind and protective of her, and is shocked when the counselor suggests that (for example) the father's recent attempt to "marry off" his daughter to a much older man is manipulative and highly inappropriate in modern-day American society. Which term MOST closely explains the behavior of the client's father?

a. Cultural bias
b. Discrimination
c. Cultural lag
d. Culture-bound syndrome

26. A social worker has been assigned to chair a task group. The most effective way of organizing the work of the group is by FIRST:

a. agreeing to a consensus form of decision-making
b. specifying the group's objectives
c. rotating the role of facilitator among group members
d. specifying the group's timeline

27. A family therapist tells her clients that one of the rules in her sessions is that "everybody talks." She asks each person to tell her what they think the main problem is, and she notices and sometimes even comments on nonverbal communications between family members that facilitate or hinder communication. What does this method do directly for the therapist, but only indirectly for the family?

a. Formulates the problem using different perspectives
b. Involves all members and gives each permission to speak
c. Identifies family rules about who speaks and who typically gives or denies permission
d. Delineates the power structure, hierarchies, and alliances in the family

28. Which does not describe a motivational obstacle arising from within the client?

a. Abulia
b. Amotivational syndrome
c. Motivation-capacity-opportunity theory
d. Apathy

29. Treatment concepts and techniques such as identification of target behaviors, antecedents, reinforcers (positive and negative), consequences, etc., along with tracking mechanisms (tally sheets, charts, etc.), journal-keeping regarding specific occurrences (when, where, with whom, etc.), and related feelings (including intensity, frequency, etc.) are all associated with:

a. behavioral therapy.
b. Gestalt therapy.
c. psychoanalytic therapy.
d. cognitive therapy.

30. A social worker has been moderating a closed membership growth group and notices group members seem to be expressing more diverse opinions among themselves. This is an indication that the group has entered which stage of group development?

a. Stage 3: Intimacy
b. Stage 5: Separation
c. Stage 4: Differentiation
d. Stage 2: Power and control

31. Treatment concepts and techniques such as clarification (feedback and illumination of misconceptions), explanation (education regarding misconceptions, thought "triggers" and secondary thoughts, beliefs, and actions), interpretation (insight development), paradoxical direction (having the client engage or continue behaviors needing correction to enhance awareness and induce a sense of control), reflection (reviewing), and writing (diagramming misconceptions and analyzing thoughts, etc.) are all associated with:

a. Gestalt therapy.
b. psychoanalytic therapy.
c. cognitive therapy.
d. task-centered therapy.

32. One advantage of group instruction over one-on-one instruction is:

a. it is more cost-effective.
b. it requires less planning.
c. it allows more time for questions.
d. it is more flexible.

33. Jane has helped her client pinpoint his biggest problem and create a list of possible ways to address it. However, the client seems to find a problem with every intervention. When Jane suggests a relevant book, the client states that he doesn't read much. He refuses to join a group, saying he doesn't want to "meet a bunch of losers." He shoots down every possible intervention, and he even claims that, although it was his presenting problem and still causes him a great deal of suffering, there are other things he'd prefer to talk about in their sessions. What does this tell Jane about her work with this client?

a. She has not found the right intervention and needs to try harder
b. The client isn't motivated to change at this time
c. She should refer this client to someone else
d. The presenting problem wasn't the "real" problem: Jane should start over

34. A social worker notices that when working with clients who have health complaints, he experiences emotional irritation and has little patience for encouraging such discussion. What should the social worker do?

a. Nothing, as every social worker has points of irritation
b. Self-examine to determine possible reasons for the reaction
c. Take steps to ensure that he no longer treats clients of this type
d. Report the difficulty immediately to his supervisor

35. A therapeutic approach that focuses solely on changing behaviors and issues that the client (as opposed to the social worker) believes to be problematic, and that views behaviors as fully conscious acts, and that views individuals as fully able to control their actions and make needed changes is called:

a. crisis intervention.
b. task-centered therapy.
c. psychoanalytic therapy.
d. cognitive therapy.

36. At what level of care would a social worker investigate persons at risk of abuse or neglect, address the situation, prevent further risk, and locate resources or better placements for that person?

a. Extended
b. Skilled
c. Intermediate
d. Protective

37. Treatment concepts and techniques such as "dialogue" (using the "empty chair" technique – i.e., talking with an absent person to reveal inner conflicts), "enactment of dreams," "exaggeration" (dramatizing a physical or verbal action in order to enhance awareness), "exposure of the obvious" (also to enhance client awareness), and "rehearsal" (practicing feelings, thoughts, and behaviors in preparation for change) are used to engage and overcome barriers such as "confluence" (a preoccupation with false similarities while ignoring or denying differences), "introjection" (an over-identification and integration of messages from others), "projection" (attributing one's own dysfunctional personality traits to others), and "retroflection" (doing to oneself what one wishes to do to another), which are all associated with:

a. task-centered therapy.
b. crisis intervention.
c. Gestalt therapy.
d. behavioral therapy.

38. The Confusion Assessment Method is a tool that covers 9 factors related to mental status. This tool is used to assess for:

a. delirium.
b. Alzheimer's disease.
c. substance abuse.
d. brain injury.

39. A therapeutic approach that sees periods of intense trauma as optimal for effecting change, and that seeks to equip clients with new and/or more effective coping skills to manage traumatic situations is known as:

a. cognitive therapy.
b. behavioral therapy.
c. task-centered therapy.
d. crisis intervention.

40. A client's main goal is to be free of conflict when called upon to make a decision. She has suffered for years with being unable to make efficient choices and never again wants to experience anxiety when debating a choice. What is likely to happen in terms of counseling?

a. The client will be happy during the course of counseling
b. Counseling will be of a short-term nature
c. She will effectively meet her therapy goal with time and patience
d. Counseling will become interminable

41. Sharon and Jack are forming a college therapy group, and they realize that the first five people to sign up have all been fairly extroverted women. They decide to place posters advertising the group in the computer labs of the chemistry, engineering, and mathematics departments. What are the coleaders trying to achieve?

a. A structured group
b. Group balance
c. Group cohesiveness
d. Group harmony

42. A problem list focuses on:

a. a prioritized list of patient problems based on assessment, history, and interview.
b. all identified patient problems based on assessment, history, and interview.
c. the patient's self-reported problems.
d. a standardized list of problems related to specific diagnoses.

43. A therapeutic approach that arises from the belief that individual in similar situations can identify with, comfort, reassure, and help one another is called:

a. group therapy.
b. conjoint therapy.
c. collective therapy.
d. systems therapy.

44. Working for the best interests of the patient despite conflicting personal values and assisting patients to have access to appropriate resources may be defined as:

a. moral agency.
b. advocacy.
c. agency.
d. collaboration.

45. Mark is 40 years old. He has been diagnosed with posttraumatic stress disorder (PTSD) and attention-deficit/hyperactivity disorder (ADHD). He has had several relationships with women that included violence. He comes to the agency as an involuntary client after receiving a ticket for texting while driving and having been fired from his job for watching online pornography. He admits to spending hours each day on porn sites, spending hundreds of dollars each month on them. Which would be the BEST hypothesis about Mark's youth?

a. He had a learning disorder
b. He had ADHD
c. He was sexually abused
d. He was addicted to drugs or alcohol

46. Which therapy involves the use of monitoring devices to allow people to control their own physiological responses?

a. imagery.
b. acupuncture.
c. meditation.
d. biofeedback.

47. Treatment concepts and techniques largely oriented around immediate problem-solving, stress reduction, coping skill enhancement, support system building, and emotional buffering are primarily associated with:

a. grief therapy.
b. crisis intervention.
c. task-centered therapy.
d. short-term therapy.

48. A client has been in therapy for several months because of depression and suicide ideation. Progress has been limited until, during a particular session, the client demonstrates a positive attitude and reports he has "turned a corner" and finally feels relaxed and happy. What should his social worker do?

a. take a position of extreme caution
b. feel good that the client has finally "turned a corner"
c. make plans to terminate counseling because the client has improved
d. continue with counseling as usual

49. Specific treatment approaches, such as the "communications approach" (which sees communication deficits as central to interpersonal dysfunction), the "structural approach" (which views interpersonal interactions as central to dysfunction), the "social learning approach" (focusing on improving interactive skills such as conflict resolution and communication), and the "narrative approach" (using personal stories, ideas, thoughts, etc., and revisions, to discover and implement new behavior patterns) are associated with:

a. group therapy.
b. cognitive therapy.
c. behavioral therapy.
d. family therapy.

50. A client is the same gender as the social worker and not homosexual. The client is seeing the social worker because of relationship issues. During the course of treatment, it becomes apparent that the client is directing feelings of a romantic nature toward the social worker. What is likely to be the cause of the client's feelings?

a. An unhealthy attachment to the social worker
b. A genuine romantic attraction to the social worker
c. Transference
d. None of the above

51. All of the following are kinds of group therapy structures EXCEPT:

a. natural groups (groups which coalesce independently, and seek a moderator only later – such as a divorce group).
b. formed groups (groups formed around a specific issue or to achieve a certain goal).
c. forced groups (groups arising from court orders, insurance mandates, or other criteria requiring attendance).
d. short-term groups (groups oriented around a crisis situation [e.g., hospitalization of a loved one] or other short-term event, such as birth preparation, etc.).

52. The best approach to solving a problem that involves 3 different departments in a hospital is:

a. forming an interdisciplinary team that works together to find a solution.
b. the administration resolves the problem independently.
c. each department proposes a solution to administration.
d. all three departments have a joint meeting to brainstorm possible solutions.

53. Kelly spends a lot of time and energy dealing with her husband's drinking problem. She hides his liquor or pours it down the drain, and then she feels sorry for him and goes to the store to buy more. When he goes "cold turkey," his suffering is so extreme that she gives him a drink "just to get him over the hump." He blames her for making him want to drink, and she accepts that if she were easier to get along with, he would be able to maintain his sobriety. What is the clinical term for Kelly's attempts to help her husband, which also helps him keep drinking?

a. Codependency
b. Enabling
c. Passive aggression
d. Misplaced empathy

54. Clients have an ethical right to self-determination. When may a social worker limit this right?

a. When there's a threat to self or others
b. If the client is choosing poorly
c. When the courts are involved
d. If the client's family is opposed to a particular action

55. According to Kübler-Ross, individuals typically pass through five stages of grief to reconcile a loss. Those stages, in order, are:

a. Anger, denial, bargaining, despair/depression, acceptance.
b. Denial, anger, bargaining, despair/depression, acceptance.
c. Denial, anger, despair/depression, bargaining, acceptance.
d. Anger, bargaining, denial, despair/depression, acceptance.

56. Which disorder MOST frequently occurs in association with addictive disorders, with approximately 30% of people with addictions also experiencing this problem?

a. Bipolar disorder
b. Anxiety
c. Depression
d. Obsessive-compulsive disorder (OCD)

57. A theoretical approach that believes that individuals, families, and groups are all part of a greater whole, with "boundaries" (invisible lines of separation) between each, that change in any one will result in change in the others, and that "entropy" describes the de-organization of any or all of these parts of the whole, but which notes that they tend toward "homeostatic balance" and resist entropy, is called:

a. integration theory.
b. group theory.
c. holistic theory.
d. systems theory.

58. An 18-year-old client presents with an aloof manner that is indifferent and withdrawn. He has no friends and spends most of his time outside of school building model airplanes. He does not fit the criteria for autism disorders. His mother tells the social worker that he's always been "different; impossible to talk to; not a bad boy, just not really there, somehow." What is the most likely DSM-5 diagnosis for this young man?

a. Schizoid disorder of adolescence
b. Schizophreniform disorder
c. Schizoid personality disorder
d. Highly introverted personality

59. A theoretical approach that focuses on the relationship between living things and their social and physical environment, that sees "adaptation" as the process by which individuals and environments accommodate each other in seeking a "goodness of fit," and that views dysfunction as a failure to cooperate and accommodate is called:

a. systems theory.
b. ecosystems theory.
c. ecological theory.
d. conservation theory.

60. A team leader makes decisions independently and strictly enforces all rules. This type of leadership is:

a. bureaucratic.
b. laissez-faire.
c. autocratic.
d. democratic.

61. A therapeutic approach that involves "field theory" (where everything that happens is interrelated through a larger network of interactions, and can only be fully understood in the context of the interrelatedness), "figure/ground formation" (which suggests that whatever is most important in the here and now becomes figural and invites attention, leaving everything else to drift into the background), exploration of "resistances," the processing of "introjects" (messages internalized in childhood), and the use of "experiments" to increase awareness and growth is called:

a. existential theory.
b. cognitive theory.
c. Gestalt theory.
d. systems theory.

62. Which of the following is NOT considered a neurobiological disorder?

a. Anorexia nervosa
b. Schizophrenia
c. Bipolar disorder
d. Major depression

63. A therapeutic approach that focuses on the multidimensional aspects of the individual (interpersonal, psychological, social, and environmental), and that engages the client in the context of his or her personal history, strengths, weaknesses, resources, wants, and needs is referred to as:

a. cognitive therapy.
b. lifecourse therapy.
c. psychoanalytic therapy.
d. psychosocial therapy.

64. In the course of explaining her marital problems, a client also alludes to various symptoms that could be diagnosed as psychotic in nature. Her social worker doesn't have training in psychosis and should:

a. continue to work with the client but research psychosis.
b. consult with a social worker trained in psychosis.
c. discontinue counseling and refer the client to another social worker.
d. discontinue counseling because the social worker isn't qualified in this case.

65. A therapeutic approach that assumes clients to be competent to co-construct goals and strategies (and that resistance is lowest when clients are conscripted in co-formulating interventions); that views that clients are experts regarding their own lives and experience meanings; that encourages change by "doing something differently", even while recognizing that only small steps need be taken (as change often "snowballs" and grows naturally); and that suggests "if it isn't broken, don't fix it" and "if it didn't work, try something different" is called:

a. solution-focused therapy.
b. cognitive therapy.
c. problem-oriented therapy.
d. systems therapy.

66. Which of the following most closely characterizes Selye's biological theory of stress and aging?

a. The body is a machine that wears out over time
b. The body's response to stress is characterized by a generalized adaptation syndrome
c. All cells and organisms have a programmed life span
d. Over time, mutations occur that interfere with body functioning and cause aging

67. A therapeutic approach that is used primarily with the elderly and with those experiencing loss (e.g., disability, bereavement, unemployment, etc.), is often adjunctive to other therapeutic interventions that focus on important survivor questions (What is the meaning of life? Why go on? What have I accomplished? How well did I utilize life's opportunities? Etc.), and that see three key paths to meaning (creativity, experiential values [finding beauty], and attitudinal values [a posture toward positive coping]) is called:

a. group therapy.
b. logotherapy.
c. psychosocial therapy.
d. crisis intervention.

68. A client reveals to his social worker that he has recently entered into a business relationship with the social worker's spouse. Is this likely to present a concern?

a. Yes, but only if the counseling relationship has just begun
b. Yes, but only if money is involved
c. Yes, under all circumstances
d. No

69. A therapeutic approach that is based on "fundamental units of social intercourse" and "fundamental units of social action" (called "strokes"), carried out through stimulus-response patterns (including words, tones, and expressions) mediated by "ego states" (the "parent" [concepts taught before age five], the "child" [feelings derived before age five], and the "adult" [learned concepts from childhood onward]), and framed in the belief of individual value, a capacity to think, and the ability to change is called:

a. social therapy.
b. psychosocial therapy.
c. cognitive therapy.
d. transactional analysis.

70. A social worker has recently entered into a counseling relationship with a client who has a past history of depression and suicide attempts. The social worker will want to give particular care to discussing:

a. the limits of confidentiality
b. the legal definition of suicide
c. his experience in treating patients who are depressed
d. the effects of suicide upon family and friends

71. There are two forms of conditioning that can be used to modify behavior. One form of conditioning is used to train autonomic responses and to associate a stimulus that normally wouldn't have any effect with a stimulus that would. The second form of conditioning creates an association between a behavior and a consequence (also called "response-stimulus" conditioning). In the order presented here, name these two forms of conditioning:

a. autonomic conditioning and learned conditioning.
b. neurological conditioning and cognitive conditioning.
c. classical conditioning and operant conditioning.
d. trained conditioning and planned conditioning.

72. A client wants to read his personal records. What should the social worker do?

a. Deny the request and explain that records are private
b. Provide the records and help to interpret them
c. Allow the client to see only those parts that are pertinent
d. Deny the request

73. A client who previously met the criteria for tobacco use disorder has not smoked in 10 weeks. He is using a nicotine replacement system, NicoDerm CQ. The client has not had any symptoms of tobacco use disorder except craving. This client should be considered:

a. not in remission, due to using a nicotine replacement medication.
b. in early remission.
c. not in remission, due to symptoms of tobacco use disorder.
d. not in remission, due to not meeting timeframe for remission.

74. The term "correlation" refers to the relationship of the sample variables to each other. This relationship is expressed via a "correlation coefficient" (symbolized as "r"). A perfect correlation (where all measurement points between two variables coincide) is statistically represented by the following correlation coefficient value:

a. 1.0.
b. 9.9.
c. 0.0.
d. 0.5.

75. An individual with whom a social worker has had a previous sexual relationship has arrived in her office seeking counseling for an addiction problem. What should the social worker do?

a. Begin counseling, because the relationship is in the past
b. Enter into a co-therapy situation
c. Design a treatment plan but refer to a colleague
d. Refer the client to another social worker

76. Following the death of a young child from cancer, a couple comes in for help in resolving complicated feelings of grief. When the couple enters the office, the social worker notes that both the husband and wife pull their chairs slightly away from each other and make no verbal, physical, or eye-contact. The social worker's best response would be to:

a. ignore the behavior.
b. explicitly address and explore the behavior.
c. mention the behavior casually.
d. confront the couple about the behavior.

77. Assessment of a substance user should always include: 1) kind of substance used; 2) frequency and quantity of use; 3) typical level of intoxication; 4) withdrawal symptom severity (if experienced); 5) duration of substance abuse (months or years, etc.); 6) mode of use (oral, inhalation, needles, etc.); 7) any related legal history; 8) comprehensive history of any prior treatment (length, voluntary/involuntary; type and methods of treatment, successful or unsuccessful program completion). All of the following should also be included EXCEPT:

a. family history of substance abuse/use.
b. social history.
c. impact of use on daily living.
d. sources where substances were obtained.

78. Five specific elements (1) a research hypothesis; 2) a null hypothesis; 3) a test statistic; 4) a rejection region; and 5) a conclusion) collectively make up what is called a:

a. theoretical construct.
b. conceptual construct.
c. statistical paradigm.
d. statistical test.

79. All of the following represent treatment modalities for substance abuse EXCEPT:

a. detoxification (ridding the body of toxins that have accumulated from drug use – which may or may not be medically supervised).
b. pharmacologic treatment (to reduce withdrawal symptoms or to induce abuser avoidant-reactions in an effort to reduce future substance abuse).
c. drug "affinity" testing to determine the level of addiction present.
d. psychosocial treatment (counseling and behavior modification, group therapy, etc.) to help establish new coping skills.

80. During an initial session with a client, it becomes apparent that the client is reluctant to disclose his primary problem. Which of the following approaches would be the least effective in overcoming the client's reluctance?

a. Developing a written contract based on specific goals and expected outcomes
b. Simply asking the client directly why he/she is unwilling to cooperate
c. Addressing the anticipated number of sessions, meeting frequency and duration, and the costs involved
d. Openly acknowledging the client's reluctance to open up and share information

81. Cognitive-behavioral therapy is the most commonly used approach to substance abuse treatment. Also used, however, is behavioral therapy, group and family therapy, and all of the following EXCEPT:

a. psychodynamic therapy.
b. psychoanalytic therapies.
c. self-help groups.
d. interventional therapies.

82. The term referring to the threshold necessary to decide whether an intervention produced an outcome, or whether it was the result of chance is "statistical significance." The actual value threshold indicating reasonable probability that the intervention produced an outcome is called the "level of significance." An acceptable probability that the null hypothesis will be incorrectly rejected (a type I error) is traditionally placed at 0.5. Where greater certitude is required, it may be placed at 0.1. This threshold value is properly referred to as a study's:

a. alpha value.
b. beta value.
c. kappa value.
d. omega value.

83. A 70-year-old man is referred to a social worker for confusion, emotionality, and unusual lethargy. In the session, he mentions having headaches and needing help organizing his daily schedule of medications. What is the FIRST thing the social worker should do for this client before working with him in therapy?

a. Have him assessed for Alzheimer's disease
b. Assess his reality orientation
c. Help him schedule an appointment for a review of his medications
d. Ask if he is depressed

84. A male client tells a female social worker that he just cannot speak with a woman and requests assignment to a male social worker. The social worker's best response would be to:

a. aid the client in exploring his difficulties in this area.
b. explain that this should not be a problem.
c. promptly terminate the relationship.
d. arrange a case transfer or referral.

85. Substance-related disorders may be grouped into 10 "classes" such as: 1) alcohol; 2) cannabis; 3) tobacco; 4) hallucinogens; 5) narcotics; 6) stimulants; 7) caffeine 8) inhalants 9) opioids 10) sedatives, hypnotics, and anxiolytics. Please classify cocaine (and the freebased form, crack cocaine) into the proper category, among which one of the following classes?

a. Opioids
b. Hallucinogen
c. Narcotic
d. Stimulant

86. Social service programs can be categorized in all of the following ways EXCEPT:

a. exceptional eligibility programs.
b. means tested programs.
c. universal programs.
d. selective eligibility programs.

87. Most anxiolytics are a subclass of what drug classification?

a. Hallucinogens
b. Stimulants
c. Depressants
d. Narcotics

88. Extensive patient and caregiver participation in interdisciplinary team discussions is important so that the:

a. patient and caregivers can be informed of the plan of care as formulated by the medical providers.
b. cost of hospice care is reimbursed by the patient's insurance provider.
c. plan of care can be crafted to meet the specific needs and goals of the individual patient and family.
d. patient and caregivers come to terms with a terminal prognosis.

89. The stages of grief as theorized by Elizabeth Kubler-Ross include denial, anger, bargaining, depression, and acceptance. What is an important fact that she discussed after publication of her work and that many practitioners are not aware of?

a. The listed stages are not relevant to people undergoing any loss but bereavement
b. The stages can only be passed through in the order listed above
c. The stages are not necessarily passed through in order, and they may even be revisited
d. The stages do not apply to people facing their own death

90. The social security program was enacted in 1935 to provide "old age survivors benefits." Individuals who are employed and paying into the social security system can earn up to four tax credits annually. To be eligible to receive social security retirement benefits, an individual must have earned a lifetime credit total of at least:

a. 80 credits.
b. 60 credits.
c. 40 credits.
d. 20 credits.

91. Significant client factors that may influence the communication process include: 1) age; 2) education; 3) ethnicity; 4) culture (and belief systems); 5) ethnicity; 6) primary language; and all of the following EXCEPT:

a. grooming and hygiene.
b. emotional state.
c. intellectual level.
d. gender.

92. A female patient scheduled for a surgical procedure is a Jehovah's Witness. What aspect of future care could be affected by the patient's religious practices?

a. Diet
b. Covering of body with a burka
c. Organ donation
d. Blood transfusion

93. When exploring a client's concerns, he begins to divulge important personal information about his marital situation. At one point he seems to be having difficulty finding adequate words to express his emotions, fears, and concerns. After two or three efforts to express a particularly sensitive issue, he seems unable to find the words to continue and a long pause ensues. At this juncture the social worker should:

a. attempt to further the discussion by suggesting what he might have been trying to say.
b. press the client to continue so as not to lose the momentum of the conversation.
c. discuss with him the difficulty he is experiencing, and encourage him to take more time.
d. ignore the pause and remain quiet no matter how long it takes.

94. Publicly funded disability insurance is available to individuals who become unemployable due to a permanent or chronic disability. At a minimum, the disability must be expected to last for a year or more, or be expected to result in death. This program is administered by:

a. each state's Department of Human Services.
b. the federal Department of Health and Human Services.
c. the federal Disabled Persons Program.
d. the Social Security Administration.

95. A social worker meets a client, and discovers that she has limited English-speaking skills. The social worker has some ability to speak her primary language, but is not fluent. At this point the social worker should:

a. terminate the meeting immediately, until it can be arranged for her to see a social worker who speaks her native language.
b. revise the meeting to cover only very basic issues until other arrangements can be made.
c. delay the meeting to find an interpreter before continuing.
d. attempt to interview her in her own language.

96. A client is seen who is in a verbally abusive relationship. She admits that he has been verbally abused, including frequent angry outbursts, routine put-downs, and name-calling. Friends and relatives have encouraged her to end the relationship, but she continues to struggle with intense feelings of attachment and affection for him. The first step should be to:

a. confront the client with the reality of the abuse.
b. acknowledge the highly ambivalent feelings she is experiencing.
c. offer reading material on abusive relationships.
d. explore the client's other relationships, past and present.

97. Maria is raising her two children alone, working full time, and caring for her mother, who has recently started wandering away from the house and becoming lost. Maria has started experiencing bouts of anger, followed by apathy. She feels she has more responsibility than she can handle and that she has little control over the financial and physical safety of her family. She continues being a responsible employee and a nurturing caregiver, but she is feeling the pressure. What is the most correct term for Maria's problem?

a. Existential crisis.
b. Identity crisis.
c. Burnout.
d. Generalized anxiety.

98. A social insurance program for individuals sustaining employment-related injuries is the:

a. Employee Assistance Program.
b. State Compensation Program.
c. Worker's Compensation Program.
d. Worker's Health Program.

99. How can a social worker best begin work with a client so that both parties have clear expectations of the goals, the time period the work will cover, and each one's responsibilities in the working relationship?

a. By having an implicit understanding naturally arise during the work
b. By discussing and writing goals, processes, and timetables at the beginning of the counseling work and reevaluating priorities at regular intervals
c. By discussing goals, processes, and timetables as the work proceeds
d. By reviewing together what's been achieved at the end of treatment

100. A client seems to frequently have difficulty formulating her thoughts. She pauses often, partially completes her sentences, presents as somewhat helpless and needy, and seems openly eager for the social worker to do most of the talking. The most appropriate response for the social worker would be to:

a. take over and lecture the client about her life.
b. confront the client and demand that she talk more openly.
c. use reflective listening techniques and allow the client more time.
d. stop talking and use silence aggressively to stimulate discussion.

101. The difference between "rephrasing" and "paraphrasing" what a client has said is:

a. rephrasing is used to correct what the client said wrong, while paraphrasing is used to repeat the same idea back.
b. rephrasing is used to elaborate on what the client said, while paraphrasing is used to reiterate it.
c. rephrasing is used to emphasize what the client said, while paraphrasing is used to show mutual understanding.
d. rephrasing is used to clarify what the client said, while paraphrasing is used to explain what the client said.

102. The government has established a "poverty line" threshold regarding income. Individuals who fall below that threshold may be eligible for means-tested public assistance. Eligible individuals include the "working poor," as well as individuals who are elderly, disabled, and/or blind. Primarily funded by the federal government, benefits are also supplemented by the state. This program is called the:

a. Indigent and Poverty Program.
b. Supplemental Security Income program.
c. Income and Poverty Assistance Program.
d. Security and Stability Income Program.

103. Active or "reflective" listening includes the use of attending nonverbal cues (sitting forward, making good eye contact, using content-appropriate affective expressions, etc.), as well as all of the following EXCEPT:

a. clarification ("Are you saying...?").
b. substitution ("What I would do is...").
c. encouragement ("Tell me more" and "Go on").
d. summarization ("What you're saying is...").

104. Symbols of alcohol misuse include all of the following EXCEPT:

a. involuntary defecation.
b. respiratory depression.
c. excessive energy.
d. confusion/disorientation.

105. Leading questions tend to stifle communication, and usually result in closed-ended ("yes" or "no" short-answer) responses. All of the following are examples of "leading questions" EXCEPT:

a. "You do know...[a certain fact]...don't you?"
b. "Could you tell me more about...[a situation]...?"
c. "But sure you wouldn't want to...[conclusion]...would you?"
d. "I think that...[decision]...would be best, don't you?"

106. In 1966 the program known as "Aid for Families with Dependent Children (AFDC)" was renamed and revised to be a transitional program from welfare to work. The new name of this program is now the:

a. Transitional Aid to Work Program (TAW) program.
b. Family Welfare Resource Transition (FWRT) program.
c. Temporary Assistance for Needy Families (TANF) program.
d. Transitional Aid for Families and Children (TAFC) program.

107. A question that contains multiple parts, potentially leaving a client confused or unclear what the question was, or at least uncertain which part to answer first, is known as a:

a. stacked or complex question
b. manifold question
c. multipart question
d. fragmented or fractured question

108. Which of the following medications are NOT indicated to treat the psychotic symptoms of schizophrenia?

a. Prozac
b. Haldol
c. Thorazine
d. Clozaril

109. When a client seems overwhelmed or uncertain how to share further, it can help to break down the concerns at hand into smaller, more manageable parts. This communication technique is known as:

a. fragmentation.
b. sequestration.
c. downsizing.
d. partialization.

110. The federal health insurance program for the elderly is known as Medicare. Exclusively for individuals over the age of 65 or the disabled, or individuals with end-stage renal disease (ESRD), this insurance has which two specific components?

a. Medical insurance and hospital insurance
b. Physician insurance and hospital insurance
c. Medical insurance and drug coverage
d. Hospital insurance and drug coverage

111. Although Sophie doesn't ignore the fact that her client has a gambling addiction and bipolar personality disorder, in sessions, she focuses on his skill at calculating statistics and his love of animals. Which perspective is Sophie operating from with this client?

a. A strengths-based perspective
b. A solution-focused perspective
c. A structural perspective
d. A behavioral perspective

112. Only one of the following food assistance and nutrition programs is not funded by the federal government. The locally funded program is the:

a. Elderly Nutrition Program.
b. Food Stamps Program.
c. Women, Infants, and Children (WIC) program.
d. Meals on Wheels program.

113. A social worker may be required to assume many roles. These include: 1) administrator; 2) advocate; 3) broker (resources and linkages); 4) case manager (resource and service coordinator); 5) counselor; and all of the following EXCEPT:

a. educator and teacher.
b. enforcer and regulator.
c. lobbyist and politician.
d. staff development coordinator.

114. According to Freud's Structural Theory of Personality Development, which part of the personality would be driving the behavior of a serial rapist?

a. The Ego Ideal
b. The Ego
c. The Id
d. The Superego

115. The social work profession is dedicated to meeting basic human needs and enhancing human well-being from a social context, including societal and environmental forces that bear on problems in everyday life. This is/these are the National Association of Social Workers (NASW) social work:

a. creed.
b. goals.
c. vision.
d. primary mission.

116. Kay is leading a group focused on expressing their feelings and needs, and standing up for their rights and beliefs. Which coping skill is being addressed MOST especially in the group?

a. Assertiveness
b. Positive thinking
c. Healthy communication
d. Stress reduction

117. In anger management training, which technique includes getting a different perspective on the situation?

a. Relaxation
b. Communication
c. Cognition
d. Environmental change

118. Erikson proposed eight psychosocial stages of development. Each stage builds on the other, and to successfully pass through any given stage, one must encounter and overcome a "psychosocial crisis." The crisis arises between two opposing personality features—one that is in harmony with one's personality and one that is not. Erikson called these two opposing features:

a. the Id and Ego.
b. the Yin and Yang.
c. ego-Positive and Ego-Negative.
d. dystonic and syntonic.

119. If a social worker witnesses, obtains evidence, or reasonably suspects abuse (physical, sexual, emotional, financial) of a child, dependent elder, or a dependent adult, or has reason to believe that a client is a danger to himself or others, confidentiality must be suspended and the issue reported to appropriate authorities based upon the social worker status as a(n):

a. evaluator.
b. case manager.
c. mandated reporter.
d. officer of the state.

120. Heinz Hartmann developed the theory of Ego Psychology to explain how individuals use the Ego portion of personality to accommodate the external environment (either changing the self, or acting upon the environment). He proposed that the ego has how many major functions?

a. 12
b. 24
c. 8
d. 36

121. During a series of home visits with an elderly, demented client, the social worker notes that increasing numbers of persons appear to be living in the home. These include purported "relatives" as well as the boyfriend of a privately hired in-home chore worker. During later visits the social worker notes a wide-screen television in the front room, and a new car in the driveway. He also notes that the client is no longer allowed in the main house, and has been moved out of the master bedroom and into a small back room. Most of her clothes also seemed to have disappeared. What primary form of abuse would the social worker suspect in this situation?

a. Physical abuse
b. Financial abuse
c. Emotional abuse
d. Sexual abuse

122. Hartmann's theory of Ego Psychology drew from and built upon Freud's Psychoanalytic Theory. However, in explaining the origin and functions of the Ego, Hartmann parted ways with Freud in one significant area. He believed that the Id and the Ego are specifically present in:

a. adults, following adequate development.
b. children, from birth forward.
c. adolescents, during pre-adult transitioning.
d. latency-aged children, following adequate development.

123. Which DSM-5 resource helps social workers clarify the impact of culture on clients' symptoms and possible treatment options?

a. The list of culture-bound syndromes
b. The cultural assimilation interview
c. The cultural formulation interview guide
d. The assessment of cultural deprivation

124. Another human development theory posits that all individuals are born with a need to develop a sense of self, a sense of others, and to build interpersonal relationships. It theorizes that the sense of self and others will affect all subsequent personal relationships. This theory is called:

a. self-psychology.
b. ego psychology.
c. integrative relations theory.
d. object relations theory.

125. The Federal Privacy Act of 1974 (i.e., PL 93-579) requires that clients be informed: 1) when records about them are being maintained; 2) that they have a right to access these records; 3) that they have a right to copies (provided they bear the costs); and 4) that the records will only be used for the purpose they were created unless they provide written release or consent otherwise. Exceptions include: 1) sharing with agency employees on a "need-to-know" basis; 2) legitimate research, if identifying information is removed; and all of the following EXCEPT:

a. providing information to government agencies for legitimate law-enforcement purposes.
b. responding to a court order or subpoena.
c. publication in a reputable professional journal.
d. responding to an emergency to protect another individual.

126. A defense mechanism that serves to repress, disconnect, or dissociate feelings that seem "dangerous" to psychic well-being is called:

a. regression.
b. isolation.
c. splitting.
d. fragmentation.

127. In 1996, legislation was enacted providing Federal protection for personal health records privacy. The legislation applies to all health care providers, health care clearinghouses, and health plan providers. It sets limits on records disclosure and uses, provides for individual access to medical records, and it establishes the right to receive notices of privacy practices. This legislation is called:

a. The Health Records Privacy Act of 1996 (HRPA).
b. The Health Records Privacy and Accountability Act of 1996 (HRPAA).
c. The Health Insurance Portability and Privacy Act of 1996 (HIPPA).
d. The Health Insurance Portability and Accountability Act of 1996 (HIPAA).

128. Louise began therapy with a presenting problem of experiencing increasing anxiety and panic attacks when driving alone or riding in the car with her husband. As the social worker took her history, she also learned that Louise has been having marital problems and is considering leaving her husband, but is terrified of being alone again. When Louise casually mentions that she doesn't feel anxious when riding with her friends as a passenger, her social worker intuits that the marriage trouble and the driving phobia are related, and that the client's panic is arising from her feelings about her marriage. Which type of content has brought the therapist to this hypothesis about her client's presenting problem?

a. Neurotic symptoms
b. Overt content
c. Manifest content
d. Latent content

129. Malpractice liability generally runs from an agency's Board of Directors, to the director, supervisory staff, and then to the front-line social worker. Employer and supervisor liability accrue under the legal theory of:

a. vicarious liability.
b. hierarchical liability.
c. substitute liability.
d. proxy liability.

130. A client is seeing a social worker for difficulties he's experiencing with family conflicts and discusses his employment in the family business. He comments, "I like working that lousy job with my brother. When all is said and done, I really respect that idiot brother of mine." Which of the following does this comment bring to mind?

a. positive communication
b. Freudian conflict
c. disqualifying communication
d. thought/feeling confusion

131. Barbara has learned that her new client, Jim, is also her mother's legal advisor, and he occasionally lunches with her mother to discuss business. Her mother is unaware of the counseling relationship between them. Barbara explains to Jim that there is a conflict of interest in their working together and that her main concern is making sure his interests and confidentiality remain protected. What is the BEST action Barbara can take next?

a. Keep working with Jim, but try to be aware of potential conflicts
b. Refer Jim to someone else
c. Ask Jim to tell her mother about the counseling arrangement
d. Terminate the counseling relationship

132. According to Lawrence Kohlberg, the stage of development in which an individual fully appreciates the need to conform to social rules and laws is:

a. the Conventional Level, stage 4.
b. the Pre-Conventional Level, stage 2.
c. the Post-Conventional Level, stage 5.
d. the Conventional Level, stage 3.

133. Individuals bound by the principles of confidentiality include social workers, agency administrators and supervisors, and all of the following EXCEPT:

a. agency volunteers.
b. other clients.
c. agency clerical staff.
d. agency consultants.

134. Responses to Pavlovian Classical Conditioning are learned in response to an environmental event (or "stimulus"). The response will either be voluntary or involuntary—also known, respectively, as:

a. explicit or incidental responses.
b. emitted or reflexive responses.
c. determined or spontaneous responses.
d. immediate or delayed responses.

135. A child described as "latency aged" will be between the ages:

a. 12-16 years old.
b. 3-6 years old.
c. 6-12 years old.
d. under three years old.

136. In seeking to overcome problems at the community level or that affect society as a whole, a social worker is functioning as a(n):

a. advocate.
b. broker.
c. educator/teacher.
d. lobbyist or politician.

137. At times the social worker may serve as a "case manager." This is because of which part of the social worker's role?

a. Facilitates staff development by means of case presentations
b. Teaches clients tools and strategies for improved functioning
c. Connects clients to needed resources and services and coordinates the delivery and application of these resources and services
d. Implements agency or organizational policies, services and programs

138. A social worker is asked to officiate at a funeral (i.e., introduce speakers and music, and offer closing remarks) for a client who recently died from a brain tumor. She agrees, knowing that the client had few living relatives and friends who could provide this service. Some days after the funeral, a thank-you card arrives. It contains a note of appreciation and a $100.00 bill. The BEST response would be to:

a. graciously accept the money and send a return note of thanks.
b. donate the funds to the local Brain Tumor foundation, thanking them for the funds and telling the family where they were sent.
c. return the money to the family with apologies and explaining that agency policy does not allow social worker's to accept such a substantial gift.
d. break the $100.00 bill and sent $80.00 back, thanking them for the gift and explaining that the agency has a $20.00 limit on gifts.

139. The BEST source for the rules, guidelines, and boundaries that define a professional relationship between a social worker and his/her client is:

a. an agency policy and procedure manual.
b. a handbook of clinical practice.
c. the *National Association of Social Workers (NASW) Code of Ethics.*
d. the social work credentialing board.

140. After a therapeutic relationship has ended, a client approaches a social worker to join in various family activities (birthday celebrations, holiday events, etc.). In light of the fact that a past professional relationship existed, yet acknowledging that it has formally ended, the social worker's BEST response would be to:

a. attend only small family gatherings as a show of care and support.
b. accept any invitation that time will allow to show uncompromising support.
c. attend some events, and invite the client out to others with them, so that the activities don't become one-sided.
d. cite the professional code of ethics, and clarify that even after a professional relationship ends, socializing is not permitted.

141. A client develops romantic feelings for his social worker, and repeatedly makes overtures and gestures indicating he would like to become involved. The BEST response would be for the social worker to:

a. refer the client to another professional promptly, emphasizing the need the client has to remain focused on resolving the important problems involved without any distraction.
b. talk about how much she wishes things were different, but cite the code of ethics as a barrier to becoming involved.
c. allow only a casually flirtatious relationship, making sure no legal boundaries are violated.
d. confront the client and demand that he/she stop behaving inappropriately.

142. If a client is to make a treatment-oriented decision, he/she must be fully informed about the purpose, risks, benefits, costs, and burdens that may be associated with the decision. The client may need to be educated about certain related features or issues in order to make a meaningful decision. While it may not be possible to foresee every eventuality, the client must receive all information that a "reasonable person" would expect in the given situation. This process of informing, educating, and reviewing prior to a treatment decision is called:

a. treatment orientation.
b. informed consent.
c. patient education.
d. legal disclosure.

143. The *NASW Code of Ethics* indicates that a client's ability to pay should be considered in setting fees. This means that a social worker may do all of the following EXCEPT:

a. decrease fees for a needy person already receiving services.
b. refer a potential to public programs prior beginning services.
c. liberally increase fees for a client who is particularly well off.
d. produce a sliding-scale fee rate that sets reasonable rates in advance.

144. An adult with an intellectual disability is in need of a medical procedure or treatment with a complex array of possible burdens and benefits with any choice that may be made. The client is able to understand many aspects of the procedure, and the immediate outcomes, but he/she may not be able to understand the full ramifications of future eventualities both with and without receiving the procedure or treatment. The best response would be to:

a. leave the client out of the decision-making process entirely.
b. turn the entire issue over to an ethics committee and don't remain involved.
c. tell the client just enough to make a decision that would be best.
d. involve the client in every aspect that he/she can properly understand, and allow his/her choices to govern where possible.

145. Social services may be paid for in numerous ways. The most obvious is by personal contribution (one pays for what they receive). All of the following are other ways that social services are funded, EXCEPT:

a. court ordered funding.
b. employer funded (direct pay).
c. government funded (i.e., direct pay or tax relief).
d. publicly funded (non-profit, public agencies).

146. The transfer of services once performed by the government to private entity providers is known as "privatization." Under these circumstances, the pay source becomes:

a. the private institution that assumes the service provider role.
b. the government continues paying (but hopes the service will become cheaper to provide).
c. philanthropic organizations that can afford to pay.
d. personal contributions.

147. Housing assistance for those with low income is provided in all the following ways EXCEPT:

a. public housing (government built and owned housing offered at reduced rent rates.
b. subsidized housing ("Section 8" and other reduced rent and maintenance programs via government contributions).
c. home loan subsidy programs.
d. co-op housing (jointly owned via the renter and the government).

148. A source of food for low-income families is a federally-funded, state-administered program that provides purchase vouchers or coupons based on a family's size, income, and resources (e.g., a selective eligibility, means-tested program) that is known as:

a. S&H green stamps.
b. blue-book coupons.
c. food stamps.
d. nutrition voucher program.

149. A federally-funded, state-administered program providing food and assistance to pregnant women, mothers of children up to five months of age (if not breast feeding), breast-feeding mothers up to 12 months after delivery, and children up to five years of age is called the:

a. Women, Infants, and Children (WIC) program.
b. Women and Children Nutrition (WCN) program.
c. Women and Children Food (WCF) program.
d. Women and Children Health (WCH) program.

150. A locally funded program that provides delivery of food to low-income individuals who are unable to leave their home is called:

a. Food on the Move.
b. Meals on Wheels.
c. Drive and Dine.
d. Moveable Feast.

Answer Key and Explanations

1. B: The most appropriate diagnosis would be bulimia nervosa, severe. The diagnosis could not be anorexia nervosa, as she has not lost substantial weight and although of post-menarchal age, she has not experienced amenorrhea (much less for three consecutive cycles). The diagnosis is bulimia nervosa, as her behavior has persisted for three or more months. The degrees of severity are as follows: Mild: purging 1-3 times/week. Moderate: purging 4-7 times/week. Severe: purging 8-13 times/week. Extreme: purging 14 or more times/week.

2. A: The parent would be best served by joining an educational group. There are 7 major group types. Educational groups are formed to provide education, information, and essential skills. This parent needs to learn ways to manage medications, changing blood sugar, dietary needs, signs and symptoms of medical compromise, and so forth. An educational group is an ideal setting to learn how to provide optimum care and cope with inevitable changes and problems. A support group focuses on coping with a common problem (i.e., bereavement, etc.), but with less of an emphasis on learning and skill development. A self-help group is focused on behavioral change (i.e., alcoholics anonymous, etc.). A task group focuses on accomplishing a singular goal. Other group forms include: remedial groups (or psychotherapy groups, focused on personal growth, such as anger management), growth groups (developing personal potential), and socialization groups (to enhance interpersonal skills).

3. B: The most likely diagnosis is bipolar I, manic episode, with psychotic features, in full remission. Hypomania does not appear appropriate, as the client's behavior would likely have resulted in hospitalization had anyone been able to evaluate him during his period of mania. Cyclothymic disorder does not appear appropriate, as the client's conduct exceeded the threshold severity for hypomania, and no information is provided regarding depressive symptoms (though he may well have them). While there are some delusions likely involved in the episode described at the amusement park, there is no indication of hallucinations or disorganized speech, and it is better explained by the manic episode of a bipolar disorder given the other symptoms than by a brief psychotic episode (see criteria C of brief psychotic episode). Finally, the Bipolar I, manic episode is identified to be in full remission, as the client's manic symptoms appear to have completely resolved.

4. A: Bloom's taxonomy describes 3 types of learning:

- Cognitive: Learning and gaining intellectual skills and mastering categories of effective learning (knowledge, comprehension, application, analysis, synthesis, and evaluation).
- Affective: Recognizing categories of feelings and values from simple to complex (receiving and responding to phenomena, valuing, organizing, and internalizing values).
- Psychomotor: Mastering motor skills necessary for independence, following a progression from simple to complex (perception, set, guided response, mechanism, complex overt response, adaptation, and origination).

5. C: The incorrect cluster is Cluster B: Violent and/or Explosive Disorders (also referred to as "aggressive and intrusive conduct disorders"). These cluster descriptions have been provided by authors in various academic sources, although they only loosely describe each cluster's content. Cluster A includes: paranoid, schizoid, and schizotypal personality disorders. Cluster B includes: antisocial, borderline, histrionic, and narcissistic personality disorders. Finally, Cluster C includes:

Obsessive/Compulsive, Avoidant, and Dependent personality disorders. Clusters tend to run in families.

166. A: Operating revenue refers to the funds derived through the provision of services and/ or goods. Operating support refers to funds derived from other sources besides the sale of goods and services (i.e., donations, grants, etc.). Expenses are the costs incurred for organizational operations. A surplus results when revenue and support exceeds operating expenses, whereas a deficit occurs when profits falls short of needed operating expenses. Gains or losses are reported from non-business operating transactions (i.e., the sale of business equipment, furniture, etc.). Net assets (after accounting for all revenue and expenses) are often referred to as the business' bottom line.

7. A: The most likely diagnosis for the young boy is attention deficit hyperactivity disorder (AD/HD). The term ADD is no longer in use, as it was excluded from a previous revision of the DSM. Conduct disorder would not be appropriate, as this child is not deliberately cruel or violent toward others. Obsessive compulsive disorder does not fit, as the child is not fixated on either ritualistic behavior or things, per se, but is simply chaotically busy. Oppositional defiant disorder is not an appropriate diagnosis, as this child is not deliberately uncooperative or argumentative. Caution is needed, however, in making the diagnosis. The behavior must not be situationally due to problems at home, and it must have persisted for six months or longer. Further, and most importantly, it must not be simple youthful exuberance or even a "high-energy" personality. Rather, the diagnosis is properly made when the behaviors are extreme, and well out of step with other peers. Having multiple involved adults complete the Connor Rating Scales (i.e., parents, grandparents, the teacher, a pediatrician, etc.) can reduce the chance of inappropriately applying this burdensome diagnosis.

8. D: Jane is attempting to fulfill the roles of wife, mother, breadwinner, and society hostess—some of the duties and time constraints of which must occasionally conflict. Although all of her assigned roles are traditionally "feminine" (even her arduous job is stereotypically "feminine") there are simply too many expectations to meet them all successfully—a condition of overload.

9. B: The social worker's practice framework may vary depending upon the issues involved, resources, etc., and thus multiple practice frameworks may be required to properly serve the needs of an agency and its clients. The practice framework is based upon time and resources available, treatment modality required, the issue to be addressed, the outcomes sought, and an appropriate theoretical framework.

10. B: This is an example of a natural group. The group occurred naturally, and pre-existed the presence of the social worker. Some concern exists in formal settings, such as a hospital, when natural groups form. A primary concern is when misinformation emerges and is perpetuated via the group. Therefore, it may become necessary for the group to be formalized. In this situation an open group structure (that allows members to join and leave as they desire) may be advantageous. A closed group typically has set meeting times and an end-date (10 weeks, etc.), fosters greater intimacy and group cohesion, and allows for graduated information and teaching. It will of necessity be a short-term structure, as pediatric patients will ultimately be discharged. Formed groups are intentionally arranged, such as a court-ordered group for drug offenders.

11. A: An ecosystems framework is largely derived from Ecological Systems Theory (also called "Development in Context" or "Human Ecology" theory). It addresses five environmental systems, and assumes bi-directional influences within and between the systems. Developed by Urie Bronfenbrenner, a developmental psychologist, the five systems are: 1) the Microsystem (family, peers, neighborhood, and other social environments; 2) the Mesosystem (the connections between these environments; 3) the Exosystem (settings which indirectly affect development, such as parental work); 4) the Macrosystem (the cultural context); and 5) the Chronosystem (events and transitions over the life course). Biology is also relevant; thus, the theory is sometimes called the "Bio-Ecological Systems Theory." The roles, norms, and rules of each system shape psychological development throughout life.

12. C: Difficulty learning to read is a particular problem for hearing-impaired students, and many hearing-impaired people grow up in families in which other members do not learn sign language, and attend schools in which there are limited opportunities to interact with teachers and students who know how to use sign language. Frustration with not being able to communicate and with not catching verbal cues can make deaf people seem rude to others. Because Rose communicates fluently with her teacher, elective mutism and autistic disorders would be ruled out in this example.

13. D: This is called a feminist framework. Although largely used only when working with female clients, the framework can be extended to male clients, especially when the presenting problem involves sex role issues, stereotypic expectations, and/or reverse role gender discrimination (female on male).

14. A: Mentoring is providing professional guidance, as well as being someone to whom a staff person can bring questions or concerns. Role modeling takes place when one nurse serves as a role for others, such as demonstrating those behaviors and responses that advocate for the patient and show care. Supervising is ensuring that delegated tasks and duties are done correctly. Coaching involves providing staff with tools and ways to respond, or procedures to follow, to help staff become more effective.

15. C: The social worker has not encountered clients from this culture before and has misinterpreted the client's lack of eye contact (or tact) and unwillingness to talk about himself (which would be rude in front of a strange professional woman). What she sees as a potential mental illness is in fact considered respectful manners in the client's culture—something the school counselor, with her familiarity of that culture, understood.

16. D: Behavior modification and compliance rates are the best determinants of the effectiveness of patient education. Patients may be satisfied, may understand, and may be able to provide a demonstration, but if they don't utilize what they have learned the education has not been effective for that patient. Behavior modification involves thorough observation and measurement, identifying behavior that needs to be changed and then planning and instituting interventions. Compliance rates should be determined by observation at necessary intervals and on multiple occasions.

17. B: The psychoanalytic approach views behavior as derived from unconscious drives and motivations, views disorders and dysfunction as emerging from internal conflicts and anxiety, and seeks to facilitate the conscious awareness of previously repressed information. This approach is built upon the concepts and theory of Sigmund Freud and others who have followed him. The approach is also sometimes called a "psychodynamic" approach.

18. B: The right to pain control is part of the Patients' Bill of Rights. Affordable healthcare and access to latest medical technology are not included. The right to sue is not directly included, but patients are entitled to a procedure for registering complaints or grievances. Other provisions include respect for patient, informed consent, advance directives, and end of life care, privacy and confidentiality, protection from abuse and neglect, protection during research, appraisal of outcomes, appeal procedures, an organizational code of ethical behaviors, and procedures for donating and procuring organs/tissues.

19. C: Transference (client to social worker) and countertransference (social worker to client) include emotions, reactions, defenses, desires, and feelings that come to bear on the relationship and/or the problem, whether consciously or unconsciously.

20. B: This should notify the social worker to focus attention on the issue of Jamie's mother. Even when a client is verbal and appears to be invested in honestly exploring significant issues, there often is some resistance to confronting the most pertinent (and painful) issues. Jamie's behavior is indicative of this type of situation.

21. C: The older couple is reacting to the stress of sharing their home, and they have lost their way as a couple. The first actions are to address the couple's feeling that their marriage is in trouble and to help them remember how important it is—so important that they are asked to work on their marriage rather than focusing on the rest of the family. Helping this couple reestablish their solidarity in the onslaught of family members will help them undertake the rest of the problems as a pair working together, rather than turning against each other.

22. D: Recruiting membership to ensure a large and diverse population, ideally consisting of more than 20 group members, is NOT integral in effective group leadership. Most theorists indicate that effective groups should not have memberships exceeding 8-12. The younger the group membership, the smaller the ideal group (preteens: 3-4; teens: 6-8; young adults: 8-10).

23. C: The behavioral approach, sometimes also simply called "behavior modification," believes that as long as a problem can be "operationally defined" (in terms of the specific change needed and the consequences necessary to induce change) virtually every problem can be resolved by resorting to behavioral modification techniques. This approach is most effective when the client voluntarily undertakes treatment, but involuntary treatment can also be successful if proper reinforcements and/or consequences can be integrated into the change process. This approach is based on principles of social learning theory, operant conditioning, behavioral theory, and classical (respondent) conditioning theory.

24. C: The legal document that designates someone to make decisions regarding medical and end-of-life care if a patient is mentally incompetent is a Durable Power of Attorney for Health Care. This is one type of advance directive, which can also include a living will, a medical power of attorney, and other specific requests of the patient regarding his or her health care. A do-not-resuscitate order is a physician-generated document that is completed when a patient does not want resuscitative treatment in an end-of-life situation. A general power of attorney allows a designated person to make decisions for a person over broader areas, including financial concerns.

25. C: In cultural lag, people maintain the standards of their original culture, which may be inappropriate in the culture that they currently live. In this case, the father's patriarchal and domineering ways, normal to his cultural background, are accepted on one level as manifestations of his caring by his daughter, but they are also causing her distress because they limit her personal freedom.

26. B: Specifying the group's objectives. All other tasks can only be successfully pursued once the group's goals and objectives have been clarified. The other options presented could actually be addressed and incorporated or dismissed during the goal and objective clarification process.

27. D: The therapist overtly helps the family formulate the problem, has each member speak, and brings covert communications into the open. She does not discuss the power issues in the family with the family members, but she can use what she observes to make further decisions about other interventions.

28. C: Whereas the other three terms are designated as lack of motivation within the client, the theory of motivation-capacity-opportunity tends to view clients as willing to participate as long as the intervention is appropriate and as long as no external obstacles prevent the client from taking part in the process.

29. A: Behavioral therapy was formulated by John Watson and Ivan Pavlov (classical conditioning) and B.F. Skinner (operant conditioning). Additional social worker work is done in analyzing client tally sheets, charts, journal entries, etc., in search of patterns and insights that would assist in refining key insights in to behavioral antecedents, and improving selected reinforcers and consequences. Collateral work must also be done regarding client- social worker contract revision and consequences for contract agreement violation, etc.

30. C: This is characteristic of Stage 4: Differentiation. During this stage, group members display opinions and differing views more readily. Stage 1, pre-affiliation, involves getting acquainted and group appraisal. Stage 2, power and control, involves the development of roles and leadership within the group. Stage 3, intimacy, refers to the development of group cohesion and solidarity. Stage 5, separation, involves preparation for termination, including goal review, anticipated loss, and closure.

31. C: Cognitive therapy utilizes treatment concepts and techniques such as clarification, explanation, interpretation, paradoxical direction, reflection, and writing.

32. A: Group instruction is more cost effective than one-on-one instruction because a number of patients/family can be served at one time. Group presentations are usually more rigidly scripted and scheduled for a particular time period, so family and patients have less control. Questions may be more limited, but group instruction also allows patients/families with similar concerns to interact. Group instruction is particularly useful for general types of instruction, such as managing diet or other lifestyle issues.

33. B: This is not an unusual situation: Even clients whose problems are wrecking their lives find it extremely difficult to change. In therapy, they may be labeled as "resistant" and "dumped," or conscientious helpers may struggle to suggest different solutions, only to find that nothing works—and to feel like they're failing the client. In this case, the social worker has done all she can and is working harder than her client (this is always a clue that something isn't right). She doesn't need to refer the client because he would probably act the same way with any helper. Jane's challenge is to stick with the client, to stop presenting him with solutions, and to wait until his problem becomes his problem again, not hers. If he is not motivated to change because his problem isn't causing him much suffering, he will drop out of therapy on his own. If the pressure on him has relaxed because he has shifted his responsibility for solving the problem to Jane, her relaxing of the hold on his problem will allow the pressure to rest on him again, which will eventually increase his motivation to change.

34. B: The social worker should self-examine to determine possible reasons for the reaction. While it may be prudent for a social worker to speak with a supervisor or colleague about what he or she is experiencing, the best first step would be self-examination. Self-awareness is an important quality in a competent social worker, which is why social workers often are urged to enter counseling themselves. It's important for a social worker to be self-aware in order to competently treat clients.

35. B: These are characteristics of task-centered therapy. It is important to note that, because this form of therapy is client-driven, with the social worker only assisting by means of facilitation, individuals who are not committed to change would not be good candidates for this form of therapy. It is generally short-term (6-12 sessions), and involves open sharing between both the client and the social worker (i.e., no "hidden agendas").

36. D: The protective level of care is that level required for children, the elderly, people with mental retardation, and people with disabilities. "Skilled" or "extended" care is usually associated with Medicaid designations for long-term nursing facilities. Intermediate care is a designation used for older people who cannot live alone but can manage activities of daily living and are not in need of full-time nursing care.

37. C: Gestalt therapy utilizes treatment concepts and techniques such as dialogue, enactment of dreams, exaggeration, exposure of the obvious, and rehearsal to overcome barriers such as confluence, introjection, projection and retroflection.

38. A: The Confusion Assessment Method is used to assess the development of delirium and is intended for use by those without psychiatric training. The assessment tool covers 9 factors:

- Onset: Acute changes in mental status.
- Attention: Inattentive, stable, or fluctuating.
- Thinking: Disorganized, rambling, switching topics, illogical.
- Level of consciousness: Altered (ranging from alert to coma).
- Orientation: Time, place, person.
- Memory: Impaired.
- Perceptual disturbances: Hallucinations, illusions.
- Psychomotor abnormalities: Agitations or retardation.
- Sleep-wake cycle: Awake at night, sleepy in the daytime.

39. D: The crisis intervention approach sees periods of intense trauma as optimal for effecting change, and seeks to equip clients with new and/or more effective coping skills to manage traumatic situation. The goal is not to produce a "cure" but to help clients more adequately cope until the worst of the crisis has passed. Once the crisis has passed, the client may well be in need of further psychotherapeutic intervention.

40. D: Most likely, counseling will become interminable. Counseling can be interminable when factors exist that limit its ability to be effective. One of those factors is when therapy goals are unrealistic. In this case, the goal of never experiencing conflict when making decisions is an unrealistic one, so counseling is likely to be interminable unless the error is noted and corrected.

41. B: The coleaders are trying to recruit "typical" students from the sciences—usually introverted, usually male—to balance out the outgoing female members. Whereas some groups are structured to meet the needs of a particular population (as in a group working on excessive shyness, in which everyone would be socially uncomfortable to some extent), others are built upon the idea that differences between members will enrich the experience for everyone. In such a group, leaders will seek variety in the group's members.

42. A: A problem list focuses on a prioritized list of patient problems based on assessment data, history, and interview. Trying to deal with all patient problems without prioritizing them to determine which are the most critical can result in ineffective care. Patients are not always aware of their own needs regarding health care or intervention, and standardized lists of problems may be used as a guide but will not always match the individual's circumstances.

43. A: Group therapy arises from the belief that individuals in similar situations can identify with, comfort, reassure and help one another. It is important to note, however, that group therapy is typically an adjunctive approach (sometimes called a "complementary therapy" or "complementary intervention"), rather than an individual's only source of treatment. The seven major types of groups are: 1) educational groups; 2) growth groups (consciousness raising); 3) remedial groups (or "psychotherapy groups" where issues, such as anger, are encountered); 4) self-help groups (such as Alcoholics Anonymous); 5) socialization groups (to improve interpersonal skills); 6) support groups (or "mutual sharing groups" for those with common concerns, such as bereavement); and 7) task groups (focused on achieving specific goals, such as job location, etc.).

44. B: Advocacy is working for the best interests of the patient despite conflicting personal values and assisting patients to have access to appropriate resources. Moral agency is the ability to recognize needs and a willingness take action to influence the wholesome outcome of a conflict or decision. Agency is a general willingness to act arising from openness and the recognition of involved issues. Collaboration is working together to achieve better results.

45. C: Mark's history of violence in his intimate relationships and his current addictions to pornography and the internet, combined with his having PTSD and ADHD, produce a constellation of conditions that points to his having been abused as a child. He may well have been addicted to drugs or alcohol at an early age because it's not uncommon for abused children to turn to drugs to attempt to numb the pain and ease the memories of abuse, and current abuse or symptoms of PTSD will look like ADHD or learning disorders in the school setting. However, there is no current indication of drug or alcohol abuse.

46. D: Biofeedback uses monitoring devices to allow people to control their own physiological responses. People use information (feedback) from ECG, EMG, EEG, galvanic skin response, pulse, BP, and temperature to differentiate between the abnormal and the desired state. People with hypertension will use the feedback about their BP to help them lower it by relaxing, deep breathing, or other activities. The monitoring devices show when their efforts are effective. Biofeedback may be used to control heart rate, BP, pain, incontinence, and muscle strength.

47. B: Crisis intervention utilizes treatment concepts largely oriented around immediate problem-solving, stress reduction, coping skill enhancement, support system building, and emotional buffering. Because engagement is during a crisis experience, and is typically short-term in nature, the focus is less on assessment than on buffering, support system building, stress reduction, etc.

48. A: The social worker should take a position of extreme caution. Suicidal clients who suddenly feel better are often not improving but rather are less conflicted because they have made the decision to take their lives. This is when extreme caution should be exercised by the social worker, because the risk to the client is actually higher.

49. D: These treatment approaches are associated with family therapy. This modality also uses the "strategic family therapy approach," which focuses on the function of family rules and behavior patterns. The goal of the social worker is to devise interventions which will elicit functional behavioral patterns, and revise those family rules which defeat or impede appropriate family relationships and conduct.

50. C: Transference is likely causing these client's feelings. Transference is a Freudian term that describes a client's placing feelings for another onto the social worker. In this case, especially because of the problematic relationship issues, the client is likely to be transferring feelings inaccurately onto the social worker.

51. C: Forced groups are not a type of group therapy structure. While some groups are formed of members under court order, there is no such group category, nor would a group, itself, seek to force attendance.

52. A: The best approach to solving a problem that involves 3 different departments is to form an interdisciplinary team of representative participants to work together and find a solution. This allows all parties to have a voice and to work toward compromise, while avoiding the confusion caused by too many competing interests. If administration makes a decision independently, or picks one of the proposed solutions over another, all or many staff members may feel their voices weren't heard. Trying to gather all members of 3 departments together for brainstorming is usually impractical, and an unnecessary use of employee time and resources.

53. B: Enabling behavior helps create situations in which the other person's dysfunction can continue. Enabling may take the form of providing the substance, but it may also happen when someone tries to deprive the addicted person of the substance, which gives that person cause for resentment and another "reason" to continue the destructive pattern.

54. A: A social worker may limit the client's right to self-determination when there's a threat to self or others. Social workers are expected to respect a client's right to self-determination. However, if a client's choice of action threatens himself or the welfare of others, a social worker may limit that right.

55. B: Individuals typically pass through five stages of grief to reconcile a loss (Kübler-Ross, 1969):

1. *Denial*, a defense mechanism that protects an individual from the full initial impact of the loss.
2. *Anger*, at the irretrievability of the loss.
3. *Bargaining*, considering all "what if" and "if only" elements that could have prevented or could restore (appeals to God, etc.) the loss.
4. *Despair/depression*, as the full meaning of the loss emerges.
5. *Acceptance*, surrendering to loss and coming to believe in eventual recovery.

56. C: Depression is strongly associated with addiction, and in many cases, it's difficult to discern which comes first. Some theories of addiction say that people become addicted in an attempt to self-medicate their long-standing and pervasive depression. In general, mental illness presents a risk for substance abuse as the patient attempts to self-medicate to overcome their struggles.

57. D: Systems theory. The systems may be "open" (accepting of outside input) or "closed" (resisting outside forces and input). Working with a system from a "horizontal approach" is to limit the scope of intervention to a specific community and those things occurring within it. In contrast, a "vertical approach" reaches well beyond the identified community, extending, for example, to policies, programs, and resources outside the community that can be brought to bear in addressing community concerns.

58. C: Because this young man's withdrawn behavior has been persistent throughout his lifespan, he would most likely be considered to have a schizoid personality. (Because he is at the age dividing adolescence from adulthood in the diagnostic criterion, without evidence that his behavior has been lifelong, he might have been diagnosed with schizoid disorder of adolescence.) Schizophreniform disorder is much less adaptive and contains features of schizophrenia, and although someone might be considered to have a highly introverted personality, introversion is not a diagnosable condition.

59. B: The ecosystems theory (also called the "Life Model Theory) focuses on the relationship between living things and their environment, sees "adaptation" as the process by which individuals and the environment accommodate each other, and views dysfunction as a failure to cooperate and accommodate. In direct practice, social workers use ecosystems theory to help clients recognize the demands of their environment and then better accommodate. In community practice, social workers use ecosystems theory to pursue community, policy, and program change in ways to make the environment more receptive to the individual.

60. C: Autocratic leaders make decisions independently and strictly enforce rules. Bureaucratic leaders follow organizational rules exactly and expect others to do so, as well. Laissez-faire leaders exert little direct control and allow others to make decisions with little interference. Participatory leaders present a potential decision and make a final decision based on input from team members. Consultative leaders present a decision and welcome input, but rarely change their decisions. Democratic leaders present a problem and ask the team to arrive at a solution, although these leaders make the final decision.

61. C: In Gestalt theory, great attention is given to the immediate therapeutic encounter as an "experience" from which to gain awareness and increased understanding of the "here and now," which is considered to be a more reliable source of understanding than processes of cognitive interpretation.

62. A: Anorexia has been associated with cultural pressures that result in body image distortions and attempts to control perceived weight gain. Although it certainly has neurobiological concomitance, its cause has not been identified as organic.

63. D: Psychosocial therapy (also referred to as "bio-psycho-social therapy") focuses on the multidimensional aspects of the individual and engages the client in the context of his/her personal history, strengths, weaknesses, resources, wants and needs. The earliest proponent of this form of therapy was Florence Hollis (1963), who was later joined by Mary Woods (who continued this work after Hollis' death).

64. B: The social worker should consult with a social worker trained in psychosis. A social worker is ethically responsible to practice only within those areas where he or she is competent. Because the client's welfare must be paramount, the social worker in this case should not discontinue counseling but should consult with someone who is competent in psychosis and proceed from there.

65. A: Solution-focused therapy sees clients as competent to co-construct goals and strategies and as experts regarding their own lives and experiences. It encourages change by doing something differently, even while recognizing the only small steps need to be taken, and suggests that "if it isn't broken, don't fix it" and that "if it didn't work, try something different." It originated at the Brief Family Therapy Center (BFTC) in Milwaukee, and Steve de Shazer was one of the primary originators.

66. B: Selye's biological theory of stress and aging states that stress is a body response to demands requiring positive or negative adaptation, characterized by the "generalized adaptation syndrome," which includes 3 stages:

- Alarm: Fight or flight response.
- Resistance: The body mobilizes to resist a threat, focusing on those organs most involved in an adaptive response.
- Exhaustion: As the body is weakened and overwhelmed, organs/systems begin to deteriorate (hypertrophy/atrophy) and can no longer cope with stress, resulting in stress-related illnesses and eventual death.

67. B: Logotherapy is used primarily with the elderly and with those experiencing loss. It is often adjunctive to other therapeutic interventions that focus on important survivor questions and that see three key paths to meaning. The originator of this therapeutic approach was Viktor Emil Frankl (author of the best-selling book "Man's Search for Meaning").

68. C: Yes, under all circumstances this presents a concern This situation may present a dual relationship that can create a conflict of interest. Conflicts of interest are not ethically allowed in counseling relationships and are to be avoided.

69. D: Transactional analysis (TA) is based on fundamental units of social intercourse and fundamental units of social action. The founder of this theory was Eric Berne, who developed it during the 1950s. Transactional Analysis is the method for studying interactions between individuals. Departing from the Freudian dialogue approach, TA social workers simply observe communication processes (words, body language, facial expressions), often in group settings, to explore a client's transactions – in light of the fact that complete communication importance is: actual word - 7%; word delivery style (tone, inflections, etc.) - 38%; and facial expressions - 55%. Through such analyses, interactive styles can be identified, and changes made (where needed) to enhance an individual's interpersonal strengths and ultimate successes.

70. A: The social worker must give care to discussing the limits of confidentiality. Confidentiality is a critical issue in social work, but there are limits, and a client should be made aware of those limits. In this case, suicide ideation may present a situation where confidentiality needs to be breached. To ensure a positive client/ social worker relationship, the client should be made particularly aware of confidentiality limits.

71. C: These two forms of conditioning, in order, are classical conditioning and operant conditioning. Stimuli that induce a reaction without training are called "primary" or "unconditioned" stimuli (US). They include food, pain, and other "hardwired" or "instinctive" stimuli. Stimuli that do not induce a desire reaction until after conditioning has occurred are called secondary or conditioned stimuli.

72. B: The social worker should provide the records and help to interpret them. Social workers have a responsibility to provide clients with their records upon request. In some cases, however, interpretation may be needed. Also, social workers should be careful that the confidentiality of other people's material in an individual's records is protected.

73. D: The client would be considered not in remission, due to not meeting timeframe for remission. Early remission starts at 3 months and continues to 12 months of symptom free except craving. Sustained remission is 12 months or more symptom free, except craving. The client has only been free from substance use for 10 weeks, so he doesn't meet either of those criteria yet.

When the client reaches 3 months, even if he is using a maintenance therapy medication he can be considered in remission, it will just be noted "on maintenance therapy". For the rest of the client's life he may experience craving, but as long as he does not have any other symptoms he will still be considered "in remission."

74. A: A correlation coefficient of 1.0 indicates a perfect relationship between two variables.

75. D: The social worker should refer the client to another social worker. It is not considered ethically responsible to enter into a counseling relationship with someone with whom the social worker previously had a sexual relationship. Professional boundaries are difficult to maintain in this situation, and harm to the client could ensue.

76. B: The social worker should thoughtfully but explicitly address and explore the behavior. Ignoring the behavior offers the couple no opportunity to address and overcome it. Mentioning the behavior only casually allows it to be equally casually dismissed. Confronting a couple who is in pain from a profound loss and already in fragile state could be perceived as overly aggressive, potentially leading to diminished rapport and/or therapeutic estrangement.

77. D: Sources where substances were obtained are not a necessary part of the assessment process. There is no reporting requirement for this, and it is not germane to the treatment process.

78. D: A statistical test is comprised of a research hypothesis, a null hypothesis, a test statistic, a rejection region and a conclusion. The research hypothesis is symbolized as "H_A," the null hypothesis is symbolized as "H_O," the test statistic is symbolized as "TS," and the rejection region is symbolized as "RR."

79. C: Drug "affinity" testing to determine the level of addiction present is not a treatment modality for substance abuse. There is no laboratory test to determine an individual's level of addiction – particularly because much of the addictive experience is psychological and not just physiological.

80. B: Simply asking the client directly why he/she is unwilling to cooperate would be the least effective approach in overcoming the client's reluctance. The direct approach is sometimes ideal. However, asking a why question can be particularly problematic in a situation of resistance because the client may feel that he/she is being judged or challenged in his response. The question itself suggests some belligerence or non-cooperation on the part of the client, and it can produce a confrontational situation that could damage the working relationship. Often asking a client to "tell me more about that" serves the same purpose, without the potential for disrupting the relationship.

81. B: Generally, deep seated issues (the focus of psychoanalytic therapy) are not dealt with in a substance abuse treatment program. Most focus on very practical strategies for increasing awareness and breaking the cycle of substance abuse relapse (changing peers, changing areas, becoming more productive and attentive to life, improving home relationships, etc.). Because most addictions are chronic in nature, individuals require long-term interventions. Cost and efficacy issues generally move individuals into long-term self-help resources, such as Alcoholics Anonymous and Narcotics Anonymous, etc.

82. A: Alpha value refers to the threshold necessary to decide whether an intervention produced an outcome, or whether it was the result of a chance "statistical significance."

83. C: Many of the elderly are overmedicated or are taking medications whose interaction effects create additional ailments, such as headaches, confusion, and emotional problems. In a medication review, each medication is considered in relation to the others, and a review may discover that medications from different doctors or for different illnesses are causing new problems for the client.

84. A: The social worker's best response is to aid the client in exploring his difficulties in this area. It would be helpful to the client to explore his reluctance further, certainly in deference to his capacity to work well in other opposite-gender relationships. If the client remains entirely unwilling to address the issue, or if subsequent exploration does not resolve the client's concerns, then a case transfer or referral out would be most appropriate.

85. D: Cocaine is classified as a stimulant. In 1914, with the Harrison Drug Act, cocaine was erroneously classified, in the eyes of the law, as a narcotic. This legal designation has never been revised, thus, identifying it as a narcotic would be "legally" correct. However, pharmaceutically and psychoactively, cocaine is a stimulant; thus, this would be the most correct answer, from an abuse and rehabilitation perspective.

86. B: Means tested programs is not a category of social service programs. Universal programs are open to everyone, without any exclusion criteria. Exceptional eligibility programs are only available to certain groups with common needs, such as the Veteran's Health Administration. Selective eligibility programs are either "means tested" (including asset evaluation) or "income-tested" (looking solely at financial income).

87. C: Most anxiolytics (anti-anxiety medications) are benzodiazepines, which makes them depressants in their action on the central nervous system. There are exceptions, however, such as buspirone (BuSpar), which is a psychotropic drug that is a serotonin receptor stimulant.

88. C: Interdisciplinary palliative care teams ensure that providers from multiple specialties (e.g., physician, social worker, nurse, chaplain) can collaborate with the patient and family to craft a care plan that meets the needs and goals of the patient. Care is directed primarily by the patient. Ideally, the team provides information and elicits patient values, preferences, and goals as they pertain to end-of-life care. Once this is completed, specific challenges can be identified and possible solutions planned. Interventions are then provided to the patient and family in accordance with the formulated plan. Reassessments and changes in the care plan are made as illness progresses or preferences or goals change.

89. C: After her work became famous, Kubler-Ross was dismayed that practitioners and lay readers conceptualized the stages in a linear fashion, when in fact, the grief process can involve cycling back to earlier stages over longer periods of time.

90. C: To be eligible to receive social security retirement benefits, an individual must have earned a lifetime credit total of 40 credits. For those born before 1960, the retirement age for maximum benefits is 65. For those born in or after 1960, the age is 67.

91. A: While the client's grooming and hygiene may indicate a great deal about the client and his or her habits, financial status, mental and physical health, etc., these factors should not have direct influence on the communication experience.

92. D: Jehovah's Witnesses do not allow transfusions of blood or blood products. Some may allow auto-transfusion for blood loss.

93. C: The social worker should discuss with him the difficulty he is experiencing, and encourage him to take more time. "Sentence finishing" often substitutes the social worker's thoughts in place of the clients, which the client may then accept to relieve the burden he is feeling. Pressing the client to continue will often make the problem worse. Ignoring the problem and waiting indefinitely may lead to premature termination.

94. D: This program is administered by the Social Security Administration, where the program is referred to as Social Security Disability (SSD).

95. B: The social worker would revise the meeting to cover only very basic issues until better arrangements can be made. Abruptly terminating a meeting may leave the client feeling rejected and upset after the efforts made to attend. Delaying the meeting can cause similar problems. Resorting to the use of one's limited language skills could lead to misunderstandings and unnecessary confusion. Therefore, revising the meeting to pursue only basic information intake and to establish simple rapport would be advantageous.

96. B: The first step should be to acknowledge the highly ambivalent feelings she is experiencing. There is a natural tendency is to hasten and point out the classic features of relationship abuse. However, this approach is likely to immediately alienate the client. Importantly, she has already expressed ambivalent feelings. Allowing her to process those feelings, and then moving on to exploring other past relationships, and eventually reality-testing this one is typically much more successful approach.

97. C: Burnout is characterized by feeling that one has more responsibility than control. (Note that there is no change in Maria's outward behavior: She is not in crisis and is not presenting with symptoms of unusual anxiety).

98. C: A social insurance program for individuals sustaining employment-related injuries is the Worker's Compensation Program. To be eligible, the injuries sustained must not have occurred through gross negligence, willful misconduct, or intoxication.

99. B: The more clearly that goals are defined, the more likely they are to be attained. Likewise, clear-cut agreements about timetables, payment, rights, and responsibilities set the stage for a transparent therapeutic alliance.

100. C: In this situation, the social worker should use reflective listening techniques and allow the client more time. Aggressive and/or confrontational techniques are unlikely to induce change in a client with a predisposition to defer to others. It becomes necessary to more skillfully apply reflective listening techniques to bring this client out. This will require the social worker to be more tolerant of a slower therapeutic pace, and carefully guard against completing the client's sentences to overcome awkward pauses and periods of silence.

101. C: Rephrasing is used to emphasize what the client said, while paraphrasing is used to show mutual understanding. Rephrasing changes only a few words that further emphasize what the client has said (e.g. "the surgery hurt" to "so, the surgery was very painful"). Paraphrasing, however, is virtually an unchanged restatement of the client's words to demonstrate that she was heard.

102. B: The Supplemental Security Income program supports individuals falling below the "poverty line" threshold, including the working poor and individuals who are elderly, disabled and/or blind.

103. B: Substitution is not an element of active listening. Telling a client what oneself would do not only turns the conversation away from him and his own thinking, but it closes off further communication as the authority figure "has spoken" and seemingly concluded that scenario.

104. C: Symbols of alcohol misuse include:

- Confusion/Disorientation
- Loss of motor control
- Convulsions
- Shock
- Shallow respiration
- Involuntary defecation
- Drowsiness
- Respiratory depression
- Possible death

105. B: "Could you tell me more about…" is an open-ended, non-leading question that encourages the client to continue and to share more.

106. C: The Temporary Assistance for Needy Families (TANF) program was renamed in 1966, stemming from the "Aid for Families with Dependent Children" program. It was revised to be a transitional program from welfare to work.

107. A: A stacked or complex question contains multiple parts, potentially leaving a client confused or unclear what the question was, or at least uncertain which part to answer first. For example, "Was the part that you didn't understand where he told you to stop, or where he asked for your supervisor, or where he said that you could be liable for that?" This question can easily leave a client confused and uncertain how to respond. Feelings such as this can make the client less willing to communicate.

108. A: Prozac is an SSRI used to treat depression. Medications used to treat the psychotic symptoms of schizophrenia include:

Old antipsychotics**:**

- Haldol (haloperidol)
- Thorazine (chlorpromazine)
- Mellaril (thioridazine)
- Stelazine (trifluoperazine)
- Prolixin (Fluphenazine)
- Navane (thiothixene)
- Clozaril (clozapine)

Newer or atypical antipsychotics:

- Clozaril
- Risperdal
- Seroquel
- Zyprexa (olanzapine)
- Abilify

109. D: Partialization is the process of breaking down the concerns at hand into smaller, more manageable parts. For example, "Well, if we take these things one at a time, maybe we can start with…"

110. A: Two components of the federal health insurance program for the elderly (Medicare) are medical insurance and hospital insurance. The hospitalization coverage portion is known as Medicare Part A, and the medical care coverage portion is known as Medicare Part B. Expansions in recent years have also resulted in Medicare Part C (a combined A & B program administered by private health insurance companies, HMOs, etc.), and Medicare Part D (prescription drug coverage).

111. A: Sophie is focusing on her client's strengths using a strengths-based perspective, which has been shown to empower clients and build resiliency. Solution-focused perspectives focus on end goals and methods to reach those goals. A structural perspective focuses on identifying the interacting elements of the client system and which areas require attention to regain stabilization. A behavioral perspective would focus on behaviors that contribute to and surround the client's gambling addiction and finding ways to control or discourage those behaviors.

112. D: Meals on Wheels is a locally funded program, not a federally funded program. Federally funded programs include the Elderly Nutrition Program, the Food Stamps Programs, and the Women, Infants and Children (WIC) program.

113. B: The social worker does not assume the role of enforcer and regulator. Quality social work is all about providing insights and options. It is not about punitive accountability, enforcement, or policing. Assuming such roles will extinguish the trust and sustaining power of the therapeutic relationship that must predominate. While social workers may be called upon to provide protective roles in investigating abuse, the law enforcement and the criminal justice system will mete out the necessary consequences, not social work staff, who must still refrain from caustic critique and recrimination.

114. C: The "Id" would be the part of the personality driving the behavior of a serial rapist. It is the most primitive part of the personality, and the libido is its most basic instinctual drive. The "Ego" is more rational, and mediates between individual wants and environmental demands. As the Ego develops, the "Reality Principle" arises, introducing compromise. The "Superego" incorporates ethical and moral constraints on behavior. It is composed of two parts: 1) the "Conscience" (i.e., the "do not do" behaviors); and 2) the "Ego Ideal" (regulating the "should do" behaviors). Development should be complete by about age five, per Freud.

115. D: The NASW social work primary mission is dedicated to meeting basic human needs and enhancing human well-being from a social context, including societal environmental forces that bear on problems in everyday life.

116. A: Standing up for oneself and one's rights are key components of assertiveness training, which are being demonstrated in this group. Positive thinking, healthy communication and stress reduction would be secondary skills utilized to foster assertiveness.

117. C: Changing one's perspective is a skill used in cognitive interventions, which teach clients new ways of thinking about problems and solutions. Notice that the other three options either assume the presence of another person (communication) or a mind-body approach, as in relaxation responses or environmental change.

118. D: Erikson called these two opposing features dystonic and syntonic. Taking Stage 1 (trust vs. distrust) as an example, one may be naturally trusting or naturally distrusting. Regardless, one part of this stage "syntonic" (in natural accord with one's personality) and one part will be "dystonic" (not easily accommodated in one's natural personality). The "crisis" is coming to terms with both. One must learn to be appropriately trusting in key situations in order to have fulfilling and meaningful relationships. Yet one must not become so trusting as to be vulnerable to abuse in situations that should not involve immediate trust. Upon resolving this dichotomy, one will be prepared to move on to the next developmental stage.

119. C: The social worker is a mandated reporter. This includes even reasonable suspicions of abuse – a client who is routinely dressed improperly for the weather, has bruises, is malnourished, is abandoned alone when supervision is needed, etc. – must all be reported, along with frank evidence of abuse.

120. C: Hartmann proposed that the ego has eight functions. The eight functions of the Ego are:

- Reality testing
- Impulse control
- Affect regulation
- Judgment
- Object relations
- Thought processes
- Defensive functioning
- Synthesis

121. B: The primary form of abuse to be suspected here is financial abuse. This is also a form of abuse that must be reported and investigated by the proper authorities.

122. B: Hartmann believed the Id and the Ego to be rudimentarily present from birth forward, therefore in all children. He also believed that the Ego has the capacity to function independently, while Freud saw the Ego functioning as a mediator (with the Id) and receiving mediation through the Superego.

123. C: The cultural formulation interview guide assists social workers in coming to an understanding of how the client's culture impacts his or her experience and current feelings and functioning. Such an interview should help social workers increase their cultural awareness and identify a change incident of cultural bias, as well as letting clients know that their heritage matters and is not being ignored or denigrated.

124. D: This theory is called the Object Relations Theory. Derived both from Freud's Psychoanalytic Theory and Hartmann's Ego Psychology, it focuses on Ego organization during the first 3½ years of life, when differentiation between self and others is emerging.

125. C: Publication in a reputable professional journal is not an exception for consent. Regardless of the compelling nature of the information, or the good it might do others, records cannot be released for publication without consent from the individual. While PL 93-579 applies only to federal agencies and settings, virtually all state and local government agencies have promulgated these same practices.

126. C: Splitting serves to repress, disconnect, or dissociate feelings that seem "dangerous" to psychic well-being. Engaging this defense mechanism can result in an individual losing touch with his or her true feelings, resulting in a "fragmented self" in proportion to the frequency and degree to which the mechanism is utilized.

127. D: The Health Insurance Portability and Accountability Act of 1996 (HIPAA) applies to all health care providers, health care clearinghouses, and health plan providers. It sets limits on records disclosure and use, provides for individual access to medical records, and establishes the right to receive nots of privacy practices.

128. D: The underlying story of this client is that the client is conflicted about leaving her husband. The client doesn't consciously connect that conflict with her car-related phobia, but the social worker notes that anxiety and panic attacks do not happen with other people. In this case, the latent content of the client's story may be that driving is a metaphor for her life.

129. A: Employer and supervisor liability accrues under the legal theory of vicarious liability. Although an agency may have liability insurance, it is usually recommended that individual social workers carry their own private coverage. Agency responsibility typically ends at the margins of the scope of the social worker's employment duties (unless agency staff knew in advance of an employee's misconduct and took no protective action). Agency liability continues even off the premises, to the degree the employee's scope of duties extends off the premises.

130. C: This type of behavior is sometimes referred to as "disqualifying communication," meaning that, by words or actions, it disqualifies what one has just said. In the example, the client makes a comment about liking his job and respecting his brother. However, his use of the words "lousy" and "idiot" run counter to the meaning behind those statements and thus disqualify what appears to be the intended message.

131. B: In this case, where Jim advises her mother on finances, which may affect her as well, it's a reasonable, sensible, and ethical decision to refer Jim to another social worker. Terminating the relationship without a referral is not for the best interest of the client.

132. A: According to Lawrence Kohlberg, an individual fully appreciates the need to conform to social rules and laws at the Conventional Level, stage 4 of moral development.

133. B: While other clients receiving services at the agency may be asked to maintain confidentiality (and this request may even be formalized in group settings) they are not professional bound to ethical standards as are social workers and support staff employed by an agency.

134. B: The responses, according to Pavlovian Classical Conditioning, will be either emitted (voluntary) or reflexive (involuntary) responses.

135. C: 6-12 years old. A "latency-aged" child is one between the ages six and twelve.

136. D: When seeking to overcome problems at the community level or that affect society as a whole, the social worker is functioning as a lobbyist or politician. Effective change at this level typically requires enhanced policy or legislation to align numerous interest groups and resources.

137. C: Because the social worker connects clients to needed resources and services and coordinates the delivery and application of these resources and services, they may be considered a case manager.

138. B: The best response would be to donate the funds to the local Brain Tumor foundation, thanking them for the funds and telling the family where they were sent. This allows the family to see the social worker's gratitude, even while making sure that the funds would be expended in a way that reflects their needs, as well.

139. C: The *NASW Code of Ethics*, most recently updated in 2018, is the best source for the rules, guidelines, and boundaries that define a professional relationship between the social worker and his/her client. While other sources may be informative there is no substitute for studying the NASW Code of Ethics. Policy and procedure manuals and clinical practice texts, in particular, are less likely to provide overarching guidelines of an ethical nature, and instead focus on practical issues for carrying out specific job duties.

140. D: The appropriate response is to cite the professional code of ethics, and clarify that even after a professional relationship ends, socializing is not permitted.

141. A: The best response would be for the social worker to refer the client to another professional promptly, emphasizing the need the client has to remain focused on resolving the important problems involved without any distraction. Feeding the behavior, allowing any level of inappropriate conduct, and confronting the client will only damage the important professional relationship that must exist.

142. B: The process of informing, educating, and reviewing prior to a treatment decision is called informed consent.

143. C: Liberally increasing fees for a client who is particularly well off is not within the ethical behavior outlined by the *NASW Code of Ethics*. Client gouging (charging rates outside of the usual and customary range) is never acceptable.

144. D: The best response for this client would be to involve the client in every aspect that he/she can properly understand, and allow his/her choices to govern where possible. For example, in situations where either a magnetic resonance imaging (MRI) scan or a computed tomography (CT) scan could produce adequate imaging for a requisite test, let the client choose. No one may know, except the client, that he/she has issues with claustrophobia that would make an MRI scan much more burdensome. Thus, asking the client would be essential to supporting his/her right to make independent decisions.

145. A: Social services are never funded via court order (unless from an estate or by some method of litigation—which falls under "personal contributions" as they come from some private individual).

146. B: Under privatization, the government continues paying (but hopes the service will become cheaper to provide). Privatization is undertaken in the hope that the service will be provided less expensively via the private sector, but the government remains the service payer. Issues of accountability sometimes arise once privatization occurs.

147. D: Housing assistance is provided through public housing, subsidized housing, and home loan subsidy programs. There are no "co-op" housing assistance programs based on public assistance.

148. C: The Food Stamps Program is a federally-funded, state administered program that provides purchase vouchers or coupons based on a family's size, income, and resources.

149. A: The Women, Infants, and Children (WIC) program is a federally-funded, state-administered program providing food and assistance to pregnant women, mothers of children up to five months of age (if not breastfeeding), breast-feeding mothers up to 12 months after delivery, and children up to five years of age.

150. B: Meals on wheels is a locally funded program that provides delivery of food to low-income individuals who are unable to leave their home.

How to Overcome Test Anxiety

Just the thought of taking a test is enough to make most people a little nervous. A test is an important event that can have a long-term impact on your future, so it's important to take it seriously and it's natural to feel anxious about performing well. But just because anxiety is normal, that doesn't mean that it's helpful in test taking, or that you should simply accept it as part of your life. Anxiety can have a variety of effects. These effects can be mild, like making you feel slightly nervous, or severe, like blocking your ability to focus or remember even a simple detail.

If you experience test anxiety—whether severe or mild—it's important to know how to beat it. To discover this, first you need to understand what causes test anxiety.

Causes of Test Anxiety

While we often think of anxiety as an uncontrollable emotional state, it can actually be caused by simple, practical things. One of the most common causes of test anxiety is that a person does not feel adequately prepared for their test. This feeling can be the result of many different issues such as poor study habits or lack of organization, but the most common culprit is time management. Starting to study too late, failing to organize your study time to cover all of the material, or being distracted while you study will mean that you're not well prepared for the test. This may lead to cramming the night before, which will cause you to be physically and mentally exhausted for the test. Poor time management also contributes to feelings of stress, fear, and hopelessness as you realize you are not well prepared but don't know what to do about it.

Other times, test anxiety is not related to your preparation for the test but comes from unresolved fear. This may be a past failure on a test, or poor performance on tests in general. It may come from comparing yourself to others who seem to be performing better or from the stress of living up to expectations. Anxiety may be driven by fears of the future—how failure on this test would affect your educational and career goals. These fears are often completely irrational, but they can still negatively impact your test performance.

Review Video: 3 Reasons You Have Test Anxiety
Visit mometrix.com/academy and enter code: 428468

Elements of Test Anxiety

As mentioned earlier, test anxiety is considered to be an emotional state, but it has physical and mental components as well. Sometimes you may not even realize that you are suffering from test anxiety until you notice the physical symptoms. These can include trembling hands, rapid heartbeat, sweating, nausea, and tense muscles. Extreme anxiety may lead to fainting or vomiting. Obviously, any of these symptoms can have a negative impact on testing. It is important to recognize them as soon as they begin to occur so that you can address the problem before it damages your performance.

Review Video: 3 Ways to Tell You Have Test Anxiety
Visit mometrix.com/academy and enter code: 927847

The mental components of test anxiety include trouble focusing and inability to remember learned information. During a test, your mind is on high alert, which can help you recall information and stay focused for an extended period of time. However, anxiety interferes with your mind's natural processes, causing you to blank out, even on the questions you know well. The strain of testing during anxiety makes it difficult to stay focused, especially on a test that may take several hours. Extreme anxiety can take a huge mental toll, making it difficult not only to recall test information but even to understand the test questions or pull your thoughts together.

Review Video: How Test Anxiety Affects Memory
Visit mometrix.com/academy and enter code: 609003

Effects of Test Anxiety

Test anxiety is like a disease—if left untreated, it will get progressively worse. Anxiety leads to poor performance, and this reinforces the feelings of fear and failure, which in turn lead to poor performances on subsequent tests. It can grow from a mild nervousness to a crippling condition. If allowed to progress, test anxiety can have a big impact on your schooling, and consequently on your future.

Test anxiety can spread to other parts of your life. Anxiety on tests can become anxiety in any stressful situation, and blanking on a test can turn into panicking in a job situation. But fortunately, you don't have to let anxiety rule your testing and determine your grades. There are a number of relatively simple steps you can take to move past anxiety and function normally on a test and in the rest of life.

Review Video: How Test Anxiety Impacts Your Grades
Visit mometrix.com/academy and enter code: 939819

Physical Steps for Beating Test Anxiety

While test anxiety is a serious problem, the good news is that it can be overcome. It doesn't have to control your ability to think and remember information. While it may take time, you can begin taking steps today to beat anxiety.

Just as your first hint that you may be struggling with anxiety comes from the physical symptoms, the first step to treating it is also physical. Rest is crucial for having a clear, strong mind. If you are tired, it is much easier to give in to anxiety. But if you establish good sleep habits, your body and mind will be ready to perform optimally, without the strain of exhaustion. Additionally, sleeping well helps you to retain information better, so you're more likely to recall the answers when you see the test questions.

Getting good sleep means more than going to bed on time. It's important to allow your brain time to relax. Take study breaks from time to time so it doesn't get overworked, and don't study right before bed. Take time to rest your mind before trying to rest your body, or you may find it difficult to fall asleep.

Review Video: The Importance of Sleep for Your Brain
Visit mometrix.com/academy and enter code: 319338

Along with sleep, other aspects of physical health are important in preparing for a test. Good nutrition is vital for good brain function. Sugary foods and drinks may give a burst of energy but this burst is followed by a crash, both physically and emotionally. Instead, fuel your body with protein and vitamin-rich foods.

Also, drink plenty of water. Dehydration can lead to headaches and exhaustion, especially if your brain is already under stress from the rigors of the test. Particularly if your test is a long one, drink water during the breaks. And if possible, take an energy-boosting snack to eat between sections.

Review Video: How Diet Can Affect your Mood
Visit mometrix.com/academy and enter code: 624317

Along with sleep and diet, a third important part of physical health is exercise. Maintaining a steady workout schedule is helpful, but even taking 5-minute study breaks to walk can help get your blood pumping faster and clear your head. Exercise also releases endorphins, which contribute to a positive feeling and can help combat test anxiety.

When you nurture your physical health, you are also contributing to your mental health. If your body is healthy, your mind is much more likely to be healthy as well. So take time to rest, nourish your body with healthy food and water, and get moving as much as possible. Taking these physical steps will make you stronger and more able to take the mental steps necessary to overcome test anxiety.

Mental Steps for Beating Test Anxiety

Working on the mental side of test anxiety can be more challenging, but as with the physical side, there are clear steps you can take to overcome it. As mentioned earlier, test anxiety often stems from lack of preparation, so the obvious solution is to prepare for the test. Effective studying may be the most important weapon you have for beating test anxiety, but you can and should employ several other mental tools to combat fear.

First, boost your confidence by reminding yourself of past success—tests or projects that you aced. If you're putting as much effort into preparing for this test as you did for those, there's no reason you should expect to fail here. Work hard to prepare; then trust your preparation.

Second, surround yourself with encouraging people. It can be helpful to find a study group, but be sure that the people you're around will encourage a positive attitude. If you spend time with others who are anxious or cynical, this will only contribute to your own anxiety. Look for others who are motivated to study hard from a desire to succeed, not from a fear of failure.

Third, reward yourself. A test is physically and mentally tiring, even without anxiety, and it can be helpful to have something to look forward to. Plan an activity following the test, regardless of the outcome, such as going to a movie or getting ice cream.

When you are taking the test, if you find yourself beginning to feel anxious, remind yourself that you know the material. Visualize successfully completing the test. Then take a few deep, relaxing breaths and return to it. Work through the questions carefully but with confidence, knowing that you are capable of succeeding.

Developing a healthy mental approach to test taking will also aid in other areas of life. Test anxiety affects more than just the actual test—it can be damaging to your mental health and even contribute to depression. It's important to beat test anxiety before it becomes a problem for more than testing.

Review Video: Test Anxiety and Depression
Visit mometrix.com/academy and enter code: 904704

Study Strategy

Being prepared for the test is necessary to combat anxiety, but what does being prepared look like? You may study for hours on end and still not feel prepared. What you need is a strategy for test prep. The next few pages outline our recommended steps to help you plan out and conquer the challenge of preparation.

Step 1: Scope Out the Test

Learn everything you can about the format (multiple choice, essay, etc.) and what will be on the test. Gather any study materials, course outlines, or sample exams that may be available. Not only will this help you to prepare, but knowing what to expect can help to alleviate test anxiety.

Step 2: Map Out the Material

Look through the textbook or study guide and make note of how many chapters or sections it has. Then divide these over the time you have. For example, if a book has 15 chapters and you have five days to study, you need to cover three chapters each day. Even better, if you have the time, leave an extra day at the end for overall review after you have gone through the material in depth.

If time is limited, you may need to prioritize the material. Look through it and make note of which sections you think you already have a good grasp on, and which need review. While you are studying, skim quickly through the familiar sections and take more time on the challenging parts. Write out your plan so you don't get lost as you go. Having a written plan also helps you feel more in control of the study, so anxiety is less likely to arise from feeling overwhelmed at the amount to cover.

Step 3: Gather Your Tools

Decide what study method works best for you. Do you prefer to highlight in the book as you study and then go back over the highlighted portions? Or do you type out notes of the important information? Or is it helpful to make flashcards that you can carry with you? Assemble the pens, index cards, highlighters, post-it notes, and any other materials you may need so you won't be distracted by getting up to find things while you study.

If you're having a hard time retaining the information or organizing your notes, experiment with different methods. For example, try color-coding by subject with colored pens, highlighters, or post-it notes. If you learn better by hearing, try recording yourself reading your notes so you can listen while in the car, working out, or simply sitting at your desk. Ask a friend to quiz you from your flashcards, or try teaching someone the material to solidify it in your mind.

Step 4: Create Your Environment

It's important to avoid distractions while you study. This includes both the obvious distractions like visitors and the subtle distractions like an uncomfortable chair (or a too-comfortable couch that makes you want to fall asleep). Set up the best study environment possible: good lighting and a comfortable work area. If background music helps you focus, you may want to turn it on, but otherwise keep the room quiet. If you are using a computer to take notes, be sure you don't have any other windows open, especially applications like social media, games, or anything else that could distract you. Silence your phone and turn off notifications. Be sure to keep water close by so you stay hydrated while you study (but avoid unhealthy drinks and snacks).

Also, take into account the best time of day to study. Are you freshest first thing in the morning? Try to set aside some time then to work through the material. Is your mind clearer in the afternoon or evening? Schedule your study session then. Another method is to study at the same time of day that you will take the test, so that your brain gets used to working on the material at that time and will be ready to focus at test time.

Step 5: Study!

Once you have done all the study preparation, it's time to settle into the actual studying. Sit down, take a few moments to settle your mind so you can focus, and begin to follow your study plan. Don't give in to distractions or let yourself procrastinate. This is your time to prepare so you'll be ready to fearlessly approach the test. Make the most of the time and stay focused.

Of course, you don't want to burn out. If you study too long you may find that you're not retaining the information very well. Take regular study breaks. For example, taking five minutes out of every hour to walk briskly, breathing deeply and swinging your arms, can help your mind stay fresh.

As you get to the end of each chapter or section, it's a good idea to do a quick review. Remind yourself of what you learned and work on any difficult parts. When you feel that you've mastered the material, move on to the next part. At the end of your study session, briefly skim through your notes again.

But while review is helpful, cramming last minute is NOT. If at all possible, work ahead so that you won't need to fit all your study into the last day. Cramming overloads your brain with more information than it can process and retain, and your tired mind may struggle to recall even previously learned information when it is overwhelmed with last-minute study. Also, the urgent nature of cramming and the stress placed on your brain contribute to anxiety. You'll be more likely to go to the test feeling unprepared and having trouble thinking clearly.

So don't cram, and don't stay up late before the test, even just to review your notes at a leisurely pace. Your brain needs rest more than it needs to go over the information again. In fact, plan to finish your studies by noon or early afternoon the day before the test. Give your brain the rest of the day to relax or focus on other things, and get a good night's sleep. Then you will be fresh for the test and better able to recall what you've studied.

Step 6: Take a practice test

Many courses offer sample tests, either online or in the study materials. This is an excellent resource to check whether you have mastered the material, as well as to prepare for the test format and environment.

Check the test format ahead of time: the number of questions, the type (multiple choice, free response, etc.), and the time limit. Then create a plan for working through them. For example, if you have 30 minutes to take a 60-question test, your limit is 30 seconds per question. Spend less time on the questions you know well so that you can take more time on the difficult ones.

If you have time to take several practice tests, take the first one open book, with no time limit. Work through the questions at your own pace and make sure you fully understand them. Gradually work up to taking a test under test conditions: sit at a desk with all study materials put away and set a timer. Pace yourself to make sure you finish the test with time to spare and go back to check your answers if you have time.

After each test, check your answers. On the questions you missed, be sure you understand why you missed them. Did you misread the question (tests can use tricky wording)? Did you forget the information? Or was it something you hadn't learned? Go back and study any shaky areas that the practice tests reveal.

Taking these tests not only helps with your grade, but also aids in combating test anxiety. If you're already used to the test conditions, you're less likely to worry about it, and working through tests until you're scoring well gives you a confidence boost. Go through the practice tests until you feel comfortable, and then you can go into the test knowing that you're ready for it.

Test Tips

On test day, you should be confident, knowing that you've prepared well and are ready to answer the questions. But aside from preparation, there are several test day strategies you can employ to maximize your performance.

First, as stated before, get a good night's sleep the night before the test (and for several nights before that, if possible). Go into the test with a fresh, alert mind rather than staying up late to study.

Try not to change too much about your normal routine on the day of the test. It's important to eat a nutritious breakfast, but if you normally don't eat breakfast at all, consider eating just a protein bar. If you're a coffee drinker, go ahead and have your normal coffee. Just make sure you time it so that the caffeine doesn't wear off right in the middle of your test. Avoid sugary beverages, and drink enough water to stay hydrated but not so much that you need a restroom break 10 minutes into the test. If your test isn't first thing in the morning, consider going for a walk or doing a light workout before the test to get your blood flowing.

Allow yourself enough time to get ready, and leave for the test with plenty of time to spare so you won't have the anxiety of scrambling to arrive in time. Another reason to be early is to select a good seat. It's helpful to sit away from doors and windows, which can be distracting. Find a good seat, get out your supplies, and settle your mind before the test begins.

When the test begins, start by going over the instructions carefully, even if you already know what to expect. Make sure you avoid any careless mistakes by following the directions.

Then begin working through the questions, pacing yourself as you've practiced. If you're not sure on an answer, don't spend too much time on it, and don't let it shake your confidence. Either skip it and come back later, or eliminate as many wrong answers as possible and guess among the remaining ones. Don't dwell on these questions as you continue—put them out of your mind and focus on what lies ahead.

Be sure to read all of the answer choices, even if you're sure the first one is the right answer. Sometimes you'll find a better one if you keep reading. But don't second-guess yourself if you do immediately know the answer. Your gut instinct is usually right. Don't let test anxiety rob you of the information you know.

If you have time at the end of the test (and if the test format allows), go back and review your answers. Be cautious about changing any, since your first instinct tends to be correct, but make sure you didn't misread any of the questions or accidentally mark the wrong answer choice. Look over any you skipped and make an educated guess.

At the end, leave the test feeling confident. You've done your best, so don't waste time worrying about your performance or wishing you could change anything. Instead, celebrate the successful completion of this test. And finally, use this test to learn how to deal with anxiety even better next time.

Review Video: 5 Tips to Beat Test Anxiety
Visit mometrix.com/academy and enter code: 570656

Important Qualification

Not all anxiety is created equal. If your test anxiety is causing major issues in your life beyond the classroom or testing center, or if you are experiencing troubling physical symptoms related to your anxiety, it may be a sign of a serious physiological or psychological condition. If this sounds like your situation, we strongly encourage you to seek professional help.

Tell Us Your Story

We at Mometrix would like to extend our heartfelt thanks to you for letting us be a part of your journey. It is an honor to serve people from all walks of life, people like you, who are committed to building the best future they can for themselves.

We know that each person's situation is unique. But we also know that, whether you are a young student or a mother of four, you care about working to make your own life and the lives of those around you better.

That's why we want to hear your story.

We want to know why you're taking this test. We want to know about the trials you've gone through to get here. And we want to know about the successes you've experienced after taking and passing your test.

In addition to your story, which can be an inspiration both to us and to others, we value your feedback. We want to know both what you loved about our book and what you think we can improve on.

SCAN HERE

The team at Mometrix would be absolutely thrilled to hear from you! So please, send us an email at tellusyourstory@mometrix.com or visit us at mometrix.com/tellusyourstory.php and let's stay in touch.

Additional Bonus Material

Due to our efforts to try to keep this book to a manageable length, we've created a link that will give you access to all of your additional bonus material.

Please visit https://www.mometrix.com/bonus948/swmasters to access the information.

Made in the USA
Columbia, SC
24 August 2022

66020057R00233